Contents

Preface

As in the previous casebook published in 1987, the cases contained in this text draw upon the authors' experience of teaching business policy and strategic management over a number of years and as such, the material contained has been tried and tested in the 'market place'.

A small number of cases from the previous book have been retained in view of their perceived popularity and enhanced teaching effectiveness. Where appropriate, these have been revised and improved, whilst retaining their original flavour and focus. Additionally, we have included a number of 'not-for-profit' cases in order to enhance the sectoral coverage.

Although the cases have been selected to complement the companion text – *Business Policy: An Analytical Introduction* (Blackwell, 1991) – we should point out that they may equally be used alongside other similar management texts and readings and indeed, we would positively encourage students to resort to wider reading in order to enhance the analytical process and to enrich classroom discussions.

In this edition we have appended notes on case analysis. This inclusion is meant to offer guide lines and provide a 'flavour', rather than to establish any rigid methodology of approach and presentation. As no two cases are the same and any one case may be looked at from a number of perspectives, the choice of analytical tools and emphasis of analysis must be considered flexible. Nonetheless, the notes should help the student adjust in the early stages of the course and they should serve as a useful form of reference from time to time at the later stages. To help in course design, we have produced an accompanying set of teacher's notes which address the major policy and strategy themes along with the teaching ideas we have discerned from their use; these notes are available to bona fide teachers and can be obtained direct from the authors or on application to the publisher.

To both student and teacher we would stress that there is no substitute for careful and comprehensive preparation of case material and that the sharing and challenging of ideas is fundamental to the learning experience.

We believe that with such a holistic subject as business policy it is essential to gain a broad understanding of strategic analysis before proceeding to some of the more specialized areas of the subject. It is often difficult for students coping with business policy studies for the first time to come to terms with its integrative nature and with its concentration on top management decision-making. The former problem is often resolved by repeated exposure to case material with the constant application of models of strategic analysis, whilst the latter problem requires more sensitive treatment in order to demonstrate how the handling of strategic problems improves the students' ability to proffer solutions and to appreciate the significance of such, as well as improving their ability to handle seemingly difficult data and opinions. Perhaps the greatest benefit of the case method is that students can potentially develop themselves as managers albeit in a risk-free environment and without the imposition of the school of 'hard knocks'.

For many students, particularly those who are to be formally examined in the subject, the learning style of the case method comes as something of a challenge. Often it is difficult for students to get specific answers from textbooks or to revise for an examination in the usual sense, and on a regular basis. Thus, the role of the teacher in extracting the lessons and principles from the case material becomes crucial.

Further, the choice and sequence of case material becomes an important aspect of the course design in business policy. In this respect the cases in this book have been selected and arranged in such a way as to facilitate the learning process, the major themes moving from concepts through to analytical techniques, thence through growth alternatives and recovery strategies and finally implementation. The broad divisions in strategic terms are as follows:

1 Business policy framework
2 Strategic analysis
3 Strategic direction
4 Growth and decline
5 Strategy implementation

The first two sections comprise the scope and variety of case histories through which students can thoroughly develop both an understanding of the concept of strategy and the associated skill of strategic analysis. For example: setting business objectives, analysing the business environment and internal company analysis.

In the remaining sections, cases have been grouped together into more specific categories in order to indicate a main theme upon which the respective cases may be focused. These groupings, however, have to some extent been designed for the convenience of presentation as many of the cases are structured to provide additional focal points for analysis.

Thus the structure, although assisting in course design, should not be interpreted as a rigid classification of content nor of the application of the cases.

On a final note, the authors stress that all of the cases making up this text have been written for the purpose of student instruction rather than to convey the notion of effective or ineffective management of a business.

Brian Kenny
Edward Lea
Stuart Sanderson
George Luffman

Acknowledgements

We are grateful to the following for permission to include case material, without which the scope and quality of the cases would have been that much less: John Edwards and Graham Inman, the School of Management University of Bath (Westbury Homes Group); Colin Clarke-Hill, Huddersfield Polytechnic (Daf-Leyland Merger); John L. Heath formerly of Leicester Polytechnic (Ariel Industries); David Yorke UMIST (Metropolitan Borough of St Helens); Ian Smith Bradford University (TI Group); and E. Bourdon (Lightwater Valley Theme Park).

We also gratefully acknowledge the co-operation of the many companies whose case histories form the body of the text. We would further like to thank the following for permission to reproduce copyright material: *Caterer and Hotel Keeper*; Euromonitor Publications; *Investors' Chronicle*; Extel Statistical Service Ltd; *Financial Times*; Times Newspapers Ltd; Mintel Publications Ltd; ICC Information group; *Wool Record*; Wood Mackenzie; British Carpet Manufacturers' Association; Pickfords Travel; Economist Intelligence Unit; Central Statistical Office; International Management; Thomas Cook; Birds Eye; *Sunday Times*; Data Stream; Monopolies and Mergers Commission; MEAL; *Journal of Long Range Planning*; Textile Statistics Bureau; Wool Industry Bureau of Statistics; British Textile Confederation.

PART I

BUSINESS POLICY

FRAMEWORK

1 Hollybank School

BACKGROUND

Hollybank School for the disabled, located in Kirklees Metropolitan Borough in the north-east of England, cared for some 40 pupils whose ages ranged from 11 to 19 years of age. The disabilities of the students were classified as 'severely physically handicapped' (SHP), with both severe communication and mobility problems. The school employed specialist staff in the fields of speech therapy, physiotherapy and educational psychology, in addition to general care and welfare personnel.

Being in the voluntary, non-maintained sector the school relied on income from a variety of charitable sources and fees from local education authorities (LEAs) whose pupils attended the centre, mainly from the north of England (see Appendix 1 for details on user and non-user LEAs).

The governing of the school was carried out by a Board of Management – a body made up of elected officials from a variety of backgrounds, and mostly located in the immediate area. The collection of expertise within the Board, by design, reflected those areas conducive to the efficient operation of the school, such as the educational, welfare, medical and financial aspects.

In 1985 the Headmaster, Trevor Hodkinson, decided the time was ripe to embark upon the expansion and development of facilities within the School. The move was based on a long-held belief that the 16-years and, more so, the 19-years-plus age-groups of severely physically handicapped pupils had little chance of being integrated into the mainstream of public education, and that the school was ideally placed to innovate in this area. Such a move would of course require considerable investment, which would include a move to larger, more expensive premises. This move was considered essential in order to accommodate at least twice the existing number of pupils and to carry the extra facilities necessary to support curriculum and welfare development.

PLANNING FOR CHANGE

Trevor Hodkinson realized that his drive and enthusiasm for developing and expanding the school would be insufficient on their own to convince the Board of Management of the viability of his plans. Having in the recent past completed postgraduate studies involving business management, he was more than aware of the need for a systematic, well-supported approach to the problem. Indeed, although he felt that the Board would be no less enthusiastic about his proposals, they would be equally critical regarding their long-term viability without a good deal of supporting evidence.

He further realized that his own LEA regarded the school very favourably with regard to the placing of locally-based severely handicapped pupils (SHPs), and that this practice would continue well into the foreseeable future.

Following presentation of his preliminary proposals, the Board of Management instructed Trevor Hodkinson to arrange for a detailed feasibility study which would indicate a strategy for the future, together with the necessary investment estimates and implementation details.

Trevor Hodkinson was aware that unlike many sectors of industry, the specialist field of education for the disabled was not blessed with specific up-to-date government statistics, nor was it exactly an attractive target for economic and other related research. Nonetheless, he realized he would need to support any subsequent plan with some firm estimates of the potential for expansion.

ESTIMATING GROWTH POTENTIAL

Problems of data collection

Before any field survey was contemplated, secondary data collection was undertaken to determine the likely size of the 'market' within the wider catchment area (see figure 1.1). This proved to be a rather unfruitful exercise, as pupil figures issued by the Department of Education and Science (DES) merely disaggregated into categories of special school type. In addition, there also appeared to be a degree of disparity in the returns from LEAs as recorded in official source material.

However, from the published data it was possible to deduce that in the wider catchment area there had been a decrease in the special school population of some 16,000 pupils between 1976 and 1985, and that some 20 special schools had been closed in that period. It was also established that about 0.205 per cent of the population were regarded as 'special' pupils, and subsequently it was estimated that approximately 33,500 pupils in the wider catchment area were in the

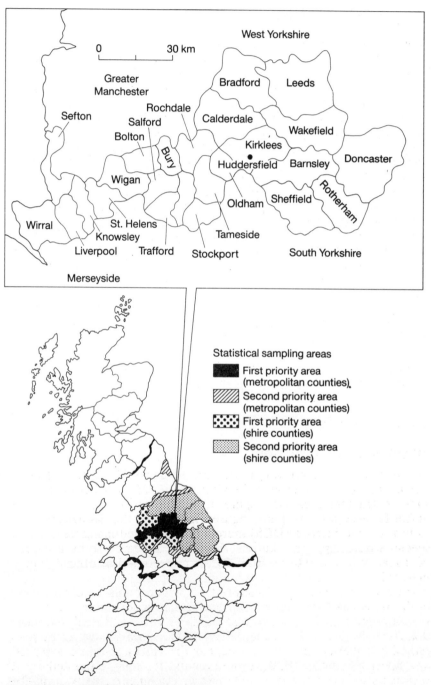

FIGURE 1.1   **Catchment area map**

special school category. Unfortunately, the disparities in statistical returns inhibited any meaningful trend analysis. Even allowing for the inconsistencies, such data on their own were only marginally useful, as they failed to identify statistics relating specifically to SHPs.

However, it was known that many SHPs suffered from cerebral palsy, and that some 21 pupils at the school were in this category. Trevor Hodkinson also uncovered some research carried out by Bleck and Nagel[1] in the United States, which showed that the predicted frequency of cerebral palsy at birth in the US population was seven in 100,000. Of these seven, one child would die and of the remaining six, two would be very severe. Of the other four, one would be very mild and one probably suitable for home care. They concluded that two to three of the sufferers would be in the totally, or the near-totally dependent category.

SURVEY OF LOCAL EDUCATION AUTHORITIES

A survey of a sample of LEAs was carried out within the wider catchment area of the school – this was limited to the metropolitan and shire counties of northern England. This geographic area was further subdivided into first priority areas – the shire and metropolitan counties from where the school could reasonably expect to attract pupils, and second priority areas, comprising those authorities that lay outside the prime catchment area for the school (see figure 1.1).

Although no reported statistics could be obtained on the numbers of SHPs within the catchment area, it was estimated that the number of SHPs placed outside the local authorities' provision had been decreasing for the past five years, assisted by falling school rolls. Day units, making special school provision, had been incorporated into secondary schools to facilitate educational and social integration. The places thereby made available were gradually being filled by more severely handicapped pupils, who previously would have been candidates for residential provision, some in out-LEA establishments such as Hollybank School.

There were no perceived short-term benefits to LEAs of adopting this policy, due to the added cost of building modifications, and higher transport costs. The geography of each LEA and the relative locations of the SHPs' homes and the special schools was a major consideration. The ideal maximum transport time of 45 minutes between home and school made for practical differences between urban LEAs and counties with sparse, scattered populations.

Many education officers saw their LEA as having a strong locally-devised policy of integrating SHPs into an appropriate point along a continuum of educational provision. Nonetheless, this emphasis on the SHP was not universally shared, particularly as these pupils were a very small minority among a vast population;

SHPs generally represented less than 1 per cent of any LEA's school population.

Objections by parents pre- or post-placement could trigger a wider search for suitable schools. However, apart from problems of location and access, some assistant education officers treated pre-placement objections as symptomatic of the difficulties in adjusting to parenthood of an SHP, and they might wait a year or more in anticipation that eventually, parents would accept the LEA recommendation. Only 36 per cent of LEAs surveyed indicated that the fulfilment of parents' wishes was a relevant criterion in the placement process.

Within the LEA decision criteria, the degree of pupils' handicap might preclude their needs being accommodated within the LEA's existing facilities. Spending an amount on local improvements equivalent to external placement fees would not achieve the level of facilities required. More confidence was detected among LEAs regarding integration of SHPs at primary age-level, but there was increasing uncertainty for secondary age-level, and even more uncertainty about future provision of further education facilities for the SHP.

The cost of placement as a very important criterion in the decision-making process was noted by only 7 per cent of the sample. However, there appeared to be an accepted price band within which LEAs expected residential fees to fall.

Regarding other noted criteria, the final decision to place outside the authority appeared to rest upon evaluation of the following factors:

- A very high standard of care and maintenance of pupils was regarded as *sine qua non*.
- Geographical location and ease of access were important both to minimize travelling time for the pupil and to enable parents to visit frequently. Proximity to road and rail systems was relevant here.
- Curriculum provision was important, and gaining in significance. The ability to match SHPs' special educational needs with teaching and learning facilities to maximize their potential was a major selling point. Like all differentiation policies, this customized service was not expected to come cheaply.

Further details regarding the LEA decision-making processes are attached at Appendix 2.

DEVELOPING A FUTURE SCENARIO

In view of the nature and level of the proposed school development, it was felt necessary to provide more support in the way of likely long-term threats and opportunities. The field survey had provided little conclusive evidence as to future integration progress, although it had been invaluable in identifying the various decision criteria. Thus, it was felt necessary to solicit further, specific opinions from less 'politically sensitive' sources in an attempt to find some convergence of views regarding likely future scenarios of direct consequence to the educational development of the SHP.

Survey design

An initial sample of respondents was drawn from national institutions and associations who had first-hand knowledge of the problems associated with the educational and community development of the handicapped. For example, these included the National Bureau for Handicapped Students (NBHS), the Educational Welfare Officers' Association, the Research Council for Special Education, the Health Visitors' Association, the Invalid Children's Association, the Council for Educational Technology, the Centre for Studies on Integration in Education, and the Association for Spina Bifida and Hydrocephalus.

The questionnaire comprised 21 statements relating to possible developments by the year 1995, against which respondents were requested to score a probability of occurrence (0–10, 25, 50, 75 and 95 per cent respectively).

Pilot run

In all, some 22 respondents took part in the pilot forecast. This was a relatively small sample size compared to the norm for the type of forecasting method adopted, but in dealing with such a narrow, specialized field within a confined geographic area and with the wide-ranging backgrounds of the respondents, it was felt that any convergence of opinions expressed would have some valid basis for assessing a future scenario.

Initial findings

In searching for convergence of opinion among respondents, individual statements with widely dispersed responses recording between 0.25 and 0.40 probability were generally disregarded, although the choice of this range was little more than subjective, in the final analysis. Ultimately, this led to the rejection of six of the original 21 statements. The highest probability related to statement number 10, which referred to decision-making between all agencies concerned with the assessment of the SHP. The lowest probability of occurrence identified – 0.116 – related to the prioritization of education for the SHP. (Appendix 3 shows the complete list of statements, and the estimated probabilities of occurrence.)

The scenario development exercise was further assisted by reference to relevant published papers, extracts of which are shown in Appendix 4.

The future

In reviewing the results of the surveys and supporting research, Trevor Hodkinson concluded that there were problems of both a long-term and a short-term nature. He realized that the current system of communicating with LEAs through the annual mailing of a school brochure was probably less than effective. For example, feedback showed that the personal contact with LEA decision-makers, as a result of the survey, appeared to have raised the level of awareness and image of the school far beyond that which regular receipt of the school brochure had achieved. Trevor also realized the need to specify and, where appropriate, quantify future long-term potential growth opportunities and expected return on investment if the Board of Management were to be convinced. In contrast, he had contemplated the wider impact of 'social objectives' which concerned the well-being and development of the SHP. How could these be reconciled with the more commercialized aims of the venture? Even taking into consideration the proceeds of the sale of the existing school site, several tens of thousands of pounds would need to be raised in order to finance the move and to equip the new school with the requisite facilities.

Appendix 1   Comparative statistics

USER AUTHORITIES

Authority	No of S/Schools		Population (000s)	
	1976	1985	1976	1985
Kirklees	13	15	370	372
Bradford	20	20	461	467
Tameside	4	7	223	217
Calderdale	7	4	194	192
Barnsley	6	15	226	224
Wakefield	10	12	303	314
Humberside	20	17	848	858
North Yorkshire	17	18	664	685
Derbyshire	21	28	892	914
Gateshead	6	6	225	210
Doncaster	6	2	283	267
Lancashire	48	46	1,345	1,378
Rochdale	13	8	279	209
Cheshire	40	26	910	900

NON-USER AUTHORITIES

Authority	No of S/Schools		Population (000s)	
	1976	1985	1976	1985
Bolton	4	7	257	261
Bury	4	4	180	175
Knowsley	9	11	196	174
Leeds	26	25	746	714
Liverpool	34	28	574	503
Cleveland	19	22	566	565
Cumbria	15	12	474	476
Durham	21	20	612	608
Lincolnshire	21	21	520	566
Manchester	32	28	542	470
Newcastle upon Tyne	13	13	304	283
Northumberland	12	11	287	301
Nottinghamshire	28	54	981	991
North Tyneside	5	5	206	197
Oldham	7	8	224	220
Rotherham	9	7	244	253
St Helens	6	5	190	189
Salford	13	12	279	247
Sefton	8	7	308	300
Sheffield	27	23	561	543
South Tyneside	5	5	172	159
Stockport	6	7	294	289
Sunderland	9	11	292	294
Trafford	7	6	240	221
Wigan	16	5	301	309
Wirral	15	11	349	339

Appendix 2   The SHP placement procedure

Under the Education Act (1981), Section 4/1, LEAs have a statutory obligation to formulate a statement of educational needs for each severely handicapped pupil (SHP) and, with the agreement of the child's parents, to meet them wherever possible within the normal educational system. Most LEAs suggest that this legal requirement is merely a formal expression of the philosophy of integration already adopted.

The Act requires each education authority to provide a named officer to whom parents of handicapped children can apply for help or information at any stage during or after the assessment of their child's needs. In some LEAs this task is allocated to an officer whose senior position makes him one of the key decision-makers, but in others the task is handled by an administrative assistant without executive power.

Each education authority has a designated assistant education officer (AEO) for special needs. Final responsibility for SHP placement decisions rests with this officer, although he in turn reports to the chief education officer or deputy CEO, depending upon the LEA's size. The AEO normally chairs any formal committee or panel meeting which is convened, wherein progress on the assessment of pupils' needs would be reported (annual reassessment is mandatory) and decisions considered.

The other key post is that of consultant on educational development and potential, the chief educational psychologist (CEP), who presents the assessment of the child's needs – made by one of a small team of peripatetic educational psychologists working for the CEP.

Beyond this core of three posts, which are critical to the placement decision, there exist other influential roles. That of administrative assistant (AA) to the AEO is instrumentally influential, because it operates the information storage and retrieval functions. It often acts as gatekeeper for the other members of the decision-making unit. The post requires no experience or qualifications in special educational needs, but its holder liaises administratively with special schools and advises the AEO on pupils' progress from LEA files. In a minority of LEAs the AA is the named officer whom parents may contact. The named holders of all the aforementioned posts are published annually in the *Educational Year Book* (HMSO), ensuring an easy flow of communication.

THE DECISION PROCESS

The framing of the Education Act (1981) ensures that the formal focus of the decision procedures is assessment of the child's

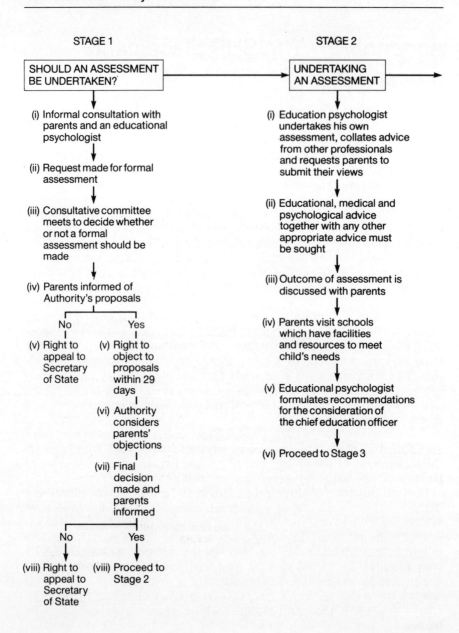

STAGE 1

STAGE 2

| SHOULD AN ASSESSMENT BE UNDERTAKEN? |

| UNDERTAKING AN ASSESSMENT |

(i) Informal consultation with parents and an educational psychologist

(ii) Request made for formal assessment

(iii) Consultative committee meets to decide whether or not a formal assessment should be made

(iv) Parents informed of Authority's proposals

No　　Yes

(v) Right to appeal to Secretary of State

(v) Right to object to proposals within 29 days

(vi) Authority considers parents' objections

(vii) Final decision made and parents informed

No　　Yes

(viii) Right to appeal to Secretary of State

(viii) Proceed to Stage 2

(i) Education psychologist undertakes his own assessment, collates advice from other professionals and requests parents to submit their views

(ii) Educational, medical and psychological advice together with any other appropriate advice must be sought

(iii) Outcome of assessment is discussed with parents

(iv) Parents visit schools which have facilities and resources to meet child's needs

(v) Educational psychologist formulates recommendations for the consideration of the chief education officer

(vi) Proceed to Stage 3

FIGURE 1.2　**Example of the procedure for making a formal assessment**

STAGE 3

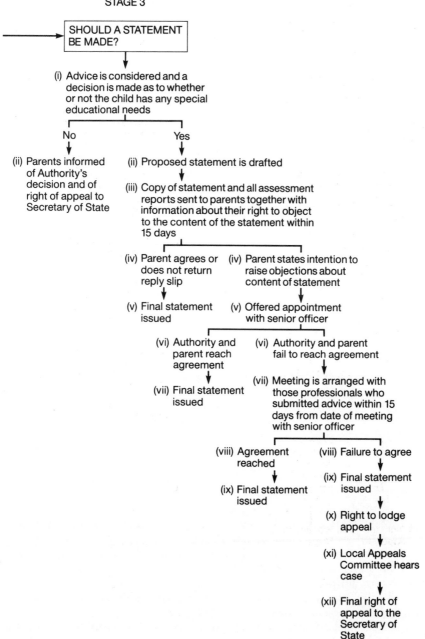

SHOULD A STATEMENT BE MADE?

(i) Advice is considered and a decision is made as to whether or not the child has any special educational needs

No

(ii) Parents informed of Authority's decision and of right of appeal to Secretary of State

Yes

(ii) Proposed statement is drafted

(iii) Copy of statement and all assessment reports sent to parents together with information about their right to object to the content of the statement within 15 days

(iv) Parent agrees or does not return reply slip

(v) Final statement issued

(iv) Parent states intention to raise objections about content of statement

(v) Offered appointment with senior officer

(vi) Authority and parent reach agreement

(vii) Final statement issued

(vi) Authority and parent fail to reach agreement

(vii) Meeting is arranged with those professionals who submitted advice within 15 days from date of meeting with senior officer

(viii) Agreement reached

(ix) Final statement issued

(viii) Failure to agree

(ix) Final statement issued

(x) Right to lodge appeal

(xi) Local Appeals Committee hears case

(xii) Final right of appeal to the Secretary of State

educational and physical potential and limitations. Each LEA operates according to its own interpretation of the 1981 Act (although a few small LEAs largely dispense with panels), but the procedures remain very similar. An example is provided by the flow chart in figure 1.2.

It will be seen that at Stage 2(iv) the parents visit potential placement schools. As early as Stage 1 (i) – the informal consultation between parents and Educational Psychologist – the recognition will occur that a placement decision may be needed. At the outset, only the parents will be facing a 'new-buy' situation. Their emotions will tend to be the most engaged, their information the scantiest, their access to other members of the decision team and other information sources determined partly by the severity of their child's handicap and the extent to which their stance is pro- or re-active.

In contrast, the Educational Psychologist is likely to be considering some known alternatives, and will be able to approach the eventual selection of educational placement as a 'modified re-buy' decision, wherein the specific needs of the child will be compared with various provisions available at known, previously used or recommended schools. The consultative committee at Stage 1(iii) brings in the CEO or AEO (Special Needs) and the LEA Advisor (Special Needs); the other professionals for whom a placement is usually a modified re-buy or limited decision process. Alternative schools may be mentioned, shaping the thoughts of key decision-makers.

At Stages 2(i) and 2(ii) the Educational Psychologist, LEA Advisor and AEO are able to compare the SHP's assessed needs with the recognized provision available in their own preferred schools. The placement shortlist is then narrowed.

Assuming parental agreement, the school selected at Stage 2 will be the destination of the SHP. Generally, a visit to check the school by the Psychologist or Advisor will only be made if a year has elapsed since the last recorded call.

Appendix 3   'Scenario' statements

1 Most disabled pupils, regardless of disability, will be fully integrated into normal schools. (Probability of occurrence = 0.188)
2 The majority of mainstream schools will have a fully resourced provision for the SHP. (0.166)
3 Local authorities will be specially funded to cater for the SHP in the maintained sector of education. (Divergent, probability = 0.316)
4 Local authorities will have a full range of education provision for the SHP at post-19 years. (0.188)
5 Post-16 years FE provision for the SHP will be the norm rather than the exception in all colleges of further and higher education. (Divergent, 0.288)

6 Most SHP students will be entitled to full-time education up to 21 years of age. (0.122)
7 Chronological age will not be considered as a basis for provision for the SHP. (0.216)
8 Education and training will be compulsory for all people up to the age of 18 years. (0.272)
9 The majority of SHPs will be placed within two hours' travelling time from home. (0.216)
10 There will be a centralized and statutory 'corporate' approach (full joint consultation and decision-making between all agencies) in the assessment of educational needs for the SHP. (0.522)
11 Education provision for the SHP will become a top priority for our society. (0.116)
12 School placements for all pupils will be at parental choice. (0.216)
13 Society's attitudes to the severely disabled will have markedly shifted so that the SHP is regarded as on a par with all other members of society. (0.216)
14 Special education facilities will be financed by direct educational support grants. (0.444)
15 The majority of special schools for the disabled will be in the non-maintained voluntary sector. (0.166)
16 No special schools for the disabled will be in the non-maintained voluntary sector. (Divergent, 0.172)
17 Most schools for the handicapped will be providing post-school occupational training for work. (Divergent, 0.327)
18 Most local authorities will be specially funded by the government to cater fully for the SHP within the maintained sector of education. (0.188)
19 The government will shift resources to the disabled in our society so that educational disadvantage for this sector of population is eliminated. (0.138)
20 There will be specialist regional centres providing for the needs of the SHP funded by a system of local authority pooling. (Divergent, 0.422)
21 There will be specialist regional centres providing for the needs of the SHP that will be funded by the voluntary sector and used as such by local authorities in their placement policy. (Divergent, 0.430)

Appendix 4   A perspective on needs and provision in further education

The Warnock Report (1978) identified the 16–19 age-group as a priority area for the further education of those with special needs. While noting some progress among a few local authorities, Bradley

and Hegarty highlighted the general plight of the severely handicapped pupil:

> In the case of special schools, leavers' courses have made prog-
> ress, albeit with more limited aims, to provide simple language
> and number skills and to encourage maximum independence.
> For those in mental hospital schools, education is concentrated
> on enabling young people to become socially acceptable and, if
> possible, to learn social sight vocabulary. However, in many
> ways the most difficult problems for those responsible for provid-
> ing educational opportunities are presented by *young people
> who, while intellectually able, are very severely physically handi-
> capped.*[2]

Warnock suggested a focus on a number of broad factors in terms of
special, further education needs:

1 the provision of special means of access to the curriculum through
   special equipment, facilities or resources, modification of the physical environment or specialist teaching techniques;
2 the provision of a special or modified curriculum;
3 particular attention to the social structure and emotional climate in
   which education takes place.

The conclusions of Bradley and Hegarty's research suggested that
while a great deal of work undertaken on the needs of the disabled
had been carried out in the school sector, little information was available on 'the epidemiology of handicap in the 14–19 age range or on
the coherence of pre- and post-sixteen curricula' (p. 29).

Their recommendations indicated the need for a high-priority focus
on curriculum development and implementations. The integration
problem, however, was not underestimated and the authors stressed
the need for further research, not least, of a concerted nature:

> Various issues stand out as requiring additional research atten-
> tion. Apart from the curriculum and teacher training which are
> discussed later, these include: the efficacy of and constraints
> associated with different forms of integration in relation to the
> needs of older pupils; the new roles that special schools can
> adopt; the forging of relationships between *special schools and
> the FE sector, employers, the local community and ordinary
> schools; and the problems of adolescence.*[3]

As recently as August 1985, it was reported that Bradford Authority
had commenced a two-year project to examine the integration of
children with special needs into mainstream education (*Times
Educational Supplement*, 23 August 1985). The project involved more
than 60 nursery, primary and secondary schools, as well as colleges
and special schools.

From the point of view of the very severely multiple-handicapped, it will be interesting to discover what particular problems are occurring and whether a truly integrated approach can work for this group. Certainly Bradley and Hegarty see some compromise solution, and the 'Bradford approach' may well point to a workable solution:

> A significant, and developing, contribution made by further education colleges is that of out-reach provision, whereby classes are held outside the colleges – for instance at centres for the disabled or in their own homes. The development of this provision would appear to have enormous potential for both school leavers and adults, not least since it offers a relatively inexpensive means of ensuring the continued education of [the disabled].[4]

PERSPECTIVES ON FURTHER AND HIGHER EDUCATION FOR THE DISABLED[5]

1 *General*

The report of the Warnock Committee in 1978 emphasized that the educational needs of those hitherto educated in special schools were one end of a continuum of special needs that encompassed as many as one in five children and young people. Notwithstanding this, it has been the belief of many in the Bureau that the needs of the very small minority of young people with severe and multiple handicaps could be overlooked in the greater emphasis on the wider school and college population. This concern, coupled with a feeling that further education has taken the 'easy option' of providing for those whose difficulties were less, resulted in the Bureau setting up a working party in 1983 to examine the particular needs of the severely and multiple handicapped.

The voluntary sector has played, and continues to play, a major role in making available post-16 education and training opportunities for those with severe handicaps. Well used to plugging gaps in statutory provision, organizations such as the Spastics Society and MENCAP have also shown they are able to respond to past advances in medical science which now result in increasing numbers of very severely multiple-handicapped young people looking for post-school opportunities.

Provision in 'ordinary' further education is still limited and few young people with severe handicaps can be sure of a welcome at their local college. In higher education the decade has seen the creation of specialist provision in Southampton, Sussex, Oxford and Essex, and many others prepared to set aside time, and accommodation. The introduction of a 'disabled students allowance' has assisted many in purchasing necessary equipment, and the establishment of a Community Service Volunteer (CSV) network, capable of meeting the personal care needs of severely disabled students, has already benefited many.

2   *Information Technology*

Many young people with disabilities do not have access to adequate training opportunities; with the help of a grant from the Greater London Council, NBHS organized a pilot residential training course on the use of computers in a business setting, which was heavily over-subscribed.

The lack of adequate funding in this area has been highlighted by the large number of applications to the COMET (Concerned Micros in Education and Training) bursary scheme. The COMET project was established in 1984 to help disabled young people who have been unable to get funding for microcomputing equipment. For each of the twelve awards granted in the last year there were ten well-qualified applicants who could not be helped.

Technological advances in a few years have brought new hope to many who were previously denied access to education alongside non-disabled students.

Much remains to be done: improved assessment of individual student needs; training in the use of new equipment; evaluation of appropriate software; co-ordination of unpublished information; and an appraisal of the role of information technology in an evolving curriculum for young people with special needs.

As it develops its role in this field in the years ahead, NBHS hopes to strengthen its links with other organizations and colleges, to ensure that the benefits of new technology are made available to anyone with a disability whose education can thereby be enhanced.

3   *The Future*

To the extent to which we continue in this country towards reduced staff and student numbers in higher education, and even towards more strongly vocationally orientated courses, then the pressure to admit more disabled students is likely to decrease. On the other hand, if we move to greater flexibility in admission procedures, to a more balanced assessment of achievement and potential, and to greater opportunities preceding higher education, then students with disabilities may yet find a welcome throughout higher education.

The young handicapped population is likely to continue decreasing, but at the same time becoming more severely disabled, continuing a trend that advances in medical science helped establish a decade or more ago. At the same time strict accounting by the Audit Commission, and rigid tests of employability by the Manpower Services Commission and others, may serve to limit the opportunities made available to a group of young people whose need for extended education and training is greater than anyone's. Nevertheless, the confidence built up by the colleges accepting less severely handicapped students will surely extend in the years to come to cover those with severe and multiple handicaps. Equally it is certain that young people themselves, and their parents, will increasingly demand the chance to be educated alongside their able-bodied peers.

Notes

1 E. Bleck and D. Nagel, *Physically Handicapped Children – A Medical Atlas for Teachers*, (Grune and Stratton, New York, 1982).
2 Judy Bradley and Seamus Hegarty, *Students with Special Needs in Further Education*, Further Education Unit, Dept. of Education and Science, October 1981.
3 Ibid., p. 8.
4 Ibid., p. 10.
5 Extracted from National Bureau for Handicapped Students, *Tenth Annual Report*, 1985.

2 BBA Group

INTRODUCTION

The origin of the BBA Group lies in the chance meeting of two men in Sweden. William Fenton, a Scotsman, was employed as weaving manager in a textile mill at Jonsered. The other was Walter Willson Cobbett, a merchant of industrial supplies, who was on holiday.

Fenton had invented a solid twill woven cotton belting. This, he thought, would improve on the current plain woven beltings that were beginning to supersede leather and canvas belts for driving machinery. Fenton was to have sole responsibility for manufacturing, Cobbett sole responsibility for selling.

Fenton left Sweden in 1879 and started up in a small factory in Dundee, calling himself a 'Belt and Hosepipe Maker' and manufacturing the belting under the brand name 'Scandura'. In 1897 the business became a joint stock company, incorporating the separate business of two sons who had started manufacturing separately in 1888. The new company required new premises, and in 1901 the business moved to Cleckheaton in Yorkshire.

In the inter-war years, the growing friction materials business necessitated the acquisition of the British Asbestos Company. The Second World War provided a significant impetus to BBA products and growth. For instance, every RAF aircraft which fought in the Battle of Britain was fitted with BBA (Mintex) brakes. BBA looms were manufacturing materials for tanks, other army vehicles, parachutes and gas masks. The plant was working 24 hours a day, seven days a week, and the number of employees rose from 400 to 1,400.

In 1960, BBA obtained a quotation on the Stock Exchange, but the Fenton and Pearson (Cobbett's descendants) families retained dominant positions on the board until 1985.

PRODUCTS AND MARKETS

Industrial

In 1945, experiments were started with PVC as a coating material in an attempt to produce a fire-resistant belt. After a disastrous fire at

Cresswell Colliery in 1950, a directive was issued by the Ministry of Fuel to the effect that all belts used in collieries were to be flame-proof. The Scandura product was, and became the first coal conveyor belting to be officially recognized as such. Today, Scandura belts carry coal, clay, copper, phosphates, potash, quarry stone and lumber, as well as products from the food industry and the packaging industry.

Other Scandura products include asbestos yarns for packing and sealing purposes, asbestos cloth for thermal insulation, as well as jointings and packings, tapes, laggings, linings and tubings. Scandura screen mats are available for the grading of aggregates, and Scandura compensating seals are fitted to ducting and pipework. Endless belts manufactured by the company are widely used on rolling machines in the cigarette industry. Scandura also produce glass cloth, webbings, and tubings for heat insulation and general industrial applications.

BBA's other industrial activities include Sovex Marshall, the conveyor makers and system-handling engineers. Their document systems are installed in many government buildings, banks, and insurance houses; Postube is a pneumatic tube system for handling documents and small parts.

Marshall Mechanization forms the other main branch of the company's activities and produces a large range of standard conveyor products. The Automotive division supplies machinery for inter-process handling of small and large automotive components.

Automotive

The company has a long history of successful innovation in the brake-lining business, Jaguar being the first major user to fix Mintex (BBA) disc brakes, in 1959. With its worldwide production facilities the BBA Group supplies more disc brake pads as original equipment than any other manufacturing group in the world. In addition, licensing agreements are in operation for the manufacture of BBA friction materials in several overseas countries.

Also prominent in the list of BBA Automotive companies is plastics bearings manufacturer, Railko. In the 1930s Railko developed a new centre-pivot bearing material – requiring no lubrication – for use in railway bogies. BBA Group obtained a 50 per cent stake in the company in 1962, and it became a wholly-owned subsidiary in 1970.

Railko have developed a wide range of bearing and controlled-friction materials which are used extensively throughout the marine, railway, automotive, mechanical handling and other industries.

Geographical

From the very first meeting of its founders in Sweden, the company has developed international connections. Export ledgers for the latter part of the nineteenth century show that the company was represented by agents in France, Germany, Spain, Australia, India, Russia, Holland, Sweden, and even in the Sudan, Brazil and Trinidad.

After the Second World War, BBA's overseas activities continued to expand. Today the company has manufacturing plants in Australia, Canada, South Africa, Spain, the USA and Germany. Of the Group's 7,000 employees, some 2,500 work overseas.

BBA PERFORMANCE TO 1984

BBA's performance in its early years as a public company was most encouraging. The company enjoyed a solid record of profit growth from the mid-1960s right through to its centenary in 1979; profits dipped in 1974, from £4.78m. to £3.96m. pre-tax as a result of the miners' strike and the three-day week, but quickly recovered to £6.3m. by 1975. With major subsidiaries overseas, a substantial proportion of profits was generated outside the UK throughout this period. Unfortunately the strengthening of sterling, combined with difficult trading conditions in some businesses, led to a rather disappointing performance in 1976 and 1977, but profits quickly advanced thereafter to a peak of £8m. in 1979. Some 83 per cent of profits in 1979 came from the automotive parts businesses, and 57 per cent of profits were generated overseas. The six year record to 1984 is summarized in table 2.1. As can be seen from the table, the group suffered a disastrous decline in profits in 1980, as BBA took the brunt of savage destocking by both car and component manufacturers; the automotive proportion of profits fell from 83 per cent to an overall loss, with Mintex moving into loss and Textar (a German friction material manufacturing subsidiary) generating a much lower overall contribution and second half losses. Regina Fibreglass and Sovex Marshall continued in loss, but Scandura Ltd put up a good performance. The German company was quick to recover in 1981 but UK losses were a persistent feature of group profits between 1979 and 1984.

Within the UK, Mintex remained in loss between 1980 and 1984, Sovex Marshall returned a small operating profit in 1984, and Regina Fibreglass (in which BBA had a 49 per cent stake) was sold to Pilkington Brothers for £1.5m. cash in 1981, after a trading loss of some £1m. in 1980. The remaining UK companies generally were reasonably successful over this period, with Scandura Ltd making good progress until it was badly affected by the miners' dispute in 1984; however, even in that year the company continued to generate profits. One major problem was that newer friction materials have a longer life (the life expectancy of clutches, for example, is now at least as long as the life of a car). Imports, although not of great significance in terms of volume penetration, have had an adverse effect on margins, which were already being affected by a price war between the

TABLE 2.1   **BBA performance, 1979–84**

	Turnover (£000)	Profit before tax (£000)	Earnings per share	Tax rate	Net dividend
1979	137,316	8,168	9.30p	31%	2.63p
1980	135,423	850	(0.90p)	215%	1.74p
1981	130,607	3,559	1.50p	75%	1.74p
1982	150,904	4,547	2.10p	73%	1.74p
1983	156,112	5,513	3.57p	56%	1.74p
1984	176,110	5,409	0.92p	77%	1.74p

TABLE 2.2   **Profit before tax, 1979–84**

	UK £000	Overseas £000	Total
1979	3,647	4,521	8,168
1980	(948)	1,798	850
1981	(754)	4,313	3,559
1982	(279)	4,826	4,547
1983	708	4,805	5,513
1984	(154)	5,563	5,409

three major manufacturers within the UK – Mintex, Don (Cape Industries) and Ferodo (Turner & Newall). After years of rationalization and restructuring at Mintex, the company seemed no nearer to achieving a position of profitable trading.

CHANGES IN 1985

Following the arrival of Dr John White as Group Managing Director at BBA, the automotive interests of Cape Industries were acquired in March 1985 for £15.75m. of which £10.5m. was paid in cash and the remainder (which attracted no interest) was payable in five years' time. The acquisition was accompanied by a 1-for-4 rights issue (14,473,316 shares) at 60p which raised £8.1m. net. The Cape deal involved the acquisition of three UK companies, Don International, Trist Draper and TBL (which collectively lost £544,000 at the operating level on turnover of £24.6m. in 1983).

Trist Draper is a wholesale distributor to the replacement market of commercial vehicle parts. It had 16 branches, about 140 employees and a turnover of £5.8m. in 1983, which resulted in £141,000 of trading losses.

TBL is a specialist manufacturer of friction materials for railways and industrial applications; the company also manufactures a range of automatic transmission components. It is based at Bristol, sharing a site with Don and has some 70 employees.

Also included in the purchase were two overseas companies, Don International SA (Don SA) of Belgium, and Svenska Broms-bandsfabriken AB (SBC) of Sweden, which together made an operating profit of £812,000 on turnover of £12.14m. in 1983, together with interests in associated companies in India, Spain, Malaysia and New Zealand. Cape's share of profits before tax for these associates in 1983 was £263,000. It is understood that the UK companies improved their operating performance during 1984, but remained in loss. Net assets of the companies acquired at 31 December 1984 were approximately £20.7m.

Overseas, progress was generally satisfactory, with Textar in Germany and Bendix Mintex, the Australian associate, being particu-larly strong performers. Scandura Inc, in the United States, has been consistently in profit, although profitability dipped sharply in 1982 as a result of a weakening of demand for industrial belting and a severe drop in demand for mining belting. The company registered a good improvement in sales and profits in 1983 and 1984.

On 24 June 1985, the Boards of BBA and Synterials announced that agreement had been reached on the terms of a recommended offer on behalf of BBA for the whole of the issued share capital of Synterials. The offer placed a value of £16.32m. upon Synterials. There were two main reasons for the acquisition: firstly the substantial cash element in the Synterials balance sheet (£12.8m.) was attractive to BBA, especially as the majority of the cash was surplus to Synterials' requirements. Secondly, Synterials would help BBA in the develop-ment of an engineering materials business, being built around Railko and TBL.

On 13 August 1985, BBA announced the acquisition of the rubber belting business of Uniroyal Inc in the US and Canada for about $US13.5m. (£9.3m.). Uniroyal was merged with Scandura Inc in the United States to form the second biggest materials handling company in that country.

SECTOR ANALYSIS PERFORMANCE 1984–5

Automotive

Table 2.3 is an estimate of the 1984 and 1985 breakdown of the operating profits of BBA's automotive companies.

UK Mintex-Don, the largest UK company within the BBA Group, manufactures friction materials, mostly for the motor industry, including brake linings, clutch linings and disc pads. The original

TABLE 2.3   **Estimate of automotive trading profits**

	1984(E) £m.	1985(E) £m.
Mintex	(2.1)	0.8
Railko	0.5	0.7
Textar	5.8	6.4
BBA France & B.G.	0.1	0.2
Frenos y Embraques	0.3	0.4
Mintex Canada & Cantex	0.4	0.4
Frima (now Mintex-Don SA)	(0.7)	0.5
Bendix Mintex	2.0	2.1
	6.3	11.5
Cape Cos (Trist Draper, TBL and associates in 1985)	(0.5)	0.1
	5.8	11.6

equipment (OE) market for friction materials is supplied via the brake and clutch manufacturers – Lucas Girling, Automotive Products and Laycock – whilst the replacement market is served, via 23 service depots, through factors and garages. Mintex enjoys a 20–25 per cent share of the UK market, with about 25 per cent of export from the UK and a turnover of about £30m. In the UK, competition comes from Ferodo, Antela (Automotive products) and imports.

The problems experienced at Mintex during the first half of the 1980s have been outlined above, and despite five separate series of redundancies, the latest of which were made during 1984 and are estimated to have removed some £2m. of operating costs, there was no sign of a return to profitable trading: the company lost almost £2m. at the operating level in 1983, and more than £2m. in 1984. Prior to the acquisition of Cape's automotive businesses it was hoped that Mintex would achieve break-even by 1985; this target became more easily attainable following the Cape purchase.

Don International formerly competed directly with Mintex in the manufacture of brake and clutch linings and their distribution via a network of depots. Turnover at Don and TBL in 1983 was £18.8m. and together the two companies lost £403,000 at the trading level.

At the time of the acquisition it was stated that Mintex and Don would be rationalized into one strong and profitable UK manufacturing operation. This process was quickly completed, with the two companies merged to form 'Mintex-Don'. In terms of manufacturing capability the companies fitted together very neatly: respective strengths were in different sectors of the market, with BBA stronger in passenger cars and Cape stronger in commercial vehicles.

Rationalization and restructuring along the following lines took place over the next eighteen months or so:

1   Mintex ceased production of commercial vehicle linings and concentrated on the passenger car market, whilst Don concentrated on the manufacture of commercial vehicle (CV) linings. Don is undoubtedly the UK market leader at the 'heavy' end of the market, and enjoys a good technical reputation in Europe. Mintex operated from two manufacturing sites and Don from four. The combined group now operates from two CV and two passenger car sites.

2   The distribution networks were significantly rationalized; both Don and Mintex operated from 22 depots (including Trist Draper), some of which were in direct competition within the same city. The rationalization to 16 depots removed approximately £1.5m. from overhead costs.

3   A material and product strategy was formulated which coordinated, much more closely than in the past, R&D and production on a group-wide scale. For example, Mintex and Textar operated more or less as autonomous units within the group; subsequently production was better co-ordinated, with spare capacity in the UK being utilized to take pressure off the Textar factories in Germany; some 15 per cent of Mintex's output is exported directly to Textar where it is packaged in Textar 'colours'. Significant cost savings accrued as a result of these developments, and increased collaboration and discussion led to improvements in the operating efficiencies of the UK companies.

4   The merger of Don and Mintex resulted in considerable savings in both fixed and operating costs including: administration; sales; finance; computing and R&D.

At the time of the Don acquisition BBA estimated that the reduction of expense would be between £2.5m. and £3m. per annum. It had been expected that some £1.5m. of sales would be lost as a result of the merger, but this figure proved far too high, with relatively few sales being lost, and the profit impact in a full year was some £4–£4.5m. In addition, there was an increase in the gross margin. Arising from the increased market share of the merged Mintex-Don (40–45 per cent), the company was able to be far more aggressive in terms of pricing, and significant price increases were pushed through (for some lines by up to 40 per cent); Ferodo, which had also been in loss in the UK and enjoyed a similar percentage share of the market, was happy to follow suit. These price increases gave BBA scope to trim unprofitable volume. The overall cost of the merger to BBA was £2.5m.–£3.5m.

The acquisition was made at a particularly favourable price since Cape, because of problems elsewhere within its group, was a forced seller. Furthermore, Don was in considerably better shape than BBA had anticipated, particularly with regard to the quality of its management and to the technological competence of the company. BBA was also impressed with the general condition of Don's manufacturing plant and fixed assets. It should also be noted that the workforce at Mintex and Don reacted positively to the measures taken towards rationalizing the two companies, realizing the dreadful state that the industry was in.

Railko manufactures reinforced plastics, bearings and components. The company made pre-tax profits of £546,000 in 1984 after net interest receipts of £64,000, on turnover up 22 per cent to £3.7m. Some 33 per cent of turnover was for export.

Overseas   Textar has been a major success story in recent years, and the company managed to increase turnover and profits in 1984, despite the impact both of lower car and commercial vehicle registrations in Germany, and the strike by the IG Metall workers. Textar, like Mintex-Don, manufactures brake and clutch linings, enjoying a 33 per cent share of the German market and some 40 per cent of exports from Germany, in competition with Jurid, Pagid and Beral.

The notably better performance of Textar compared with Mintex stems from a number of factors, including the much stronger showing of German car manufacturers compared with their UK counterparts, better manufacturing facilities and practices, and the different structure of the UK and German markets. The latter factor is important: in Germany the OE market for brake linings and disc brake pads is serviced by sale direct to the brake manufacturers as in the UK, but in Germany the car manufacturers specify the components to be used in the manufacture of the brakes. Of greater significance, the replacement market is supplied by the motor manufacturers as in the UK: the vehicle manufacturers have been able to control and hold prices in Germany much better than the brake and clutch manufacturers in the UK, and this has had a very significant effect upon margins in the replacement market.

Frenos y Embraques is an important supplier to the Spanish OE and replacement markets, enjoying a 15 per cent share of the home market and 20 per cent of exports from Spain.

Fressek (Spain) is one of the companies brought into the Group under the terms of the acquisition of Cape's automotive interests, and is now a 43 per cent owned associate of BBA.

Subsidiaries or associate companies in France, Canada, South Africa, Belgium and Australia sell Mintex-Don products; rationalization reduced costs without any loss of revenue.

Industrial

Table 2.4 is the estimate of the 1984 and 1985 breakdown of the operating profits of BBA's industrial companies.

TABLE 2.4   **Estimate of industrial trading profits**

	1984(E) £m.	1985(E) £m.
Scandura Ltd[a]	0.50	1.20
Synterials		0.20
Scandura Inc (including Uniroyal)	0.90	1.80
BBA Properties	0.25	0.25
Comprehensive Computer Services	0.25	0.25
Regina Glass Fibre Ltd ⎫ Vivian-Regina Ltd ⎬	−0.50	0.55
Sovex Marshall ⎭	0.10	0.35
	2.50	4.60

[a] including Mulcott Belting

UK Scandura Limited is the largest company within the industrial division, having in an average year a turnover of some £15m. per annum. During 1984 Scandura was badly affected by the miners' dispute, and in September that year moved into monthly losses of about £100,000. Nevertheless, the impact of the strike was mitigated to some extent by sales of belting to other outlets, both in the UK and overseas.

Scandura's activities can be subdivided into two main categories: belting, and industrial textiles and seals. The larger of these two subdivisions is belting: both heavy and lighter beltings are manufactured. The largest single user of heavy belting is the NCB (which accounts for 40 per cent of Scandura's total turnover), to whom Scandura is one of four technically-approved suppliers, the others being Fenner, TBA and Dunlop. Scandura's sales to the NCB have doubled in the last ten years and the company supplies 30 per cent of the NCB's requirements, although NCB orders fell by some 40 per cent in 1984 as a result of the strike. Exports of heavy duty belting are significant, particularly to Canada, India, Spain, New Zealand and Scandinavia.

Within industrial textiles and seals, a high proportion of turnover is made up of inter-group sales of dry asbestos yarn which is used in the manufacture of automotive friction materials, although nevertheless some 45 per cent of Scandura's yarn-based products are exported. The only significant competitor in the UK for asbestos yarns and fabrics is Turner & Newall. Asbestos cloth is also made for use in the manufacture of laminates and for protective clothing. Scandura also manufactures sheet rubber and asbestos jointing for automotive gaskets and for flanged joints in petrochemical installations. Scandura has an estimated 12 per cent share of the UK market for these products.

Scandura has considerable experience and expertise in weaving, and it is BBA's intention to expand from this base, and by utilizing some interesting product innovations (including new types of belting), move into the more general field of industrial textiles. It is in this area that BBA's next major corporate move is expected – probably initially in the UK, but eventually a further move may be made into the US market.

BBA Properties makes a useful profit each year, largely as a result of rental income on surplus properties, but also from time to time from development. Comprehensive Computer Services provides computer bureau services and generates a small, but useful profit.

Sovex Marshall supplies standardized mechanical handling systems and equipment for unit handling. Principal customers include the Post Office, the printing trade, document handling, baggage and freight at airports and seaports. There are a large number of competitors in this area, including GEC-Elliott, Fenamec, Lamson, Crabtree-Vickers, Denag and Desicon. Sovex Marshall was at one time a persistent loss-maker, but measures to improve the performance were taken in 1984 and these resulted in a return to trading profits (after losses of some £200,000 on turnover of about £3m. in 1983).

Overseas   In the United States, Scandura Inc manufactures heavy-duty solid woven PVC belting for coal conveying and for the conveying of grain and feed. A somewhat thinner version is used for the conveying of citrus fruits in California, Florida and Texas. Recently, the company has successfully introduced belting into the food processing industries and for use in warehouses, supermarkets and department stores. Scandura Inc has a good trading record and has remained consistently profitable; profits of up to £2m. were being earned a few years ago, although they have now been reduced to below £1m. as a result of the fall-off in demand from the mining industries. The move out of solid-woven and into plastic belting for the food processing industries, combined with a management shake-up, should lead to a recovery in profits over the next couple of years.

The Uniroyal companies, acquired in August 1985, were to be merged with Scandura Inc because the rubber belting produced by Uniroyal is manufactured using a similar method to the PVC belting of Scandura; both are attached to a loom-woven fabric or canvas. Rubber is more suitable than PVC for various applications (and is particularly heavily used by the open-cast mining industry and for transporting aggregates). There is very little direct competition between PVC and rubber belting, but there would be considerable cost savings on the merger of the two companies. Uniroyal's businesses returned to profit after a number of years of losses, but BBA saw further scope for cost reduction and margin improvement. Turnover of the combined grouping was anticipated to total about

£55m. in 1985, of which the Uniroyal business would contribute the greater proportion. This would place the combined company in a strong position as number two in the US market, behind Goodyear. Prospects for gains in market share were thought to be good, particularly following the withdrawal of Goodrich from the market. Given the potential for cost-saving and improvements in volume for the enlarged company, good progress was anticipated in the US market. Early inspection of the Uniroyal manufacturing plants encouraged BBA that it had made a good purchase.

AUTOMOTIVE PRODUCTS (AP) 1985

Automotive division

This division accounts for approximately one-third of AP Group turnover and manufactures a range of products for the original equipment (OE) manufacturers. For example, AP clutches have a high (possibly 90 per cent) market share in the UK, and a growing share in Europe. The division also includes brakes and steering and suspension systems, and some other products in which sales are relatively small in comparison with the aforementioned products.

Automotive–replacement parts

Replacement Parts are sold both through the OE manufacturer and also through AP's own distributor network, Antela. Antela has 89 depots through which it distributes spares to the garage trade. It has a turnover of £25m. and a market share of under 2 per cent. Approximately 30 per cent of Antela's turnover is accounted for by AP products. In a weak, over-supplied market AP has moved to franchising, and over 50 per cent of the depots are now franchised. Profits have been on an improving trend over the last two years.

Precision hydraulics

The division manufactures flying control and landing gear for civil and military aircraft, and hydraulics for military and defence applications. Turnover in 1985 was about £14m. An industrial relations problem was resolved, and turnover was expected to reach £19m. with good margins.

On 27 January 1986 BBA offered 56.25 million BBA shares, valuing Automotive Products at approximately £113.6m.

GUTHRIE 1988

After 1985 there were significant improvements in EPS achieved, without a major acquisition. However, in 1988 BBA acquired Guthrie, which was approximately one-third the size of BBA in terms of sales and assets.

In April 1988, Permodalan Nasional Berhad accepted BBA's £135m. cash for its 61 per cent stake in Guthrie. BBA were offering 2.7 cumulative convertible preference shares (at 6.75 per cent) for each Guthrie share which, with BBA shares at 154p, valued the cumulative preference shares at 292p, against a pre-bid price for Guthrie of 198p and a cash alternative of 270p.

The BBA convertible preference shares are convertible into BBA shares at the option of the holder on 31 May in any of the years 1990 to 2005 (both dates inclusive) by notice given during the period of 278 days on the relevant conversion date, at the rate of 54.64 BBA shares for every £100 nominal of BBA convertible preference share capital, equivalent to a conversion price of approximately 183p per BBA share. Subject to the provisions of the Companies Act 1985, the BBA convertible preference shares not previously converted of redeemed will be redeemed by BBA on 31 May 2006. Full conversion will increase the current issued share capital of BBA by 47,391,020 BBA shares, representing approximately 18.8 per cent of the current issued ordinary share capital of BBA as enlarged by such conversion. The BBA convertible preference shares to be issued pursuant to the offer will be allotted, credited as fully paid, initially on renounceable allotment letters.

Reasons for the offer

In the automotive components business, Guthrie's concentration in North America complemented BBA's activity in Europe and Australia. Guthrie's activity in structural plastics for the automotive industry in the USA would facilitate BBA's further growth in this area in Europe.

BBA had sought for some time to extend its activity in niche markets in industrial textiles for a wide range of end-users. Guthrie's hose and floor-covering business would provide a major step forward in this regard.

The spread of businesses of the two groups in North America, Europe and Australia offered an excellent geographical fit, protecting the enlarged group from exposure to any one economy. The sector spread of the new group would markedly improve the industrial balance of the two companies' activities.

The business of Guthrie

The activities of Guthrie are structured under six operating divisions: Automotive Components, Aviation Services, Electrical Equipment, Fire Protection Equipment, Textiles and Floor Coverings, and Trading.

The Automotive Components division consists principally of Butler Metal, based in Ontario, and Butler Polymet, which has plants in Toronto and North Carolina and a research centre in Detroit. Butler Metal is a major supplier to General Motors and has contracts for the supply of important motor components for the GM-10 series of intermediate cars. Butler Polymet manufactures and assembles structural plastic mouldings and has major contracts with Ford for the load floor for the Taurus and Sable estate cars and for bumper assemblies. Both companies have been awarded high quality ratings from General Motors, and Butler Polymet has gained Ford's prestigious Q.1 rating.

The Aviation Services business is conducted through Page Avjet Corporation, an aircraft sales and service business which provides a range of products and services to general and commercial aviation in the USA. It provides aircraft and passenger services to general and commercial aviation in the USA. The principal base is at Dulles, and there are other significant operations at Orlando, Miami, Detroit and Minneapolis. Page has one of the largest independent aircraft modification and maintenance centres in the world and has an established reputation for the design and installation of high-quality interiors. It also undertakes specialized engineering projects, including supplemental fuel tanks for Boeing 727 and 737 aircraft, engine noise reduction kits for DC-8 aircraft, and cargo doors. Page also operates a Jet Sales Division which buys and sells executive jet and airline passenger and cargo aircraft, and has a franchise with the Beech Aircraft Corporation.

The Electrical Equipment division consists of Ajax Magnethermic Corporation and Trench Electric. Ajax is one of the world's leading manufacturers of induction heating and melting equipment and its products are widely used in steel mills, foundries and the metal processing industries. Its headquarters and research and development centre are in Ohio and it has manufacturing facilities in Kentucky, North Carolina, Canada and the UK. Trench Electric, based in Toronto and with a marketing subsidiary in Germany, designs and manufactures specialized high voltage electrical transmission equipment for public utilities and major electrical contractors throughout the world.

Angus Fire Armour is one of the world's leading suppliers of fire-fighting and fire-protection equipment. Its principal customers are fire brigades, industries with high value installations, and government and military departments, but its products have widespread applications and are used in most countries in the world. Its principal products include Angus Duraline, the best selling fire hose in the UK, fire-fighting foam, fixed fire protection systems, extinguishers and sprinklers.

The principal UK company in the Textiles and Floor Coverings division is Duralay, which is the largest manufacturer of carpet underlay in Europe. 'Super Duralay' is the UK market leader, and Duralay also supplies retailers such as Harris Queensway, Allied Carpets and John Lewis with own-brand underlays. Duralay has developed a new range of floor-covering accessories, and further growth will result from the acquisition of P.C.Cox (Newbury) Limited, a manufacturer of adhesive and mastic applicators.

In Australia, Tascot Templeton manufactures Wilton, Axminster and bonded carpets for the Australian market and also has an active export trade. Palm Beach Towel is the second largest towel manufacturer in Australia and supplies a broad range of high-quality towels and towelling products.

The Trading division consisted largely of the group's wholesaling, retailing and packaging interests in Malawi, which were sold in March 1988. Guthrie Export Services provides export and buying services for government and private customers.

In the year ended 31 December 1987, the Guthrie Group had turnover of £319.8m. (1986: £321.0m.), profit before taxation of £22.6m. (1986: £17.6m.), and earnings per share of 21.8p (1986: 19.1p). Net tangible assets attributable to shareholders at that date amounted to £106.9m., and net cash balances were £13m.

Appendix 1   BBA Group PLC

FINANCIAL ANALYSIS, 1978–88

Year To 31.12		1978	1979	1980	1981	1982	1983	1984	1985	1986	1987	1988
Turnover (£m.)		120.5	137.3	135.4	130.6	150.9	156.1	176.1	229.5	553.2	672.6	1011.9
Net profit before int & tax (£m.)		9.27	10.36	4.08	7.73	8.39	8.78	8.86	16.7	36.0	56.7	89.3
Net profit before tax (£m.)		7.66	8.00	0.35	3.56	4.55	5.51	5.41	12.0	22.7	44.2	64.1
Net capital employed (£m.)		48.0	54.0	73.2	69.5	69.6	72.1	75.8	79.8	125.5	304.9	320.4
EPS (25p ord. share) (P)		10.1	10.5	–	2.6	3.4	4.6	2.2	8.2	10.3	17.5	20.8
Dividend cover (adjusted) (P)		3.2	2.8	–	1.1	1.4	1.9	0.9	3.0	3.0	3.3	2.4
Share price: high (P)		52	55	48	39	39	40	59	147	288	248	188
low (P)		36	35	21	19	21	23	25	50	114	102	139
ROCE line 3	%	16.0	14.8	0.5	5.1	6.5	7.6	7.1	15.0	18.1	14.5	20.0
line 4												
Margin line 2	%	7.7	7.5	3.0	5.9	5.6	5.6	5.0	7.3	6.5	8.4	8.8

Appendix 2

INDUSTRIAL AND GEOGRAPHICAL ANALYSIS, 1981–8 (£m.)

Industrial	1981	1982	1983	1984	1985	1986	1987	1988
Sales								
Industrial	36.8	42.0	41.8	46.2	54.8	93.6	106.5	227.0
Automotive	93.8	108.9	114.4	130.0	174.7	459.6	566.1	694.3
Aviation								90.6
Profit								
Industrial	1.18	2.04	1.89	2.57	4.41	12.4	10.4	20.6
Automotive	7.55	6.35	6.76	6.48	12.69	26.4	41.4	52.9
Aviation								10.4
Net Assets								
Industrial	15.5	16.1	20.2	22.6	31.9			
Automotive	30.1	30.6	38.1	36.0	52.0			
Geographical Sales								
UK				48.1	66.3	172.8	214.1	287.0
W Germany				57.7	72.9	109.1	120.3	131.0
R O Europe				33.6	47.0	131.5	156.5	188.0
N America				24.1	28.8	67.3	66.0	231.9
Other				12.6	14.5	72.5	115.6	174.0
Profit								
UK				0.71	3.41	5.93	18.1	26.8
W Germany				3.74	5.28	7.76	7.5	7.1
R O Europe				1.62	2.93	7.30	7.5	13.2
N America				1.33	2.86	8.20	7.7	19.6
Other				(0.31)	0.93	8.17	8.9	13.3

Appendix 3   T & N PLC

FINANCIAL ANALYSIS, 1984–8

Year ended December	1984	1985	1986	1987	1988
Turnover (£m.)	520.3	535.1	540.8	961.2	1048.8
Profit before interest & tax (£m.)	50.8	49.7	53.9	95.3	106.4
Profit before tax (£m.)	38.1	39.6	44.3	77.1	93.9
Net capital employed (£m.)	328	351	304	521	520
EPS (per £1 ord share) (P)	26.6	27.1	24.7	24.2	29.7
Dividend cover	8.1	4.1	2.4	2.1	2.3
Share price: high (P)	108	114	240	321	200
: low (P)	60	74	80	139	154
ROCE line 2 (%) line 4	15.5	14.2	17.7	18.3	20.9
Margin line 2 (%) line 1 (%)	9.8	9.3	10.0	9.9	10.3

Appendix 4   Automotive products

FINANCIAL ANALYSIS, 1981–5

	1981 £m.	1982 £m.	1983 £m.	1984 £m.	1985 £m.
Trading					
Turnover	201.9	203.3	223.5	242.8	260.2
Group operating profit on continuing activities	7.3	1.3	14.3	13.2	17.2
Trading losses of operations sold[a]	–	(2.0)	(3.1)	(0.9)	–
Interest (net)	(7.0)	(8.5)	(7.2)	(7.8)	(9.5)
Exceptional costs	(2.5)	(4.9)	–	(0.6)	(0.2)
Result before taxation	(2.2)	(14.1)	4.0	3.9	7.5
Taxation	(1.2)	(0.6)	(0.8)	(1.0)	(1.1)
Result after taxation	(3.4)	(14.7)	3.2	2.9	6.4
Extraordinary items	–	1.5	(1.7)	(2.0)	(2.5)
Dividends	(2.5)	(1.1)	(1.4)	(1.7)	(1.4)
Transfer to/(from) reserves	(5.9)	(14.3)	0.1	(0.8)	2.5

continued

continued

	1981 £m.	1982 £m.	1983 £m.	1984 £m.	1985 £m.
Employment of capital					
Fixed assets					
Tangible and intangible assets	68.3	72.7	69.4	72.4	75.4
Investments	5.2	5.9	3.9	5.4	3.8
Working capital (excluding bank balances and short term loans)	74.2	73.3	75.0	80.6	75.9
	147.7	151.9	148.3	158.4	155.1
Capital employed					
Capital and reserves	100.3	87.8	87.4	86.9	88.2
Net borrowings including obligations under finance leases	47.4	64.1	60.9	71.5	66.9
	147.7	151.9	148.3	158.4	155.1
Ratios					
Earnings per share–net basis[b]	(7.54p)	(27.70p)	4.18p	3.72p	9.92p
Operating profit return on average capital employed[c]	5.2%	0.9%	9.5%	8.6%	10.9%
Ordinary dividend per share including imputed tax credit	4.286p	0.714p	1.429p	2.143p	1.429p
Number of employees at year end	10.493	9.285	9.186	8.552	8.172

[a] Trading losses of operations sold have not been identified prior to 1982
[b] Earnings per share is calculated on the results after taxation and preference share dividends, but before extraordinary items
[c] Adjusted to exclude operations sold from 1982 on onwards

Turnover and profit on ordinary activities

The geographical analysis of Group turnover and profit is

	Turnover		Operating profit	
	1984	1985	1984	1985
	£m	£m	£m	£m
Companies in:				
United Kingdom	187.7	189.0	10.5	14.6
Europe	28.5	46.0	0.9	1.0
Rest of the world	19.4	25.2	1.6	2.1
	235.6	260.2	13.0	17.7
Discontinued activities	7.2	–		
	242.8	260.2		

The market analysis of turnover is as follows:

UK 55% (1981 58%) Europe Other EEC 26% (1984 18%) Rest of the world 19% (1984 24%). Income arising from trading operations carried on outside the United Kingdom amounted to £118.4m. (1984 £102.0m.). Goods and services exported direct from the United Kingdom amounted to £55.4m. (1984 £62.1m.) which included £8.2m. (1984 £8.0m.) to overseas subsidiaries. The value of goods sold by the Group in the United Kingdom to vehicle manufacturers and then exported by them is estimated to total £24.6m. (1954 £23.5m.).

Appendix 5   Guthrie Group

FINANCIAL ANALYSIS, 1983–7

Consolidated profit and loss accounts

The following is derived from the consolidated profit and loss accounts of the Guthrie Group for the five financial years ended 31 December 1987:

	1983 £000	1984 £000	1985 £000	1986 £000	1987 £000
Turnover	280,504	359,467	332,083	321,023	319,844
Operating profit	11,063	16,803	18,238	19,720	22,282
Interest	(4,374)	(5,373)	(4,143)	(2,083)	314
Profit on ordinary activities before taxation	6,689	11,430	14,095	17,637	22,596
Taxation	1,269	2,381	2,253	2,883	4,676
Profit on ordinary activities after taxation	5,420	9,049	11,842	14,754	17,920
Minority shareholders' interest	93	(12)	179	80	75
Profit before extraordinary items	5,327	9,061	11,663	14,674	17,845
Extraordinary items	(1,949)	4,516	(1,199)	–	327
Profit after extraordinary items	3,378	13,577	10,464	14,674	18,172
Dividends	–	–	–	2,624	5,084
Retained profit for year	3,378	13,577	10,464	12,050	13,088
	Pence	Pence	Pence	Pence	Pence
Earnings per ordinary share	7.5	12.8	16.5	19.1	21.8
Dividends per ordinary share	–	–	–	3.2	6.2

Consolidated balance sheet

The following is the consolidated balance sheet of the Guthrie Group as at 31 December 1987:

	£000
Fixed assets	
Tangible assets	54,298
Investments	1,484
	55,782
Current assets	
Stocks	46,556
Debtors	57,502
Cash	42,370
	146,428
Creditors due within one year	70,605
Net current assets	75,823
Total assets less current liabilities	131,605
Creditors due after more than one year	24,399
Net assets	107,206
Capital and reserves	
Called up share capital	20,501
Share premium account	36,310
Capital redemption reserve	14,948
Profit and loss account	35,168
	106,927
Minority shareholders' interest	279
	107,206

continued

continued

Analysis of operating profit and turnover by activity

	Operating profit £000	Turnover £000
Automotive components	5,612	65,039
Aviation services	5,967	78,670
Electrical equipment	2,722	51,447
Fire protection equipment	3,676	56,735
Textiles and floor coverings	3,475	56,483
Trading	830	11,470
	22,282	319,844

Analysis of operating profit and turnover by geographical source

	Operating profit £000	Turnover £000
Africa	1,048	11,348
Australia	1,691	14,190
Canada	4,275	63,683
United Kingdom and Europe	3,217	92,035
United States of America	12,051	138,588
	22,282	319,844

Analysis of turnover by geographical market supplied

Africa	14,467
Australia	15,076
Canada	25,642
United Kingdom and Europe	83,368
United States of America	160,789
Other	20,502
	319,844

Other income

Income from fixed asset investments:

Listed	117
Unlisted	251
	368

Appendix 6   *Acquisitions Monthly* profile of Dr John White

If Dr John White makes running a public company sound and look perfectly simple, it must be due to his clear-sighted, highly organized, tough, no-nonsense approach to business. This self-confessed workaholic was appointed Group Managing Director of BBA Group at the beginning of 1985. Since his appointment as a director of BBA in October 1984, the company's share price has risen from 32p to 149p. Impressive enough.

The Yorkshire-based component manufacturer has had its share of problems. In recent years, although BBA's overseas subsidiaries made good returns, the UK businesses produced losses. It is for this reason that White was chosen to steer the company on a more profitable course.

A key element in his strategy is making acquisitions. In 1985 alone, BBA made eight acquisitions in the UK and overseas worth a total of around £44m.

White, himself, has vast experience of making acquisitions. He says he handled his first takeover at the age of 26 and, now aged 43, has completed 23 acquisitions, only one of which proved unsuccessful. These purchases were all part of the 'corporate turnarounds' which seem to be White's trademark in his career to date.

He feels his first big break came in 1967 when Professor Roland Smith offered him a senior research fellowship at the Institute of Science & Technology at Manchester, drafting him on permanent secondment to Staveley Industries. For Staveley, he investigated the problems and necessity of applying modern marketing to the machine tool industry.

Armed with this experience and a well-earned doctorate, White went to Bullough Limited where he was first of all a member of a team running a holding company which comprised eight engineering and two chemical companies. A man with a keen eye for a good acquisition, he identified recovery possibilities at Newton Derby, a small public company. On behalf of Bullough, White was involved in acquiring Newton Derby and then restructuring and running the company as Managing Director.

From 1975 to 1978, White used his expertise to good advantage for the Hepworth Iron Company and its parent company Hepworth Ceramic Holdings Ltd. As assistant Managing Director of Hepworth Iron, his executive workload was the formation of a European group in the clay pipe industry. An organization of four companies in West Germany, Holland, Belgium and France was built up by acquisition and rapidly formed into a successful cohesive group.

Tarmac Plc recruited White in October 1978. To appreciate White's contribution to Tarmac over a period of six years, one has only to look at the figures. He was first in charge of Permanite, a building materials subsidiary, just breaking even on a £20m. turnover. Over the next years, he was responsible for creating the 20-company strong Tarmac Building Products Ltd with sales of £210m. and profits of £12.2m.

The Pearson and Fenton families who ran BBA for three generations must have felt themselves fortunate to head-hunt White. BBA is a small (£176m sales and profits of £5.4m in 1984) multi-national engaged in the manufacture of friction materials for the automotive industry and industrial textiles, principally for conveyor belting. White says that BBA will remain as a furnisher of components and expansion will be made within its core businesses.

BBA's first major acquisition since White's arrival was that of a major UK competitor to BBA's friction materials subsidiary, Mintex. It acquired Don, Cape Industries' subsidiary, for £15.8m. in April of this year and both companies are to be reorganized to achieve lower costs all round. Other major purchases have been the acquisition of the US rubber belting subsidiary of Uniroyal Inc., for £13.5m. and the takeover of a high-tech USM company, Synterials, which is involved in the design and manufacture of complex precision moulds.

Target companies for BBA are those within its own core businesses where there is a high cost of market entry and the company is producing a good cash flow within a dying industry. The price should reflect a hefty discount to net assets.

White says that BBA's small board – the Chairman, himself as group MD, Finance Director and one non-executive director – can quickly respond to proposals or decisions and this is of great importance on the acquisition front. White goes after acquisitions himself, doing the necessary research, identification and negotiations without the assistance of intermediaries. 'If someone brought a company to me that I did not already know about, I would worry that I am losing my touch.'

When considering a takeover in a particular sector, he normally has a list of ten potential companies and then chooses just one to go for. When it comes to the actual purchase, he says that if the chairman of the target company leaves, as is often the case, he likes 'the original executives to have the first option on filling the top management position in the new subsidiary.'

White has produced a fascinating corporate philosophy check-list for BBA's own management. In it, he talks of 'grit and gumption as preferable to inertia and intellect' and says that long-term growth requires 'resources – notably men and money' as well as 'sustained performance rather than superficial genius.'

In many ways, this philosophy draws on his deep religious faith. White is a member of the Central Board of Finance of the Methodist Church, and has just completed 24 years as a local lay preacher.

He says he will always finish every task he has set himself before he goes to bed at night. This tenacity is presumably the quality which helps him to engage in his favourite hobby of dry-stone walling in his Leicestershire smallholding. He says he sees an analogy between this hobby and his business life – 'taking small pieces and fitting them together to make a solid object.' (*Acquisitions Monthly*, December 1985)

Appendix 7

BBA – A CORPORATE PHILOSOPHY

The inertia of history is a powerful influence on corporate philosophy. BBA in its 103 years of existence has strayed little from:

1   Yorkshire paternalism;
2   weaving of heavy textiles;
3   friction technology via woven or pressed resin media.

The philosophy of BBA for the next few years will be to adapt rather than abandon the inert.

Management

1   Grit and gumption are preferable to inertia and intellect.
2   The Victorian work ethic is not an antique.
3   One man can only serve one master, to whom he is responsible for a minimum number of succinctly defined tasks.
4   Most companies owned or yet to be acquired possess adequate people waiting to be transformed by dedicated leadership.
5   The effectiveness of an organization is in inverse proportion to the number of hierarchical layers.

Markets

We shall concentrate in markets where:

1   The products are in a state of maturity or decline – 'Sunset Industries'.
2   The scale of our presence in a market segment will allow price leadership.
3   The capital cost of market entry is high.
4   Fragmentation of ownership on the supply side facilitates rapid earnings growth by acquisition of contribution flows.

Money

1   The longer run belongs to Oscar Wilde, who is dead.
2   The key macro and micro variables of our business are so dynamic that poker becomes more predictable than planning and reactivity more profitable than rumination.

3   Budgets are personal commitments made by management to their superiors, subordinates, shareholders and their self-respect.
4   The cheapest producer will win.
5   The investment of money on average return of less than three points above market should be restricted to Ascot.
6   Gearing should not exceed 40 per cent. The location from which funds emanate should be matched to the location from which the profit stream permits their service.
7   We are not currency speculators, even when we win.
8   Tax is a direct cost to the business and, accordingly, should be eschewed.
9   Victorian thrift is not an antique.
10 Nothing comes free, cheap assets are often expensive utilities.

Monday
Our tactic is to:

1   Increase the metabolic rate of BBA through directed endeavour.
2   To increase profit margins by drastic cost reduction.
3   To massage and thereby extend the life cycle of the products in which we are engaged.
4   To become market dominant in our market niches by:
    (a) outproducing the competition;
    (b) transforming general markets where we are nobody to market niches where we are somebody;
    (c) buying competitors.
5   Use less money in total and keep more money away from the tax man and the usurer.
6   Avoid the belief that dealing is preferable to working.
7   Go home tired.

Maybe

1   The replication of our day-to-day tactic provides long-term growth.
2   We need to address 'Monday' this week and what our reaction will be to what may be on 'Monday' for the next three years.
3   Three years is, in the current environment, the limit of man's comprehension of what may be.
4   Long-term growth necessitates:
    (a) Resource – notably men and money.
    (b) Sustained performance rather than superficial genius.

Appendix 8

CAR AND COMMERCIAL VEHICLE PRODUCTION IN THE UK
1974–88

	Cars (000s)	Commercial vehicles (000s)
1974	1,534	403
1975	1,268	381
1976	1,333	372
1977	1,316	398
1978	1,223	384
1979	1,070	408
1980	923	389
1981	954	229
1982	888	269
1983	1,045	245
1984	909	225
1985	1,048	266
1986	1,019	229
1987	1,143	247
1988	1,227	318

3   Ariel Industries

In 1988 the Board of Leicester-based manufacturing group Ariel Industries plc announced its plans for reverting the company to private status.

Following his appointment in 1962, Chairman Kenneth Edwards, with his unique brand of management style, had shaped and steered the company full cycle from turnaround and healthy growth during the 1960s and 1970s, through recession in the mid-1980s. After four years of sustained losses from 1984 to 1987, the company finally appeared to be making a recovery.

BACKGROUND

The Ariel Group has its origins in a small company established in 1920 to supply accessories to the foundation garment industry. The company was associated with an American manufacturer from whom it purchased machinery of advanced design for the manufacture of these products.

Largely as a result of this technological advantage, the company enjoyed a period of high profitability and growth. By the mid-1950s, however, with the post-war boom over and no new products available, the company began to feel the effects of much stiffer competition, and earnings declined.

Consultants were called in and at intervals over a period of several years they introduced work study, production planning, sales forecasting and other schemes, but these had little lasting effect.

Early in 1962, the family directors were advised to go to the market for a professional manager. Acting on consultants' advice, they invited Mr Kenneth Edwards to join Ariel as general manager of the main operating company. This he did, in the belief that Ariel was a company big enough to do something with, but small enough to enable his style of management to be applied.

Mr Edwards had grown up on his parents' farm where business in general buying, selling, and the affairs of the farm in particular were topics of family conversation in which the Edwards children were immersed from an early age. He had been encouraged by his father to take initiatives and follow them through to their conclusion.

These started in a small way, but at all times a high degree of realism was achieved by the father insisting that the children use their own money. Whether they were buying and selling produce or rearing cattle, they were responsible for the initial outlay and for all subsequent decisions right through to eventual marketing.

Kenneth Edwards's association with manufacturing industry had originally been intended to be of strictly limited duration. On leaving Cambridge University in 1952, he had decided to take a job in industry for six months to see what it was like.

Joseph Lucas Ltd had been chosen from his list of potential employers as the company he would least mind embarrassing by resigning from after only six months. In the event, however, on his first day with the company, he had felt compelled to confess his short-term intentions to the education officer who had recruited him. It had been suggested that it would be helpful to all concerned if these limited objectives were not widely circulated.

However, at the end of six months when he finally explained his position he had been offered a series of interesting assignments which had induced him each time to delay his resignation.

Ten years passed, punctuated by a succession of challenging appointments at Lucas, but his inherent interest in farming remained strong. Eventually, at Leicester a satisfying compromise was found; a new challenge with Ariel, but close enough to his farming interests to offer something of both worlds.

PROBLEMS FACING THE NEW MANAGER

At this time, Ariel's management was facing severe labour relations problems and their products were in the last few years of their life. Earning power was totally in the areas which were about to collapse, and other areas which had a future just had not been developed.

Mr Edwards soon saw that for a rescue operation to succeed he would first of all have to get management back in control of the company, and then quickly diversify into product areas with growth potential. To provide the wherewithal to fund the diversification he would have to find ways of releasing capital from the declining areas of the business. To shore up the operation until the new ventures paid off, he would need to squeeze the last drop of earnings out of the older products.

The company was in an overdraft position at this time, and although asset-heavy, considerable reorganization would be necessary before under-utilized assets could be released. The business was still under family control and decision-making was highly centralized. For example, even quite minor items of expenditure in both domestic and overseas operations required approval of the managing director. There was some reluctance to come to terms with the major decisions that needed to be taken if the company was to be re-established on a profitable basis. It had to be made very plain that unless firm action was taken in a number of areas, there would be no future for the company.

During the difficult few years following Mr Edwards's appointment there was pressure from some shareholders to sell off certain areas of the business in which the break-up value was considered to be greater than that of a going concern. This suggestion was resisted by Mr Edwards, who began to buy shares heavily in the company himself at this time to strengthen his opposition to such a move.

During this period he set up an employee share bank as a trustee company, through which employees had an indirect, risk-free stake in the equity of the group. Interest on these investments was related to dividends declared on Ariel shares.

By the end of 1973 Mr Edwards's shareholding was approximately 20 per cent and the share bank held some 14 per cent of the equity. No other shareholder held more than 10 per cent.

GROWTH AND DEVELOPMENT OF ARIEL

Reorganization

In February 1969 Mr Edwards was appointed chairman of the holding company, and in presenting his first report, for the year ending 30 November 1968, he noted the considerable cost of the company's diversification programme, and the continuing decline in demand for the traditional range of foundation garment accessories, which together had resulted in a fall in pre-tax profits of 30 per cent compared with the previous year.

However, by the end of 1970 he was able to report that the company had completed the reorganization programme it had set itself, and that he was pleased with the way new product lines were developing. He stated:

> The main ones are industrial fasteners, light engineered products including automatic assembly equipment and polyurethane formulations and components. These give us a product range which is wide enough to insulate us from the fluctuations in fortune in any particular industry, without losing for us the flexibility and good communications which a company of this size can enjoy.
>
> What is equally important is that the products themselves are

to some large extent complementary, and the management skills required to run them are very similar. We are in the happy position where we have adequate cash resources to take every opportunity which presents itself to supplement these lines with profitable additions.[1]

In 1974, formal planning was based upon a requirement that there should be 15 per cent growth in net assets in real terms each year, so that capital employed doubled approximately every five years. This objective was coupled with a wish to pay a dividend of 5 per cent on capital employed each year. Under 1973–4 tax arrangements these goals required pre-tax earnings of about 35 per cent on capital employed.

In discussing his company's future, Mr Edwards explained that it was his intention to obtain separate stock market quotations for each operating subsidiary as soon as it had a satisfactory five-year track record.

I do not believe in large companies, and I am not convinced that economies of scale are as clearly defined as is often believed. A turnover of, say, £3,000,000 from 300 people, turning in about half a million pounds a year, is a meaningful company. I believe that a company of that size is, in terms of performance and employee relations, an optimum unit.

In reorganizing Ariel, a number of people had developed certain talents for this type of operation, which made it important in Mr Edwards's view to adopt a strategy which would allow the company to capitalize on these reorganizational skills. It was also considered that the company had considerable management expertise in making simple products in very large quantities, and selling these to industry. Everything the company touched was said to fit precisely into that pattern.

Mr Edwards emphasized that in his opinion the key to corporate planning was not so much in setting objectives, but getting the necessary action to achieve those objectives: 'We put stress on making sure we have action going, consistent with what we want to achieve, but do not bother too much about the decimal points of the objective.'

There were considered to be very few technical factors limiting company achievement: a more significant constraint on growth was felt to be the amount of disruption that people can stand: 'Generally, you come up against the fact that if you push very hard you have to make a great many changes, and there is a limit to what you can do without making people unhappy,' commented Mr Edwards.

In 1972 the group was enlarged by acquisition, and the possibility of future acquisitions was causing the company to review its management structure. It was hoped to organize the company in such a way that Ariel's direct management style and now excellent employee relationships were not endangered. Within the group it was hoped that subsidiaries could grow independently until they reached a stage where some part of their equity could be given a separate stock market quotation. Reorganization would make each major subsidiary an operationally autonomous unit. Mr Edwards explained the company's organization in March 1974 as follows:

Ariel Industries Ltd is the public holding company. In line beneath this, but not in importance, we have Ariel Management Services Ltd employing a small number of people who are the central team: myself, our data processing and central accounting staff; altogether about 20 people.

Everyone else is employed in subsidiary companies under a chief executive with his own structure. We have developed a style of management where we have effort all the way down the line. I think we have harnessed our people's imagination better than most. I do not see management as brilliance. The need for the genius is totally overrated. Our success is due to depth of interest rather than brilliance at any one level. Every operation is organized on such a scale that we get intelligence all the way down.

The emphasis on the all-rounder by Business Schools is wrong. Management is a matter of getting together a team of people each with a particular cutting edge that is well honed. One of the things I have to do is to stop my people who have been on business courses from trying to dabble in things they are not good at. It is important to realize the business you are in and not to think that you can do everything. There is a world of difference between knowing the management techniques and being able to make things happen. The problem is to find people in the market place with any entrepreneurial streak. We are after people whose instincts are right, who in a business situation can make things happen – these are the sort of men I want, not the smart alecs.

We do have failures of course, perhaps one out of three. Some want to sit in the office and apply theory, but that does not make things happen. I bring people in at a lower level, and give them project work, throw them in and even let them make a mess of it at times. A man in his late twenties or early thirties may be put in as a general manager of something small, but something that is his. If he makes a success of that he moves on to something bigger and we are away. That is how I think managers are bred.

Acquisition of Thomas Hunter Limited

In July 1972 the shareholders of Thomas Hunter Ltd accepted a £1.8m. cash offer from Ariel for the whole of the issued share capital of their company. Hunter's was a long-established private company manufacturing and marketing metal closures for the food industry, and equipment for applying those closures.

The company had a good profit record, but recently a change in marketing policy by some major food manufacturers had caused a swing away from closures of the type produced by Hunter. This change in demand, coupled with a totally inadequate investment programme, had caused a marked decline in earnings.

It was Ariel's intention to make whatever revenue and capital expenditure was necessary in order to regain business lost over the previous two years, and reverse the downward trend in profits. At the time of the acquisition, Hunter had approximately £900,000 in cash, surplus to requirements of the existing business.

On completion of the sale, Hunter's previous board of two directors retired and Mr Edwards and Mr George Beebee, a fellow director of Ariel, were appointed to the Hunter board. It was their intention to make as few changes as possible in the staffing of Hunter's and to build the new management team substantially from existing executives. Reorganization at Hunter's was expected to be completed during the second half of 1974. Although cash resources were used to purchase Hunter, Ariel was able to free enough cash from subsidiaries to clear its overdraft and leave a substantial amount of cash in hand by the end of 1972, which it was considered would put the company in a good position in its search for further acquisitions during 1973. It was stated Ariel policy not to become involved in asset-stripping, but to find a company complementary to its own and which would benefit from joining the group. An acquisition would only be of interest to Ariel if it could be left operationally intact, and given positive help in its development.

GRETONE LIMITED

Gretone, Ariel's engineering subsidiary, was located in north-west England, at St Anne's-on-Sea, about 150 miles from its parent company's Leicester base.

In addition to mould and die manufacture, the company also produced test pieces and other components on a batch production basis for the aircraft and atomic energy industries. In 1973, about 25 per cent of Gretone's output was for the aircraft industry.

The company occupied a new freehold factory, purchased in 1972, with adequate space for a threefold expansion if required. Manufacturing facilities included jig borers, profile grinding machines, lathes, milling machines, cylindrical and surface grinding machines. There were also fabricating and some heat-treatment facilities.

Gretone operated as an autonomous unit under its managing director, Mr Alan Armitage, earning a pre-tax profit of £86,000 in 1973 on a turnover of £360,000, from its 70-strong, skilled work-force.

At the end of 1973, Ariel acquired SOB Engineering Co Ltd, a smaller company than Gretone, and situated at Blackpool, a few miles north of St Anne's. This business was acquired as a result of a legal action by Ariel against the company's former owner, who had also been an executive of Gretone. The value of this acquisition to Gretone was considered to be primarily its skilled labour force of 40 men.

Mr Armitage had transferred one of his own staff to SOB as works manager, but it was also occupying his own time to a significant extent in March 1974. Gretone had a full order book for the whole of 1974 with sufficient work for both factories. There was no intention at this time of combining operations at one site. It was considered doubtful, in any case, whether many of the men would be prepared to travel the few miles involved if operations were centralized at St Anne's. Because of the demand for skilled labour in the area, SOB employees would have little difficulty in finding alternative employment close to their present workplace.

Mr Armitage's main activity was in developing new business and negotiating with existing customers. Although located in the north-west of England, Gretone's work was also obtained from firms in other parts of the UK. The Republic of Ireland, too, was an important outlet, accounting for about 10 per cent of Gretone's sales in 1973.

Both Mr Armitage and his planner/estimator considered it necessary for Gretone to have its own product. In common with other subcontractors in the engineering industry, the company was considered to be vulnerable to the economic fluctuations of that sector, and would be among the early sufferers of a down-turn in business. Nevertheless, in early 1974, subcontract toolmaking was a very profitable activity for Gretone.

Mr Armitage considered that about 35 people was probably an ideal size for a toolmaking business, providing rather more flexibility than Gretone enjoyed, especially when work was less plentiful. However, by careful planning and estimating, Gretone was able to compete successfully with smaller companies, especially on delivery, even though they might be undercut on price from time to time by their competitors. Gretone required a product of its own to provide some insulation from the economic fluctuations of its industry, and also to provide the basis for growth. Mr Edwards considered this so important that he devoted much of his time in the spring of 1974 to analysing how this might be achieved.

'Gretone is a very successful unit, but not yet large enough to be totally independent,' he commented. 'We need to buy something to put with Gretone to achieve two things. Firstly, to build up the company to the right size, and secondly, to give it an "own product" content in its sales.' Mr Armitage did not envisage this to be a mass-produced product, but rather one which would utilize the company's precision engineering skills.

The group continued its traditional line of business through to the 1980s, but during the period 1980–3, profits were ploughed into new product developments such as systems for soilless crop growing (hydroponics) and associated chemicals. The company had seen the necessity to diversify away from the traditional business as the economic recession began to bite into the traditional core activities.

Gretone continued to be a major profit contributor through the difficult period from 1984 to 1987, through its main aerospace activities.

FINANCIAL PERFORMANCE

In April 1973, Ariel increased its authorized share capital from £750,000 to £1,750,000 in order to achieve three objectives:

1   To provide for a one-for-one scrip issue to shareholders as a step towards creating a freer market in the company's shares.

2   To provide a block of unissued shares which could be used as part of the consideration in any future acquisitions.

3   To qualify the company for trustee status.

With regard to the second of these objectives, whilst the company was primarily interested in cash acquisitions, it was recognized that cases could arise where equity was required as part of the consideration, and for this reason unissued shares should be available. There was little merit, in Mr Edwards's opinion in 'throwing paper around'. If one company issued shares to buy another, a larger company resulted but what contribution did that make to the economy? 'To finance our acquisitions we release cash from existing operations. If I had to issue equity to do it, who would I be fooling?'

Gearing had not been used by the company in its expansion programme, but it was anticipated that this might become necessary in the future. To this end the company would be prepared to accept one pound of debt capital for every two pounds of equity assets.

However, the company had not resorted to raising capital, relying hitherto mainly on retained profits up to 1988, although plummeting profits from 1983 saw bank overdraft rise to almost £2m. in 1988 (£1.5m. in 1987).

By 1988 the company was experiencing an improvement in performance, assisted to some extent by the upturn in the United Kingdom economy and new product development pay-offs (See Appendix 1 for performance figures.)

EMPLOYEE RELATIONS AND OWNERSHIP

Mr Edwards expressed his strong belief in free enterprise, but had certain reservations about the way in which the rewards of free enterprise were distributed. He had sought, and felt that he had to some extent succeeded in achieving, a system whereby salary increases were determined solely by performance and were not left to the subjective judgement of himself or any other member of the company. By developing a mathematical model which clearly showed the economic outcomes of each of the main strategies open to the company, he was able to develop and agree with the work-force and their unions, a wages policy which guaranteed automatic awards as the 'value added' within the company increased.

At Ariel, suggestions were invited from all sections of the company regarding future programmes, which were then jointly determined. It was agreed in advance what proportion of value added should be paid out, taking into consideration the need to plough back sufficient earnings to support the company's desired level of growth.

Programmes were measured in advance to determine expected yields, and employees knew in advance their salary expectations for that year. Rewards were paid month by month, according to value added, as the programme was achieved.

The scheme was seen as an important breakthrough by Mr Edwards, and had fundamentally altered a situation from one in which the company simply reacted to trade union demands, to one in which the company took the initiative in developing its reward system.

During the period 1980–2 Mr Edwards strove to maintain the viability of the employees' share trust and in a letter to shareholders (Appendix 2) he put forward a proposition to outside shareholders which involved an invitation to sell their shares to the trust at a price of 30p (which was well above the 'low' of that year). Although dividends were held constant over this period, the chairman was pessimistic regarding the prospects for 1983 and thus anxious that shareholders should have the opportunity to cut their own 'losses' in the short term.

By 1985 only about 10 per cent of Ariel's shares were held by outside shareholders, the rest being held jointly by the share trust and the directors. In September 1983 the employee trusts – of which there were then three, owning, in total, 75 per cent of the equity – considered buying the company's older engineering businesses, Steels and Busks and S & D Rivet (industrial fasteners). This was a move basically to protect jobs, and although neither business was particularly profitable, S & D Rivet was considered to have firmer long-term prospects.

By 1987 the company was still negotiating disposal of these companies for around £2m., and it had the backing of the employee trusts – a major pre-condition of the disposals was the need to demonstrate that the businesses were ongoing and that they could offer long-term viability and thus continued job security for the existing employees. It was a policy of the group to encourage participation at every level of employment and to ensure that employees were well informed at all times of current and future developments.

In the middle of 1988 the company announced its intention to revert to private status (see Appendix 3) and to buy back shares from the small number of outside investors, who held only about 10 per cent of the total shares issued.

The main shareholder interests as at 31 March 1988 were:

	No of shares
Ariel Industries Employees' Share Trust	1,794,000
Ariel SA	1,389,447
Ariel Employees' Holdings Limited	1,297,256
C.K. Edwards	911,670

Appendix 1

CONSOLIDATED PROFIT AND LOSS ACCOUNT FOR THE YEAR ENDED 31 MARCH 1988

	£
Turnover	11,146,430
Profit on ordinary activities, before taxation	522,317
Taxation on profit on ordinary activities	(237,627)
Profit on ordinary activities, after taxation	284,690
Proposed dividend	(120,000)
Retained profit for the financial year	164,690
Earnings per ordinary share	4.74p

CONSOLIDATED BALANCE SHEET FOR THE YEAR ENDED 31 MARCH 1988

	£	£
Fixed assets		
Tangible assets		4,211,989
Investments		322,198
		4,534,187
Current assets		
Stocks	2,438,786	
Debtors	2,680,537	
Cash at bank and in hand	1,206,537	
	6,325,860	
Creditors: amounts falling due within one year		
Bank overdraft	(1,650,142)	
Other	(1,927,435)	
	(3,577,577)	
Net current assets		2,748,283
Total assets less current liabilities		7,282,470
Creditors: amounts falling due after more than one year[a]	(29,400)	
Provisions for liabilities and charges	(195,072)	
		(224,472)
		7,057,998
Capital and reserves		
Called-up share capital		1,500,000
Reserves		5,557,998
		7,057,998

[a] Corporation Tax

COMPARATIVE RESULTS 1978–87

	1978 £000s	1979 £000s	1980 £000s	1981 £000s	1982 £000s	1983 £000s	1984 £000s	1985 £000s	1986 £000s	1987 £000s
Turnover	6,229	6,778	8,056	7,175	7,702	8,906	8,481	9,995	9,837	10,058
Net profit (loss) before tax	717	813	1,028	137	27	35	(120)	(198)	(370)	(13.5)
Fixed assets	3,036	3,694	4,120	6,146	6,350	6,250	6,195	5,752	5,301	5,064
Net current assets	1,861	1,880	2,247	1,876	1,592	1,467	1,517	1,739	1,778	1,968
Earnings (loss) per share (p) (after tax)	10.55	12.40	17.13	2.299	0.02	0.04	(0.56)	(2.34)	(4.91)	(0.81)

Appendix 2   Chairman's letter to shareholders[2]

TO THE MEMBERS OF ARIEL INDUSTRIES PLC
11 AUGUST 1982

Dear Member,

In my statement contained in this year's Report & Accounts I mention that the directors have decided that there is a need for them to extend the application of the employees' share trusts so that these trusts can resume their long-standing role as 'last resort' buyers of the company's shares. The purpose of this letter is to explain the background to this decision, the steps which are being taken to implement it, and exactly how shareholders can take advantage of it if they so wish.

The initiative stems from our awareness that the future for the manufacturing sector of industry in this country is far from bright and consequently that there is a need for us to embark upon a major diversification programme. To do this, without recourse to share-holders for more capital, we shall need to reinvest the bulk of our earnings for the next four or five years, and this will inevitably restrict the amounts available for dividends. Being aware that a number of our shareholders rely upon dividend income and so will not be happy to accept a reduced payout for some years, we feel under an obligation to ensure that there is a ready market for their shares at some reasonable price should they wish to sell.

As you can see from the resolution to be put to members at the forthcoming Annual General Meeting, the directors are asking for authority to make available to the trustees of the employees' share trusts financial assistance not exceeding £1 million to enable the trustees to continue to operate as 'last resort' buyers of the company's shares. The intention is that the share trusts will, through their stockbrokers, undertake to buy at 30 pence any shares that are offered to them for a period of one calendar month commencing on Monday 23 August 1982. As the purchases will be made through the Stock Exchange shareholders can expect to receive $29\frac{15}{16}$ pence less the normal commissions. It is necessary for the purchases to be made in this way because the employees' share trusts cannot offer to purchase the shares direct without making a formal bid, and this would be expensive due to the professional fees involved.

The sum of £1 million has been arrived at to cover the possibility that all outside shareholders may wish to sell. To keep funds of this magnitude available is expensive, and so it is the present intention of your directors to limit the offer to one month. However, should the number of acceptances be such that the residual outside holdings are not sufficient to maintain a listing on the Stock Exchange, the offer will be automatically extended and I shall write to all remaining shareholders explaining the position as it then stands.

As shown in the latest Report & Accounts I have an interest in 1,208,899 shares which represent 20.1 per cent of the issued capital of the company. This includes 100,000 shares held by my wife and 206,000 shares in my family trusts. My fellow directors hold a total of 7,900 shares (.1 per cent) and the trustees of the Ariel Industries Employees' Share Trust (previously known as S & B Employees' Share Bank) hold a total of 1,794,000 (29.9 per cent). In addition, the trusts established for overseas employees currently hold 12,022 shares.

I have been informed by the trustees of each of the employee trusts that it is not their intention to take advantage of this offer and further-more, to minimize the funding required, your directors have agreed not to sell any of the shares they hold personally. However in my capacity as trustee of family trusts I must reserve the right to recommend acceptance for the shares held in those trusts.

The trustees' offer is at a price considered to be a fair one by Messrs Thomas May & Co, the company's auditors. It is being made so that existing shareholders who wish to sell can dispose of their holdings, in whole or in part without any concern that the size of the market will not be sufficiently large to take all the shares offered. Sadly the market in our shares has for many years been a narrow one, as was shown in April and May of this year when the price dropped below 20 pence. It recovered only when we announced the current initiative. Since then uninformed press comment has caused a further rise which your directors feel is not likely to be sustained.

Current trading levels still reflect the continuing recession and it is likely that the group as a whole will break even in the six months to 30 September 1982. I feel duty bound to point out that dividend prospects are uncertain and consequently that is likely that when the current offer lapses the share price will drift to significantly lower levels.

I wish to emphasize that the company will endeavour to maintain its listing on the Stock Exchange and that members wishing to retain their holdings on a long-term basis are free to do so. As early indications are that the resolution will be approved at the Annual General Meeting, it is important that those who wish to sell should instruct their stockbrokers accordingly. The present offer is for a limited time and it is by no means certain that there will be any subsequent offers, and so I strongly recommend those shareholders who are unsure as to whether or not they should take advantage of it to consult their professional advisers. Those who have no professional advisers are free to contact the company brokers, Messrs Smith Keen Cutler, Exchange Buildings, Stephenson Place, Birmingham B2 4NN, Telephone No 021-643 9977, who will give them all necessary help and advice.

Appendix 3

CHAIRMAN'S STATEMENT [3]

Now that the major part of our reorganization is complete it is interesting to look at the future structure of the Company. Our consolidated balance sheet shows net assets of some £7 million of which approximately £4 million will continue to be deployed within our three main operating units: Gretone Ltd which manufactures airframe components for the aerospace industry; Thomas Hunter Ltd which manufactures closures and machinery for food processing; and Ariel Industries Pty Ltd which offers formulated polyurethane systems in Australia.

We shall retain the buildings on the Temple Road site as investment properties, but are planning disposals of other assets of around £2 million to clear our overdraft and to leave us with just over £1 million in cash.

The proposed disposals are firstly, as I mentioned in my statement last year, S&D Rivet Ltd and Steels & Busks Ltd, the two companies on the Temple Road site. The trustees of the Employee Trusts are in principle willing to offer asset value, which is around £2 million, for these operations to protect the interests of their members who work there. The only pre-condition is that we must demonstrate to the workpeople concerned that the ongoing businesses have long-term viability and hence can offer continued job security. I am confident that we shall be able to demonstrate this within the next few months to the satisfaction of both the trustees and the workpeople so that the offer can become unconditional.

The other disposals we are planning are the Applied Filters business in Australia as this is no longer a mainstream activity, and the Omnia Foods' sites, at Aldingbourne in Sussex and Almeria in Spain, now that we have substantially completed our research and development programmes. When we have firm proposals on all these disposals we shall circularize details and convene an Extraordinary General Meeting.

Our work on hydroponics has provided us with useful technology which we plan to exploit in two distinct market areas; firstly, we have commercially viable systems for growing crops in hostile environments, and these will undoubtedly augment our expertise in food processing so that Hunters can offer comprehensive turnkey projects in a number of developing countries. Secondly, we have the means of growing extremely high quality produce in controlled environments and are hopeful that we shall be able to demonstrate the commercial viability of out-of-season production in the main industrialized countries.

Demand for our aerospace products at Gretone continues at a high level and we have entered this year with a full order book. Our work on software for computer-controlled machining is proceeding well and undoubtedly gives us a competitive advantage.

Our polyurethane systems business in Australia is growing rapidly. We are competing in a market area which is normally the preserve of major multinational companies, but we are carving out a very worthwhile niche for ourselves by offering extremely high levels of quality and service.

This year Mr Jim Simons retired after 49 years service during which time he held several senior appointments and since 1972 has been a main Board director. I thank him for his support and for the undoubted contribution he has made. We all wish him well in the years ahead.

I am happy to report that each of our operations is trading well and that the current year should see a major upturn in our earnings which, together with the improved liquidity which should flow from the disposal of non-mainstream activities, will enable us to resume dividend payments. I believe the Company has a bright future before it and am very grateful for the support I have received from both shareholders and employees alike during the period of reorganization.

As you will see from the Notice convening the Meeting we are planning to put before shareholders the proposal that the Company reverts to private status. It is a move which will be of considerable significance to certain of our outside shareholders and so we are making it a Special Resolution to bring it to everyone's attention.

Over the years the number of shares in the Company held by outside shareholders has progressively decreased to the point where it now amounts to little more than 10 per cent, and consequently there has been a very limited market in our shares. On a number of occasions your Directors have had to consider whether the stage has been reached where we should finally relinquish our listing on the Stock Exchange. We have naturally been reluctant to do this and, as you will see in my statements for the last few years, have taken the view that the optimum strategy remained that of hiving off the older operations and concentrating the resources of the quoted company on those activities which offered growth potential.

However we have had to be mindful of the fact that there is only a small minority of shareholders keen to follow this path and that our outside shareholder base is so small that we would have great difficulty in getting enough shares into circulation to create a free market. Reluctantly we have concluded that the most logical step now is to privatize the whole Company whilst ensuring that adequate safeguards are provided for outside shareholders who prefer to sell their holdings rather than to see them locked into a private company.

To this end we are asking the Company Pension Fund and Employee Trusts to make sufficient funds available to purchase at £1 per share all shares offered to them through the Stock Exchange before 31 December 1988. Shareholders accepting the offer will receive £1 per share less the normal commissions. This represents an exit price/earnings ratio of 21 on last year's post-tax earnings. It reflects the improvement in the Company's fortunes since we completed the reorganization, and compares well with the price of around 20p to which the shares had dropped in August 1984 when we last asked the Employee Trusts to enter the market. Shareholders who are in any doubt as to whether they should accept this offer should consult their professional advisers.

Shareholders wishing to avail themselves of this offer should either consult their own stockbrokers or other agents through whom they made their original purchase, or, alternatively, forward their share certificates before 31 December 1988 to Smith Keen Cutler Limited, Stockbrokers, Exchange Buildings, Stephenson Place, Birmingham B2 4NN, with written instructions to sell the shares on the basis of the terms set out in this statement. Smith Keen Cutler, acting as agents, will purchase them on behalf of the Company Pension Fund and Employee Trusts. Normal Stock Exchange settlement procedures will apply. Smith Keen Cutler will charge shareholders a reduced minimum commission of £25 or 2 per cent (plus VAT), whichever is the greater.

Naturally I am pleased to see our earnings beginning to rise again. Currently, of course, we are benefiting from the sustained boom in the UK economy, but I am happy that our company is now soundly based and will continue to cope well even when there is a slow down to more sustainable rates of growth.

I am in many ways sad that our days as a public company are numbered, and wish to record my appreciation of the support I have received from all those shareholders who have stayed with the Company during its difficult years.

Kenneth Edwards

Notes

1 This quotation and those which follow are from company sources.
2 Source: Ariel Industries, 1982.
3 Source: Company Reports 1987/88.

4 Smiths Industries

The company was founded in 1851 by Samuel Smith, a London watch and clockmaker, and remained solely concerned with horological instruments and jewellery until 1904 when the first manufacturing part of the business was formed with the purchase of a motor accessory business.

The founder's grandson, Allen Gordon-Smith, was largely responsible for building the company into a manufacturing business covering automotive, aviation, marine and industrial products. S. Smith and Sons (Motor Accessories) Ltd became a public company in July 1914.

The 1920s were difficult years, but by the early 1930s the company was in a position to look for opportunities for expansion. Speedometer and spark plugs businesses were bought, and the clock-making activities re-established. In 1931 the first synchronous electric clock was produced and Smiths English Electric Clocks was formed. This was strengthened by acquisitions and Smiths were soon producing large numbers of eight-day clocks for automobiles and domestic use.

The company continued to grow up to 1939, at which time 8,000 people were employed, compared with 5,000 in 1935. After the war further businesses were acquired in car radio manufacture, watch mass production (a joint venture with Ingersol) and, after considerable research, the first all-electric automatic pilot was produced. The latter had a very significant impact in the world of aviation and established Smiths' name as an avionics company of world-wide importance. At the same time the company expanded overseas into North America and Australia.

In 1966 the company was renamed Smiths Industries Limited, to more accurately reflect the diverse nature of the organization. By the end of the 1960s the core activities were in automotive components and aircraft instrumentation. The clock and watchmaking businesses, although still active, had been in decline for some time. The embryonic medical business of single-use plastic products was no more than a small research activity within another business at that time. Many parts of the industrial divisions were at the same stage of development, including polymer products, specialized conduit, multi-pin connectors and environmental controls.

DEVELOPMENTS IN THE 1970s

Throughout the 1970s the company's repeatedly-stated objective was to achieve consistent growth in profits and return on capital employed in its traditional industries. The period was characterized by a series of UK acquisitions and investment in the core UK automotive original equipment business. Appendix 1 lists the company's acquisitions in chronological order since 1972, together with the prices paid and the type of activities involved. In 1973 Mr R. G. Cave succeeded Mr R. G. Smith as Chairman, and announced that Smiths Industries' aim was to become a multi-divisional, multi-product manufacturer and distributor of light engineering and electronic products, suggesting that the company seek out new product markets in new geographical regions. However, the group remained heavily committed to the UK automotive original equipment component industry. The company acquired a car radio business and a battery clock company.

By 1978 the company was beginning to recognize that its UK markets were showing very slow growth. The Chairman, by now Mr E. R. Sisson, described the company's aim of seeking out export markets for its automotive component products. Appendix 2 contains details of the UK car market in the 1970s.

In 1979 Mr R. Hurn became Managing Director, and for the first time the top management acknowledged that the company's motor industry business was in decline. Mr Hurn called for a restructuring of the automotive business, a de-emphasizing of its importance, and a new focus on medical systems and overseas growth opportunities. He also sought collaboration with other European companies involved in the European Airbus project and announced the formulation of Smiths' Aerospace and Defence Systems division.

THE EARLY 1980s

The 1980s began with a wide acceptance within the company that if it were to succeed in the medium to long term, it must reduce its current heavy reliance on the automotive industry in general and the UK economy in particular. It saw itself as too small and parochial an operator to continue to succeed in a declining market with intensifying competition. It realized that it must look elsewhere for growth. This was summarized in the Chairman's report to the shareholders in 1980, in stating the company's strategic objectives in the coming years as:

To seek acquisitions in the US to give the company a greater geographical balance.

To look to other overseas markets for growth rather than the UK.

To reduce the importance to the company of its automotive original equipment and marine businesses.

The year 1981 was a sad one for many of the company's older employees, when the remaining parts of Smiths' clockmaking business were sold off. In 1982 IAS was acquired, and the motor accessory shops were sold off. Car radio manufacture ceased and the furniture business was sold to its management. In his review of 1982 the Chief Executive expressed his concern that the UK motor vehicle original equipment business was performing poorly and and had been doing so for many years. Operating losses were incurred in this part of the business in both 1982 and 1983.

THE AUTOMOTIVE COMPONENTS BUSINESS 1974–83

Overall the company maintained its margins at between 9.4 per cent and 9.7 per cent throughout the 1970s. However, the automotive parts of the company invariably performed below that figure, and by the 1980s Smiths were incurring operating losses.

During the 1970s turnover and profits were constant at approximately £130m. and £13m. respectively (at 1974 prices). This was achieved despite the automotive industry core business, rather than because of it. Smiths were assisted by the purchase of the Godfrey Holmes distribution chain, which helped to safeguard their non-original equipment business, along with an increase in employee productivity. The forward integration into retailing with the Holmes acquisition, whilst safeguarding distribution, was also in fact responsible for a decline in profitability.

Given the strategic decision to remain committed to the declining automotive industry, the company was good at maintaining its profitability. This strategy, though, was inappropriate as it resulted in no growth overall, with the expanding medical and avionics systems parts of the business effectively being used to support the struggling automotive side.

On his appointment as CEO in 1981, Roger Hurn stated his company's intention of reducing its heavy commitment to the declining automotive business in the UK. The sudden downturn suffered in 1981 and 1982 left Smiths with four options:

1   Stay in the UK automotive industry and fight to maintain/improve position.
2   Stay in the automotive industry and seek to concentrate the industry via the acquisition of competitor companies.
3   Shift automotive-related operations overseas to areas where the vehicle industry showed growth potential.
4   Exit and seek opportunities for growth in other areas.

The latter policy was pursued, and the majority of the business was sold to Lucas Industries and Hanson Trust in 1980, with the remainder going to GKN in 1984.

DEVELOPMENTS FROM 1984 TO 1988

The increasing geographical diversity and product/market concentration of the early 1980s was accompanied by an increasingly diversified management structure. This process culminated in 1984 with the formal reorganization of the company into the three major international operating divisions of Aerospace and Defence, Medical Systems and Industrial. Profits increased in 1984 for the first time since 1979. This reflected the company's strategy of moving from the old, low margin and increasingly competitive mechanical engineering markets to the more attractive, higher value added high-technology electronics markets. Research and development spending was concentrated in aerospace-related areas.

By 1985 company profits came approximately equally from each of the three divisions. Medical Systems provided the greatest return on turnover, and Industrial the lowest. This reflected the growing and increasingly attractive market for disposable medical equipment, a field in which Smiths were becoming increasingly important internationally.

Unlike Aerospace and Defence, Medical Systems achieved much of its growth in the 1980s organically. The market for one-time-use medical supplies was growing world-wide and reputed to be worth $US2 billion in the US alone. Here 90 per cent of the equipment used in situations where there was a danger of cross-infection was disposable, the US medical scene being particularly cautious because of the country's highly litigious nature. By comparison, the corresponding UK usage was just 60 per cent. Japan was the fastest-growing market for medical products at this time, and by 1988 was larger than the UK market, for the first time.

Sir Alex Jarrett became the Chairman in 1985 and reaffirmed the company's policy of achieving growth by careful and considered acquisitions. In 1986 Smiths Industries disposed of all its South African interests, as involvement in that country was considered inappropriate and could potentially damage business elsewhere in the world. The majority holding in SIDK of Australia was sold, representing the final withdrawal from the automotive component business world-wide. By 1987 the declining profitability of the Industrial division was causing some concern. This division consisted of 19 companies with products falling into four categories: connectors, specialist conduit, environmental controls and specialist engineering. Appendix 6 lists the company's subsidiaries by operating division, and product details are given in Appendix 7.

During 1987 Aerospace and Defence was established as the major part of the company's business. Within the division business was split approximately evenly between defence contracts and major civil aviation contracts with Boeing, Airbus Industries and British Aerospace, in the US, Europe and UK respectively.

In September 1987 Smiths beat off competition from GEC to purchase Lear Siegler Avionics in the US for $US350m. (then $US223m.), approximately doubling the size of the company. Table 4.1 shows LSA's trading record for the five years preceding the acquisition by Smiths.

The capital for this acquisition was raised entirely by the issue of 71. 9 million new shares at £3.10 each. In the October stock market crash that followed shortly after the acquisition, Smiths' share price dropped to £2.82 and fell even lower during 1988, to an average of £2.47 (1988 low of £2.20 and high of £2.78).

The activities of LSA (subsequently renamed SLI) were expected to complement Smiths Industries' business by adding flight control, flight management, gyroscope and air navigation products to their portfolio. Smiths Industries hoped that this would provide an increased defence equipment operation in North America for Smiths' other products through SLI's existing contracts with the Pentagon.

Although its US defence contracts provided it with a $US600m. orderbook, SLI was not seen as being a member of the 'first division' of US defence contractors. This acquisition meant that 70 per cent of Smiths aerospace and defence business was now in military contracts.

The purchase of SLI constituted a change of strategy for the company, in that its previous growth had been step-by-step, with a succession of relatively small acquisitions allowing entry into niche growth areas in both aerospace/defence and medical disposables markets.

At the end of the 1988 financial year Smiths Industries had £98 million net cash. It had also spent £94 million on R&D activities, which served to illustrate the commitment to high-technology, high-margin businesses. Continued product development and innovation was held to be the company's policy, as was the constant search for new market opportunities. To this end, during 1988 the company were investigating a potential £3 billion new market in modernizing and retro-fitting ageing combat aircraft for Third World air forces. There were an estimated 900 such fighters in the eight to ten-year-old

TABLE 4.1   **Lear Siegler Electronics – trading record**

	1983	1984	1985	1986	1987
Sales ($USm.)	248	290	321	353	417
Profit ($USm.)	29	36	34	29	35
Margin (%)	11.5	12.4	10.4	8.2	8.4

TABLE 4.2   **Smiths Industries – trading profit (ignores non-trading profit)**

	Six months to 28 Jan. 1988 £m.	Six months to 28 Jan. 1989 £m.
Aerospace and Defence	22.4	25.0
Medical Systems	8.8	8.2
Industrial	6.1	7.4

age-group, suitable for refitting with up-to-date avionics, at a cost of approximately £30m. each. A presence in this market would be particularly advantageous to Smiths, as there was a potential sales gap between declining Tornado work up to 1990 and the introduction of the European Fighter Aircraft in 1993–4. Smiths were hoping to win their first EFA contracts in the near future.

Smiths' principal customer was Boeing, for whom it was the main flight management systems supplier for the 737, the world's best-ever selling jet airliner. Boeing's order book at the time consisted of 1,500 aircraft totalling about $75 billion, of which 500 were 737s, enough to keep them busy into the mid-1990s. Other civil aircraft manufacturers had nearly equally buoyant order books. Boeing produced 15 737s per month, but were looking to increase this to around 20 per month by 1990. Whether this was achievable would depend to a large extent on its suppliers. Appendix 8 gives a summary of the demand for aircraft.

In his 1988 report to the shareholders, the Chairman stated that the company aimed to maintain a balance between each of the three divisions, preventing the company from becoming over-exposed, and therefore vulnerable in any one field. The profits announced for the six months up to 28 January 1989 were up by 13 per cent to £47m. on the same period the previous year. Interest receipts also increased to £6.6m. from £3.5m. This was attributable to higher interest rates and increasing cashflow. Despite spending £30m. on acquisitions in this six months (see Appendix 1), the group ended the period holding £83m. in cash. Turnover for the same interim period was £308m., up from £307m. Divisional profits are given in Table 4.2.

Appendix 1a   Acquisitions

1972	Godfrey Holmes Ltd (Motor Component Distributor)	£1.5m.
	Garage Supply Factors Ltd	£1.3m.
	Several small motor component manufacturers and distributors including: Smallbone Factors; Colbridge Motor Factors Ltd; Autospares and Acessories Ltd; LTR Distributors Ltd; F. Medcalf & Co Ltd	} £1.1m.
1973	Masons Motor Factors & Battery Electrics Ltd	£720,000
	Car Radio Services	
	Claude Rye Ltd	
1974	Tudor Accessories Holdings	£162,000
1976	G. Maclellan Holdings Ltd	
1977	Simonsen & Nielson	
	Miller & Edwardes Ltd	
1979	Concord Laboratories Inc. USA	
1982	Integrated Air Systems	
1983	Xionics Ltd	
1984	Downs Surgical PLC	
1986	I. D. Potter	} £850,000
	Camper & Nicholson Marine Equipment	
1987	Lear Siegler Avionics Systems	£219m.
1989	Times Microwave Systems	$US53.5m.
	Avon Medicals	£3.5m.
	PVB (WG) Medical Products	£13.5m.

Appendix 1b   Divestments

1981	Clock interests sold.	
1982	Sale of motor accessory shops.	
	Kitchen/bedroom furniture manufacturer sold – MBO.	
	Car radio manufacturing ceased.	
1983	Withdrawal from OE automotive supply business.	
	Vehicle Instrumentation Systems sold to Lucas.	
	Hanson Trust purchased vehicle heater business.	
1984	Godfrey Holmes sold to GKN.	
1985	Australian automotive activities sold.	
	All South African interests sold.	
1987	Integrated Air Systems	$US1m.
	Mecro – MBO	} £4.5m.
	Xionics – MBO	
1988	SI-Tex Marine Electronics	$US2.5m.
	Australian non-medical & aerospace operations	$A40m.
1989	Closure of Aero Electronic Connector Company, USA.	
	Closure of surgical instruments business, UK.	

Appendix 2

CAR AND COMMERCIAL VEHICLE PRODUCTION IN THE UK 1974–88

	Cars (000s)	Commercial vehicles (000s)
1974	1,534	403
1975	1,268	381
1976	1,333	372
1977	1,316	398
1978	1,223	384
1979	1,070	408
1980	923	389
1981	954	229
1982	888	269
1983	1,045	245
1984	909	225
1985	1,048	266
1986	1,019	229
1987	1,143	247
1988	1,227	318

Appendix 3   Smiths industries PLC

FINANCIAL ANALYSIS, 1974–88

	1974	1975	1976	1977	1978	1979	1980	1981	1982	1983	1984	1985	1986	1987	1988
Turnover (£m.)	135.8	157.5	180.8	224.1	254.8	284.6	319.8	367.6	385.9	380.7	388.7	383.0	401.2	429.9	666.4
Adjusted[a]	135.8	126.8	124.9	133.6	140.3	138.2	131.6	135.2	130.7	123.3	119.9	111.4	112.8	118.2	175.8
Trading profit (£m.)	13.2	15.1	17.5	21.7	24.1	27.5	30.1	30.8	32.3	31.4	39.2	48.9	55.7	62.2	89.9
Adjusted[a]	13.2	12.2	12.1	12.9	13.3	13.4	12.4	11.3	7.1	10.4	12.1	14.2	15.7	17.1	23.7
Margins (%)	9.7	9.6	9.7	9.7	9.5	9.7	9.4	8.4	5.4	8.4	10.1	12.8	13.9	14.5	13.5
Dividend (p)			1.6	1.8	2.0	2.4	2.5	2.6	2.7	2.9	3.5	4.5	5.5	6.5	7.5
Dividend cover			2.6	3.8	4.1	3.7	3.7	3.6	3.0	2.9	2.9	2.8	3.0	3.0	2.9
EPS (p/25p share)			4.3	7.0	8.4	9.2	9.3	9.4	8.3	8.4	10.2	12.9	16.4	19.4	22.5
t6 per employee (£)[a]	5,853	6,009	6,153	6,549	6,911	6,910	6,784	7,726	8,086	9,341	10,705	10,127	9,724	10,649	13,022
EBIT per employee (£)[a]	569	578	596	632	655	670	639	646	438	788	1,080	1,291	1,353	1,541	1,756

[a] Adjusted to 1974 prices

Appendix 4

ANALYSIS OF PROFIT MARGIN BY DIVISION

%	1974	1975	1976	1977	1978	1979	1980
Vehicle manufacture	4.2	2.7	6.2	10.0	5.7	3.2	2.5
Aerospace	11.8	12.4	12.6	9.6	6.2	11.5	11.1
Marine	5.0	9.2	8.5	4.5	7.6	1.4	1.9
Other	9.2	10.8	11.5	12.6	16.0	14.7	15.3
Distributive	11.8	11.6	10.0	10.5	11.7	11.1	8.3
Overseas	8.4	6.1	6.7	6.4	5.4	7.4	8.9

%	1981	1982	1983	1984
Aerospace	14.3	13.4	13.0	11.4
Automotive	loss	loss	loss	–
Distribution	3.0	1.9	2.4	–
Industrial	10.7	9.4	8.4	9.3
Marine	8.8	7.6	7.5	9.2
Medical	21.1	25.3	25.1	20.4
Australia/S. Africa	9.4	5.2	1.5	5.7

%	1985	1986	1987	1988
Aerospace &	11.9	14.7	14.4	12.0
Defence	20.3	19.5	20.4	19.7
Medical Systems	11.3	9.4	10.6	13.7
Industrial	7.9	10.8	9.4	11.9
Australia				

ANALYSIS OF TURNOVER AND PROFIT

	1985		1986		1987		1988	
	% of sales	PBT	% of sales	PBT	% of sales	PBT	% of sales	PBT
Aerospace &	39	36	40	42	44	43	66	59
Defence								
Medical	20	31	22	31	23	33	15	22
Systems	34	29	32	22	26	19	16	16
Industrial	7	4	6	5	7	5	3	3
Australia								

ANALYSIS OF TURNOVER BY GEOGRAPHICAL REGION

%	1984	1985	1986	1987	1988
UK	63	62	63	66	48
North America	26	28	24	21	44
Australia	8	7	7	7	3
Rest of World	3	3	6	6	5

Appendix 5

BALANCE SHEETS

	1988 £000	1987 £000
Fixed assets		
Tangible assets	99,866	75,093
Investments and advances	801	823
	100,667	75,916
Current assets		
Stocks	112,088	96,750
Debtors	142,819	101,922
Investments	56,238	25,527
Cash at bank and on deposit	63,767	41,692
	374,912	265,891
Creditors due within one year	159,436	109,138
Net current assets	215,476	156,753
Total assets less current liabilities	316,143	232,669
Creditors due after one year	35,932	23,668
Provisions for liabilities and charges	25,901	11,641
Net assets	254,310	197,360
Capital and reserves		
Called-up share capital	72,114	53,959
Share premium account	553	1,006
Revaluation reserve	4,640	7,002
Other reserves	2,682	1,931
Profit and loss account	174,321	133,402
Shareholders' funds	254,310	197,360

Appendix 6

SUBSIDIARY COMPANIES

AEROSPACE & DEFENCE GROUP

UK
Smiths Industries Aerospace & Defence Systems Ltd
Kelvin Hughes Ltd
Micro Circuit Engineering Ltd

USA
Smiths Industries Aerospace & Defense Systems Inc
SLI Avionic Systems Corp
SLI International Corp

Other overseas
Smiths Industries Australia Pty Ltd
Smiths Industries North America Ltd (Canada)
A/S Kelvin Hughes (Denmark)
Smiths Industries SA (France)
SLI International SRL (Italy)
SLI Pacific Operations Pte Ltd (Singapore)
Kelvin Hughes (Singapore) Pte Ltd
SLI International GmbH (West Germany)

MEDICAL SYSTEMS GROUP

SIMS Healthcare
Portex Ltd
Concord Laboratories Ltd
Laboratoire Portex SA (France)
Eschmann Bros & Walsh Ltd
Grosvenor Surgical Supplies Ltd
Laboratoire SIMS SA (France)
SIMS SA (Spain)
Medic-Eschmann GmbH (West Germany)
SIMS Pte Ltd (Singapore)

Simcare
Surgical Companies
Eschmann Bros & Walsh Ltd
Downs Surgical Ltd
Surgical Equipment Supplies Ltd
Smiths Industries Medical Systems Pty Ltd (Australia)

SIMS North America
Concord Laboratories Inc (USA)
Portex Inc (USA)
Downs Surgical Inc (USA)
Smiths Industries Medical Systems Inc (USA)
Smiths Industries Medical Systems Canada Ltd

INDUSTRIAL GROUP

Connectors
Hypertac Ltd
SI-TAC Connectors Inc (USA)

Specialist Conduit Companies
Icore International Ltd
Icore International GmbH (West Germany)
Fliteline Ltd
Icore International Inc (USA)
Flexible Ducting Ltd
Flexschlauch Produktions GmbH (West Germany)
Kopex International Ltd

Environmental Controls
Smiths Industries Environmental Controls Co Ltd

Specialist Engineering Companies
Sifan Systems Ltd
Hefac Engineering Ltd

Smiths Industries Hydraulics Co
  Ltd
Unitex Ltd
MacLellan Rubber Ltd
Automated Engineering Products
  Ltd
Medcraft Bros Ltd
Lodge Ceramics Ltd
SIMAC Ltd

CORPORATE

Smiths Industries Management
  Ltd
Smiths Industries Inc (USA)
SI Properties Ltd
Henry Hughes & Son Ltd
Ming Instruments Ltd
Smiths Industries Japan Ltd

Appendix 7 Main Product Areas by Division, 1988

AEROSPACE AND DEFENCE

Autopilot; autothrottle: flight management systems; head-up displays; head-down displays; display computers; flight deck instruments; missile management systems; data business systems; interface computers; electronic engine control; ignition equipment; fuel gauging; naval defence systems; gyros; accelerometers; flight data recorders; data transfer systems; navigation systems.

INDUSTRIALS

Multi-pin electronic connectors; pressure hoses; plastic and metal conduit; time switches; heating controls; home security; air moving equipment; hydraulic power packs; rubber sheeting; aluming ceramics; ignition and spark-plug products.

MEDICAL SYSTEMS

Anaesthesia, respiratory, therapy and intensive care equipment; thoracic and general wound drain systems; urology equipment; blood gas analysis kits; operating equipment and instruments; sterilization equipment; ostomy and incontinence equipment.

Appendix 8 Notes prepared from the 1988 *Financial Times* Aerospace Review

FUTURE DEMAND FOR AIRCRAFT

It is estimated that about one-third of the cost of a civil airliner is accounted for by onboard avionics. In the case of the military sector the proportion of the cost attributable to avionics is much higher and is likely to increase as more aircraft operating functions are taken over by electronic systems. The world's major aircraft manufacturers are currently enjoying a boom in sales of jet transports of all kinds that seems likely to continue into the early 1990s. This also appears to be true of the suppliers to the aircraft industry. Two factors are causing this increased demand. Firstly the continued growth in world air traffic, and secondly that many of the bigger airlines are starting to replace their ageing fleets.

During 1988 the world's scheduled air traffic rose by 4 per cent to 1.1 billion passengers. Growth is generally expected to be around 5 to 7 per cent in the future and by the year 2000 the number of passengers will have doubled to 2.2 billion. To cater for this increased demand airlines are going to have to invest heavily in new aircraft. Boeing estimates that between now [1988] and 2005 $US342 billion will be spent on acquiring new jet airliners of all kinds. Of this sum $US242 billion will be spent on new aircraft while $US100 billion will be spent on replacing ageing aircraft. It is estimated that by 2005 the world fleet will consist of 11,700 aircraft compared with 7,800 at the end of 1988, representing an increase of 3,900 aircraft (50 per cent).

Within the military sector, over the next 11 years spending is likely to be in the region of $US700 billion of which $US550 billion will be spent on new tactical combat aircraft and $US150 billion on military transports and specialized aircraft.

FUTURE TECHNOLOGICAL DEVELOPMENTS AND MARKET TRENDS

With the increasing amount of air traffic, navigation and communication systems are going to have increasing sophistication. The International Civil Aviation Organization on Future Air Navigation Systems (FANS) concluded last year that satellite technology could provide the necessary global solution to current shortcomings in air navigation and in-flight communications systems. Other developments in avionics include changing cockpit layouts to incorporate cathode ray tubes to display information, instead of electro-mechanical devices, and 'fly-by-wire' techniques.

With these new technological advances development costs will increase markedly. It is thought that this will lead to a concentration of the avionics industry by a number of mergers and international collaborative ventures.

Appendix 9   Dowty Group PLC

Dowty is an international high-technology engineering and electronics group manufacturing advanced systems and products for aerospace, defence, marine, information technology, mining and industrial markets.

FIVE-YEAR FINANCIAL RECORD

	1984	Adj. 1974	1985	Adj. 1974	1986	Adj. 1974	1987	Adj. 1974	1988	Adj. 1974
Sales (£m.)	403	125	463	134	519	145	574	155	625	163
EBIT	37.2	12	43.8	13	49.3	14	58.5	16	72.1	19
Margin (%)	9.2		9.5		9.5		10.2		11.5	
ROCE	16.7		19.4		19.3		20.7		22.9	
PBT	36.5	11	44.2	13	47.6	13	55.7	15	64.1	17
Sales growth (%)			8.5		8.2		8.1		5.1	
PBT growth (%)			14.2		4.1		14.4		11.0	

AEROSPACE DIVISION

The division is one of the worlds' leading suppliers of aircraft landing gear, flight control systems and propellers. Its customers include Airbus Industries, Boeing, British Aerospace, Fokker and Saab. The business is 54 per cent civil and 46 per cent military. North America accounts for 41 per cent of sales. A major part of the business is the sale of spares and carrying out repairs, which accounts for 43 per cent of sales.

	1984	1985	1986	1987	1988
Sales (£m.)	131	137	154	177	210
EBIT	16.3	16.5	19.3	25.6	29.6
Margin (%)	12.4	10.7	12.5	14.5	14.1
Sales growth (%)		12.8	8.6	12.3	14.4
PBT growth (%)		(4.4)	12.8	29.6	11.5

ELECTRONICS DIVISION

Active in a number of military and civil niche markets, especially in the areas of missile, submarine and aircraft systems. Products include submarine command systems, engine control systems, afterburner engine systems for high-performance fighter aircraft, mine-detection systems and batteries.

	1984	1985	1986	1987	1988
Sales (£m.)	82	102	116	119	134
EBIT	10.7	11.1	10.4	9.3	12.0
Margin (%)	13.0	10.9	9.0	7.8	9.0
Sales growth (%)		17.4	9.9	0.2	8.6
PBT growth (%)		(2.1)	(9.7)	(12.8)	24.2

INDUSTRIAL DIVISION

This division operates in two main market areas – polymer engineering and hydraulic equipment. Presence in North America was increased in 1988 by the acquisition of Woodville Polymer Engineering Inc.

Dowty is a world leader in high-quality custom-engineered mouldings and seals. Other products include 'stealth' materials for submarines and surface vessels, automotive safety systems, gear pumps, railway retarders and hydrojets.

	1984	1985	1986	1987	1988
Sales (£m.)	48	56	60	63	83
EBIT	1.9	5.0	7.3	6.0	10.5
Margin (%)	4.0	8.9	12.2	9.5	12.7
Sales growth (%)		10.1	1.8	2.6	27.1
PBT growth (%)		282.0	41.1	(19.7)	68.6

PERCENTAGE OF GROUP PROFIT AND SALES BY DIVISION

Division	1984		1985		1986		1987		1988	
	Sales	PBT	Sales	PBT	Sales	PBT	Sales	PBT	Sales	PBT
Aerospace	44	44	40	38	40	39	31	44	33	41
Electronics	14	29	19	25	20	21	20	16	21	17
Industrial	12	5	12	11	12	15	11	10	13	15
Other	30	22	29	26	28	25	38	30	33	27

In the 1988 annual report the Chairman stated that the Group's central strategy was to concentrate on areas where they are already successful. Consequently the hydraulic undercarriage business would remain as a core business (the system was invented by Sir George Dowty in the 1930s). This early business led to electronic development and defence applications, into which the company expanded. The Group therefore sees all its products as developed on the basis of interlocking technologies and markets and is more homogeneous than is sometimes supposed. The Group intended to maintain this strategy and anticipated little change in its direction. Hence when an opportunity to enter a new area of missile technology for the MOD was presented the company declined, as it would have required an unusually high degree of diversification for the company. The Group is essentially conservative.

Appendix 10　Lucas Industries

FINANCIAL ANALYSIS, 1982–8

	1982	1983	1984	1985	1986	1987	1988
Group turnover (£m.)	1,220.3	1,216.8	1,518.5	1,588.2	1,715.6	1,820.4	1,972.1
Adjusted to 1974 base (£m.)	414.9	389.4	470.7	460.6	480.4	491.5	512.7
Operating profit (£m.)	35.3	20.1	58.1	83.5	114.8	137.3	169.2
Profit before tax (£m.)	20.2	2.4	35.8	59.8	95.2	114.5	146.3
Capital employed (£m.)	454.3	462.1	477.4	450.2	533.2	499.6	677.6
Gearing (%)	28	29	23	33	29	43	24
ROCE (%)	4.5	0.5	7.4	13.2	17.8	22.9	21.6
Margin (%)	1.7	0.2	2.4	3.8	5.5	6.7	7.4
Turnover/CE (%)	2.7	2.6	3.2	3.5	3.2	3.6	2.9
Current ratio	1.7	1.8	1.5	1.6	1.7	1.6	1.6
Sales/employee (£)	–	–	23,340	23,112	25,266	26,699	31,045

Appendix 11   Environment trends 1977–86

SELECTED IMPORTS (£m.)

Year	Road vehicles	Other transport	Gen. ind. machinery	Electrical machinery
1977	2,133.5	1,037.8	1,651.1	1,331.9
1978	2,796.9	1,069.2	1,837.6	1,398.6
1979	3,943.2	856.6	1,960.3	1,457.4
1980	3,351.6	1,488.9	2,316.8	1,798.6
1981	3,408.1	1,111.1	2,305.7	1,758.7
1982	4,489.6	1,103.8	2,411.8	2,117.0
1983	5,753.7	1,275.9	2,334.2	2,292.3
1984	5,957.6	1,482.9	2,577.1	2,805.3
1985	6,800.6	1,765.6	2,937.5	3,380.1
1986	7,939.7	1,434.4	3,035.2	3,383.0

IMPORT/EXPORT BALANCE (IMPORTS/HOME DEMAND)

Year	Electrical & e'tronic eng.	Motor vehicles & parts
1977	30	35
1978	31	35
1979	31	41
1980	31	39
1981	36	42
1982	39	47
1983	42	52
1984	44	51
1985	47	50
1986	47	51

MEAN BANK BASE RATES

Year	Rate(%)
1977	8.0
1978	9.5
1979	13.9
1980	15.0
1981	14.5
1982	11.4
1983	10.0
1984	10.1
1985	12.6
1986	10.9

UK DEFENCE SPENDING (£m.)

Year	Total	Air Eqmt
1977	6,158	844
1978	6,787	1,010
1979	7,455	1,214
1980	9,178	1,427
1981	11,187	2,059
1982	12,607	2,458
1983	14,412	2,640
1984	15,487	3,057
1985	17,122	3,494
1986	19,943	3,296

PART II

STRATEGIC ANALYSIS

5   Dunlop Holdings

INTRODUCTION

In 1888 John Boyd Dunlop invented the first usable pneumatic tyre and Dunlop came into being. By the turn of the century the Dunlop Rubber Co., as it became known, had two factories in Birmingham, then the centre of the UK car and bicycle industry.

The next twenty years were a period of growth and expansion. Investments were made in rubber estates in Malaya, and tyre factories were opened in Japan and the USA. The product range expanded through the acquisition of a wheel manufacturer and the addition of golf balls and aircraft tyres. Also textiles used in the tyres were now manufactured in mills owned by Dunlop.

As with many other companies, the collapse in world trade in 1929 was almost fatal for Dunlop. The dramatic fall in commodity prices and in particular the price of rubber was the major cause of the problem. Under new management the company recovered slowly, widening its range of products which usually included components based on rubber technology.

World War Two offered the company considerable opportunity to increase sales of existing products and to develop and manufacture new products for military use. However, on the negative side, plantations were seized in Malaya, and German and French factories were bombed. The end of the war saw another period of expansion. The experience and expertise developed in the war were now used to develop civil applications from the knowledge gained. At the same time military spending remained at a high level for several years, providing a profit base for such expansion. The range of sports goods expanded to include footwear. Rubber belting and hose had many new applications, and flooring materials provided a further extension to the product range. The company continued its policy of expansion largely by selling to new geographical markets in the 1960s.

TECHNOLOGICAL CHANGE IN THE 1960s

In the 1960s a change took place in tyre technology with the development of the radial tyre which was expected to replace some or all of the sales of the cross-ply tyre. The radial could be steel- or textile-based, with the steel-based tyre giving greater durability (over twice the mileage of a cross-ply tyre) but the textile tyre providing greater adhesion to the road in wet conditions. Michelin was the first company to make a significant commitment to the radial tyre and it chose the steel-based version. Dunlop opted for the textile-based tyre, which was the wrong choice, and by the time they had changed to the steel-based version Michelin were market leaders.

THE 1970s AND THE DUNLOP–PIRELLI UNION

The vicious price war which developed in the early seventies forced companies such as Uniroyal to withdraw from Europe. In an attempt to combat the threat of Michelin, Dunlop and Pirelli entered into an unusual form of agreement whereby a union would result through the exchange of minority interests; maybe this was seen as a prelude to a full merger of the two companies.

The balance of the union suffered in the first year, when Pirelli made huge losses and Dunlop were obliged to make a £41.5m. provision against their original investment.

As part of the deal, shares held by Pirelli in Dunlop Limited were redesignated to 'preferred' shares; any losses suffered by Dunlop Limited in the future would be borne entirely by UK shareholders. Thereby, Pirelli would not be entitled to any of the profits of Dunlop Limited until Industrie Pirelli returned to profit.

In the early 1970s, Dunlop consequently refused to invest money in Pirelli until it returned to the black. As a result of this, Dunlop's stake was eventually reduced to 19 per cent.

The agreement was terminated in October 1981. A statement showing the effect of the Union between 1970 and 1976 is shown in table 5.1

The history of Dunlop through the 1970s can be seen through the following extracts from company reports.

1972 UK TYRE MARKET

The level of business in the replacement market was sustained for the greater part of the year. Then, to end a discount war which was confusing to the public, recommended retail prices were discontinued. There are signs that the policy is proving effective.

TABLE 5.1   **Attributable profit of the Dunlop–Pirelli union, 1970–6**

£m.	1970	1971	1972	1973	1974	1975	1976
Union-attributable profit	10	1.3	3.7	17.3	20	28	40
Dunlop share of							
union-attributable profit	7	10.4	12.7	10.5	11	14	19
Pirelli share of							
union-attributable profit	3	(9.1)	(9)	6.8	9	14	21

Some progress was achieved in volume and market share, but increased costs were not fully recovered and profits were slightly reduced.

Preparations for the launch of the Dunlop 'Denovo' – the 'Total Mobility Tyre' – are well advanced. Vehicle manufacturers are showing increasing interest and two models fitted with this revolutionary new safety tyre are expected to appear at the London Motor Show. The Department of Trade and Industry and safety organizations in Britain and abroad are well aware of its unique qualities.

Germany

Although the German economy grew slightly faster than in 1971, the demand for tyres was below industry expectations. However, demand for steel-braced radial-ply car tyres continued to rise and capacity is being extended. An independent survey of tyres of this type available in the German market gave an exceptionally high rating to the Dunlop SP4 tyre.

Turnover of Dunlop AG was a little below the 1971 level, but the fall in profits was rather greater, owing to intensive price competition coupled with rising costs.

1973 TYRE MARKET IN EUROPE

The second half of the year was adversely affected by rising raw material and other costs, which were not fully recoverable and then only with some delay. In addition, industrial disruption in our own and customers' factories in the United Kingdom lost the company an estimated £3.75m. and the employees £1.5m.

In the European Economic Community, the problem of over-capacity in the car tyre business was aggravated by the effects of the energy crisis in the latter part of the year, and profits were depressed, especially in France and Germany. In product areas outside the automotive industry, however, results were better than in 1972.

Rubber market losses

As explained more fully in the Directors' Report, contrary to company policy, certain forward sales of latex and dry rubber were left unhedged. With rising prices, this failure to hedge gave rise to losses of £4.8m., £3.2m. after tax. Of this latter amount £1.9m. was attributable to Dunlop Holdings.

Denovo launched

Denovo, the total mobility tyre, was launched at the London Motor Show and fitment to two models (Rover 3500S and Mini 1275GT) was announced. During the year, development work continued with car manufacturers in the UK and overseas. The Denovo development team was honoured by being chosen for the MacRobert Award from the Council of Engineering Institutions to mark the outstanding engineering achievement of the year.

1974 CHAIRMAN'S REPORT – EXTRACT

It was clear from the start that 1974 would be uncertain and difficult, imposing considerable strains on private-sector companies. The energy crisis, inflation, price controls, politics, currency instability, industrial unrest, and recession all combined to ensure this.

So the management had four objectives – to control the use of funds tightly and to safeguard the liquidity of the business; to maintain profitable growth as far as possible; to be highly selective in the use of resources; and to seek additional savings, particularly in oil-based materials and energy.

In the United Kingdom, trading activity recovered well after the three-day week and, as a result of increased operating efficiency and cost savings, UK operations contributed a larger share of the group's profit than in the previous year. This improvement would have been greater but for price control which bore heavily on a number of operations.

In continental Europe, the car tyre business continued to be depressed, with fierce competition from imports in Germany which resulted in a trading loss; France and Spain were unable to recover costs quickly enough because of price restraints.

1975 CHAIRMAN'S REPORT – EXTRACT

Recession, or high inflation, or both, were experienced in almost every area in which we operate. Indeed many of the countries experienced the worst recession for decades. All product groups were affected, not least the motor industries in developed countries with car manufacture particularly hard hit.

However, Dunlop achieved record attributable profits of £15m., nearly 50 per cent more than in 1974 (before an 'extraordinary item'). The improvement owes much to careful control of resources – as well as to gains in efficiency, particularly in the United Kingdom. There was a strong performance by our Engineering and Industrial Groups, a good growth in exports, and a useful upturn in Germany.

Our interests in overseas Pirelli activities also contributed significantly to the improved profits.

Changes in world markets have created opportunities as well as problems. Technical innovation in products for the off-shore oil industry, for irrigation, for fire protection, and for conveyor belting already yield good results and again illustrate the renewal and widening of the group's product range. The carbon fibre brakes for Concorde, now in service, were another 'Dunlop first' and are already being developed for other advanced aircraft, military and civil.

1976 CHAIRMAN'S REPORT – EXTRACT

1976 saw the end of the post-OPEC recession and Dunlop has emerged a stronger company than when we first began grappling with the severe problems of 'stagflation' brought about by the oil crisis.

For the third successive year, there was a significant improvement in group profits and the sharp increase in 1976 owed much to our broad international spread. Both Dunlop and Pirelli activities outside continental Europe contributed substantial increases in earnings; operating profits in the UK also showed a marked increase, although when adjusted for inflation, they are still less than is required for the expansion of the home businesses.

During the past year we have re-appraised the group's objectives and set new and stretching targets, basing them on a longer-term view of our world markets, as should be expected of a multinational group. We are now moving into a period when greater emphasis will be given to the faster development of certain of our businesses. In a phrase, we have changed from selective containment to selective expansion.

1977 CHAIRMAN'S REPORT – EXTRACT

A year ago, we reported a change in general policy 'from selective containment to selective expansion'. This was based on improving results and a financial position which was strengthening internally and could then be supported by the rights issue of May 1977. These encouraging conditions persisted with improved results for the first half-year. Towards the end of the year, however, results were disappointing though the financial position remained satisfactory.

Attributable profits for the year 1977 fell by 20 per cent from the previous year, but it is encouraging that the profits from activities other than tyres increased. They now represent approximately two-thirds of total profits compared with 55 per cent last year.

What happened? The greater general growth in demand which governments were seeking, without renewed inflation, was not realized. In the industrialized countries particularly, excess production capacity or price controls or both, depressed margins, particularly for tyres. In the United Kingdom, the so-called re-entry from precise wage control towards more general guidelines caused frustration and more industrial disruption than I can ever remember in Dunlop factories. This was supplemented by stoppages among customers. Fortunately, resultant losses were partly offset by more satisfactory results in other parts of the group, but then the rise in the general value of sterling between June and the year-end reduced the apparent profits accruing both in Dunlop and associated Pirelli international operations.

This is the last Annual Report which I shall have the privilege to present to you. Accordingly, I take this opportunity to express sincere appreciation to all my colleagues on the Board and fellow employees in Dunlop for the encouragement, co-operation and support which they have given in fair and rough weather.

Sir Campbell Fraser, whom the Board have selected as their new Chairman, has served the Company since 1956 and has been Managing Director since 1971. During these eight years he has built round him a team which represents not only a deep knowledge of the business but a mixture of talent and experience well suited to present conditions and the political and social environment in which business is carried on at home and abroad. Times are not easy but objectives are clear, the management team is in good heart and I wish every success to them and all who are concerned with the future of Dunlop worldwide. – *Reay Geddes.*

At this point in Dunlop history it will be useful to take a more detailed look at Dunlop operations. The detail appears in the appendices (10 and 11) in order to avoid interruption to the general flow.

1978 CHAIRMAN'S REPORT – EXTRACTS

Tyres in Europe

It is generally accepted that the companies making tyres for the European market have more capacity than is needed. The major reasons for this over-capacity are: widespread factory construction in the late 1960s; the halt in the growth of motoring mileage following the oil price increases of 1973–4, and its aftermath; and the growing use of the steel-radial tyre which provides the motorist with twice the life or more of the cross-ply tyre which it has been replacing.

Dunlop, in common with the other tyre makers, has supported the British Rubber Manufacturers' Association in its applications to the Department of Trade and the European Commission to prevent 'dumping' by any foreign manufacturer.

With severe competition, tyre prices have fallen sharply in recent years, so that the real cost to the motorist in pence per mile has fallen, in a decade, by between 30 per cent and 40 per cent. The customer has been exceptionally well served by the industry in value for money.

The result for the Dunlop European tyre business was a drop from profit into loss at the operating level between 1977 and 1978, reflecting a serious deterioration in the United Kingdom results, only partly offset by slightly better figures in continental Europe. During the year a detailed examination of the situation was carried out. [For report see appendix 12.]

Other activities

While grappling with these special problems Dunlop has not stood still in other respects. There was an increase in total operating profit outside the European tyre market, many product divisions and subsidiaries contributing to this improvement.

The broad economic picture in the industrial world in 1978 saw increases in real personal incomes in some countries, notably the United Kingdom. At the same time, there was little sign of a real increase in the pace of industrial output in the major economies. This pattern is closely reflected in Dunlop's own results.

The most dramatic improvement came in consumer goods; in industrial products it was more difficult to make progress, although there were notable achievements. There were also very real signs of advance in many parts of the world with satisfactory profits earned in the Far East, Africa and in the group's plantations.

The task ahead

The task facing your board is to ensure that the European tyre business returns to good health speedily. It will be a hard slog, but it will be tackled with realism, vigour and determination. [A review is provided in appendix 12.]

1979 CHAIRMAN'S REPORT – EXTRACTS

At this time last year, I said that the major task for the company was to restore the European tyre business to good health, and that whilst this would be tackled with vigour and determination, it would be a hard slog. And so it proved in 1979 - a year which began in the United Kingdom with the transport drivers' strike, followed in the autumn by the engineering dispute, by strengthening sterling and by the steady rise in interest rates generally.

The losses due to industrial disputes, taking account of their direct and indirect effects on customers and suppliers, were £10m. for the group worldwide, of which £8m. was in the UK.

Tyres in Europe

I commented last year on the extent of the over-capacity in tyres in Europe and the measures that were in hand to cope with it. In the market place, competition has remained intense, but the closure of several tyre plants in Europe has begun to bring supply and demand a little more into balance. During the year further rationalization and modernization of our tyre facilities in the UK continued, with new product development being given enhanced priority. The UK is the development centre for the group's tyre activities world-wide and we shall continue to strengthen this base. The first results can be seen in the introduction of new ranges of car and commercial vehicle tyres earlier this year, to be followed soon by additional new car tyres. There are, in fact, more new tyres in the development pipeline than ever before.

At the same time, the policy of selective acquisitions to build on our strengths continued. Two companies were bought during 1979 – a specialist manufacturer of printing plates to reinforce our market strength in printers' blankets, and a specialist distributor of health and fitness equipment to enable the Sports Group to build up their stake in this growing part of the market.

Outside Europe, the real growth and profitability of our overseas operations was maintained, notably in the Far East and Africa, where the tyre markets are both expanding and remunerative, and where the group commands substantial market shares. And our plantations companies again achieved record profitability, helped by favourable prices and further increases.

The way ahead

There will be no lessening of our efforts to achieve a turnround in the results of our European tyre business – that remains a central task. Good progress has been made, but much remains to be done.

At the same time, we intend selectively to reinforce our other businesses in Europe and to continue to seize every opportunity to capitalize on the real growth that is possible in our overseas businesses.

DUNLOP IN THE EIGHTIES

The eighties began where the seventies left off with rationalization and retrenchment in Europe, particularly with respect to tyres. Much of the rationalization in tyres led to very substantial improvements in productivity. The tyre factory at Inchinnan was closed in 1982, the factory at Cork was closed and the French company was placed into receivership. The union with Pirelli was dissolved with a £21m. payment for 'adverse cash flow'. Also the rubber plantations in Malaysia were sold. The National Tyre Service, the group's retail and wholesale distribution chain, increased the number of outlets to over 500 in the UK. The greater geographical spread, increases in volume and operating efficiency significantly improved profitability.

However, continued overcapacity together with increased import penetration persuaded Dunlop to sell its European manufacturing facilities to Sumatomo. Discussions were started in 1983 in which the Japanese company was to pay £82m. over a 15-month period and £41m. would be paid to Dunlop immediately. Included in the deal was the purchase of Dunlop's tyre inventories which were estimated to be £30m. approximately. As the book value of the assets was £94m. and there would be additional rationalization costs, there would be a loss on the deal of £25m. which would have to be written off as an extraordinary item.

Rationalization and divestment took place in other parts of the group, mostly in those businesses associated with the automotive industry. Whilst top sportsmen were achieving significant results with Dunlop equipment (McEnroe, Bernhard Langer, Geoff Boycott), the Sports Division was operating at very low levels of profitability.

Aviation, oil, and marine hose and belting products were the bright spots in the portfolio, with, in respect of the first two, a world market reputation and leadership and, for all three businesses, products which were technologically advanced for the industry in which they operated.

Chemical products including a range of DIY adhesives produced steady performances, whereas industrial and consumer footwear and the flooring products were subject to much greater volatility in profits.

A new business division was seeking to build up businesses which would be suitable diversification opportunities so that ultimately they could be transferred to a fully commercial operation.

However, by late 1984 the company was in serious financial difficulty. In November Michael Edwardes was appointed to the board to effect a financial reconstruction and turn-round. Before this had really begun, BTR bid for the group and, after increasing the initial offer price, the board eventually recommended acceptance at a price valuing the company at £101m.

TABLE 5.2 **The world tyre market in 1982**

Company	Market share	Country of origin
Goodyear	22	USA
Michelin	19	France
Firestone	10	USA
Bridgestone	8	Japan
Dunlop	6	UK
Pirelli	6	Italy
Goodrich	4	USA
General Tire	4	USA
Continental	4	USA
Uniroyal	3	USA
Yokohama	3	Japan
Sumitomo	2	Japan
Others	9	–

Source: *The Economist*

THE TYRE MARKET IN THE EIGHTIES

Structure of the market

In 1982 the world tyre market was worth $US27 billion with Goodyear and Michelin being the market leaders as can be seen from table 5.2.

The Japanese companies, although with only a small market share, had grown rapidly and increased share significantly over the previous twenty years as a result of the worldwide success of their motor industry. Furthermore, now that the Japanese car manufacturers were setting up plants in other parts of the world, for example in the USA and the UK, the Japanese tyre firms were following them.

Overcapacity in the European tyre market was still a problem in spite of the closure of 15 plants in Europe over the period 1978–81. In fact, employment in European tyre manufacturing fell from 45,000 (1978) to 25,000 (1983).

Channels of distribution

Traditionally tyres were sold through garages but, by 1983, 85 per cent of replacement tyres were sold through specialist distributors offering a 'while you wait' tyre change service. In the UK there were estimated to be approximately 2,500 of the outlets. A large proportion of those outlets were owned by tyre manufacturers as can be seen from table 5.3.

TABLE 5.3   **Ownership of tyre distributors in 1983**

Name of distributor	Number of outlets	Ownership
National Tyre	550	Dunlop
Michelin	420	Michelin
Tyre Services GB	280	Goodyear
Motorway Tyres	200	Avon
Kwik-Fit Euro	200	(not owned by tyre manufacturer)

Marketing

Brand loyalty, if it can be called such, results from the car owner replacing the tyres on the car with 'another set of the same'. However, brand awareness is low and it is unlikely that the owner will replace tyres until it becomes legally necessary.

In order to combat this lack of brand awareness tyre manufacturers increased expenditure on direct advertising in the early eighties: Goodyear by £1.9m., Michelin by £1.8m., Dunlop by £1.3m. and Kwik-Fit Euro by £2.45m.

Appendix 1

DATA FROM THE COMPANY REPORTS, 1968–84 (£m.)

Source	1968	1969	1970	1971	1972	1973	1974	1975	1976	1977	1978	1979	1980	1981	1982	1983	1984
Sales	450	495	541	585	636	750	888	1,015	1,289	1,361	1,475	1,569	1,386	1,456	1,525	1,603	1,582
Operating PBIT	32.6	33.0	34.6	42.6	43.0	47.6	58.2	66.7	87.0	75	64	64	50	52	41	63	71
Total PBIT	35.3	36.1	38.4	50.9	53.4	55.5	70.0	80.1	105.9	87	78	76	59	45	49	68	78
PBT	27.7	27.4	26.9	38.0	39.9	35.7	44.0	52.0	73.3	57	43	29	10	–	(7)	17	27
Net profit	11.9	11.0	9.1	11.6	13.4	9.8	11.0	15.0	19.3	20	11	–	(15)	(41)	(52)	(28)	(15)
Inv. Inc./Assoc. Coy.	1.8	2.1	2.5	6.8	8.8	11.0	10.0	13.4	18.9	12	14	12	9	(7)	8	5	7
Fixed assets	130.7	144.6		192.8	212.9	237.7	256.9	263.4	302.1	309	340	304	313	332	373	345	237
Investments	10.0	11.6		88.0	54.0	62.0	70.9	80.5	101.3	110	115	123	134	46	79	37	25
Net working capital	132.7	151.1	158.5	174.2	190.1	215.7	252.4	268.1	347.6	364	386	364	301	332	353	142	136

Total	273.4	307.3	326.3	455.0	457.0	515.4	580.2	612.1	751.0	783	841	791	748	710	805	524	398
Shareholders' funds	105.4	122.2	122.6	149.0	123.7	142.5	167.8	189.8	229.3	254	251	253	235	253	251	110	48
Preference shareholders' funds	14.7	14.7	14.7	14.7	14.7	14.7	14.7	14.7	14.7	15	15	15	15	15	15	15	15
Minority shareholders' funds	26.5	27.7	29.2	94.9	105.2	121.3	142.3	152.6	180.7	200	200	179	166	73	113	127	57
Debt & loans	89.1	84.0	101.9	137.1	151.4	163.0	161.1	162.8	228.4	245	294	272	264	288	305	61	66
Overdraft & acceptances	27.2	38.0	35.4	29.2	24.6	38.7	59.0	55.4	75.4	65	78	68	64	135	156	149	163
Other	10.5	20.7	22.5	30.1	37.4	35.2	35.3	36.8	22.5	4	3	4	4	(54)	(35)	62	49
No. of Pref. Sh.				14.7	14.7	14.7	14.7	14.7	14.7	14.7	14.7	14.7	14.7	14.7	14.7	14.7	14.7
£ of Ord. Sh.				49.1	49.1	49.1	49.1	49.1	49.1	65.5	66.2	66.4	68.6	71.9	71.9	71.9	71.9
No. of Ord. Sh. 50p.	98.2	98.2	98.2	98.2	98.2	98.2	98.2	98.2	98.2	131.0	132.4	132.9	137.2	143.8	143.8	143.8	143.8
EPS P/Share	11	10	8	11	13	9	12	16	23	16	8.1	–	(11.3)	(29.4)	(36.7)	(20.4)	(10.8)
Exports (£m.)				52	49	61	80	98	126	141	152	155	146	129	125	130	139
Employees (thousands) UK	52	52	52	52	52	52	52	49	48	48	48	48	36	29	25	22	20
O/seas	54	54	54	54	54	57	53	51	54	54	52	54	45	46	34	31	22
R&D (£m.)											17	20	26	33	36	34	31

Appendix 2

FINANCIAL ANALYSIS

	1968	1969	1970	1971	1972	1973	1974	1975	1976	1977	1978	1979	1980	1981	1982	1983	1984
1. Current ratio	2.4	2.5	2.4	2.6	2.4	2.4	2.4	2.3	1.8	1.8	1.7	1.8	1.6	1.4	1.4	1.0	0.9
2. Acid test	1.2	1.3	1.2	1.2	1.3	1.2	1.1	1.1	0.9	0.9	0.8	0.9	0.8	0.7	0.7	0.5	0.6
3. Gearing	44	43	45	39	42	42	40	38	42	40	44	43	44	55	55	45	66
4. Interest cover	4.5	4.2	3.4	4.0	4.0	2.8	2.7	3.3	3.2	2.9	2.2	1.6	1.2	1.0	0.9	1.3	1.6
5. Stock turnover	4.1	4.1	4.0	3.9	4.1	4.0	3.8	4.1	4.2	4.0	4.0	4.9	4.5	4.1	4.2	4.8	6.1
6. Drs/Sales	82	88	85	80	83	78	77	73	79	75	77	74	72	80	75	10	2.8
7. Sales/Fixed assets	3.44	3.42		3.03	2.99	3.15	3.46	3.85	4.26	4.40	4.34	5.16	4.37	4.39	4.09	4.65	6.45
8. Sales/Total assets	1.71	1.68		1.59	1.58	1.66	1.74	1.91	1.98	2.02	2.03	2.34	2.26	2.19	2.10	3.29	4.24
9. EBIT/Sales	7.24	6.66	6.40	7.28	6.76	6.35	6.57	6.75	5.51	4.34	4.08	3.61	4.26	2.69	2.69	3.93	4.49
10. EBIT/Total assets	12.40	11.19		11.61	10.67	10.51	11.43	12.54	13.38	11.14	8.81	9.58	8.14	7.83	5.65	12.94	19.03
11. PBT/Capital employed	10.13	8.91	8.24	8.35	8.73	6.93	7.58	8.50	9.76	7.28	5.11	3.67	1.33	—	(0.87)	3.24	6.78
12. Dividend	61	78	94	76	39	40	35	40	35	27	26	40	—	—	—	—	—
13. Retained profit	39	22	6	24	61	60	65	73	74	60	—	—	—	—	—	—	—

DEFINITIONS

Shareholders' funds = Ordinary shareholders' funds + Preference shareholders' funds + Minority shareholders' funds

Total debt = Debt and loans + Overdraft and acceptances

Total assets = Fixed assets + Net working capital

Capital employed = Total assets + Investments

Operating PBIT = Operating profit before interest and tax

Profit before Tax (PBT) = PBIT + Investment income – Tax

Net profit = PBT – Tax

1 Current ratio: $\dfrac{\text{Current assets}}{\text{Current liabilities}}$

2 Acid test: $\dfrac{\text{Current assets} - \text{Stocks}}{\text{Current liabilities}}$

3 Gearing: $\dfrac{\text{Total debt}}{\text{Total debt} + \text{Shareholders' funds}}$ %

4 Interest cover: $\dfrac{\text{Earnings before interest and tax}}{\text{Interest payable}}$

5 Stock turnover: $\dfrac{\text{Sales}}{\text{Stocks}}$

6 Average collection period: $\dfrac{\text{Debtors}}{\text{Sales}}$ (days)

7 Fixed asset turnover ratio: $\dfrac{\text{Sales}}{\text{Fixed assets}}$

8 Total asset turnover ratio: $\dfrac{\text{Sales}}{\text{Total assets}}$

9 Operating profit margin: $\dfrac{\text{Operating profit}}{\text{Sales}}$ %

10 Return on total assets: $\dfrac{\text{Operating profit}}{\text{Total assets}}$ %

11   Return on capital employed: $\dfrac{\text{Total profit before tax}}{\text{Capital employed}}\%$

12   Dividend payment: $\dfrac{\text{Dividend}}{\text{Net profit}}\%$

13   Retained profit%: $\dfrac{\text{Retained profit}}{\text{Net profit}}\%$

Appendix 3   Product and business analysis

RESULTS BY PRODUCT (£m.)

	1971	1972	1973	1974	1975	1976	1977	1978	1979	1980	1981	1982	1983
Sales													
Tyres	368	401	463	528	615	776	815	871	897	743	838	872	953
Industrial	68	71	84	114	133	163	182	210	231	244	210	201	198
Consumer ⎱ Sport	101	116	142	170	188	155	167	189	204	170	167	207	218
Engineering	40	38	45	52	57	77	84	90	96	99	108	119	137
Plantations	–	–	–	–	–	74	77	87	95	73	82	98	97
Other	8	10	16	24	22	30	36	40	46	57	51	28	–
Total	585	636	750	888	1,015	1,275	1,361	1,487	1,569	1,386	1,456	1,525	1,603
Profit													
Tyres	30.8	30.0	29.9	29.6	38	42	25	18	22	13	24	25	41
Industrial	3.4	4.5	7.3	12.2	12	19	20	10	14	13	9	9	7
Consumer ⎱ Sports	5.7	6.8	7.9	8.7	8	5	8	10	9	7	2	9	11
												(1)	1
Engineering	2.8	2.6	1.9	4.7	4	6	6	4	3	3	2	3	3
Plantations	–	–	–	–	–	7	8	6	7	5	8	–	–
Other	1.4	0.7	2.3	4.8	3	4	8	8	9	9	7	(4)	–
Total	44.1	44.6	49.3	60.0	65	83	75	66	64	50	52	41	63

TOTAL BY PRODUCT (%)

	1971	1972	1973	1974	1975	1976	1977	1978	1979	1980	1981	1982	1983
Sales													
Tyres	63	63	62	59	61	61	60	59	57	54	60	57	59
Industrial	12	11	11	13	13	13	13	14	15	18	15	13	12
Consumer ⎱	17	18	19	19	19	12	12	13	13	12	12	14	14
Sports ⎰	–	–	–	–	–	6	6	6	6	7	8	8	9
Engineering	7	6	6	6	6	6	6	6	6	5	6	6	6
Plantations	–	–	–	–	–	3	3	3	3	4	4	–	–
Other	1	2	2	3	2	–	–	–	–	–	–	2	–
Profits													
Tyres	70	67	61	50	58	50	33	27	34	26	46	61	65
Industrial	8	10	15	20	18	23	27	30	22	26	17	22	11
Consumer ⎱	13	15	16	15	12	6	11	15	14	14	4	22	17
Sports ⎰	–	–	–	–	–	8	8	6	5	6	4	(2)	2
Engineering	6	6	4	8	6	8	11	9	11	10	15	7	5
Plantations	–	–	–	–	–	5	11	12	14	18	13	–	–
Other	3	2	5	8	5	–	–	–	–	–	–	(10)	–

RESULTS BY BUSINESS (£m.)

	Sales		Profits	
	1984	1983	1984	1983
Turnover				
Dunlop Slazenger	153	128	1	2
Dunlop Consumer	274	274	3	9
Dunlop Engineering	61	63	(1)	(2)
Dunlop Aerospace	53	46	8	7
Dunlop Industrial	135	133	5	4
Dunlop Tire and Rubber	346	273	28	24
Dunlop South Africa	111	118	14	20
Dunlop Overseas	120	113	11	12
Divested discontinued businesses	329	455	2	(13)
Total	1,582	1,603	71	63

OPERATING PROFITS OF UK ACTIVITIES, 1976–80 (£m.)

	1976	1977	1978	1979	1980
Tyre	10	7	(8)	(13)	(22)
Non-tyre	21	23	26	15	7
Total	31	30	18	2	(15)

Appendix 4

RESULTS BY REGION (£m.)

	1971	1972	1973	1974	1975	1976	1977	1978	1979	1980	1981	1982	1983	1984
Sales														
UK	252	259	286	345	393	463	537	591	618	552	498	498	504	506
Rest of EEC	132	149	182	225	255	336	349	384	420	251	243	406	394	277
Rest of Europe	5	5	6	8	10	12	13	14	14	15	12	12	13	15
Asia & Australia	67	77	97	129	133	183	187	204	212	240	283	145	166	181
Africa	49	53	70	78	105	100	104	125	138	169	202	154	165	148
N America	73	85	99	94	119	172	161	160	159	147	203	263	337	428
C & S America	7	8	10	9	}	9	10	9	8	12	15	19	24	27
Other	–	–	–	–	–	–	–	–	–	–	–	28	–	–
Total	585	636	750	888	1015	1275	1361	1487	1569	1386	1456	1525	1603	1582
Profits														
UK	10.8	12.9	11.7	21.7	21	31	30	18	2	(15)	(13)	(10)	–	8
Rest of EEC	11.6	8.6	7.0	5.3	7	4	2	4	11	9	4	(6)	(4)	3
Rest of Europe	(0.2)	–	–	0.2	–	–	–	–	–	–	1	1	–	(1)
Asia & Australia	7.2	6.6	13.3	15.3	15	21	21	23	27	28	27	17	16	14
Africa	0.7	6.5	9.7	10.5	13	10	9	13	17	23	21	26	26	17
N America	6.0	8.6	8.4	7.3	9	17	12	8	7	4	11	15	22	27
C & S America	8.0	1.4	1.2	(0.3)	}	–	1	–	–	1	1	2	3	3
Other	–	–	–	–	–	–	–	–	–	–	–	(4)	–	–
Total	44.1	44.6	49.3	60.0	65	83	75	66	64	50	52	41	63	71

TOTAL BY REGION (%)

	1971	1972	1973	1974	1975	1976	1977	1978	1979	1980	1981	1982	1983	1984
Sales														
UK	43	41	38	39	39	36	39	40	39	40	34	33	31	32
Rest of EEC	23	23	24	25	25	26	26	26	27	18	17	27	25	18
Rest of Europe	1	1	1	1	1	1	1	1	1	1	1	1	1	1
Asia & Australia	11	12	13	15	13	14	14	14	14	17	19	10	10	11
Africa	8	8	9	9	10	8	7	8	9	12	14	10	10	9
N America	12	13	13	11	12	13	12	11	10	11	14	17	21	27
C & S America	1	1	1	1	—	1	1	1	1	1	1	1	1	2
Other	—	—	—	—	—	—	—	—	—	—	—	2	—	—
Profits														
UK	24	29	24	36	32	37	40	27	3	(30)	(25)	(24)	—	11
Rest of EEC	26	19	14	9	11	5	3	6	17	18	8	(15)	(6)	4
Rest of Europe	—	—	—	—	—	—	—	—	—	—	2	2	—	(1)
Asia & Australia	16	15	27	26	23	25	28	35	42	56	52	41	25	20
Africa	2	15	20	18	20	12	12	20	27	46	40	63	41	24
N America	14	19	17	12	14	20	16	12	11	8	21	37	35	38
C & S America	18	3	2	—	—	—	1	—	—	2	2	5	5	4
Other	—	—	—	—	—	—	—	—	—	—	—	(10)	—	—

Appendix 5

CAPITAL EXPENDITURE (£m.)

	1976	1977	1978	1979	1980	1981	1982	1983
By Product								
Tyres	31	35	34	34	37	40	37	39
Industrial	5	9	11	10	9	9	11	12
Engineering	2	2	3	2	2	2	5	8
Consumer	2	3	5	5	3	5	5	3
Sports	2	4	2	2	3	3	3	3
Plantations	1	1	1	1	1	1	–	–
Total	43	54	56	54	55	60	61	66
By Region								
UK	17	23	23	22	25	27	21	22
Rest of EEC	13	14	13	16	10	11	13	10
Asia & Australia	3	6	9	9	8	10	5	8
Africa	8	5	5	5	8	7	9	12
North America	2	6	5	2	4	4	10	13
Central & South American	–	–	1	–	–	1	3	1
Total	43	54	56	54	55	60	61	66

Appendix 6

DIRECTORS, 1972–83

	Age in 1983	Date joined company	84	83	82	81	80	79	78	77	76	75	74	73	72
Executive															
Lord				CE[a]	CE	CE	CE	CE	✓	✓					
Gardener	57	1975		✓	✓	✓	✓	✓	✓	✓	✓	✓			
Harvey	51	1959		✓	✓	✓	✓	✓	✓	✓	✓	✓			
Hope	51	1976		✓	✓	✓	✓	✓	✓	✓	✓				
Johnson	58	1974		✓	✓	✓	✓	✓	✓						
Marsh	56	1951		✓	✓	✓	✓								
Wheater				✓											
Campbell Fraser	60	1956			CH[b]	CH	CH	CH	CE	CE	CE	CE	CE	CE	CE
Bexon					✓	✓	✓	✓	✓	✓	✓	✓	✓	✓	✓
Dent							✓	✓	✓	✓	✓	✓	✓	✓	✓
Geddes										CH	CH	CH	CH	CH	CH	CH
Ward													✓	✓	✓	✓
Baker																✓
			84	83	82	81	80	79	78	77	76	75	74	73	72
Non-executive															
Hodgson				CH	✓	✓										
Baring				✓	✓	✓										

continued

continued

	Age in 1983	Date joined company	84	83	82	81	80	79	78	77	76	75	74	73	72
Eng				✓											
Ghafar Baba				✓											
Knight				✓	✓	✓									
Menzies Wilson				✓	✓										
Read				✓	✓	✓	✓	✓	✓	✓	✓	✓	✓	✓	✓
Carroll						✓	✓	✓	✓	✓	✓	✓	✓	✓	
Lever								✓	✓	✓	✓	✓	✓	✓	
Partridge								✓	✓	✓					
Pirelli								✓	✓	✓	✓	✓	✓	✓	✓
Shelbourne								✓	✓	✓					
Spinks							✓								
Roberts									✓	✓	✓	✓	✓	✓	✓
Melville										✓	✓	✓	✓	✓	✓
Forbes												✓	✓	✓	✓
Weir													✓	✓	✓
Flunder														✓	✓

[a] Chief Executive.
[b] Chairman

Source: Company accounts

Appendix 7   Stock market data

FINANCIAL TIMES ACTUARIES' ALL SHARE INDEX

	High	Wt. ave.	Low
1973	219	184	136
1974	150	106	61
1975	160	133	62
1976	172	153	116
1977	226	191	150
1978	242	216	191
1979	283	245	219
1980	313	271	225
1981	338	308	265
1982	389	342	306
1983	470	435	383
1984	593	517	465

Source: Financial Times

DUNLOP SHARE PRICE

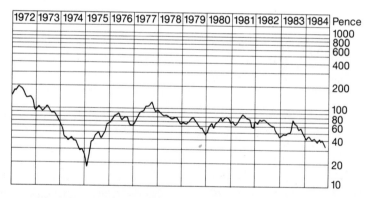

FIGURE 5.1 **Dunlop share price**

Source: Extel Handbook of Market Leaders

Appendix 8   Tyre market statistics

NUMBER OF CAR TYRES (MILLIONS)

	Cross ply	Radial	Total	Imports	Exports	Home cons.	Inflation index for tyres
1972	13.0	14.8	27.8	3.5	4.5	26.8	65
1973	9.6	17.1	26.7	3.7	5.2	25.2	67
1974	7.6	16.7	24.3	4.3	5.4	23.2	83
1975	6.2	17.5	23.7	3.9	6.0	21.6	100
1976	5.3	20.2	25.5	4.7	7.6	22.6	113
1977	4.1	19.9	24.0	5.7	6.8	22.9	139
1978	3.6	21.2	24.8	6.5	7.5	23.8	149
1979	3.0	21.2	24.2	7.0	7.6	23.6	167
1980	2.1	22.5	24.6	5.6	10.2	20.0	192
1981	1.6	20.2	21.8	6.7	NA	–	197
1982	1.2	21.4	22.6	6.6	9.1	20.1	211
1983	0.9	22.3	23.2	8.5	9.1	22.6	217
1984	1.0	20.4	21.4	8.5	8.0	21.9	227

ALL TYRES – VALUE (£m.)

	Car tyres						Other UK mftr tyres[a]	Total UK mftr tyres
	UK manufacture					Home cons.		
	Cross ply	Radial	Total	Imports	Exports			
1972	51.0	72.5	123.5	13.7	20.0	117.2	120.2	243.7
1973	41.1	85.6	126.7	16.2	25.6	117.3	133.4	260.1
1974	41.3	105.1	146.4	24.4	34.1	136.7	164.3	310.9
1975	38.9	138.7	177.6	26.0	47.3	156.3	206.7	384.3
1976	37.1	179.2	216.3	38.9	70.9	184.3	267.0	483.3
1977	35.2	207.8	243.0	54.3	71.2	226.1	291.0	534.0
1978	33.6	235.5	269.1	62.6	80.3	251.4	289.3	558.4
1979	30.7	258.4	289.1	73.5	87.8	274.8	322.7	611.8
1980	23.7	301.2	324.9	66.3	123.4	267.8	326.0	650.9
1981	17.0	254.3	271.3	85.5	NA	–	313.2	584.4
1982	14.9	285.1	300.0	83.7	113.7	270.0	257.6	557.6
1983	11.0	314.8	325.8	117.2	126.4	316.6	282.9	608.7
1984	12.5	307.9	320.4	122.2	124.0	318.6	284.6	609.0

[a] Includes tyres for lorries, buses, tractors, earthmoving equipment, etc.

Source: *Business Monitor* PQ491, PQ4811.

Appendix 9   Car and transport statistics

ESTIMATED ROAD TRAFFIC IN GREAT BRITAIN (THOUSAND MILLION VEHICLE KILOMETRES)

	1974	1975	1976	1977	1978	1979	1980	1981	1982	1983	1984
All motor vehicles	208.09	209.84	220.35	225.18	234.30	223.70	247.58	251.86	259.33	264.20	274.54
Cars and taxis[a]	163.90	165.39	173.38	178.23	185.92	184.93	197.26	201.39	208.77	213.17	221.79
Two-wheeled motor vehicles	3.22	3.84	4.74	4.76	4.74	4.92	5.92	6.69	6.91	6.30	6.24
Bus and coaches	2.95	2.90	2.97	2.86	2.91	2.93	3.06	3.01	3.00	3.11	3.20
Total goods vehicles	38.03	37.71	39.27	39.33	40.72	40.92	41.33	40.79	40.66	41.62	43.30
Light vans[b]	19.01	18.88	19.41	19.77	20.34	20.27	21.03	21.26	21.25	21.39	22.40
Other goods vehicles	19.02	18.84	19.85	19.56	20.39	20.65	20.30	19.53	19.41	20.23	20.90
Pedal cycles	3.24	3.77	4.21	5.11	4.25	3.80	4.20	4.49	5.27	5.19	5.04

[a] This category includes three-wheeled cars: excluding all vans whether licensed for private or for commerical use.
[b] Not exceeding 30 cwt unladen weight.
[c] Provisional.

Source: Department of Transport

CAR PRODUCTION AND IMPORTS

	Production		Car imports as % of new UK registrations
	Cars (millions)	Comm. veh. (thousands)	
1969	1.717	466	
1970	1.641	458	
1971	1.742	456	
1972	1.921	408	23
1973	1.747	417	27
1974	1.534	403	28
1975	1.268	381	34
1976	1.333	372	38
1977	1.316	398	45
1978	1.223	384	49
1979	1.070	408	56
1980	0.923	389	56
1981	0.954	229	56
1982	0.888	269	58
1983	1.045	245	
1984	0.909	225	

Appendix 10   Dunlop review of operations, 1977

EUROPE

Tyres

The keen competition experienced in the markets in 1976 continued throughout the year. Sales of radial car and truck tyres continued to grow; a new radial winter tyre was successfully introduced and fitment of the Denovo safety tyre was increased. Overall results, however, were down on 1976.

In the United Kingdom the strengthened pound brought an increase in tyre imports with consequent pressure on prices in the second half of the year, and the results of both United Kingdom Tyre Division and Pirelli Limited were also affected by industrial relations problems. The tyre distribution companies had a good year.

Dunlop SA in France continued to trade throughout the year under the burden of price controls bearing no relationship to cost escalation. Losses were incurred, and the strongest representations were made to the authorities.

In Germany Dunlop AG again experienced keen competition in tyre trading, but vigorous management action brought improvements in all parts of the business.

Industrial products

The Dunlop Industrial Group improved its profitability in 1977, again with an impressive export performance accounting for 34 per cent of total sales.

Hydraulic Hose Division established a new plant for the manufacture of rigid hose assemblies. New product development was a major feature of the group's activities.

With its expanded production facilities in the United Kingdom, Angus Fire Armour Limited achieved record turnover and profits in 1977 and gained its second Queen's Award for the export of irrigation hose; total exports accounted for 69 per cent of the United Kingdom activity.

Engineering products

Wheel, Suspensions and Redditch Mouldings Divisions all benefited from some improvement in demand from the motor industry whilst Plant and Equipment Division maintained the improvement of the previous year, earning a satisfactory profit and return on funds.

Considerable attention was given during the year to the development of new products and new markets, with both Aviation and Suspensions Divisions undertaking major sales drives in the USA. In addition, a range of new products for industry based on the Dunlop Thermimax Burner was launched.

Consumer products

The overall profitability of Consumer Group improved in spite of the fact that demand for consumer products remained as depressed as in 1976. Both Dunlop Textiles Limited and Dunlopillo Division showed worthwhile gains and, in particular, Dunlopillo GmbH Germany had a good year.

Sports products

Owing to the continuing stagnation of consumer spending in many major markets and the over-supply of some major products, 1977 was a difficult year for sporting goods throughout the world. In these circumstances, the sports goods operations did well to increase sales turnover in the United Kingdom and the rest of Europe; but with increased competition, notably from the Far East, operating margins were generally lower.

The main emphasis in capital spending was on improved production methods as part of a continuing cost reduction programme.

During the year, a number of new products including a new range of garden games for the family to be marketed under the generic name Dunlop 'Playsport' was developed for the forthcoming season.

Asia and Australasia

In India a decline in the growth rate for tyres and industrial products coupled with the commissioning of new production capacity resulted in very severe competition and lower margins. In the circumstances Dunlop India Limited did well to achieve a 2 per cent growth in sales volume and to earn a modest profit.

The plantations in Malaysia and New Zealand recorded exceptionally good figures, due mainly to high prices for palm oil and cocoa. Only modest profits were earned from rubber.

In Indonesia construction work was begun during the year on a Dunlopillo factory which should be on stream by the end of 1978 and the new tennis ball manufacturing facility in the Philippines is expected to begin production in April 1978.

The Malaysian golf ball operation continued to improve in efficiency.

Africa

In Nigeria the continued rapid expansion of the economy placed considerable strains on the infrastructure of the country. As a consequence Dunlop Nigerian Industries Limited was short of power supplies throughout the year and this substantially reduced tyre output. Imports of Dunlop tyres were increased, but the results in total were well below those of the previous year.

The South African sports goods business had a particularly successful year with both sales and profits well ahead of 1976.

North America

Intensely competitive conditions in both tyres and sporting goods held back the Dunlop Tire and Rubber Corporation's turnover in each of these product groups to little more than in 1976 in local currency and contributed to some narrowing of margins.

Economy programmes mitigated the effects of this, but profits after taxation were some 20 per cent lower than in the previous year.

During 1977 a new manufacturing plant was established in the USA for the production of both fire and irrigation hose, in line with the policy of expanding Angus Fire Armour's North American activities.

In a generally static market for racquet sports and golf equipment, price competition intensified and results were lower than in 1976.

In Canada, the cable market went through a difficult year with falling demand and a serious deterioration of prices. As a result Pirelli Canada Limited sustained a loss.

Dunlop International Projects Ltd

Dunlop International Projects Limited was organized in December 1976 to obtain and manage contracts for the supply of factories and technology to outside customers on a turnkey basis, and the contract signed during 1977 for a factory to produce latex foam articles in the USSR is an example of the type of operation being undertaken.

Appendix 11 Corporate planning at Dunlop (1977)

Extracts from an article in Long Range Planning *No. 12 (February 1979) pp. 17–21 (Pergamon Press) by A. M. Rossiter, manager of corporate planning. The lecture was originally given on 10 March 1977.*

1 We are much concerned with rebalancing our funds employed, so that new investments are carefully channelled into those areas where profitable growth commensurate with risk can be maximized. Equally, we are concerned, without detriment to the quantum of profit upon which we substantially depend, to restrict those parts of our business where the prospects are perceived to be less promising.

2 Operational features of corporate planning (CP) at Dunlop.

    (a) CP tends to take the helicopter view which gives a broader view but loses some definition. However, interesting sightings can be examined in closer detail.

    (b) CP tries not to get too bogged down in detail, but seeks to spot significant trends and outline their relevance to the firm.

    (c) CP seeks to paint a comprehensive picture.

    (d) CP is concerned with the right balance between centre-led and bottom-up initiatives.

    (e) CP is responsible for the discipline of the planning cycle.

    (f) CP develops and disseminates the overall and devolved objectives (usually in terms of profit and profitability) and with allocation of funds to different cost centres.

3 We vet all major capital expenditure plans. We have to try to 'pick the winners'. First we analyse the market in which the business operates and then our own strengths and weaknesses in that market. The results are then plotted on a simple form of 'directional policy matrix'.

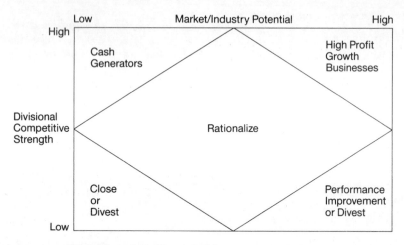

FIGURE 5.2   **Directional Policy matrix**

Market/Industry Criteria	*Divisional Competitive Criteria*
Market Growth	Profitability
Industry Profitability (particularly margins)	Market Share
Capacity v Demand	Product Quality and Performance
Opportunity for Specialization	Innovative Ability & Resources
Complexity of Products/Services	Marketing Strengths

4   Allocation of resources is the actual sum advised to divisions and includes both fixed and working capital requirements for three years.

5   Having categorized each unit according to its prospects for growth and profitability, the object is to expand the funds employed in the growth areas of high profitability, while containing and in real terms contracting those in low-growth and less profitable areas.

6   The CP system will be in a constant state of change as experience is gained and the environment changes. However the change should be evolutionary rather than revolutionary (unless the system is manifestly inadequate) in order not to destroy continuity. Also the system should never be so sophisticated as to deny ready comprehension at all levels.

Appendix 12   Review of European tyre operations, 1978

In 1978 Dunlop took steps to strengthen its position as a competitor in the difficult European tyre market. A growing proportion of our output was of the most modern steel radial car and truck tyres, continuing to secure the basis for an improving reputation for our products. There was also progress toward a standardized range of tyres for the European market.

All aspects of the business were scrutinized to find more efficient operating methods, and output per man-hour showed good improvements in France and Germany.

A broader base of business with vehicle manufacturers – the essential original equipment market – was secured and in some markets shares of the replacement tyre business rose. There were two notable improvements in Dunlop technology for tyres and wheels. In November the company announced the 'Denloc' system of keeping the tyre bead in place on the wheel rim in case of puncture or deflation. This major advance in tyre safety commended itself to the National Highway Traffic Safety Administration in the United States of America.

The system has also been incorporated in the improved Denovo run-flat tyre. The Denovo 2 will be available on British, French, Italian and Japanese cars brought out during 1979.

The trading results of the tyre business in Europe were much less satisfactory. Losses were suffered by all the tyre manufacturing businesses, where competition was extremely severe, with markets showing little or no growth as the result of the longer life of tyres. Prices could not be raised to cover cost increases, and in some cases even fell. Some competitors have been forced to withdraw from the business, or scale down operations. Imports into EEC have increased, often at uneconomic prices, which have brought additional pressure on price level.

All the same, the tyre industry in Europe remains the second largest in the world after North America. It has led the world in tyre technology, and still does so. During the year, Dunlop strategy in this extremely important market was examined in depth, and as a result, the company will attack in Europe the major segments of the market with an appropriate concentration of investment.

The main impact of this policy will be in the UK manufacture of tyres, and in January of this year the ending of tyre making at Speke was announced, and at the same time a plan to invest £75 million in modernization at the three remaining tyre factories at Fort Dunlop, Inchinnan, Renfrewshire, and Washington, Co. Durham. This investment is designed to reinforce Dunlop's position as a leader in the European and worldwide tyre business.

Appendix 13   Review of operations, 1983

TYRES EUROPE

Competition in tyre markets generally throughout Europe remained intense and, although there was evidence of some recovery in demand as the year progressed, the market for truck tyres remained depressed throughout.

With overcapacity leading to unacceptably low price levels, there was a significant move towards products with demonstrable marketing advantages such as reduced fuel consumption or improved safety features. A number of new vehicles are being equipped with the new TD tyre – most noteworthy is the fitment to Metros.

United Kingdom

Compared with the very low levels of 1982, demand for original equipment car tyres rose by 20 per cent, and for replacement car tyres by 13 per cent. Dunlop sales to vehicle manufacturers rose similarly, but there was little improvement in price levels owing to the continuing influx of cheap imports.

A minimal loss of market share in the truck tyre market was more than offset by an improving export performance, but during the year production of earthmover tyres ceased as part of the rationalization plan.

France

At the beginning of October, it was decided that the parent company could not continue to support further losses and the judicial receiver was appointed.

Germany

The German company reported a year of considerable progress. The high performance premium range of 'D' tyres gained replacement market share as well as original equipment fitment on prestige vehicles. Dunlop tyres were again successful at the Le Mans 24 Hour race won by a Porsche equipped with special tyres incorporating the Denloc bead-locking system.

The high capacity utilization of car tyre production lines at the two German factories more than offset the difficult market conditions for truck and earthmover tyres.

Ireland

As a result of the unsatisfactory performance of the Cork factory, it was decided to announce closure in the middle of the year.

Rest of Europe

The European selling companies experienced a particularly difficult and unprofitable year with selling prices at very low levels throughout the region.

DIVERSIFIED PRODUCTS

Extensive rationalization and reorganization of the diversified products activities in 1982 enabled the group to enter 1983 with a greater degree of flexibility. Consequently, as the year progressed, there was a steady improvement in trading profit which rose by more than 60 per cent compared with that of the previous year.

Engineering

Lower airline traffic worldwide during 1983 affected Aviation Division on two fronts. Demand for replacement equipment for aircraft in service was reduced and the deferment of new aircraft purchases delayed offtake of original equipment. Despite these difficulties, the division was able to exploit its service network to the full and recorded increased profits. The investment programme in new production facilities for the Boeing 757 carbon brake contract continued.

The low level of demand for pipes in the UK municipal and utility sector and the deep recession in the American phosphate mining industry led to disappointing results for Dunlopipe Division factories at Coventry and in Florida.

Automotive Engineering Division returned to operating profit during 1983. The status of sole supplier of steel wheels to BL was maintained, supplemented by significant increases in business with Ford and Vauxhall in the UK as well as BMW in Germany. The latter part of the year saw the commercial introduction of the revolutionary TD wheel which is being fitted to 1984 Metro models and will appear on other new models. Although the commerical vehicle market remained in deep recession, increased sales of the advanced air suspension systems for buses, coaches, and heavy trailers were obtained. A number of development projects, in conjunction with UK, European and American vehicle manufacturers, were initiated during the year. The potential market for both advanced engine and vehicle suspension systems is considerable.

Consumer

Dunlopillo Division consolidated the progress made in moulded car seating during 1982, and with production brought together into one building at Hirwaun, the benefits of rationalization showed through in a return to profit. Retail activities were restructured and a new range of mattress/divan combinations are currently being brought to the market. The continuing research and development effort being devoted to flameproof materials has met with significant success and resulted in a contract from the Department of the Environment for mattresses to be used in prisons and other institutions.

Growth continued at Chemical Products Division with a consequent increase in profits. A new range of structural adhesives and the planned introduction of a range of 'car care' products in 1984 will provide the base for further growth. Contract Services Division maintained profit levels although the level of activity in the construction industry was depressed.

Industrial

Oil and Marine Division continued to dominate the offshore floating hose business with a further increase in market share. The new high-pressure flexible pipe (HPFP) project moved forward late in the year with the installation of initial production equipment and the winning of a substantial order to supply to the new Morecambe Bay offshore gas field. With full production of HPFP scheduled to come on stream in 1984, the division is well placed to maintain its pre-eminence in its field.

Trading conditions for both Hose and Belting Divisions remained difficult throughout the year with the lower demand situation exacerbated by an influx of cheap hose imports. Nevertheless, as a result of rationalization measures taken in late 1982, Belting Division managed to maintain its profit level, and losses were reduced in Hose Division.

In the automotive industry, after a static first quarter, Fluid Seal Division experienced an improving trend for the remainder of the year, increasing their share of business with original equipment manufacturers. For the year as a whole a profit was recorded. Polymer Engineering Division also felt the steady improvement in the UK car market, and made progress in other fields with notable orders being obtained on new rapid transit rail suspension systems in the USA and Canada.

With new orders for the British Aerospace 146 airliner and the SAAB Fairchild SF340 commuter aircraft, and an expansion in the range of products for the medical field, Precision Rubbers Division continued its growth pattern of recent years.

Dunlop Medical Products also increased its product range with the introduction of traction and physiotherapy exercise equipment, and the commencement of clinical trials for carbon implant products.

General Rubber Goods Division significantly improved on the previous year's results with increased sales of Dracones, collapsible containers, and printer's blankets. Benefits also resulted from the computerized mixing facility installed at the Manchester factory.

The Americas

Dunlop Tire & Rubber Corporation again achieved a significant increase in profits. The company is now the undisputed market leader in motorcycle tyres, and taking advantage of the strength of the dollar, made a major penetration into the steel truck tyre market with imported tyres. Productivity improvements were achieved at both factories in Huntsville, Alabama and Buffalo, N.Y., aided by a significant capital expenditure programme and trade union co-operation.

The Caribbean Tyre Company Ltd (formerly Dunlop Trinidad) maintained the profit improvement of 1982, expanding and modernizing to meet growing local demand for tyres.

Dunlop (Canada) Inc achieved a return to profit after the disappointing results of 1982. After a number of start-up problems, the joint venture roofing company now has a good forward order book for both domestic and export markets.

In Brazil, the new printers' blanket company is now fully operational. Dunlop Argentina reported a good year's trading with an expanded product range.

Africa

Dunlop South Africa maintained its level of profitability despite the impact of the recession on supplies to the mining and construction industries. These shortfalls were, however, offset by improved trading results of the tyre and Dunlopillo foam operations.

Foreign exchange shortages for the purchase of certain essential raw materials and replacements parts proved to be a depressing factor for operations in Zimbabwe. Despite productivity gains, government price controls made it impossible to recover all increased costs, so that the company recorded a reduced level of profit.

Far East and Pacific Basin

During the year, a £2m. programme to modernize existing industrial hose production and introduce new product lines was completed by Dunlop India. In contrast, trading conditions in the tyre market, particularly for truck tyres, were extremely competitive, but overall trading profits were ahead of 1982.

The improvement in commodity prices came too late in the year to influence company trading levels in Malaysia where sales and profit levels fell slightly below the previous year. An important diversification was the commissioning of a spring mattress factory to complement the existing Dunlopillo foam plant.

With a government-imposed wage and price freeze, Dunlop New Zealand Ltd maintained profit levels from an increased turnover. During the year the company acquired the tyre manufacturing operations and marketing outlets of the Reid brand from Feltex New Zealand Ltd. Reid was New Zealand's third largest tyre company and its acquisition consolidates Dunlop's market dominance.

TECHNOLOGY

Technology Division placed major emphasis during 1983 on supporting the development programmes in carbon brake technology for Aviation Division and high-pressure flexible pipe technology for Oil and Marine Division. The advances achieved in materials design and application will have potential elsewhere in the group, particularly where the application of high performance composites will give access to high value technology markets such as medical carbon implants.

In the field of dynamic research, new concepts in suspension systems designed to absorb noise, vibration and harshness characteristics in vehicles are also being developed in conjunction with the operating divisions.

6 Marks and Spencer

For the financial year end in March 1989 Marks and Spencer (M & S) reported sales of over £5 billion and pre-tax profits of over £500m. Although these results had maintained M & S's position as the UK's pre-eminent retailer, there had nevertheless been some uncomfortable moments for them in the 1980s. (See Appendix 1 for financial information.)

Michael Marks set up his first 'Penny Bazaar' on Leeds market in 1884. A Leeds wholesaler called Isaac Dewhirst gave Michael Marks trade credit, and the business relationship formed then still existed over 100 years later, with I. J. Dewhirst Plc being one of the major suppliers to M & S. Tom Spencer, although he knew Michael Marks in 1884, did not become a business partner until 1894, and the work of those two founders was carried on by Simon Marks and brother-in-law Israel Sieff, with a member of the family as chairman of the company until 1984, when Lord Raynor took over following the retirement of Lord Sieff (grandson of Michael Marks).

The trading principles of M & S were established in 1884 and restated in 1984 in the Chairman's annual report:

1   To offer our customer a selected range of goods of high quality and good value.
2   To work in close co-operation with our suppliers to develop this catalogue.
3   Always to buy British providing the goods the British suppliers produce represent high quality and good value.
4   To develop and maintain good human relations with our staff, our suppliers, and our customers.

He went on to say 'Our principles are sacrosant, our policies flexible – which departments to expand, which to contract, what new departments to introduce, where to build stores and what their size should be.' (Annual report, 1984).

The basis of M & S's success over the years was founded on textiles and clothing products, although more recent years have seen most growth in foods and housewares. By building close relationships with clothing manufacturers M & S was able to enjoy most of the benefits of having its own manufacturing base, whilst having few of the responsibilities, and in turn many of the clothing manufacturers had prospered. In this way the company demonstrated the ability of the UK clothing industry to provide well-designed clothes giving good value for money.

M & S issue 'demand specifications' to their suppliers, many of whom supply a high proportion of their output to the retailer: e.g. S. R. Gent (ladies' outerwear, 95 per cent, I. J. Dewhirst (men's suits, 90 per cent), N. Corah (underwear, 75 per cent). In return for their loyalty M & S take an interest in their suppliers' profitability, and assist in ensuring healthy progression. There is a never-ending search for efficiency, allied with strict quality control, in order that M & S can claim that their 'St Michael' brand provides the best value for money, rather than simply the highest quality. That being a supplier to M & S is considered worthwhile is shown by the fact that 45 suppliers have supplied M & S for over 40 years, and 134 for over 25 years.

By 1989 M & S had 281 stores in the UK with a total sales area of 8.78 million square feet, a further 402,000 square feet of sales area in mainland Europe (13 stores), and 3.93 million square feet in North America and the Far East (in 371 stores).

Each week over 14 million customers shopped at M & S's UK stores. This very success pointed to the company's problems in maintaining the growth rate expected of it. Providing for such a large market meant that it couldn't afford to make many mistakes and this encouraged them to be rather conservative when it came to fashion clothing. M & S had introduced 'Miss Michelle' clothes in 1979 aimed at the more fashion-conscious teenage market, but the customers had decided the clothes offered were not fashionable enough, and far too expensive. At the same time they had offered more expensive clothing to other age groups, e.g. silk blouses, but the timing proved wrong, as the onset of the recession made it more difficult to sell at higher prices.

Textiles was one of the three trading groups in the company, the others being foods and housewares, but textiles was much the biggest. The organizational structure for these trading groups involved a senior executive in charge, supported by two merchandise managers and several selectors (M & S's name for buyers). New product ideas were generated in two ways: first, by developing ideas out of existing areas, and secondly, by moving into totally new product areas. The latter route was obviously more risky, where M & S's expertise at laying down specifications could not be so easily deployed. Having found new product areas, through various methods, the company needed to distinguish good ideas from bad. The company did not undertake quantitative or qualitative marketing research, but preferred to put new products straight into the high street by trying them in about 20 stores, always including their two major London stores.

In the mid-1980s M & S had begun to respond to new challenges in the retail clothing sector by:

- cutting lead times for orders;
- ordering in smaller quantities;
- moving towards more co-ordinated fashion ranges, especially for the 25 to 35-year-old market;
- including new more fashionable clothing products;
- taking advantage of new technology to increase control over stockholding, and providing better sales information.

These challenges in the clothing sector were exemplified, first, by the growth and development of the so-called lifestyle retailers, such as *Burtons* and *Next*, which had segmented the clothing market and aimed specifically at certain age-groups, secondly, by the relatively slow growth of consumer expenditure on clothing generally in the UK, and thirdly, by the increased penetration of the clothing market by overseas manufacturers in the face of the M & S policy to buy British.

Consumer expenditure on clothing, furniture and floor-coverings in the United Kingdom represented a significant proportion of total expenditure. However, a number of environmental changes through-out the 1970s and 1980s had posed both opportunities and threats to retailers. Although total consumer expenditure continued to grow, these expenditures exhibited different patterns and volumes (see table 6.1).

Changes in clothing retailing had been profound, with the entry into the market of food retailers, and fundamental changes in strategy by existing clothing retailers. Throughout the 1970s and 1980s superstore numbers grew rapidly. In 1970 there were 33 superstores, defined as having a sales area of over 30,000 square feet. In 1980 this number had reached 278, and by 1986 there were 457 superstores in the UK with an average sales area of 32,700 square feet. These stores were typically on edge-of-town sites, and offered plentiful car parking spaces.

Over 90 per cent of these stores sold clothing, which was a relatively new product line for them. Clothing was the fifth most common item in these stores, after food, meat, vegetables, wine and spirits and confectionery. A major reason for this entry into clothing by super-stores had been the slow-down in the growth of food sales, especially in the 1970s. A further major change was the trend to more casual clothing. Large chains of menswear retailers, which had come to prominence with the made-to-measure suit, suffered because of this trend.

During the 1970s and early 1980s the UK economy suffered two major recessions due to the oil crises of 1974 and 1979, with conse-quent effects upon consumer expenditure on retailing.

TABLE 6.1   **Personal disposable income, consumer income and expenditure, 1977–88 (£m.)**

	Personal disposable income	on all items	on all items	on clothing	on carpets and floor-coverings	on textiles and soft furnishings
		Consumer expenditure:				
	Current prices	Current prices	1985 prices	1985 prices	1985 prices	1985 prices
1977	96,557	86,887	176,016	8,244	1,222	1,346
1978	113,124	100,219	185,950	8,988	1,320	1,372
1979	135,721	118,652	193,794	9,644	1,417	1,323
1980	160,009	137,896	193,806	9,608	1,270	1,256
1981	176,084	153,566	193,832	9,593	1,234	1,256
1982	191,081	168,545	195,561	9,868	1,224	1,266
1983	205,955	184,619	204,318	10,545	1,310	1,326
1984	220,764	197,494	207,927	11,202	1,334	1,321
1985	237,802	217,023	215,267	12,298	1,409	1,513
1986	259,333	239,156	229,105	13,368	1,403	1,562
1987	278,996	261,698	241,382	14,425	1,479	1,781
1988	307,170	293,569	257,918	15,275	1,631	2,050

Source: Annual Abstract 1990, Tables 14.2 and 14.9

The major factors influencing clothing sales remained population size and structure, and income. Changes in these variables coupled with changes in habits (e.g. towards more casual clothing) had contributed to changes in the pattern of demand for clothing.

There were approximately 10,000 shops specializing in menswear, and 22,000 specializing in womenswear. The numbers in both markets had been slowly decreasing over the decade. Major changes in menswear and womenswear had included a general trend away from formal wear in the menswear market, and the emergence of new classes of customer in the womenswear market. Generally the womenswear market had been more resilient to environmental pressures. The 1980 government retailing inquiry found that gross margins in menswear were 40 per cent, with a stockturn of 4.2, whilst for womenswear the comparable figures were 37 per cent and 4.8.

A number of important developments took place during the 1970s, beginning with the development of clothing boutiques, followed by the development of clothing chain or multiple stores in the 1980s.

Many of the major retail chains turned to design specialists such as Conran Associates (e.g. Hepworths and Miss Selfridge) or Fitch (e.g. Burton) to help them not only in attracting the right kind of consumer, but also to get them to spend more money. This showed an

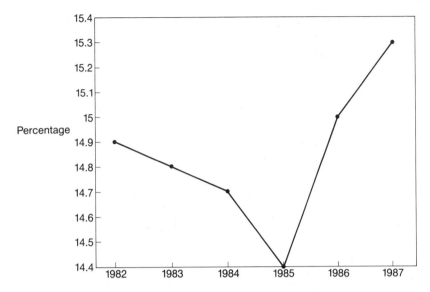

FIGURE 6.1   **Marks and Spencer's share of the UK clothing market**

appreciation that it was not sufficient to maintain volume increases by relying on inflation. Thus the Habitat Stores of Terence Conran beginning in the 1960s had set standards for design and image creation, whilst lessons were also learned from the food retailers with respect to productivity (higher rates of sales per square foot of sales space). As a consequence, the clothing retailers had to achieve a balance between attracting the appropriate target audience and then giving them sufficient space to enable clothes shopping to be a pleasurable experience.

In the mid-1980s the M & S share of the clothing market dipped (see figure 6.1). Following relatively poor financial results, M & S made plans to:

- develop out-of-town sites in collaboration with Tesco;
- refurbish existing stores and extend sales areas wherever possible, with 700,000 square feet planned for 1986/87;
- introduce the M & S Chargecard nationally, which had been piloted in Scotland where it had recorded 6 per cent of sales in the larger city stores in Scotland;
- introduce new products, including furniture and financial services/unit trusts;
- create 'dedicated' stores, i.e. stores carrying only one product group;
- open 'satellite stores', i.e. smaller stores close to original M & S stores, which would concentrate on specific product areas. The first

two of these were the 'man's shop' in Huddersfield, and 'childrenswear' shop in York. The latter would compete directly with
Mothercare, had 5,000 square feet of selling area, and was 200
yards from its parent store.

In late 1988 M & S announced their entry into the unit trust industry
by offering to their customers the opportunity to invest in a special
unit trust (the Marks and Spencer Investment Portfolio), set up on
behalf of the company by outside financial institutions with the
marketing and distribution handled by M & S, aimed mainly at their 2.
2 million chargecard customers.

Also in 1988 the company acquired two businesses in the USA.
These were *Brooks Brothers*, an upmarket menswear retailer with 47
stores and sales of $US300 million, at a cost of £436 million, and *Kings
Supermarkets*, a food retailer, which operated 16 shops with a sales
area of 265,000 square feet in New Jersey and had 1988 sales of
$US258 million and pre-tax profits of $US4.9 million, at a cost of £63
million.

During the same year the company opened its first store in Hong
Kong and began to open a chain of *Brooks Brothers* stores in Japan.

The company had experience of North America, since it had
entered the Canadian market in 1972 with the purchase of a half-share
in the D'Aillards chain of departmental stores. In 1979 M & S took a
majority holding in the company and created three divisions, one of
which carried the M & S name, but it took until 1984 before they were
profitable at the operational level. In 1986 they took full control by
buying out the minority shareholder.

Appendix 1   Marks and Spencer PLC

PROFIT AND LOSS ACCOUNT

Year ended March	*1988* £m.	*1989* £m.
Turnover	4,577.6	5,121.5
Cost of sales	3,163.4	3,458.5
Gross profit	1,414.2	1,663.0
Other expenses	905.7	1,099.3
Operating profit	508.5	563.7
Net interest payable/(receivable)	(5.6)	21.6
Profit before tax	514.1	542.1
Profit sharing	12.4	13.1
Tax	178.4	185.1
Minority interests	–	1.0
Profit for the year	323.3	342.9
Dividends	135.8	149.7

BALANCE SHEETS

Year ended March	1988 £m.	1989 £m.
Fixed assets		
Tangible	2,150.8	2,283.9
Financial Activities	81.4	71.6
Current assets		
Stocks	287.9	364.4
Debtors	130.4	192.6
Investments	15.5	13.9
Cash	276.1	88.2
	709.9	659.1
Current liabilities		
Creditors: amounts due within one year	623.5	743.1
Net current assets/ (liabilities)	(86.4)	(84.0)
Total assets less current liabilities	2,318.6	2,271.5
Creditors: amounts due after 1 year	160.6	343.7
provisions for liabilities	–	5.1
Net assets	2,158.0	1,922.7
Capital and reserves		
Shareholders' funds	2,158.0	1,918.6
Minority interests	–	4.1
	2,158.0	1,922.7

GROUP RESULTS 1982–9

Year ended March	(£m.)	1982	1983	1984	1985	1986	1987	1988	1989
Turnover									
Clothing		1,226.0	1,353.0	1,493.6	1,613.3	1,866.0	2,118.4	2,249.9	2,522.3
Homeware		172.4	216.3	216.8	366.9	439.8	516.7	551.6	611.7
Foods		774.7	902.9	1,060.6	1,216.2	1,410.0	1549.1	1,730.2	1,923.0
Financial activities		–	–	–	11.7	19.0	36.6	45.9	64.5
		2,173.1	2,472.2	2,771.0	3,208.1	3,734.8	4,220.8	4,577.6	5,121.5
Operating profit		na	na	na	306.0	361.0	434.6	508.5	563.7
Profit before tax		222.1	239.3	279.3	304.1	365.8	432.1	501.7	529.0
Shareholders' funds		1,140.0	1,226.8	1,325.3	1,325.3	1,452.4	1,578.8	2,158.0	1,918.6
Earnings per share (p)		–	–	–	6.9	8.4	10.4	12.2	12.9
Dividend per share (p)		–	–	–	3.4	3.9	4.5	5.1	5.6

MARKS & SPENCER COMPARATIVE STATISTICS, 1982–9

	1982	1983	1984	1985	1986	1987	1988	1989
Geographical contribution to operating profit (£m.)								
UK	n.a.	n.a.	n.a.	290	342	417	488	535
Europe	n.a.	n.a.	n.a.	6.8	9.6	12.4	17.3	12.0
North America and Far East	n.a.	n.a.	n.a.	9.5	9.7	5.4	3.2	16.4
Number of stores								
UK	256	260	262	265	269	274	282	281
Europe	7	8	9	9	9	10	11	13
Canada	203	209	213	227	243	263	271	371
North America and Far East	–	–	–					
Selling area (000 sq. ft.)								
UK	6,624	6,825	6,971	7,216	7,486	7,942	8,487	8,781
Europe	200	236	262	268	276	308	341	402
Canada	2,116	2,195	2,220	2,304	2,394	2,545	2,594	3,936
North America and Far East	–	–	–					
Average store size (000 sq. ft.)								
UK	26			27				31
Europe	28			30				31
Canada	10			10				11
North America and Far East	–							
Sales per store (£m.)								
UK	7.9			10.9				15.9
Europe	6.2			9.2				9.9
Canada	0.5			0.8				1.2
North America and Far East								

7 Sears PLC

In December 1987 Sears plc offered to buy the mail order catalogue company Freemans. This was at the end of a year in which share prices on the London Stock Exchange, and elsewhere, had reached record peaks, with an average rise of over 50 per cent from January to October 1987, when the market crashed. During this time Freemans' share price rose from 190p to 310p, then fell with the market back to 151p.

Sears' share price, similarly, had been affected by the rise and fall of the stock market and also by the attentions of potential predators who viewed the property assets of Sears' shops on the UK high streets as a potential source of profit if the company were to be broken up. Various companies and individuals were rumoured to be considering making a takeover offer for Sears, but one constant name had been that of Robert Holmes à Court, an Australian businessman, who had bought a 9.97 per cent share of Sears; following the market crash, however he sold it on to House of Fraser plc (then owner of Harrods) in November 1987.

During 1987 Sears' share price rose from 113p to 189p, falling back to stand at 129p in December 1987.

BACKGROUND

Sears plc was created in the 1950s and 60s by Sir Charles Clore who, following a career in property investment, turned to retailing, and through a series of takeovers built up one of the largest retailing organizations in the United Kingdom. The first of these was Trueform Shoes, bought for £5m. in 1953, followed by a series of others, such that when Sir Charles Clore retired in 1976, Sears had sales of £793m. and profits of £45m.

Sears had interests in a wide variety of products, and like other UK retailers had benefited from the rise in the volume of UK retail sales

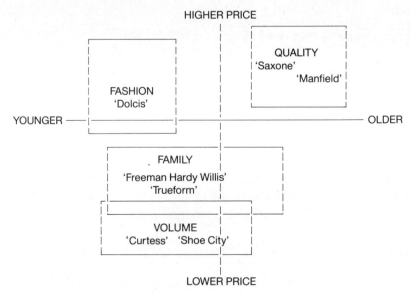

FIGURE 7.1 **Sears' footwear operations**

during the 1980s. By the end of 1987 the UK volume of retail sales index stood at 135 (1980 = 100). In its year ending 31 January 1987, Sears reported turnover of £2.48 billion. (See Appendix 1.)

With more than 5,750 retail outlets, largely in the UK but including the USA and Continental Europe, Sears was one of the UK's largest retailers, with major interests in the areas detailed below.

Footwear retailing This division was the largest UK retailer of shoes, with 1987 sales of £800m. traded through 2,500 stores in the UK under the names Dolcis, Bertie, Saxone, Manfield, Roland Cartier, Trueform, Curtess, Shoe City, and Freeman, Hardy & Willis.

During 1987 the division had been restructured into consumer-led strategic business units to address clearly-defined market segments. See figure 7.1.

The footwear operations were extremely efficient, in comparison with competitors, on measures such as profit margins or return on assets, but there were still opportunities in the market, as 50 per cent footwear in the UK was sold by independent retailers.

In Holland the company traded under the Manfield name with 56 outlets, and in the USA there were 500 outlets under the names Dolcis, TipToe, and International.

Women's fashion There were 112 Wallis and 82 Miss Selfridge outlets in the UK, accounting for approximately 2 per cent of the UK womenswear market. In the USA Sears operated through the Miss Erika name. The Miss Selfridge outlets were being expanded at the rate of ten a year.

Department stores   Sears owned 12 department stores, the best-known being Selfridges in London, and the rest Lewis's.

Men's fashion   Foster's, bought by Sears for £115m. in 1985, was the second largest menswear retailer in the UK, with 500 outlets. Jargon concentrated on sales to young men, whilst Esquire provided executive clothing and Dormie formal dress hire. Zy and Your Price were new developments, and brought the total number of retail outlets in the UK to over 600.

Sports and leisurewear   Olympus, Supasports and Sportsave, with over 100 outlets, provided sportswear, whilst in 1986 Sears added the outdoor activity retailer, Milletts, to its own outdoor activity chain, bringing it up to 173 retail outlets.
    During 1987 the first expansion of sportswear shops in Holland took place.

Childrenswear   Childrenswear was sold through the Adams chain of 120 outlets, concentrating on the up-to-eight-year-old child.

Jewellery   This division comprised Mappin & Webb with 21 outlets and Garrards with one outlet, both specializing in high-quality, high-value items. During 1987 In-Time was launched to sell lower-priced watches. In Garrards the price of a typical piece of jewellery ranged from £2,500 to £25,000, with higher prices not being uncommon. Until recently it had relied largely on the UK market but, following sales slumps associated with the oil crises of the 1970s, had looked abroad for export sales and by 1987 60 per cent of sales were exports. There were also plans to open new outlets around the Pacific Rim.

Licensed betting   Sears owned the William Hill chain of licensed betting offices which, with 870 offices, was the second largest in the UK. In Belgium, William Hill operated 405 licensed betting offices.

Housebuilding and property investment   This covered a building firm (950 houses sold in 1987) and interests such as the Amsterdam Marriott Hotel, and office construction developments in Germany and Scotland.

Sears' chargecard   Sears also operated its own chargecard, which could be used in over 1,500 retail outlets in the UK and had 350,000 cardholders.

Geoffrey Maitland Smith took over as chief executive in 1978 and as chairman of Sears in 1985, and began organizational changes which resulted in a more streamlined and refocused approach to its markets expressed as a concentration on four specific areas – specialist retailing, footwear, leisure and property. Following these decisions the company sold its motor vehicle and engineering business for £87m. In 1986, to assist with the planning, the chairman had brought in from the Imperial Group as deputy chief executive Mr Michael Pickard, who had previously had five years' experience with Grattan's, the mail order company.

Together Maitland Smith and Pickard set out to change the corporate culture at Sears, introducing profit-related pay throughout the group to encourage initiative. Not all their experiments were successful – at the Gateshead Metro Centre, a group of shops were put under the Sears banner, rather than under individual brand names, and this only confused consumers.

MAIL ORDER

The mail order industry had traditionally operated by selling its goods through agents, who earned 10 per cent commission by selling to their acquaintances and workmates. Customers, who were largely in the C1 and C2 socio-economic groups, were given the opportunity to pay for goods weekly over 20 or 40 weeks, and by 1976 the industry had grown to reach 7.3 per cent of the UK non-food retail sales of £23.81 billion in current prices. Catalogues were usually about 1,000 pages long, featuring between 10,000 and 20,000 products, and cost on average approximately £4 each to produce in 1987. The customer base fell from 20.4 million in 1981 to 17.6 million in 1986, and of the 40 per cent of households with a catalogue, many invariably had more than one.

Selling their products through the use of agents and a catalogue, five companies dominated the industry. Great Universal Stores had 42 per cent, Littlewoods 25 per cent, Freemans 14 per cent, Grattan 10 per cent, and Empire Stores 6 per cent. Between 1980 and 1987 the fortunes of these companies had varied, as both GUS and Freemans had increased their market shares, whilst those of both Littlewoods and Empire Stores had declined; Grattan had revived strongly over the last two years. Nevertheless, all five had involved themselves in cost control measures, e.g. weeding out non-productive agents and improving stock control procedures, and in better marketing developments, e.g. using telephone systems for ordering, rather than relying on the post. This latter development had been pioneered by Freemans and followed by the rest.

Other developments included a shift to direct mail, as opposed to agency, to about 15 per cent of the sales. Mail order companies had different cost structures compared with high street retailers, with lower overall costs but higher advertising, delivery and staff costs. When a mail order company ran out of stock it was not immediately apparent to their customers, who continued ordering, whilst stock which did not sell was difficult to shift, there being no window for sales. One of the major problems in mail order, however, was the high proportion of returned goods, which was estimated at 40 per cent of fashion goods and 25 per cent of electrical goods. By 1987, mail order sales had grown to £3.6 billion out of UK non-food retail sales of £57.97 billion in current prices.

The problem facing the industry of attracting new customers had been compounded by the increased competition on the high street between the so-called lifestyle retailers competing for new market segments. As approximately one-third of mail order sales were in women's and childrenswear, this increased competition accentuated the rather drab image the industry had. The main response of the mail order companies was an attempt to attract new customers by introducing new catalogues called 'specialogues', which were designed to appeal to defined segments of consumers. In addition, links were formed with high street retailers to take advantage of well-known brand names. For example, Empire Stores carried inserts for Burton's Top Shops, and the most notable link was the merger in 1986 between Grattans and Next, when the latter paid £300m. to take over Grattan. The expectation behind these links was that the retailers' flair for design could be combined with the database systems of the mail order companies, to produce highly targeted catalogues.

The first new catalogue from Next and Grattan was a 360-page catalogue called 'Next Directory', with the promise of a 48-hour delivery based on a telephone ordering service and courier delivery. To assist with this, Next had also bought a chain of newsagents' shops, called Dillons. The 'Next Directory' was unveiled in early 1988, and 500,000 copies were ordered. It had taken eighteen months to produce, had cost a total of £24 million, including £11 million in stocks, and offered an exclusive range of Next products (not those currently in the Next high street shops). It was targeted to break even in six months, make profits within a year, and reduce returns to 15 per cent. Traditionally in the industry, new catalogues had taken two years to break even.

MAIL ORDER COMPANIES

Great Universal Stores GUS was a major retailer as well as a mail order firm, with stores such as Burberry's, Times Furnishing, Hector Powe, and Scotch House. It operated a number of catalogues including John England, Trafford, and Kays (which had the largest circulation in the country) amongst others. It also owned large shareholdings in Harris Queensway, a carpet retailer, and in Freemans.

Littlewoods Warehouses Ltd This was a subsidiary company of Littlewoods Group, a privately-owned company which operated retail stores and football pools, as well as mail order – which accounted for about half of the group's sales. Its catalogues included Brian Mills, Janet Fraser, Burlington and John Moores.

Grattan Prior to its takeover by Next, this company issued about 1.3 million catalogues to its agency customers, under names such as 'Streets of London' and 'You and Yours' and many millions of its direct response catalogues under the names of 'Scotcade' and 'Kaleidoscope'.

Empire Stores This company had entered the specialogue business with catalogues aimed at the mothercare market and at the consumer durable market.

Information on these companies is shown in table 7.1.

Freemans reported turnover for the year ended 31 January 1987 at £405m. (see Appendix 2), 90 per cent of which was accounted for by its normal catalogues, sold via 690,000 agents. The customer service provided by the company encouraged agent loyalty and Freemans had contributed to this when they were the first mail order company to introduce telephone ordering in 1980, which by 1987 accounted for 70 per cent of all orders. Processing of returned goods was computerized, and the proportion returned was about the industry average. About 83 per cent of Freemans' deliveries were made by the Post Office, and the rest by their own vans in London and the North West, where the agents were most concentrated. Returned goods were sold through the company's own chain of 12 clearance shops called 'Stage 1', located in East Anglia.

Freemans had bought Warehouse, which had 23 shops in the UK and had a 13-strong in-house design team led by Jeff Banks, in June 1986 for £11.9m. Warehouse had just produced profits of £680,000 for the year, on sales of £9.4m. This purchase was a reflection of the growing interest by mail order companies in retail connections. Even Marks and Spencer had joined with N Brown, a small mail order firm with a 2 per cent market share, to issue a direct mail pamphlet to its chargecard customers.

With Warehouse, Freemans created its second specialogue, called 'Bymail', which was a special catalogue containing only Warehouse products for women and men. Its first specialogue had also been a joint venture, called 'Together', but by the end of 1987 Freemans had sold its 50 per cent share in that.

Unfortunately, Freemans suffered problems with the launch of its two new catalogues. The decision to launch them was taken very quickly after the acquisition of Warehouse, and consequently they were not able to co-ordinate the availability of both stocks and

TABLE 7.1   **Mail Order Companies**

	Great Universal Stores[a]	Empire Stores	Grattan
Sales (£m.)			
1984	2,033.0	153.6	195.3
1985	2,098.0	156.5	219.0
1986	2,270.0	162.8	266.0
PBT (£m.)			
1984	226.5	1.5	3.5
1985	261.0	3.1	9.6
1986	297.7	5.8	16.0
ROCE (%)[b]			
1984	15.5	3.8	5.8
1985	16.6	7.0	13.8
1986	15.1	12.0	18.3
Stockturn (x)			
1984	8.6	8.2	6.4
1985	8.2	8.2	6.8
1986	8.5	7.3	6.0

[a] GUS figures include all its businesses

[b] This is $\dfrac{\text{profit before tax}}{\text{capital employed}}$

catalogues. There was a resultant two-month delay, which was predicted to produce a loss on the venture for the year ending January 1988.

A further factor affecting mail order sales was a proposed strike by the postal services prior to Christmas 1987, the threat of which had deterred many prospective buyers, according to a Freemans' spokesman.

When Freemans reported their interim results for the half-year ended on 15 August 1987, they revealed flat profits based on a sales increase of 16 per cent. After taking account of sales from Warehouse and from the 'Together' specialogue, this left a sales increase of only 9 per cent for the normal catalogue business by comparison with a year earlier. The company attributed this poor performance to reduced sales due to unseasonal weather conditions which lasted up to the end of June, and to losses on sales of surplus stocks.

With respect to its prospects for the future, Freemans forecast that profits for the year ending January 1988 would be at the same level as in the previous year.

Sears had expressed interest in the mail order industry on three previous occasions. In 1971 it had bought a 21 per cent shareholding in Freemans in an attempt to create a merger, but following a lack of

TABLE 7.2 **Pro forma balance sheet for Sears and Freemans combined at 31 January 1987**

	SEARS £m.	+ FREEMANS £m.	= 'COMBINED' £m.
Fixed assets			
Tangible assets	860.2	27.7	887.9
Investments	21.0	0.2	21.2
	881.2	27.9	909.1
Current assets			
Stocks	363.4	62.8	426.2
Debtors	137.2	146.0	283.2
Assets in course of disposal[a]	87.2	–	87.2
Cash	140.3	0.2	140.5
	728.1	209.0	937.1
Creditors (due within one year)	(327.5)	(111.7)	(439.2)
	400.6	97.3	497.9
Assets less current liabilities	1,281.8	125.2	1,407.0
Creditors (due after one year)	(227.3)	(2.5)	(229.8)
Provisions for liabilities	(28.0)	(1.3)	(29.3)
Minority interests	(14.7)	–	(14.7)
Net tangible assets	1,011.8	121.4	1,133.2
Adjusted to reflect cash payment consideration for the acquisition of Freemans			(477.0)
			656.2

[a] During 1987 Sears had agreed to sell its interests in motor vehicle distribution to Lex Service plc, and awaited payment

success sold the shareholding in 1975. Then in 1981 Sears attempted to get Grattan and Empire Stores to merge, with Sears taking a 20 per cent interest in the newly-formed company. That effort was also unsuccessful, and the third attempt was in 1986 when Sears made unsuccessful overtures to Freemans to merge.

Just prior to making its 1987 bid, Sears bought 15, 176, 940 Freemans shares in the market, which represented 10.1 per cent of all Freemans' ordinary shares, and then made an offer of 315p a share in cash to the remaining shareholders. This valued Freemans at a total of £477 million. According to Sears, if the two companies were merged it would then produce a pro forma balance sheet for the combined company as shown in table 7.2.

Appendix 1   Sears PLC

PROFIT AND LOSS ACCOUNT FOR THE YEAR ENDED 31 JANUARY 1987

	1987 £m.	1986 £m.
Turnover	2,480.3	2,277.9
Cost of Sales	(1,754.9)	(1,607.3)
Gross Profit	725.4	670.6
Distribution costs	(429.1)	(413.5)
Administration costs	(77.6)	(73.8)
Trading profit	218.7	183.3
Share of associated company profits	4.1	4.8
Other income	7.0	7.3
Interest paid	(11.1)	(8.6)
Profit before tax	218.7	186.8
Taxation	(77.5)	(64.0)
Profit after tax	141.2	122.8
Minority interest dividends paid	(0.6)	(0.6)
Extraordinary items	1.0	(3.7)
Profit attributable to Sears plc	141.6	118.5
Preference dividends paid	(0.2)	(0.2)
Profit attributable to ordinary shareholders	141.4	118.3
Ordinary dividends paid	(59.7)	(50.4)
Retained earnings	81.7	67.9

BALANCE SHEET FOR THE YEAR ENDED 31 JANUARY

	1987 £m.	1986 £m.
Fixed assets		
Tangible assets	860.2	824.9
Investments	21.0	25.4
	881.2	850.3
Current assets		
Stocks	363.4	368.4
Debtors	137.2	153.6
Assets in course of disposal	87.2	–
Cash	140.3	109.0
	728.1	631.0
Creditors (due within one year)	327.5	287.9
Net current assets	400.6	343.1
Assets less current liabilities	1,281.8	1,193.4
Creditors (due after one year)	227.3	202.2
Provisions for liabilities	28.0	19.2
Minority interests in subsidiaries	14.7	14.7
	270.0	236.1
	1,011.8	957.3
Capital and reserves		
Called-up share capital	376.0	373.3
Share premium account	1.4	1.1
Reserves	634.4	582.9
	1,011.8	957.3

FIVE-YEAR FINANCIAL RECORD

	1983 £m.	1984 £m.	1985 £m.	1986 £m.	1987 £m.
Turnover	1,590.5	1,839.0	2,019.4	2,277.9	2,480.3
Trading profit					
Footwear retailing	65.6	84.8	87.7	75.3	87.4
Stores and fashion	23.8	35.3	46.2	61.8	73.0
Licensed betting	6.5	11.1	11.5	17.0	24.1
Housebuilding/Property	9.7	15.4	15.6	17.7	23.1
Motor vehicles	9.3	8.7	10.2	11.5	11.1
	114.9	155.3	171.2	183.3	218.7
Other income	4.0	7.7	11.5	12.1	11.1
Interest Paid	(3.4)	(1.2)	(2.6)	(8.6)	(11.1)
Profit before tax	115.5	161.8	180.1	186.8	218.7
Profit after tax	69.8	99.1	115.0	122.8	141.2
Minority interests/preference dividends	(0.8)	(0.8)	(0.8)	(0.8)	(0.8)
Extraordinary items	(3.0)	–	–	(3.7)	1.0
Ordinary dividends [a]	(25.1)	(33.6)	(40.4)	(50.4)	(59.7)
Retained earnings	40.9	64.7	73.8	67.9	81.7

continued

	1983 £m.	1984 £m.	1985 £m.	1986 £m.	1987 £m.
Fixed assets	–	666.1	728.7	850.3	881.2
Current assets					
Stocks	–	255.8	327.0	368.4	363.4
Cash	–	170.7	136.1	109.0	140.3
Creditors	–	126.8	136.6	153.6	224.4
	–	553.3	599.7	631.0	728.1
Current liabilities	–	253.7	294.0	287.9	327.5
Total assets less current liabilities	–	965.7	1,034.4	1,193.4	1,281.8
Creditors (due after one year)	–	189.6	174.4	236.1	270.0
Capital	–	776.1	860.0	957.3	1,011.8
		339.2	339.3	373.3	376.0
Reserves	–	436.9	520.7	584.0	635.8
	–	776.1	860.0	957.3	1,011.8

[a] Ordinary shares in issue:
   1983: 897 million
   1984: 1345 million
   1985: 1345 million
   1986: 1453 million
   1987: 1487 million

TURNOVER AND TRADING PROFITS, 1983–7

	1983 £m.		1984 £m.		1985 £m.		1986 £m.		1987 £m.	
	Turnover	Profit	Turnover	Profit	Turnover	Profit	Turnover	Profit	Turnover	Profit
By division										
Footwear retailing	564.5	65.6	671.9	84.8	763.8	87.7	789.9	75.3	800.3	87.4
Stores & fashion retailing	375.9	23.8	435.8	35.3	475.1	46.2	644.9	61.8	755.1	73.0
Licensed betting	390.5	6.5	429.2	11.1	479.1	11.5	540.3	17.0	597.7	24.1
Housebuilding & Property	34.7	9.7	33.8	15.4	38.2	15.6	47.1	17.7	62.8	23.1
Motor vehicles distribution[a]	185.3	9.3	225.9	8.7	239.7	10.2	255.7	11.5	264.4	11.1
	1,550.9	114.9	1,796.6	155.3	1,995.9	171.2	2,277.9	183.3	2,480.3	218.7
Geographical analysis										
United Kingdom	1,367.0	95.6	1,556.5	128.0	1,707.4	151.4	1,962.4	164.5	2,146.5	197.9
USA	131.6	7.1	189.4	15.9	230.0	9.6	233.7	9.6	208.2	8.9
Continental Europe	98.1	10.5	93.1	10.7	82.0	7.8	81.8	9.2	125.6	11.9

[a] This division was subsequently sold during 1987

Appendix 2   Freemans

FINANCIAL ANALYSIS, 1983–7

	1983* £m.	1984 £m.	1985 £m.	1986 £m.	1987 £m.
Sales (exc.VAT)	278.6	281.9	317.8	362.6	405.4
Profit before tax	6.4	14.1	22.0	28.0	32.4
Profit after tax	4.8	7.7	12.1	17.6	20.5
Extraordinary item	–	(2.8)	–	–	5.2
Dividends	(2.9)	(3.2)	(3.9)	(5.0)	(6.2)
Transferred from reserve	–	0.1	0.1	0.1	0.1
Retained profits	1.9	1.8	8.3	12.7	19.6
Fixed assets	–	21.2	22.4	26.1	27.9
Current assets					
Stocks	–	37.5	51.5	56.0	62.7
Debtors	–	98.5	116.6	135.1	146.0
Cash	–	0.2	0.2	0.1	0.2
	–	136.2	168.3	191.2	209.0
Current liabilities	–	76.3	101.4	113.6	111.7
Net current assets	–	59.9	66.9	77.6	97.2
Total assets less current liabilities	–	81.1	89.3	103.7	125.2
Creditors (due after one year)	–	3.7	3.4	4.1	3.8
		77.4	85.9	99.6	121.4
Capital	–	17.6	17.7	17.9	18.8
Reserves	–	59.8	68.2	81.7	102.6
		77.4	85.9	99.6	121.4

Number of ordinary shares
  1983: 137 million
  1984: 140 million
  1985: 141 million
  1986: 142 million
  1987: 144 million
* for year ended January

ANALYSIS OF TURNOVER

	1983 £m.	1984 £m.	1985 £m.	1986 £m.	1987 £m.
Clothing and footwear	173.3	178.4	211.4	244.1	285.6
Household textiles, carpets and curtains	67.7	67.5	71.4	80.2	83.2
Audio, sports, gardening, DIY and insurance	73.9	73.2	76.8	85.8	89.5
Less VAT	(36.3)	(37.2)	(41.8)	(47.5)	(52.9)
Total	278.6	281.9	317.8	362.6	405.4

8   Sirdar PLC

The company was founded in 1880 in the West Riding of Yorkshire as a worsted spinning company under the family name of Fred Harrap. One hundred years later the company had changed its name to Sirdar plc, and was the brand leader in the UK hand-knitting yarn market, a product area to which it had moved in the early part of the twentieth century. This had been followed by a marketing decision to sell their product direct to the many retail shops around the country which stocked the various colours and qualities, even holding them for their customers who sometimes preferred to buy them ball-by-ball on a weekly basis as their knitting progressed, rather than lay out all the cash in advance.

Fred Harrap died in 1960 and his daughter, Jean Tyrrell, took over. In 1971 she brought in a new managing director, K. Palmer, whose appointment was followed by those of two new board members: G. Lumb as secretary, and G. Hampton as marketing director. The 1970s proved to be a difficult decade for most of British industry, marked as it was by the major recession of 1973–4 following the quadrupling of the price of oil by OPEC, and the later recession beginning in 1979, again caused by an oil price rise following the ousting of the Shah of Iran.

Wool, the basic raw material used by Sirdar, had always been a volatile commodity in price terms; the year-to-year changes in the price of specific wools with respect to the average price for a given period was second only to rubber for fluctuations. Not only was the wool price a volatile variable, but the industry faced difficulties over the qualitative variability of wool and other fibres used, which made successful buying and blending critical. Indeed the wool industry was famous for people and firms whose fortunes were based on wool-buying expertise, rather than woollen manufacturing.

In 1973 the company made two significant moves. It decided to reduce its dependence upon wool by increasing the proportion of synthetic fibres used, and it acquired the business of Hayfield Yarns,

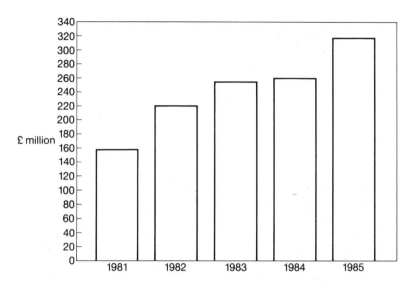

FIGURE 8.1   **UK market for hand-knitting yarns, by retail value 1981–5**

retaining it as a different brand of knitting yarns to Sirdar, which tended to be of higher quality and higher price. Hayfield was also interested in hosiery manufacture, but this was discontinued within two years, allowing further expansion of the hand-knitting yarn capacity.

The UK hand-knitting yarn market experienced a large decline in volume terms in the first half of the 1970s, when it fell by over 30 per cent between 1970 and 1976, and only really recovered in 1978 with the advent of a fashion trend towards more chunky garments. These garments used more wool, and hence led to higher sales by manufacturers, so the market demand was led by fashion design as much as by interest in hand-knitting as a pastime. The market during the period 1981–5 is shown in figure 8.1.

Of this market, about one-third of sales were of unbranded wool, and the balance of the branded market was shared by a number of manufacturers, of which the most important were Sirdar (including Hayfield) with a 35 per cent market share, Patons with 25 per cent market share, Robert Glew (Robin and Emu) with 20 per cent, and Carter & Parker (Wendy) with 8 per cent. These percentage shares referred to the branded sector. The most significant importer was Phildar (France) which operated its own chain of franchised shops in the UK and had about 4 per cent of the market.

About half the market sales were retailed through small specialist wool shops which mainly concentrated on the branded, higher-priced yarns; the balance was sold through other retail outlets like market stalls, department stores and variety chains, within which Littlewoods played a significant role as retailers, with about 10 per cent of the market concentrated on own-label brands.

By 1985 Sirdar had sales revenue of over £36m. and profits before tax of nearly £10m. (see appendix 1), attributing their success to three major factors:

1   The small and hence flexible organization of the company, based as it was on a board of directors with only five members.
2   Brand leadership of the market, which they achieved in 1981 and had maintained.
3   Continuing expenditure on the latest equipment available.

This latter factor was inspired, in part at least, by the Wool Textile Industry Scheme begun by the UK government in 1973, with a second stage in 1976, the aim of which was improvement of the industry's competitive position, by providing assistance to modernize production facilities, improve industrial structure, and eliminate uneconomic excess capacity.

By the mid-1980s Sirdar was established as the leading manufacturer in the UK market for hand-knitting yarns.

Appendix 2 shows comparative financial data for Robert Glew.

Appendix 1   Sirdar PLC

PROFIT AND LOSS ACCOUNT

Year ended 30 June	1983 £ thousands	1984 £ thousands	1985 £ thousands
Turnover	30,021	33,122	36,495
Costs and overheads	22,854	24,762	27,437
Operating profit	7,167	8,360	9,058
Interest and other income received	479	648	475
Profit on ordinary activities before taxation	7,646	9,008	9,533
Taxation	2,813	3,004	3,504
Profit on ordinary activities after taxation	4,833	6,004	6,029
Extraordinary item	–	247[a]	–
Profit for year	4,833	5,757	6,029
Dividends	1,196	1,566	1,983
Profit retained	3,637	4,191	4,046

[a] Extraordinary item arose from closure of subsidiary company in Switzerland which had been making losses. (Sirdar had closed other subsidiary companies in South Africa and Australia in 1974.)

BALANCE SHEET

As at 30 June	1983 £ thousands	1984 £ thousands	1985 £ thousands
Fixed assets			
Tangible assets	11,997	14,540	16,091
Investments	–	336	730
	11,997	14,876	16,821
Current assets			
Stocks	5,907	7,611	8,638
Debtors	5,185	5,446	6,216
Investments	6,668	8,752	8,678
Cash at bank and in hand	60	129	377
	17,820	21,938	23,909
Creditors			
(due within one year)	7,194	10,594	9,806
Net current assets	10,626	11,344	14,103
Creditors			
(due after one year)	2,599	2,002	2,671
Net working capital	8,027	9,342	11,432
	20,024	24,218	28,253
Capital and reserves			
Called-up share capital	6,184	12,167	12,167
Profit and loss account	13,840	12,051	16,086
	20,024	24,218	28,253

FOURTEEN-YEAR RECORD

	Sales £m.	PBT £m.	Fixed assets £m.	Net current assets £m.	Total assets £m.	No. of employees	Capital expenditure £m.	Stocks £m.
1972	6.6	0.635	1.316	1.276	2.592	1051	n/a	2.147
1973	9.5	0.842	2.640	1.432	4.072	1601	n/a	3.168
1974	10.5	0.609	2.739	1.482	4.221	1535	n/a	2.789
1975	11.57	0.812	2.977	1.815	4.792	1565	0.443	3.338
1976	13.51	0.942	3.640	2.146	5.786	1512	0.952	4.674
1977	16.43	1.136	4.472	3.505	7.977	1484	1.250	4.880
1978	19.28	2.110	5.851	3.080	8.931	1457	1.896	4.860
1979	21.35	3.197	7.640	3.445	11.085	1414	2.640	5.290
1980	22.99	3.726	8.825	3.997	12.822	1278	2.209	5.370
1981	27.65	5.314	9.879	5.199	15.078	1243	2.349	5.650
1982	29.63	6.175	11.401	6.540	17.941	1212	2.911	5.650
1983	30.02	7.646	11.997	10.626	22.623	1152	2.861	5.907
1984	33.12	9.008	14.540	11.344	25.884	1137	4.168	7.611
1985	36.49	9.533	16.091	14.103	30.194	1157	3.346	8.638

GEOGRAPHICAL ANALYSIS OF TURNOVER (£ thousands)

	Total	UK	Ireland	Europe	Asia	Africa	N. America	Australasia	Rest of world
1982	27,282	24,167	996	865	493	106	304	337	14
1983	30,021	25,956	1,016	947	920	32	455	631	64
1984	33,122	28,049	1,092	1,235	1,147	30	826	728	16

Appendix 2   Robert Glew

CONSOLIDATED PROFIT AND LOSS ACCOUNT, 1980–4

Year ending December	1980 £ thousands	1981 £ thousands	1982 £ thousands	1983 £ thousands	1984 £ thousands
Turnover	12,246	13,537	15,200	17,934	21,695
Changes in stocks	n/a	n/a	(352)	(484)	(2,448)
Raw materials	n/a	n/a	6,413	7,858	10,820
Other external charges	n/a	n/a	3,814	4,500	6,232
Staff costs	n/a	n/a	3,486	3,807	4,464
Depreciation	140	207	254	358	454
Interest payable	269	113	121	150	266
Profit/(loss) before tax	1,092	1,446	1,464	1,745	1,907
Corporation tax	347	351	522	567	761
Deferred tax	–	–	–	–	130
ACT recoverable	(26)	–	–	–	–
Overseas tax	–	–	4	13	36
Prior year adjustment	(7)	(41)	(16)	(17)	(26)
Total taxation	314	310	510	563	901
Profit/(loss) after tax	778	1,136	954	1,182	1,006
Preference dividends	1	1	1	1	1
Profit after pref. divs	777	1,135	953	1,181	1,005
Ordinary dividends	36	53	60	69	90
Extraordinary items	–	–	–	–	118
Retained profit/(loss)	741	1,082	893	1,112	797
Average number of employees:	621	588	563	554	612

GEOGRAPHICAL ANALYSIS OF TURNOVER

	Total	EEC	Others
1982	15,200	13,702	1,498
1983	17,934	16,070	1,864
1984	21,695	19,389	2,306

CONSOLIDATED BALANCE SHEET

Year ended December	1982 £ thousands	1983 £ thousands	1984 £ thousands
Fixed assets			
Tangible	2,109	2,578	3,178
Current assets			
Stocks	3,436	3,920	6,368
Debtors	4,454	4,795	6,217
Prepayments	201	226	151
Investments	1	1	1
Cash	17	18	324
	8,109	8,960	13,061
Creditors (due within one year)			
Bank overdraft	401	242	1,787
Advances	158	175	1,095
Creditors	2,232	2,469	2,858
Tax provision	937	1,023	1,136
Accruals	198	225	301
Dividends	70	80	90
	3,996	4,214	7,267
Net current assets	4,113	4,746	5,794
Net assets			
(total assets less current liabilities)	6,222	7,324	8,972
Creditors (due after one year)			
Government grants	152	142	266
Loans	–	–	507
Employees' benefit fund	34	34	34
Deferred tax	–	–	213
	186	176	1,020
	6,036	7,148	7,952
Capital	1,580	1,580	1,580
Profit and loss account	4,456	5,568	6,732
	6,036	7,148	7,952

Annexe 1   Inflation Index

Year	Index
1970	1.000
1971	0.940
1972	0.860
1973	0.803
1974	0.735
1975	0.633
1976	0.510
1977	0.437
1978	0.377
1979	0.349
1980	0.307
1981	0.274
1982	0.254
1983	0.253
1984	0.226
1985	0.213

Example 1	*1970*	*1971*	*1972*	*1973*	*1974*	*1975*
Figures	120	170	204	310	502	590
Corrected figures (to 1970 base)	120	160	175	249	369	373
	($\times 1.000$)	($\times 0.940$)	($\times 0.860$)	($\times 0.803$)	($\times 0.735$)	($\times 0.63$)

Example 2	*1974*	*1975*	*1976*	*1977*	*1978*	*1979*
Figures	502	590	620	690	710	720
Corrected figures (to 1974 base)	502	508	430	410	364	342
	$\left(\times \frac{0.735}{0.735}\right)$	$\left(\times \frac{0.633}{0.735}\right)$	$\left(\times \frac{0.510}{0.735}\right)$	$\left(\times \frac{0.437}{0.735}\right)$	$\left(\times \frac{0.377}{0.735}\right)$	$\left(\times \frac{0.349}{0.735}\right)$

TABLE 8.1   **Using the information in Appendices 1 and 2, complete the following:**

	Sirdar PLC			Robert Glew	
	1985	1984	1983	1984	1983
Gearing					
Return on capital employed[a]					
Stockturn					
Net assets per share					
Gross profit margin[a]					
Operating profits/PBT per employee					
Sales per employee					
Earnings per share[b]					
Dividend cover					
Price/earnings ratio					
Share price[c] (pence)	123	135	101	167	187

Year end for Sirdar plc was June;
Year end for Robert Glew Ltd, was December.
[a] Using profit before interest and tax.
[b] Sirdar had issued 47.868 million ordinary shares, and Robert Glew 6.32 million.
[c] High for the year stated.

TABLE 8.2 For Sirdar plc, complete the following:

Year	Actual sales (£m.)	Inflation adjusted sales[a] (£m.)	Actual PBT (£m.)	Inflation adjusted PBT[a] (£m.)	PBT/Sales as %	Stock turnover rate	Fixed asset turnover	Net asset turnover	ROCE as %[b]
1972	6.6		0.635						
1973	9.5		0.842						
1974	10.5		0.609						
1975	11.137		0.812						
1976	12.961		0.942						
1977	15.636		1.136						
1978	18.174		2.110						
1979	20.028		3.197						
1980	21.37		3.726						
1981	25.384		5.314						
1982	27.282		6.175						
1983	30.021		7.646						
1984	33.122		9.008						
1985	36.495		9.533						

[a] Corrected to 1972 base, e.g. 1985 = 1985 sales * 0.213/0.860 (see annexe 1)
[b] Using PBT, as PBIT is not available for the full series.

9 Lightwater Valley Theme Park

In 1989, like other UK theme parks, Lightwater Valley was a privately-owned enterprise. It formed part of the estate of Robert, Viscount Staveley and his wife Lynn, who in addition to Lightwater Valley, controlled a number of other business activities. These comprised a stone quarry (Staveley Quarries), an intensive farm (rearing mainly pigs, but also chickens), a small bistro in the nearby village of North Stainley, and a ladies' dress shop in Ripon.

Whilst the activities of the quarry, the shop and the bistro are quite separate to the running of the theme park, the pigs and chickens are an integral part of Lightwater Valley, since the predominant 'theme' of the park is farming – though this is by no means the overriding feature of the site.

BACKGROUND

The Lightwater Valley enterprise began in the early 1970s, with the opening of a self-pick fruit farm on land which had previously been farming land. The whole idea of 'pick-your-own' fruit was then an entirely new concept in the North Yorkshire area where the estate was situated, and thus for a number of years the operation was able to command good prices and return a reasonable profit. Having witnessed the success of the business, other local farmers jumped on the bandwagon; competition increased, and prices started to fall. By the late 1970s it was becoming apparent that margins were being squeezed too severely for the operation to make a reasonable return, so alternative uses for the land were sought.

Because of the pleasant country environment, just outside the small town of Ripon, and the experience of the proprietors in running a business that catered mainly for the weekend leisure market, it was decided that investment in a relatively small-scale leisure activity park could provide a more profitable use for the land. Hence in the summer of 1979, Lightwater Valley Theme Park opened its gates. It comprised a 125-acre parkland site offering a variety of attractions.

THE DEVELOPMENT OF LIGHTWATER VALLEY

In its early days, Lightwater Valley concentrated on two major features. Firstly, the farm: the intensive farm on the site was tastefully converted into a 'spectator' farm, where visitors could witness at first hand the rearing of pigs, chickens, and originally calves, in a true commercial environment (and this is probably still the only modern visitor farm in the country). Because of the intensity of the operation, it was possible for visitors to witness the birth of piglets, or chicks hatching out of eggs, on almost any day of the week. The drawback, of course, was that some visitors' illusions of the 'farmyard', where animals are allowed to roam at will, were shattered, and some took offence at the crowded conditions under which animals were reared for food.

The second main attraction on the site was the fairground rides and other types of activities for children, such as go-karts, boating lakes, and a miniature railway. This ensured that while the educational dimension of the farm was provided to persuade parents and teachers of the benefits of a visit to Lightwater Valley, the children were satisfied by the provision of more active and entertaining pursuits.

Over the years, a number of other features were added to the park. A few 'white-knuckle' rides were introduced (precipitated by the success of 'Alton Towers' in creating a theme park with a reputation for exciting rides, which encouraged customer expectations of all theme parks to move in that direction). These included 'The Rat' – an underground roller-coaster – and 'The Soopa-Loopa', the only double-loop roller-coaster in Britain. In an attempt to encourage a wider age-range to visit the site, pursuits such as croquet, crazy-golf, and a full-size nine-hole golf course were introduced. The cattle farming was discontinued due to its unprofitability following the implementation of European Community quotas, and the world's first visitor snail farm was established to replace it. A number of shops and cafés were opened, to encourage discretionary expenditure on top of gate money. Also, a carvery with an exceptional reputation for quality and value for money was established, though this was only open out of season, during the evenings and for Sunday lunch, and was not really considered to be a part of the mainstream Lightwater Valley business. Lynn Staveley took personal responsibility for its management. (In the summer, the carvery was used to provide a 'chips-with-everything' menu, as a suitable lunchtime venue for families with children.) The carvery seemed to have cashed in very successfully on the growth of eating-out as a leisure activity since the mid-1970s.

The organizational structure

As the park had developed, a team of managers had gradually been appointed, with responsibility for its day-to-day running. A number of full-time administrative staff were recruited to work all year round, but the majority of staff on site had always been employed as casual labour during the summer months only. (Lightwater Valley was never open between the end of September and Easter, because it was so reliant on reasonable weather, and on holiday-makers.)

The organizational tree (appendix 1) shows the two directors heading up the business. The general manager (Gary Blades) was responsible for the operation of the site and had a team of managers reporting to him.

A DECISION TO SEEK ADVICE

In 1988, following a season when visitor numbers had increased by only 1.7 per cent (see appendix 2) and profit levels were considered to be inadequate, Gary Blades approached the Training Agency (formerly the Manpower Services Commission) with a view to obtaining some advice about (and financial help with) staff training. In particular, he was keen for some management development to take place, as he was conscious that most of his management team (and he included himself in this) had little knowledge of the textbook skills of professional management. Many of his team had risen to levels of authority and responsibility because of their ability to do a job, and particularly lacked confidence in the areas of decision-making and people management. The Training Agency recommended that Lightwater Valley should be contracted to take part in the Business Growth Training (BGT) programme.

The BGT programme is a four-stage business consultancy programme which takes place over a 12-month period. The Training Agency agrees to fund 50 per cent of consultancy fees for the programme, up to a maximum grant of £7,500, and recommend an appropriate consultancy to undertake the work.

Phase 1 of the programme involves a business review, focusing on the marketing activity of the organization to enable the creation of a strategy for business development. This is followed by an audit of human resources, and a training needs analysis. The intention is that a management development programme can then be set up to help managers acquire the skills necessary to bring about any desired change in the organization.

Management training and development commence during the second phase, when new organizational structures have to be implemented and new teams brought together. The third phase continues with a learning programme for key managers and supervisors, to compensate for gaps in knowledge and facilitate the management of change. During the final phase, work continues from previous phases, but in addition the project is reviewed and evaluated. The aim is that the client should become independent of the consultant at this stage, since systems have been set up, and plans developed to carry the firm forward.

A project proposal submitted by Trinity and All Saints' College Business Development Unit was accepted by the Training Agency as the most appropriate for the task in hand, and in February 1989 the first meeting was held between the three parties concerned.

THE MARKETING REVIEW

This first phase of the programme was seen as the most critical stage, since any objectives set and recommendations made would influence the pattern of future development.

In particular, the review would have to take a number of environmental threats into consideration. Increased competition in the leisure industry was seen as a particularly pressing problem. The growth of other theme parks in the area (such as 'Flamingoland', situated between Lightwater Valley and the east-coast resorts of Whitby, Scarborough and Bridlington) was thought to pose a direct threat, but the influence of the 'retail revolution' was thought to be a more serious long-term problem. New shopping-mall leisure developments like 'Metroland' were due to be opening in the Yorkshire area within five years, and there was the possibility of Sunday trading being introduced, which could alter weekend leisure patterns tremendously.

Demographic changes were also giving cause for concern. The size of the 'family' market was seen to be falling rapidly, with numbers of 'young teens' (10–16 years) in particular contracting rapidly, relative to the 25–40 and retired age-groups (see appendix 3).

Imminent legislation covering school trips was seen as a threat to the important midweek market. From April 1989 it would be illegal for schools to charge for school trips, and there was a likelihood that this type of activity would be curtailed in schools which found it difficult to gain voluntary contributions from parents.

The effect of certain schools opting out of local education authority control was also an unknown factor. It was hoped, however, that the growth of private-sector education and the emphasis of practical and vocational education in the new GCSE format would offset those problems.

Lightwater Valley had always been heavily weather-prone, but the media had magnified this concern by drawing attention to 'the greenhouse effect'. The worry was that wetter summers would threaten traditional high-season activity. Conversely, warmer, drier winters were predicted, but of course Lightwater Valley was closed at that time of year. The winter of 1988–9 had been an exceptionally mild one, with temperatures well into the 60s (°F) in January and February.

A final cause for concern was the 'Green' movement. Issues such as conservation, recycling, healthy living, and animal rights had all been coming to the fore in recent years, and a continuance of this trend could mean that the spotlight would fall on intensive farming techniques. A consumer backlash could be very damaging to the basic 'theme' of the park.

The formal review was ultimately based on data, information and opinions from a number of sources.

First of all, a group discussion was conducted with the two directors (Robert and Lynn Staveley), the general manager (Gary Blades), the company accountant (Mike Jones) and the marketing manager (Sue O'Sullivan). The intention was to ascertain the precise nature of the corporate mission and corporate objectives, and also to identify what the organization itself perceived as its own strengths and weaknesses.

A subsequent interview with the marketing manager revealed the nature and extent of marketing activity currently being undertaken. Various pieces of documentation, such as the results of a 1987 visitor survey, a project report produced by a consultant from the Manpower Services Commission in 1986, a few statistics from the British Association of Theme Parks, and certain financial information about the organization, were also made available. The one notable deficiency in the information to hand was a reliable baseline visitor survey, so a proposal was written for primary research to be carried out on the site during the opening week of the season (see appendix 4).

Finally, a number of personal visits were made to the site, in different weather conditions, on different days of the week and on a bank holiday, to get a personal viewpoint on the activities and the ways in which visitors used the park.

Budgetary limitations meant that the marketing objectives and an operational marketing plan for Lightwater Valley would have to be formulated on the basis of this information, plus any additional material that could be obtained from library sources.

The findings from these different areas of investigation were as shown below.

A review of marketing activity at Lightwater Valley

The group discussion The aim of this meeting was to identify an explicit overall purpose and direction for the business, and to start to assess the basis for organizational development.

It emerged that the directors' vision was that Lightwater Valley should be seen as providing a 'high-quality' and 'tasteful' leisure service – to be 'the Marks and Spencer' of the theme park industry. A mission statement had been developed that read as follows:

Lightwater Valley is in the leisure and entertainment business, and wishes to be perceived as a provider of tasteful and high-quality countryside leisure park facilities, offering good value for money via mainly active, but also passive pursuits for all age-groups, regardless of weather.

Explicit corporate objectives were more difficult to pin down. Financial ratios were not a part of the business control mechanism, and the stated objectives were 'to increase turnover', 'to increase profit' and to 'improve cash flow'. Numerical targets were set for visitor numbers, and budgets were prepared on the basis of those forecasts. The cash-flow objective was seen as being particularly crucial, since seasonal opening and dependence upon holiday trade and good weather meant that year-round overheads had to be financed in a short trading period.

To gain an accurate perception of the strengths and weaknesses of a business of which one has an intimate knowledge is a notoriously difficult task. However, the group identified a number of areas where they considered Lightwater Valley to score highly in the leisure market.

The pleasant country environment of Lightwater Valley, about an hour's drive from the major conurbations of Leeds/Bradford and Newcastle, and served by quiet road-links just off the A1 trunk road, was seen as a plus point (despite the fact that the immediate area was very sparsely populated, and public transport to the area very limited, as Ripon station had been closed since the 1960s). Getting out of the city at weekends was thought to be a priority for families taking children on outings. The facilities on the site were also thought to be very attractive to the family market (though a weakness was perceived in provisions for other groups, such as the 18 to 25-year-olds). A spacious site, with ample parking, picnic facilities, restaurants, cafés and fast-food outlets, shops, sporting activities, rides and the farm seemed to offer something for the whole family, and Lightwater Valley was thought to be very good value for money for a whole day out, particularly in comparison with some other theme parks which charged almost twice as much for entrance (see appendix 5). Attention to detail, and an emphasis on cleanliness, tidiness and hygiene on the site were thought to be appropriate for the 'wholesome' country image that Lightwater Valley was trying to put across.

A number of weaknesses were more easily identified, as these were seen as being the major reasons for poor profit performance. Vulnerability to the vagaries of the British climate topped the list. Although some indoor activities were available (including the shops and cafés and farm), children were mainly interested in the rides, which were of limited appeal in the rain or cold, thereby limiting the open season to the summer months. This in turn meant that the winter months incurred high overheads with low income (mainly from the carvery) and cash flow was a significant problem. Indeed, it was not uncommon for profitable trading to take place only during July and August, losses being sustained for ten months of the year.

Financial restrictions due to undercapitalization were seen as a major barrier to business development. A number of investments were desirable, including the provision of more undercover weatherproof activities, and also the purchase of some minor rides which were currently being hired for the season at quite heavy rental rates. However, the most urgent investment was seen to be the installation of a third 'white-knuckle' ride. Major rides were thought to be the main reason why people came to Lightwater Valley (if there was nothing 'new' on the site, it was thought that people would be loath to make return visits in consecutive seasons). The directors believed that the most fundamental weakness in the facilities on offer was the lack of a significant number of such rides. Therefore, despite the fact that the cost of such an installation would be in the region of £1m., planning was under way for a new major ride for the 1990 season.

Another weakness perceived at Lightwater Valley was in the retail outlets. Spend-per-head in the shops was known to be poor in comparison with other theme parks, and this was obviously a lost profit-opportunity.

Personnel issues also proved to be a perennial problem. A high turnover of casual staff, brought in for the season, meant that recruitment took up a disproportionate amount of management time. This was partly attributed to the relatively low wage rates being paid. The good staff proved to be highly mobile, and retaining them for a complete season was unusual. This was seen as a particular weakness from the point of view of customer relations. Training of temporary staff was not cost-effective if these employees had no intention of staying for a reasonable period of time, yet it was these very staff who were in face-to-face contact with the public, and on whom visitor perceptions of the level of service at Lightwater Valley would depend.

An interview with the marketing manager   Sue O'Sullivan explained some of the current marketing policies operating at Lightwater Valley:

> The park first opens at Easter and closes for the winter at the end of September. Daily opening times have recently been changed. In previous seasons, other than during July and August, the park was only open at weekends, bank holidays and on Wednesdays and Thursdays. The decision was taken to open every day of the week all season and also to open on Sundays during October, in an attempt to gain some marginal trade. Projected daily attendance figures were estimated on this basis. The maximum capacity of the park is about 9,000 visitors per day. On occasions, on hot bank holiday Mondays, Lightwater Valley

has been forced to turn away visitors who arrive during the afternoon.

Opening hours vary according to the season and the weather. Gates open at 10.30 a.m. and closing time is either 5 p.m. or 5.30 p.m. The decision on this is made daily, and visitors are advised of this as they enter.

When visitors stop to pay their entrance fees, they are given a brochure containing a map of the park and a list of attractions (appendix 6). Although publicity material advertises 'over 70 great attractions', this number does include various shops and fast-food outlets.

Pricing structures are kept as simple as possible, though a number of concessions are in operation. Most visitors pay a basic daily entrance fee of £4.95. Having paid this at the gate, all activities on the site are then available at no extra cost. The purchase of food and drink, goods from the shops and gaming machines are the only other areas of possible expenditure. Children under three years old are admitted free of charge, and senior citizens can enter for £2.95 on weekdays outside of July and August. Coach parties of 20 or more are admitted at £3.95 each, with one free 'organizer's' ticket given to parties of 20–44, and two free tickets to parties of over 45 people. School parties are given special discounts, because they provide valuable revenue during weekdays outside school holidays. One teacher is admitted free with every ten pupils. Pupils are charged £1.95 in April, £2.50 in May, £2.95 in June and September and £3.95 in July. A few other concessionary schemes are running, linking up with other organizations. For example, members of the Halifax Building Society 'Xtra' Club are admitted at four for the price of three.

Promotional activity takes place in a multitude of forms. A budget of £330,000 is allocated between TV advertising (£150,000), press advertising (£40,000) and miscellaneous other activities, including the printing of maps and brochures.

TV advertising takes place over all the bank holiday weekends, and slots are booked on Yorkshire, Granada and Tyne Tees stations. A small production company in Leeds prepares the ads, which this year are taking the theme 'Lightwater Valley – something for everyone'. Also at bank holidays press ads are placed in numerous local newspapers from Lincolnshire to Tyneside, and as far west as Manchester. For the first time this year, these ads will carry a 'four for the price of three' offer, and a coupon. It is hoped that the addresses on the returned coupons will provide some useful market data. Occasionally, if a good deal can be negotiated, ads will be placed in national press, such as the *Daily Mail* or *Daily Express* Saturday holiday pages, or women's magazines. Space is always taken in appropriate tourist guides and year books. Post Office 'Nu-Media' is being tried out this year for the first time.

Sales promotion, in its broadest sense, is also important to Lightwater Valley. Leaflet distribution comes into this category. Tourist information offices and hotel foyers are both important areas for visibility, though it can be difficult getting the leaflets well displayed. Obviously they compete with material from numerous other competitive attractions. A mobile exhibition caravan is used to attend various exhibitions and country shows, where leaflets and stickers are given out. Direct mail is used for the schools market (which is contacted twice a year) and also for encouraging coach companies to plan open excursions to Lightwater Valley. Special packs are designed for the schools, and the coach companies are sent a quarterly newsletter. A new venture this year is a link into a scheme being run by the British Association of Theme Parks in conjunction with Cadbury's. Free tickets (again, four for the price of three) are being offered in exchange for chocolate bar wrappers. The offer applies to theme parks throughout the UK, and Lightwater Valley has decided to participate.

PR activities have always proved very time-consuming and have never really attracted a great deal of press interest. The RAC rally used to use the park as a stage on the route, but Lightwater Valley was hardly given a mention in any news coverage. Local radio roadshows and charity days for underprivileged children have had more success, but the costs and effort involved in staging the events have been thought to out-weigh the benefits. A recent change in corporate identity, following the appointment of a new design agency, is one attempt to improve the public profile of the park.

Personal selling does not really play a part in the promotional mix at Lightwater Valley, other than a little negotiation with coach companies, and some discussion with tour operators at trade exhibitions.

The survey   The baseline survey revealed a great deal about visitor characteristics and opinions of Lightwater Valley. The research was conducted between Friday 24 March and Sunday 2 April 1989, which included an Easter bank holiday weekend. Visitors were interviewed as they walked around the theme park; selection for interview was random. The eventual sample size was 834. Only the over-16s were questioned, but responses relevant to children were covered under 'family groups'.

The questionnaire used and the raw scores are shown in appendix 7. Cross-tabulation revealed some significant relationships between certain variables (these findings hold at the 1 per cent level). These are listed below:

1   Respondents in social class E were less likely than other groups to be enjoying their visit.
2   People who came with friends, or who looked around the park in an organized group, were less likely to have a very enjoyable time than other visitors.
3   Visitors who brought a picnic had a more enjoyable time than those who did not.
4   Although those who had a 'very enjoyable' time were less likely than other visitors to be critical of the value for money offered by the food and drink available, they were still negative about it:

Food and drink value:	Very enjoyable	Quite enjoyable
Good	26	14
Average	44	44
Poor	30	42

5   Picnickers were most likely to be between the ages of 25 and 54; 61 per cent of families with children brought a picnic to Lightwater Valley.
6   Those who had seen the TV advert were more likely to perceive Lightwater Valley as being like a funfair, and much less likely to see it as being like an adventure playground.
7   Only 8 per cent of families with children thought Lightwater Valley was most like a funfair: the comparable figure for all other types of party was twice that.
8   For every age group, 'adventure playground' was the most favoured response in terms of what Lightwater Valley should be like, though the 16–24s were much more inclined than any other group to wish for a move towards a 'funfair' conception. Families with children were least likely to wish that development should be in this direction (only 10 per cent did) and were most likely to wish that it would move towards the 'adventure playground' concept (50 per cent of them did).
9   People who had seen the TV advert were more likely to feel that Lightwater Valley should approximate to the 'fairground' conception than those who had not.
10 Those who purchased a full meal, rather than a snack, were more likely to be pleased with the value for money obtained:

Value for money:	Meal	Snack
Good	41	20
Average	36	44
Poor	22	36

11   21 per cent of visitors had seen both the TV ad and the press ad, but 34 per cent had seen neither.

12   Men were more likely to claim that no one persuaded them to come to Lightwater Valley, that they had made their own mind up. Male relatives, whether children or adults, feature more heavily as 'persuaders' for female visitors than for male visitors.

A personal visit   Three visits were made to Lightwater Valley during the early season. The first two were made for general 'acclimatization' purposes, and took place at weekends.

> The park seemed much as described in the literature. Only the sheer size of the site, and the distances that had to be walked between attractions, were surprising. The location was pleasant, not too crowded, very clean, tidy and well-kept. Lawns were neatly cut, equipment in good condition and staff friendly. Although the weather was quite cold, it was bright and there was no threat of rain. Although some negative comments were overheard about the pig farm and the sad life that the animals lead, there was a general air of great enjoyment.
>
> A subsequent visit was made on a weekday, with the specific purpose of identifying and evaluating each attraction and undertaking a thorough audit of the services provided. Unfortunately, the chosen date was very cold and rain threatened. A diary of that visit was compiled (appendix 8). Gate receipts on the particular day in question totalled £297.

Appendix 1   Lightwater Valley Ltd organizational structure

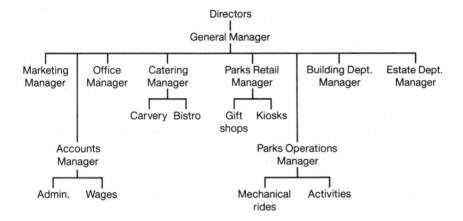

Appendix 2   Visitor statistics

Year	No.	Increase	%
1979	100,000		
1980	303,698	+203,652	+203.6
1981	265,794	−37,904	−12.5
1982[a]	419,853	+154,059	+58.0
1983	493,766	+73,917	+17.6
1984	404,962	−88,804	−18.0
1985	350,560	−54,402	−13.4
1986	332,556	−18,004	−5.1
1987	413,000	+80,444	+24.2
1988	420,000	+7,000	+1.7

[a] 1982 marked the introduction of an all-inclusive entry price

Appendix 3   UK Population: age 5–14 ('000)

1975	9,198		
1976	9,176		
1977	9,085		
1978	8,930		
1979	8,694		
1980	8,424		
1981	8,147		
1982	7,845		
1983	7,588		
1984	7,403		
1985	7,286		
1986	7,157		
1987	7,038		
1988	6,971		
1989	6,963		
1990	7,016		
1991	7,094	}	Prediction
1992	7,210		
1993	7,470	}	Estimate
1994	7,580		

Appendix 4   Research proposal

The initial marketing investigation at Lightwater Valley (based upon existing data and discussion with directors and managers) indicates the need for certain market information:

1 *Visitor profile*   (by age, sex, social class, family life cycle and group membership). Accurate targeting of future visitor types will depend upon a knowledge of the existing visitors and their attitudes and preferences.
2 *The visit influencer*   If we know the process by which the customer decides to visit Lightwater Valley, a more active and encouraging role can be played in that process. This is particularly relevant in terms of targeting advertising and promotions.
3 *Past experience*   Information about visit frequency will indicate levels of satisfaction and also illustrate the positioning of Lightwater Valley in visitors' routine annual leisure patterns.
4 *General perceptions*   By understanding visitor expectations and actual perceptions, it is possible to direct future promotional activity towards those market segments which are attracted by the reality, and avoid disappointing those for whom the Valley, in all honesty, has little to offer.

5 *Main attraction (strengths)*   Identifying the primary purpose of the visit may be achieved by discovering the key features of Lightwater Valley from the visitors' points of view.

6 *Main drawback (weaknesses)*   Weaknesses in the Lightwater Valley facility provision need to be identified, to indicate areas for improvement and investment.

7 *Shopping facilities*   Knowing why visitors do or do not purchase from the shops will indicate areas of potential improvement and profit.

8 *Catering facilities*   As for shopping facilities.

9 *Media*   It is important to evaluate the effectiveness of the two main areas of media-spend, in case more efficient use can be made of the allocated budget.

Appendix 5   Theme Parks and Safari Parks

A COMPARISON OF ENTRANCE FEES AND VISITOR NUMBERS, 1986

	Entrance fee	*Visitor numbers*
Alton Towers, Staffs.	£7.99 adult £7.99 child	2,300,000
Thorpe Park, Surrey	£6.00 adult £5.50 child	1,050,000
Windsor Safari Park, Berks.	£5.00 adult £4.40 child	600,000
West Midland Safari Park, Staffs	£4.50 adult £3.50 child	420,000
Pleasurewood Hills, Suffolk	£4.50 adult £4.50 child	407,000
Woburn Leisure Park, Bucks.	£4.50 adult £3.50 child	400,000
Camelot Theme Park, Lancs.	£3.95 adult £3.95 child	383,000
Lightwater Valley, N. Yorks.	£3.75 adult £3.75 child	333,000
Lions of Longleat, Wilts.	£3.00 adult £2.00 child	350,000
Knowsley Safari Park, Merseyside	£6.00 per car	260,000
Total:		6,503,000

Appendix 6   Lightwater Valley Theme Park visitor attractions

ACTION, ADVENTURE AND THRILLS

ROLLERSKATING
SNAKE TRAIN
SPIDERS WEB
BMX RACERS
FORT WILLIAM
ADVENTURE
   PLAYGROUND
MOON CARS
GRAND PRIX KARTING
CANOE LAKE
SOOPA LOOPA
SKATE KARTS
THE RAT
CHAIR-O-PLANES
THE DEVIL'S CASCADE
SWINGING GYMS
SKYOSCOPES
BRONCO BIKES
HELLSLIDE
DARKSLIDE
HALL OF MIRRORS
DEN OF INIQUITY
DODGEMS
VIC'S SHAK SHOOTING
GALLERY

LEISURE AND PLEASURE

CRAZY GOLF
CRAZY GOLF CLUB HIRE
LIGHTWATER RAILWAY
FORT WILLIAM STATION
MOONSHINE SHOOTING
GALLERY
JUNIPER STATION
9 HOLE PAR THREE
GOLF COURSE
CAROUSEL
HELTER SKELTER

CROQUET
BOWLING GREENS
PUTTING
BOATING LAKE
ROWING BOATS
PEDAL BOATS
LOCO SHED
AVIARY
SNAIL FARM
POULTRY UNIT
PIG FARM
THE MARKET SQUARE
REMOTE CONTROL BOATS
REMOTE CONTROL CARS
PET SHOP AND AQUARIUM

YOUNG FUN

PADDLE BOATS
BALL POND
BOUNCY BED
ACTIVE FUN PLAY AREA
KING RAT'S MAGIC CIRCLE
LEARNER TOYS
JUNIOR DRIVERS
SWINGBOATS
SWINGS
SEESAW
ROUNDABOUT
SLIDES
SANDPITS

FOOD AND DRINK

LOG CABIN GRUB
FORT WILLIAM
   REFRESHMENTS
GRAND PRIX KIOSK
THE CONSERVATORY
GOLDEN NUGGET BURGER
   BAR

THE DOUGHNUT SHOP
AMANDA'S COFFEE SHOP
FORUM ICES
THE FARMERS BAR
PIG INN

GIFTS AND GOODIES

PLANT SHOP
THE GIFT SHOP
THE SWEET SHOP

THE TOY SHOP
R SHARP ARTICLES OF
   DISTINCTION
J G BLADES
JAMES STAVELEY
THE GALLERY
THE RAT SHOP
RAT PHOTO SHOP
THE TRAIN SHOP
THE SPORTS SHOP
KODAK KIOSK

Appendix 7   Lightwater Valley questionnaire and datafile, Easter 1989

'Good-day, Lightwater Valley is carrying out a survey. Can you spare a minute to help?'

1   'Has your visit here so far been very enjoyable, quite enjoyable, or not really enjoyable?'

			%
	VERY	1	68
	QUITE	2	31
	NOT	3	1

2   'And how did you arrive here today?'   CAR   1   94
PROBE AS NEEDED   SERVICE BUS   2   0
                                          COACH   3   5

3   ASK *ONLY* IF CAME BY COACH
'What sort of coach outing did you come on?'   WORKS   1   9
                                               SCHOOL   2   6
PROBE AS NEEDED   CLUB/SOCIAL (note sort below)   3   32
....

                       COACH COMPANY EXCURSION   4   53

4   'and, as you look round here, what sort of group are you in?'

	WITH NO ONE ELSE	1	1
	WITH PARTNER	2	11
PROBE AS NEEDED	WITH FAMILY (NO UNDER-16s)	3	3
	WITH FAMILY (INCLUDE UNDER-16s)	4	72
	WITH FRIENDS (CAN INCLUDE FAMILY)	5	13
	STAYING IN ORGANIZED GROUP	6	1

5   'Have you been to Lightwater Valley before?'   NO   1   46
IF *YES* ASK 'Did you come last year?'

                                    YES, BUT NOT IN '88   2   30
IF *DID COME IN '88* ASK 'How often did you come in 1988?'
                                    CAME ONCE IN '88   3   13
                                    2 VISITS IN '88   4   7
                                    3+ VISITS IN '88   5   4

6   'Can you remember who it was, if anyone, that persuaded you to make this visit?'

	NO ONE, DECIDED ON MY OWN	1	61
	CHILD MALE RELATIVE	2	11
	CHILD FEMALE RELATIVE	3	7
	ADULT MALE RELATIVE	4	4
PROBE AS NEEDED	ADULT FEMALE RELATIVE	5	6
	ADULT MALE FRIEND	6	5
	ADULT FEMALE FRIEND	7	5
	CAN'T SAY	8	2

GIVE CARD 'A'

7 'Looking at this card, what would you say Lightwater Valley was *most like*? Choose just *one* of the descriptions on the card.'

FUNFAIR	1	10
COUNTRY PARK	2	27
ADVENTURE PLAYGROUND	3	52
FARM CENTRE	4	1
CAN'T SAY	5	10

8 'and, still looking at that card, what do you think Lightwater Valley *ought to be most like*, as you would ideally like it to be?'

		%
FUNFAIR	1	13
COUNTRY PARK	2	24
ADVENTURE	3	44
PLAYGROUND	4	2
FARM CENTRE	5	17
CAN'T SAY		

TAKE BACK CARD 'A'

9 'Is there anything you would improve here?'

	BIG RIDES	1	38
PROBE AS NEEDED	SMALL CHILD PROVIS.	2	23
CODE *AND* NOTE	TOILETS	3	9
NATURE OF SUGGESTED	CATERING FACILITIES	4	27
IMPROVEMENT BELOW	ADULT SPORTS PROV.	5	4
....	GAMING/SLOT MACHINES	6	1

10 'Is there any *single* thing about Lightwater Valley that you can pick out, that makes it worth coming?'

FARM	1	6
BIG RIDES	2	22
FOOD/RESTAURANTS	3	1
SHOPS	4	0
COUNTRYSIDE/WALKING	5	4
SPORTS/ACTIVITIES	6	4
OTHER (NOTE LEFT)	7	43
NO, CAN'T SAY	8	21

11 'Have you visited the shops here yet?'

IF YES ASK 'Did you buy anything there?'

IF *DIDN'T BUY* ASK 'Could you tell me the reason you didn't buy anything in the shops?'

PROBE AS NEEDED FOR CODING

	NO VISIT	1	52
	VISITED & PURCHASED	2	27
	PRICES TOO HIGH	3	4
	GOODS UNINTERESTING	4	5
	OVERCROWDING/LONG WAITS/ POOR SERV.	5	0
....	OTHER (NOTE LEFT)	6	8
	NO, CAN'T SAY	7	5

12   'Have you had anything to eat or drink while you've been here?'
PROBE, EXPLAINING THAT YOU ARE INTERESTED IN
ANYTHING AT ALL THAT MIGHT HAVE BEEN CONSUMED,
FROM A HUMBUG TO A THREE-COURSE MEAL, AND
THEN CODE AS APPROPRIATE

	BROUGHT A PICNIC	YES	1	57
		NO	2	43
13	BOUGHT A SNACK AT LIGHTWATER	YES	1	50
		NO	2	50
14	BOUGHT A FULL MEAL THERE	YES	1	7
		NO	2	93
15	BOUGHT ICE-CREAM OR SWEETS	YES	1	46
		NO	2	54
16	BOUGHT DRINK	YES	1	68
		NO	2	32

ASK *ONLY* IF BOUGHT FOOD OR DRINK AT LIGHTWATER!

17   'Would you say the food and drink you bought here was good, average,   %
or poor value for money?'

GOOD	1	22
AVERAGE	2	44
POOR	3	34

18   'Do you remember seeing a TV commercial for Lightwater
Valley recently?'
IF *YES* ASK 'Was that commercial unimportant, *fairly* important,
or *very* important in your decision to come here today?'

NOT SEEN	1	55
UNIMPORTANT	2	30
FAIRLY IMPORTANT	3	7
VERY IMPORTANT	4	7

19   'Do you remember seeing an advertisement for Lightwater
Valley in a newspaper or magazine – recently?'
IF *YES* ASK 'Was that advertisement *un*important, *fairly*
important, or *very* important in your decision to come her today?'

NOT SEEN	1	57
UNIMPORTANT	2	24
FAIRLY IMPORTANT	3	9
VERY IMPORTANT	4	10

GIVE CARD 'B'

20   'Would you please tell me which of the age categories on that
card you belong to?'

16–24	1	19
25–34	2	37
35–54	3	39
55+	4	5

TAKE CARD 'B' BACK

21 'And, finally, do you mind telling me what your occupation is?'
SEEK DETAILS AS NEEDED. IF THE ANSWER IS
'HOUSEWIFE' OR 'UNEMPLOYED' ASK POLITELY FOR
THE PARTNER'S OCCUPATION WHERE THIS IS APT.

AB – PROFESSIONAL/EXECUTIVE	1	34
C1 – OTHER WHITE COLLAR	2	21
C2/D – ALL MANUAL JOBS	3	33
E – RETIRED ONLY	4	4
E – UNEMPLOYED/STUDENTS ETC.	5	9

SAY 'Thank you very much for your help, do enjoy the rest of your
visit here, Goodbye.' THEN CODE THE FOLLOWING:

22 SEX	MALE	1	53
	FEMALE	2	47

23 WEATHER PREVAILING AT TIME OF INTERVIEW			
	SUNNY DRY	1	45
	DULL OR OVERCAST BUT DRY	2	54
	WET	3	1

CHECK THE QUESTIONNAIRE THOROUGHLY NOW!!!

NOTES ON INTERPRETING THE QUESTIONNAIRE AND DATAFILE

Q.3   The figures for this question relate only to those who travelled
by coach – 43 individuals in all.

Q.9   The percentages here relate to the 464 respondents who gave
one of the answers coded on the questionnaire. Other responses that
were written in include: more covered seating; more signs; more rides;
and more for under 5s.

Q.10   The 'other' responses here concerning what makes it worth
coming to Lightwater Valley include: all-in price; not too commercial;
facilities for young children; Soopa Loopa; the Rat; go-karts; clean;
well laid-out; good day out; and the variety of the general environment.

Q.17   The figures here relate only to the 694 who were able to pass an
opinion on the food or drink.

APPENDIX 8   Diary of a visit to Lightwater Valley Friday, 21 April, 1989

Arrived 11.30; very quiet, not many people about.

Disappointed to see that a number of attractions are closed for part of the day (see end of Appendix 8).

Pleasant man at the gate, very helpful and cheerful.
Car park nice and close to the site.

Used map for direction around the site (this fell apart into three pieces within an hour).

Plant Shop. Are the plants outside the toilets opposite for sale? Why is this shop selling ice-cream? (It's rather a small shop, compared to the garden centres I usually frequent – is it worth looking around?)

Pig Inn. Looks like a nice restaurant, but no menu outside – how much would it cost for lunch? – anyway it's closed.

Farmers Bar. How do you get in? Is it up the stairs, or is that all part of the Pig Inn?

Gift Shop. Seems to sell everything but the kitchen sink: toys, T-shirts, hats, rulers, mugs, badges, sunglasses, kitchen utensils, handbags, flip-flops, camera film, perfume, jewellery, ornaments, odds and ends.

Pet Shop and Aquarium. Very pleasant, no signpost outside though – I nearly missed it.

Pig Farm. Absolutely wonderful – superb graphics: could have done with a direction sign to steer people through in the same direction.

Poultry Farm. Very interesting.

Active Fun Play Area. Looks great for kids: also includes attractions No. 48 and 49 [ball pond and bouncy bed]. (Particularly nice mural.)

Aviary. Half empty! Are the birds dead, or in hibernation?

Snail Farm. Quite revolting, but I'm sure it would be fascinating for kids (especially boys!).

Hall of Mirrors. Couldn't find this: had to ask directions from an assistant. No signpost.

Darkslide. Where is this? I never found it.

Hellslide. Do you seriously expect me to jump off the edge? Needs to be demonstrated for full appreciation.

Golden Nuggett Burger Bar. Closed: very few seats nearby, just a couple of park benches.

Slide. Looks OK for young children.

Swinging Gyms
Skyoscopes
Broncobikes } No one using these. They need to be demonstrated to understand their effects

Remote Control Boats
Remote Control Cars } Not a lot of fun on your own.

Crazy Golf Club Hire
Crazy Golf } Very uninspiring in concrete. Needs green carpet and moving (or at least colourful) obstacles.

Forum Ices. Closed

Paddle Boats. Looks good for children

Sweet Shop. Sweets and ice-creams (but no Mars Bars or Kit Kats) plus crockery, jams, cookery books, and pig ornaments.

R Sharp and J Stavely (shops). All one shop – not two: a vast array of goods ranging from children's books to hologram pictures and ladies' scarves.

Amanda's Coffee Shop. No hot snacks served, so I thought I'd try the Conservatory for lunch instead.

J G Blades. Shells, perfumery and toileteries as indicated, but also cooking pots, sponge bath mats and hot potato baskets!

Toyshop. I'm not an expert here, but it all looks rather 'cheap' (except the prices).

Doughnut Shop. Closed.

Railway. Not open 'til 12.30.

Loco Shed and Train Shop. Closed. Through the window it looks like a general toy museum and shop.

Den of Iniquity. Most slot machines turned off. It's not much fun on 'bumper cars' on your own. (Closed until 12.30) – includes attractions no. 21 and 22 [dodgems and Vic's shak shooting gallery].

Devil's Cascade. Nobody about, but it looks as if it should be open.

Conservatory. Stopped here for lunch. Didn't want any 'junk food', which narrowed the choice down to a jacket potato. Chose potato and cheese and cup of tea – seemed expensive at over £1.50. Served in a paper tray/paper cup with plastic cutlery. Had to change tables as the cutlery fell through the holes in the table. Had to get up again to find a bin to dispose of my teabag. Tea tasted horrible. Potato OK, but couldn't cut the skin properly with the plastic knife.

Sandpit.
Learner Toys } Didn't test these myself!

Skate Karts. Looks good

Sports Shop. Closed – looks as if it sells mainly sweets, T-shirts and children's toys.

Carousel. Could take my mother on this.

Golden Valley Arcade. – can't find this on the map – seems to be a sweet and candy floss stall.

Golf Course. Looks like a good place to learn, or ideal for a round of golf when time is tight.

Canoe Lake. Speaks for itself.

Grand Prix Karting. My husband would love this.

Grand Prix Kiosk. Closed.

Soopa-Loopa. Only for the brave.

Chair-O-Planes.
Helter Skelter. } Good traditional fairground rides

The Rat. Couldn't muster up the courage for this one.

Junior Drivers.
Moon Cars. } OK

Rat Shop. On a theme of 'magic' and 'spooks', but could be better – needs the atmosphere of a traditional joke shop. Photos a good idea.

Boats.
Paddle Boats. } self-explanatory

Log Cabin Grub. A take-away selling drinks, sausage, beans, chips, chilli and taco shells.

Snake Train. OK

BMX Racers. Look in good condition.

Roller Skates. Do adults use these as well as children?

Spider's Web. OK

Fort William. Looks superb, I bet children love it.

Fort William Refreshments. Closed – seems to sell fast-food snacks.

OPENING TIMES FOR RIDES AND ATTRACTIONS TODAY

Grand Prix Karting	12.30 p.m. – 5 p.m.
Devils Cascade	12.30 p.m. – 5 p.m.

Rat Ride		12.30 p.m. – 5 p.m.
Soopa Loopa	10.30 a.m. – 12.30 p.m.	1.15 p.m. – 5 p.m.
Auto Scoots	10.30 a.m. – 12 noon	12.30 p.m. – 5 p.m.
Snake Train		12.30 p.m. – 5 p.m.
Train	10.30 a.m. – 1 p.m.	1.30 p.m. – 5 p.m.

All other rides and activities will be open from 10.30 a.m. until closing time.

Catering
The following are open all day:

Conservatory – open for fast food
Amanda's Coffee Shop – coffee, tea, sandwiches and snacks
Fort Kiosk – sweets and drinks
Log Cabin – fast food
Bar – open lunchtime (12 noon to 2 p.m.)

Appendix 9   Lightwater Valley Ltd

PROFIT AND LOSS ACCOUNT

	Year ended *31 March 1988* *£*	*9 months to* *31 March 1987* *£*
Turnover	2,349,933	1,212,040
Cost of sales	1,254,616	618,277
Gross profit	1,095,317	593,763
Other operating expenses (net)	832,339	507,715
Operating profit	262,978	86,048
Interest payable	(217,529)	(139,465)
Profit/(loss) on ordinary activities before taxation	45,449	(53,417)
Taxation	48,803	916
Loss for the year	(3,354)	(54,333)
Adverse balance at 1 April 1987	(54,333)	–
Adverse balance at 31 March 1988	£(57,687)	£(54,333)

BALANCE SHEET

As at 31 March	1988 £	1988 £	1987 £	1987 £
Fixed assets				
Intangible assets		115,627		129,642
Tangible assets		3,483,420		2,245,467
		3,599,047		2,375,109
Current assests				
Stock	104,387		58,925	
Debtors	101,094		133,258	
Cash in hand	9,866		1,732	
	215,347		193,915	
Current liabilities				
Creditors: amounts falling due within one year	2,434,137		2,133,525	
Net current liabilities		(2,218,790)		(1,939,610)
Total assets less current liabilities		1,380,257		435,499
Creditors: amounts falling due after more than one year		(1,298,809)		(398,222)
Provision for liabilities and charges		(139,133)		(91,608)
		£(57,685)		£(54,331)
Capital and reserves				
Called-up share capital		2		2
Profit and loss account		(57,687)		(54,333)
		£(57,685)		£(54,331)

STATEMENT OF SOURCE AND APPLICATION OF FUNDS

	Year ended 31 March 1988		9 months to 31 March 1987	
	£	£	£	£
Source of funds				
Profit/(Loss) on ordinary activities before taxation		45,449		(53,417)
Adjustments for items not involving the movement of funds:				
Depreciation	213,376		111,027	
Loss on disposal of fixed assets	3,455		9,181	
Amortization of goodwill	14,015		10,511	
		230,846		130,719
Funds generated from operations		276,295		77,302
Funds from other sources				
Proceeds of sales of fixed assets	3,043		3,600	
Hire purchase agreements	465,975		137,000	
Bank loans received	900,000		–	
		1,369,018		140,600
Total source of funds		1,645,313		217,902

Application of funds			
Purchase of tangible fixed assets	1,457,827		375,847
Purchase of partnership business	–		93,590
Bank loans repaid	334,204		80,447
Higher purchase agreements	51,183		–
		1,843,214	(549,884)
Net application of funds		£(197,901)	£(331,982)
Represented by the following movements in working capital:			
Increase/(decrease) in stock		45,462	(48,499)
(Decrease)/increase in debtors		(32,164)	65,606
Increase in creditors falling due within one year		(417,791)	(5,091)
		(404,493)	12,016
Increase/(decrease) in net liquid funds:			
Bank overdraft	198,458		(338,864)
Cash in hand	8,134		(5,134)
		206,592	(343,998)
		£(197,901)	£(331,982)

10   International Computers

In May 1981 changes in the senior management of ICL were announced. These involved the appointment of Mr C. Laidlaw as chairman in place of Mr Philip Chappell who had become chairman in February 1980; the appointment of Mr R. W. Wilmot as managing director; and the appointment of an additional non-executive director, Mr J. A. Gardiner. These appointments were approved by the British Government which, although not a shareholder in ICL, had become involved when the company ran into difficulties in 1980. The government had decided in March 1981 to guarantee loans for the company of up to £200m., which encouraged the company's four principal UK bankers to increase their facilities to a total of £270m. for a period of up to two years. The 'price' of the government guarantee was the right to make senior management changes.

DEVELOPMENT OF ICL

International Computers was created in 1968 by an amalgamation of International Computers and Tabulators, and the computer interests of English Electric. These in their turn had comprised a variety of computer operations, including parts of Ferranti, Elliott Automation, Marconi, and EMI. The UK Government was a main sponsor of the formation of ICL in an attempt to create a 'national champion' of sufficient size to compete with the American multi-nationals such as IBM. In 1965 ICT (one of the companies which subsequently helped to form ICL) had a 30 per cent market share in the UK, and a £55m. turnover, based on its 1900 series of computers launched in 1964 at an estimated development cost of £50m. ICT sold its 1900 series computers at 10–15 per cent below the equivalent IBM System 360 prices, but this depressed its return on capital in 1965 to 2 per cent. The 1964 Labour Government soon saw the significance of the UK computer industry, and in 1965 offered ICT a £5m. grant to further develop the 1900 series. The 1966 Industrial Reorganization Corporation (IRC) selected the computer industry as a major target. In 1967 it started talks between English Electric, the main shareholder in English Electric Leo Marconi (EELM) and Elliott Automation. A merger was agreed and the IRC provided £15m. cash. Later that year the Ministry of Technology initiated merger talks between English Electric Computers and ICT. In spite of the incompatibility of their products, negotiations continued until March 1968 when their merger was announced.

The government agreed to provide grants totalling £13.5m. over four years for research and development, and to purchase through the IRC £3.5m. of equity in the new company, International Computers Ltd (ICL). ICL was then the largest European computer company and ranked fifth in the world. In 1969 it held just under half of the UK computer market, with sales of £115m. The UK was maintaining its position as the only European country where IBM was denied more than 50 per cent of the market.

Plessey, a major UK electronic components company, acquired its share for £18m. at the outset. Shortly after EELM and ICT merged, English Electric was acquired by GEC.

ICL AND THE COMPUTER MARKET

The public sector represented about 30 per cent of the total UK market of which ICL held the major share in 1973 (approximately 60 per cent) followed by IBM (approximately 30 per cent).

ICL gradually concentrated on specific industry/market sectors such as central and local government, finance, retailing and distribution and manufacturing. This approach led to the recruitment of industry specialists and to the improved training of its salesmen in techniques and market requirements. ICL's stated objective over the five years 1973–8 was to double sales, to improve profitability and to increase exports up to 50 per cent of turnover. (See appendix 1.) Within its chosen market sectors, it aimed to win sales where mass data storage and remote access were vital and where the scope for communications development was considerable.

ICL's market shares in France and Germany were 3 per cent and 1 per cent respectively compared with IBM's 60 per cent + in both countries. In fact IBM's position within the European Economic Community had become so dominant that the EEC Commission decided to undertake a formal investigation in 1974. In traditional Commonwealth markets ICL was stronger. It also had a strong position in Eastern Europe where its share of imports into Comecon was 35–40 per cent compared with IBM's 25 per cent.

ICL had virtually no North American sales. Protective tariffs (typically 9 per cent) discouraged imports generally, and the US

Government Defence Agencies applied discriminatory preference factors loaded up to 50 per cent against imported computers. The private sector was also firmly encouraged to buy American. Moreover, the indigenous competition was aggressive.

In Western Europe US companies were generally dominant. Using sales and installed capacity as measures of market share they had in 1972 nearly 85 per cent of the French market and 78 per cent of the West German market.

The US companies also encouraged computer exports from their European subsidiaries. Paradoxically, the French industry, which was the weakest in terms of indigenous producers, had a good export position with a positive balance of trade of nearly £13m. in 1970.

In the UK, ICL had an equal share of the market with IBM – 35 per cent, whilst half of its sales were exports (25 per cent of sales in continental Europe). In total, ICL's 3 per cent share of the world market for large computers put the company into eighth place in the international sales league.

A feature of the computer industry was the importance of the 'customer base'. This arose because of the high cost of switching computer suppliers (associated mainly with software development), and the result that users became virtually 'locked in' to their computer supplier. (See appendix 3 for an explanation of this problem.) Replacement and expansion of installations accounted for nearly 80 per cent of the market, and thus 'locking-in' was a significant market advantage.

PROBLEMS OF THE INITIAL ORGANIZATION

ICL's formation in 1968 inevitably created stresses and conflicts within the organization, particularly within engineering and technical groups where old allegiances were sustained. The widely differing systems that ICL became responsible for maintaining in the field stretched its facilities considerably. Besides the 1900 and System 4 series, ICL was committed to maintain fifteen other systems. It soon became a vulnerability, as existing users felt little obligation to renew obsolescent equipment with ICL computers.

Profitability suffered in 1971 and 1972, and there were rumours that Plessey and GEC would sell out. Burroughs announced that it was prepared to take over ICL, and for a while it seemed that the government (still wedded to a policy of 'no lame ducks') would agree. Before this happened, Mr Tom Hudson, a Plessey board member and the man who had built up IBM's UK operation, was appointed ICL chairman. He appointed Mr Cross from Univac as managing director in May 1972. Previously ICL was run by an executive board responsible to the main International Computers (Holdings) Board. Now the executive board was confined to statutory duties while the management of ICL was delegated to a three-man executive committee of the holding board, consisting of Mr Hudson, Mr Cross and Mr Humphries, the vice-chairman. The manufacturing and marketing divisions were completely reorganized, thereby integrating ICL's activities. ICL adopted a new marketing oriented posture in line with Mr Cross's broad approach to the computer business. The quality of middle management was also strengthened by improving functional responsibility, by improving financial controls and by hiring able personnel, particularly from Univac.

During the period 1972 to 1979 ICL achieved growth rates well above the norm even for such a fast-expanding industry as computers and associated equipment. From a lowly £3m. profit before tax on sales of £154m. in 1972, the succeeding years to 1979 saw an average yearly sales growth of almost 25 per cent and a corresponding growth in profits of 28 per cent. This was even more remarkable considering that other sectors of the economy had been hit by recessions during this period.

By the end of 1979, however, ICL's competitive position in the world markets suffered a severe erosion due to the high level of UK inflation, and the strength of sterling. Combined with a significant increase in the group's fixed-cost base, the company were ill-prepared to react swiftly to the sudden halt in growth caused by the UK recession. The support of the British Government had, however, provided some breathing space for the radical new measures taken to put the company back on its feet.

ICL'S PRODUCT RANGE

The 1900 series was ICL's most profitable system and over 1,500 had been installed world-wide. It generated about 75 per cent of the ICL's sales in 1973, with prices from £90,000 upwards. The 1900 series was the most popular computer of its type in Europe after IBM's 360 series and 1400 series. It compared well with IBM's 370 series, but existing 360 users who wished to upgrade to the 370 specification could not do so with ICL equipment. IBM, by contrast, developed certain parts of their 370 range to emulate the 1900 series, but the incompatibility of their respective data files was still a major problem. ICL deliberately protected the 1900 series from the IBM attack by a competitive price/performance policy intended to be 10–15 per cent ahead of IBM and by strategies designed to lock in customers to ICL products.

The System 4 series had not been promoted since the 1968 merger. Market development was restricted to existing users who required an upgrade, to new customers attracted by the System 4's real time communications capability, and to Comecon customers attracted by its compatibility with Russian RIAD computers. System 4 compared well with IBM's System 360 and had compatible architecture, but little operating system compatibility.

1973

The 2903 series was introduced in April 1973 and in its first 15 months it won over 500 orders. It was compatible with the 1900 series, though ICL was keen to avoid 1900 users moving down to the smaller systems. Rather it was aiming at the first-time commercial users in the £1m. turnover range. The 2903 was technically advanced, with a major selling and operating advantage in that it required no air conditioning. A typical 2903 installation was priced at £40,000. It competed with IBM's System 3, though IBM were expected to introduce a competitive new system within 18 months.

1974

The larger 2900 series computers were aimed at the market covered by the IBM 370 series, but offered a better price/performance. The conversion from 1900 series and 370 series to the 2900 series was designed to be straightforward.

By the end of 1974, ICL's range was:

Small Systems	2903
Medium Systems	1900 series
	System 4 series
Large Systems	2970 (P3)
	2980 (P4)

Its range covered most of the mainframe market. ICL also marketed a wide range of peripheral equipment, but it tended increasingly to purchase peripherals from specialist producers, rather than making them itself.

1976–1981

Developments within the product range continued with larger machines (2976) and smaller (2903/20), thus lengthening the product range. During 1976 the next major shift occurred with the takeover of Singer Business Machines, bringing with it System Ten (smaller than any existing ICL computer), the 1500 series of terminals and the Point of Sale terminal. This takeover also took ICL into markets in which it had not previously been involved (e.g. Italy, Spain, Norway and Finland), and also added 2,500 customers to ICL's customer base of 5,000. And in the following years there were continual modifications and developments around the wide product range offered (e.g. 1978 saw the introduction of the 9500 Retail Business Systems and the 9600 Factory Terminals). 1978 to 1980 brought major new product developments with the addition to the range of the 7700 Information Processor, 'Distributed Array Processor' (DAP) which gave ten times more power for 20 to 50 per cent cost increase, and ME29 (successor to the 2903): a new range of systems offering more facilities, greater terminal connectivity and processing power. ME29 gained 100 orders within a month of its introduction. The cost of the ME29 (according to the number of workstations it supported) ranged from £35,000 to £250,000.

Thus by 1980 ICL was operating across the broad scale of the mainframe computer business in competition with IBM. The only area in which these two were not involved at the time was the home/personal computers market dominated by Commodore (PET), Apple and Tandy.

COMPETITION

IBM was the main competitor for most data-processing systems based on medium and large-sized computers. The company operated on a world-wide basis backed by a comprehensive range of models, extensive software support and aggressive marketing. After IBM, Sperry-Univac was ICL's major competitor in the UK middle market, which included Honeywell, Burroughs and NCR. The latter three companies also operated at the smaller end of the market along with Philips, the Dutch-based organization. The US-based Digital Equipment Corporation (DEC) had established itself in the UK market with its versatile PDP range of mini-computers, originally in process control and scientific applications, and more recently in the data processing field.

Historically, ICL's main competition both in the UK and world-wide was clearly identifiable. With the changing nature of the market, however, competition in the small computer sector had become much more fragmented and more difficult to identify. With the advances in technology and the increased entry of 'new' suppliers, cross-competition occurred across a spectrum of data-processing applications, both large and small. These 'new' suppliers consisted of first-time entrants and existing companies capitalizing on the rapidly developing area of business communications and information processing. At least 30 different manufacturers were supplying a variety of mini-computers and small business systems to the UK market in 1981.

PERSONAL COMPUTER MARKET

In August 1981 IBM announced its new personal computer. The machine was said to have an edge over its competitors, not because of any complex electronics but because it put together for the first time a series of advanced and tested concepts into one machine. The strategy had backfired on IBM, however, because they completely underestimated the demand the low prices would create and they found themselves unable to meet the orders. Even worse for IBM were the repercussions this had on its leasing business with older machines, and the net result was IBM's first drop in profits since 1951. However, the lessons of the pricing error seemed to have been absorbed, and though the new personal computers were competitively priced there was no attempt to undercut the competition drastically. The IBM view seemed to be that with its resources it could be assured of capturing a large share of the business and the market itself was going to be so large that there would be room for all. The pressures in this market would show over the longer period as machines became more sophisticated and cheaper, whilst development costs continued to rise and would affect the weaker companies.

The strategic implications of the IBM move were very significant. The personal computer market was expected to grow to annual sales of 4m. units by 1985 with a value of £2,200m. IBM did not reveal its proposed ouput level, but market expectations were a capacity in the first year of 100,000 units and rapid growth thereafter. This meant IBM was moving towards being a low price/high volume consumer electronics firm – a somewhat different business from the one in which it had traditionally excelled.

During 1981 IBM was expanding at the other extreme and involving itself in the data transmission market: global communications, in which computers and people anywhere in the world are linked together by satellite and 'talk' to each other. As a market for the following decade, personal computers would provide enormous potential but the development costs would be exceptionally high.

PROBLEMS LEADING TO THE REORGANIZATION OF ICL

In November 1980, despite a 10 per cent rise in mid-year profits to £20.5m. the company warned that rising costs, along with a fall in demand, would have a 'significant and adverse' effect on 1979/80's full results. Like the rest of British industry, ICL was battling against recession, inflation and high interest rates in the home market, while the strength of sterling was taking its toll overseas. Despite a sales increase to £715m., ICL revealed a 1979/80 plunge in pretax profits of over 40 per cent to £25m. and cash balances of £16m. replaced by an overdraft of over £10m. On the announcement of the news, the shares fell to 79 pence, having reached a peak of 196 pence in September 1980.

It had seemed that the government, after being involved in the formation of ICL in 1968, had finally allowed the company complete independence when the National Enterprise Board had sold its 25 per cent shareholding in ICL in 1980 for £38m., making a profit of £25m.

At the end of 1980 when ICL ran into difficulties, the government was faced with a delicate situation. Having participated in the creation of ICL as a 'national champion', and subsequently returned the company to private enterprise, the possibility of its collapse was both embarrassing and could have posed strategic problems. ICL was the provider and service maintainer of most large UK government computers.

The options which seemed to be available were:

1   Allow the company to solve its own problems. This might have ended in liquidation or takeover by another company or perhaps survival on its own. Clearly there were political and strategic risks attached to these possible outcomes.
2   Arrange for an 'orderly' takeover by an approved British company or approved computer company.
3   Enable the company to be refinanced with loans and/or guarantees, and ensure that the management (if necessary a new team) solve its problems.

Eventually the government settled on option 3, but there was little doubt that attempts were made on variations of option 2 during the year. Even after the government guaranteed the £200m. loans for ICL, there was pressure to arrange a takeover. Within days of the announcement of the 1979/80 collapse, the Department of Industry had approached BP and Shell to see if they would be prepared to take a stake in the clearly ailing ICL. They, and GEC in turn, politely declined to mount a rescue. With net debt heading for £250m., pressure mounted from ICL's bankers for a detailed recovery strategy.

In early May 1981 Sperry-Univac of USA was preparing a bid. Sperry hoped that it would be able to take over ICL's enviable list of customers in a world market stretching from Australia to South Africa and from Germany to Hong Kong. It also hoped that it would be able to take over ICL's 35 per cent share of the UK computer market – much of it in profitable government contracts.

Sperry expected to pay ICL shareholders only a small return for the takeover, offering only pence above the current market price – and to have the right to close down major ICL factories, lay off more than half of the ICL workforce, and virtually to end primary computer research and production in Britain. The harsh terms of the bid shocked senior ICL managers, but it won the support of the Treasury and was given a tacit go-ahead by industry secretary, Sir Keith Joseph. Sperry was not, perhaps, the perfect choice, but it was the best under the circumstances.

Sperry and ICL had problems common to all competitors of IBM in attempting to stay in the same broad market as the American multinational whose R&D budget was about equal to the whole of ICL's sales turnover. ICL had attempted to compete with IBM across the wide span of the computer market, whereas Sperry had adopted the approach of specializing in certain market segments. Sperry was recognized to be an efficient organization and its chairman had been influential in developing Sperry's specialized approach and tight financial control. In 1971 Sperry had taken over the customer base of RCA for a very small cash outlay and succeeded in persuading nearly 90 per cent of the customers to stay with Sperry.

A good deal of pressure was brought to allow ICL to be saved from takeover, and part of the plan was to allow a new management team the opportunity of nursing ICL back to health. Supporters of the plan prepared a thick file of reasons in its favour, ranging from the protection of jobs to the protection of the government's computerized PAYE system, from the reputation of Britain in overseas markets to questions of national security. Proponents of the 'sell it off at any price' policy argued that this was one last chance for the government to show that it still believed in the free power of market forces.

The decision was taken finally by the Prime Minister after consultation with a ministerial committee on ICL made up of Sir Keith Joseph and Kenneth Baker from the Department of Industry, Nigel Lawson from the Treasury, and Barney Hayhoe, the Civil Service minister whose responsibility was to present the interests of ICL's government customers. The arguments were complex and finely balanced. And in the end the government decided on an independent ICL but with a new management team.

What was the right strategy for ICL, and the British computer industry? There were industrial, financial and political implications in the decision to be made between the Sperry bid and its alternative. The most politically sensitive aspect of ICL's position was the government's reliance on the company for its own computers. Sir Keith Joseph made this clear when he voiced his support to the House of Commons on the new loan guarantees to the company. He pointed to the fact that ICL computers, to a value of more than £300m., supported vital operations in some 20 departments, including defence, revenue assessment and collection, agriculture, health and social security.

Government ministers recognized that new management would be very likely to seek further government financial support. The risk remained that ICL would need more than the guarantee for loans of £200m. already provided. There was also no certainty that ICL would be able to repay or reduce its loans by the time the guarantees ran out in 1983. (See appendix 3 for financial information.)

NEW MANAGEMENT

Rob Wilmot (then aged 36 years and an electronics engineer) was recruited from Texas Instruments, the world's biggest independent manufacturer of micro-electronic components, whose UK subsidiary he had been running since 1978.

For the second time in less than ten years, ICL turned for leadership to a young British executive who had gained his experience working for a large American electronics company. The government hoped that he would be able to repeat the successful recovery in the company's fortunes engineered in the mid-1970s by Mr Geoffrey Cross. Mr Cross was recruited from Sperry-Univac of the US to become ICL's managing director during its financial trouble in 1972. He is remembered for installing effective management controls and completing the development of ICL's 2900 series of bigger computers. One of the major challenges that faced Mr Wilmot was to chart a new product strategy, enabling ICL to diversify away from its heavy dependence on mainframe machines. Mr Cross left ICL in 1977, after having seen sales and profits rise from £154m. and £3.3m. to £419m. and £30m. whilst he was managing director (1972–7).

ORGANIZATION AND STRATEGY

The new chairman stated in the company's Interim Statement in June 1981 that:

> it remains part of our strategy over time to pursue collaborative ventures aimed at improving our product range in the future, and we shall be looking particularly for associations which provide synergy to our own product range and markets. It must again emphasise that any associations which ICL may seek must fulfil the criteria of safeguarding customer investment, both current and future, in ICL products... the primary task of the Board and Management... is to restore profitability. In regaining profitability, we will exploit even more strongly our excellent product range.

Rob Wilmot's emphasis was on the need for faster reactions at ICL, and he stressed that the company had to shorten dramatically the time needed for products to be developed and brought to the market. The twin elements of the strategy would be to rationalize the existing product range so that upgrades between products could be made in the field, and to introduce an element of 'managed risk' to allow faster development from the latest technology. His clear emphasis on developing products with inherent reliability was a contrast to his encouragement of more risk in product development. With an urgent need to save money, but a similar need to maintain R&D, Wilmot directed development teams to use the latest technology, and to allow for an element of risk in bringing it into new products. He consequently split up ICL's Product Development Group (PDG) into manageable sections. Mr Wilmot argued that the 5,000 redundancies were necessary because with a payroll of 30,000 the company needed a growth rate of 25 per cent in real terms to keep paying them.

The primary task became one of restoring the company to profitability and the new catch-phrase within the company became 'profits before growth'. Previously the company had enjoyed years of expansion, with growth often over 20 per cent p.a., and in the expansionist period of 1972–7 this growth had been supported by a period of sterling depreciation. From 1977 to 1981 the company had striven to maintain its growth objectives, but this period had been one of sterling appreciation and this laid a heavy burden on the company.

ORGANIZATION

From 1981 onwards the long-range organizational goal was to introduce product-line accountability in order to ensure that the selling and manufacturing operations responded promptly to market and company needs. This involved:

1   the establishment of a new product marketing division to increase emphasis on the formulation and implementation of marketing strategies;
2   the creation of a strong team to develop standard applications software to increase sales of ICL products to new customers;
3   the consolidation of product supply and inventory control functions within the manufacturing operation to provide a focal point for the reduction of worldwide inventory levels;
4   the creation of separate development divisions for distributed systems, for mainframe computers and also for networking strategy.

PRODUCT AND MARKETING STRATEGY

ICL's 1981 strategy was based on the concept of 'information technology' dependent on distributed computing and the convergence of telecommunications with information processing systems. These needs highlighted the concept of a Networked Product Line in which the products ICL offered would be increasingly capable of communicating both with each other and with equipment from other suppliers. The complexity of networking had prevented many organizations from enjoying the full benefits of the equipment at their disposal. The 1981 strategy of ICL was to solve this problem by offering a linked product line.

1   *Product Developments*
    (a)   June 1981: System 25 was launched (based on System 10 from Singer which had 9000 installations worldwide). System 25 was a small system capable of handling 20 jobs simultaneously and supporting up to 200 terminals. It could be

linked to a mainframe computer (including non-ICL main-frames).

(b)   October 1981: Series 20 was announced; this was ICL's new Distributed Resource System (DRS 20). The DRS 20 was a range of multi-micro-based work stations for use in local area networks (LANS) and aimed at the growing market for office systems and distributed processing.

(c)   November 1981: Major addition were announced to the 2900 series based on the same central processor technology as the successful 2966. Over 200 orders were taken for the 2966 between its first delivery in June 1981 and November 1981. (See Appendix 4 for information on product compatibility and comparability.)

2   *Marketing and Distribution Developments*

(a)   'Trader Point' was a new ICL based organization established to help penetrate the market for products at the smaller end (e.g. System 25, DRS 20 and PERQ work stations). 'Trader Point' brought together up to eighty dealers in computers, software, etc., and ICL supported them with publicity and in other ways. Such a move to using dealers as part of the marketing effort was unusual in the computer industry.

(b)   Introduction to forty 'Computer Point' centres around the world to provide local demonstration and direct sales.

3   *Collaborative Ventures*

Of all the developments undertaken by ICL's new management, the joint ventures with Japanese and American manufacturers created most interest.

(a)   Fujitsu: In October 1981 ICL announced that agreement had been reached with Fujitsu of Japan. Early access to Fujitsu mainframe advanced-chip technology would enable ICL to develop highly competitive mainframe products without massive investments in in-house specialist chip technology, allowing ICL development efforts to be focused on creating ICL's Networked Product Line whilst providing an assured growth path for existing 2900 customers.

(b)   In September 1981 ICL announced a collaborative agreement with the Three Rivers Computer Corporation of USA which enabled ICL to market the PERQ scientific graphics work-stations outside USA and Japan. Production would be in the UK with expected sales of around 1000 p.a. The PERQ provided the scientific and engineering user with an easy-to-use computer capable of linking into local area networks (LANS).

(c)   In October 1981 ICL announced that they would market under the ICL label (DNX 2000) the new MITEL all-digital private telephone exchange (PABX) based on CMOS VLSI technology. The Mitel-ICL venture represented a further step on ICL's Networked Product Line concept and brought together into one product line the two competing approaches for office automation, that is, the PABX-based network and the computer-based 10m bit local area network (LAN).

(d)   In March 1982 ICL announced they had concluded an agreement with the National Enterprise Board (NEB) transferring the assets relating to the NEXOS 2000 word processor to ICL (at book value). ICL would produce a variant of the NEXOS 2000 and market it alongside its own ICL 7700 Information Processing which provided both word and data processing. (Nexos came about as part of the NEB's electronics industry strategy in 1979 as the marketing arm for the electronic office of the future.)

NETWORKING STRATEGY

Rob Wilmot indicated that the focus for ICL would drive product activity in the direction of a Networked Product Line. ICL's traditional mainframes could already participate in advanced wide-area networks (WANS) and all future ICL products would fit into the network strategy. Also ICL could support local area networks (LANS) which can interconnect equipment on the same site (see figure 10.1).

Thus, with the growth in office technology, hardware compatibility and inter-connectability across a range of devices represents a distinct competitive advantage, not only because of the expansion and update of facilities, but also due to the cost of ownership in terms of equipment and maintenance and support.

Networking encompasses the integration of whole product ranges based upon advanced systems architecture developments. IBM first launched its Systems Network Architecture (SNA) in 1974 and this was followed by ICL's Information Processing Architecture (IPA) introduced in 1980. In the words of Gordon Peake, business manager of IPA:

> We wanted this architecture to encompass developments which we don't even know of, including office-of-the-future technology.... By 1985 half ICL's total sales will be dependent on IPA.[1]

Part of ICL's strategy was to aim at the large IBM market, with the ability to 'talk' to IBM mainframes, to supply plug-compatible processors and to encircle an IBM site with ICL peripherals.

IPA already operated between ICL's UK head offices and its operations in South Africa and Australia. This was providing a relatively cheap form of data transfer and, with expansion to other parts of the international operation, unit data transfer costs would decrease

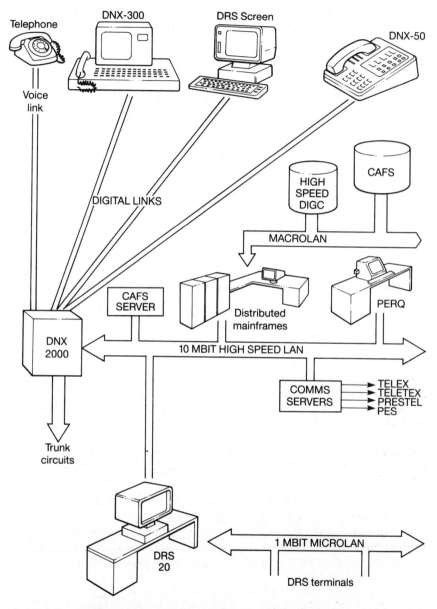

FIGURE 10.1   **ICL DNX-2000 Distributed network exchange**

significantly. The future role of data processing and transmission links was summed up by Gordon Peake:

> Data processing and telecommunications will be ultimately linked in a new discipline – telematics. And to succeed in selling computers each company will have to allow free transfer of data. IPA allows ICL users to do that today.... There could well be great advantage in linking up with British Telecom (BT) in 1983 after liberalisation of its services.... BT is thinking aggressively about its future position and a telecommunications link up would greatly strengthen our ability to sell IPA.[2]

Thus, it appeared that ICL was facing a major challenge in meeting the changing needs of the 1980s. The questions remained, however, whether the organization's new strategy would succeed in the face of rapid changes in information technology and whether the necessary resources could be sustained, given the pressures for a return to profitability.

Appendix 1

EVIDENCE GIVEN TO THE SELECT COMMITTEE ON SCIENCE AND TECHNOLOGY OF THE HOUSE OF COMMONS – JANUARY 1973[3]

In a memorandum to the committee, ICL stated:

It is the objective of ICL Group to double its turnover during the next five years, with half its business coming from outside of the UK.... The ICL Group is a total systems company that aims to meet all the data processing needs of its customers.

It is now useful to restate a number of key determinants of ICL's marketing and product strategies.

(i)   the need to conserve the investment made by individual users of ICL systems
(ii)   the ability at the same time to offer continued freedom to upgrade, develop and extend their application
(iii)   the need to offer the economies made possible by improvements in technology
(iv)   the determination to provide in all respects a service of the highest standard
(v)   the ability to make choices in system design which allow continuous adaptation to the developing use of computers.

It is frequently argued that in order to succeed in competition with IBM it is necessary to adopt a policy of new identity with current IBM systems (although the looser term 'compatibility' is generally used). ICL considers that such a policy violates several of the criteria listed

above. In particular, it involves such complete loss of free choice that
(v) is totally unsatisfied.

   This is further supported by other arguments concerned with
commercial viability of such a policy and the practical impossibility of
following it with any success for more than a very limited time
and at some distance behind IBM. 'IBM compatibility' virtually
precludes the offering of any significant price/performance advantage
over IBM. Our policy is, therefore, to maintain such a degree of
compatibility with IBM products as will permit reasonable ease
of communication with or conversion from IBM systems while pre-
serving the desired freedom of design choice necessary if we are to
continue to compete successfully with IBM on the direct merits of our
systems and support abilities.

Appendix 2

RESULTS FOR THE YEAR TO 31 MARCH 1981 (£m.)

	1981	1980
Turnover	711.1	715.8
Trading (loss)/profit	(18.7)	51.4
Interest	31.1	26.3
(Loss)/profit before taxation	(49.8)	25.1
Taxation	5.4	7.4
(Loss)/profit after taxation	(55.2)	17.7
Minority interests	0.2	–
(Loss)/profit before extraordinary item	(55.0)	17.7
Extraordinary item[a]	78.1	7.7
(Loss)/profit attributable to shareholders	(133.1)	10.0
Dividends	–	4.0
Net (loss)/profit	(133.1)	6.0
(Loss)/earnings per 25p share before extraordinary item	(41.22p)	13.26p

[a] Redundancy and rationalization programme costs.
Source: Company Reports

BALANCE SHEET AT 30 SEPTEMBER 1981 (£m.)

	1981	1980
Employment of capital		
Equipment on rental to customers	63.6	56.5
Other fixed assets	63.1	72.3
Total fixed assets	126.7	128.8
Investments	21.4	17.3
Deferred assets	19.7	16.0
	167.8	162.1
Current assets		
Inventory	139.6	183.2
Less progress payments	7.6	10.5
	132.0	172.7
Receivables	170.5	155.5
Bank and cash balances	36.9	34.4
	339.4	362.6
Current liabilities		
Payables	132.1	132.7
Provisions	47.2	1.3
Taxation	5.2	4.5
Bank overdrafts and short-term loans	97.4	44.9
Credits for exports	11.6	23.4
Dividends	–	2.7
	293.5	209.5
Net current assets	45.9	153.1
	213.7	315.2
Capital invested		
Share capital	83.4	33.4
Reserves	(11.8)	108.0
Shareholders' funds	71.6	141.4
Minority interests in subsidiaries	1.5	2.1
Medium- and long-term loans	92.3	116.8
Deferred liabilites	48.3	54.9
	213.7	315.2

ICL

	1980 (£m.)	1979 (£m.)	1978 (£m.)	1977 (£m.)	1976 (£m.)	1975 (£m.)	1974 (£m.)	1973 (£m.)	1972 (£m.)
Turnover	715.8	624.1	509.4	418.7	288.3	239.8	200.5	168.6	154.3
Trading profit	51.4	63.7	49.4	37.0	28.6	21.3	17.4	14.1	7.2
Profit before taxation	25.1	46.5	37.5	30.3	23.1	16.2	13.4	10.9	3.3
Taxation	7.4	11.2	10.7	11.7	8.3	9.0	6.4	4.9	2.3
Profit after taxation	17.7	35.3	26.8	18.6	14.8	9.4	7.0	6.0	1.0
Minority interests	–	0.2	0.3	0.5	0.3	0.2	0.2	0.3	–
Dividends	4.0	4.0	2.8	2.5	1.7	0.2	0.2	0.2	–
Net profit retained	6.0	31.1	23.7	15.6	12.8	9.0	6.6	6.3	1.0
Employment of capital									
Fixed assets	128.8	142.6	120.7	101.8	72.3	65.3	55.1	54.2	50.4
Investments	17.3	15.6	15.0	14.7	17.8	8.4	7.8	7.8	7.9
Deferred assets	16.0	14.4	17.5	18.9	17.3	11.1	6.9	6.0	4.4
Net current assets	153.1	140.3	132.0	111.6	101.2	88.1	75.0	68.0	60.9
	315.2	312.9	285.2	247.0	208.6	172.9	144.8	136.0	123.6
Capital invested									
Shareholders' funds	141.4	146.8	124.6	103.7	89.7	75.9	64.6	59.3	50.4
Minority interest in subsidiaries	2.1	2.2	2.1	2.1	1.8	1.9	1.7	1.7	1.4
Medium- and long-term loans	116.8	99.0	87.9	77.4	80.6	63.2	55.4	57.9	56.7
Deferred liabilites	54.9	64.9	70.6	63.8	36.5	31.9	23.1	17.1	15.1
	315.2	312.9	285.2	247.0	208.6	172.9	144.8	136.0	123.6

continued

continued

	1980	1979	1978	1977	1976	1975	1974	1973	1972
Number of employees at end of year	33,087	34,401	33,978	32,156	27,317	28,069	29,178	28,798	27,701
Ratios									
Earnings per 25p share	3.26p	26.30p	19.86p	13.56p	10.90p	6.05p	5.09p	4.92p	0.83p
Dividends per 25p share – net	2.98p	2.98p	2.07p	1.86p	1.30p	0.16p	0.17p	0.18p	–
Net assets per 25p share	1.06p	£1.10	£0.93	£0.78	£0.67	£0.57	£0.48	£0.44	£0.38
Turnover per employee	£21,600	£18,100	£15,000	£13,000	£10,600	£8,500	£6,900	£5,900	£5,600
	%	%	%	%	%	%	%	%	%
Profit before taxation as a percentage turnover	3.5	7.4	7.4	7.2	8.0	6.8	6.7	6.5	2.1
Trading profit as a percentage of capital invested at end of year	16.3	20.4	17.3	15.0	13.7	12.3	12.0	10.4	5.8
Profit before taxation as a percentage of shareholders' funds at end of year	17.8	31.7	30.1	29.2	25.8	21.3	20.7	20.9	6.5

Appendix 3

PRODUCT COMPATIBILITY AND COMPARABILITY

A constant feature of the industry has been the dominance of IBM, and an understanding of this can be gained from the reaction of other manufacturers to IBM's introduction of their Series 360 and 370. These IBM computers which were first introduced in 1964 resulted in a situation whereby two out of every three computer installations were IBM products by 1970 and IBM outsold its nearest five competitors put together. Although much of IBM's success had always depended on its marketing strength and user support, when IBM introduced its Series 360 the technology was so far in advance of all others since then that the 360/370 range essentially defined the terms by which all IBM's competitors must compete.

The response of most manufacturers was to develop new products based on direct compatibility with the 360/370 designs. A major feature of the 360 Series was that it was a true range of computers which were software-compatible with each other. This meant that a program written for one machine in the series could be used on any of the others. Specifically the whole range was 'upwards-compatible' which means that a user could move up to a larger machine and still use the original software program. Also the range was 'forwards-compatible' which meant that users could be confident that when models were introduced they could change to them and continue using their original software.

This feature of software compatibility proved to be crucial in enabling a rapid expansion of computer sales in the UK (e.g. there were 220 computers in use in 1960 and this had grown to 6500 by 1970). This 'generation' of computer models formed a considerable advance on the machines of the 1950s with which they were software-incompatible. When software was simple and the cost of its production minute compared to the cost of the hardware this had not been important, but subsequently software became more complex (and hence expensive) and at the same time integrated circuit developments reduced the cost and increased the power of the hardware. This became the basis of a 'customer base' as users became reluctant to switch manufacturers when changing their computer models because of the costs of rewriting their software.

As an example of the high costs of software conversion, it is estimated that to convert all the software regularly run on a typical mainframe installation from one system to another could take 25 man-years of programming effort. So for a computer manufacturer not able to offer 'forward-compatibility' it has a worse effect than just placing a burden on the user of the machine, for when the time comes to change their machine the users are no longer 'locked in' to that computer manufacturer.

ICL, during the period of IBM's introduction of the 360/370 Series, was producing two different series. The 1900, introduced in 1964, was itself highly developed architecture with similar 'upwards' and 'forwards' compatibility to the 360, and ICL had sold over 1000 installations by 1968. Also ICL at this time had the System 4 range (inherited from English Electric) which, although it had sold very few, was in fact software-compatible with IBM's 360. System 4 was therefore a forerunner of the large number of 360-compatible ranges produced in the late 1960s by manufacturers who had become convinced that the advantages of the IBM architecture were such that it was essential to copy it.

ICL faced a dilemma in that it was extremely expensive to support two systems and therefore it had to choose between continuing the development of the 1900 Series or maintaining System 4 as a potentially lucrative entry in the rapidly growing IBM-compatible market. IBM introduced a price-cutting policy which caused severe difficulties to its copiers and led to some of them leaving the industry (e.g. RCA). ICL's response was to decide to replace both its ranges with a new series. This meant enormous development costs and continuous marketing expenses for two series (1900 and System 4) until the new series arrived. A further potential difficulty was that in attempting to move to a new 'generation' of machines ICL would create a problem of 'software compatibility'.

The new series became known as 2900 Series and its introduction in late 1974 coincided with developments in the industry of minicomputers and small business systems. In the UK the first of these new mini-computer systems was Computer Technology Ltd (CTL) formed by Ian Barron, and it was followed by others including Ferranti and GEC. ICL's entry into this small systems market came about as a result of its takeover of Singer Business Machines in the mid-1970s. The System 10 from Singer became successful and later accounted for almost a third of ICL's turnover. Although the 2900 Series's incompatibility with the 1900 inevitably lost ICL a number of important users to other computer manufacturers, the new series eventually established itself as a technological success.

Notes

1 *Computing*, 4 January 1982.
2 *Ibid.*
3 HMSO *Second Report on the UK Computer Industry* (First Part), 1973.

PART III

STRATEGIC DIRECTION

11 Grand Metropolitan

INTRODUCTION

Grand Metropolitan's capital employed rose from £138m. in 1970 to £3,700m. in 1988. The growth of the company had stemmed largely from an acquisition policy, which in the early 1970s had been stated by the chairman thus:

> We only acquire companies which we consider are capable of expansion. We have made three major acquisitions during the past two years and in each, with guidance from Grand Metropolitan, the existing management and staff have increased profits substantially. We do not believe in interfering in day-to-day management but the financial resources and central managerial services of Grand Metropolitan are available to all our subsidiaries.[1]

In September 1989 the Brent Walker leisure and property group agreed in principle to purchase Grand Metropolitan's William Hill and Mecca high street betting shops, for a price in excess of £680m.

This move was less than a year after Grand Metropolitan had bought the William Hill shops for £331m. from the Sears Group, and little more than a year following on from its record take-over of the US-based Pillsbury group for more than $US5 billion.

THE DEVELOPMENT OF GRAND METROPOLITAN

Early Growth Stages

In 1961 Mount Royal Ltd became a public company and, following a number of acquisitions, changed its name to 'Grand Metropolitan Hotels'. In 1973 the name was shortened to 'Grand Metropolitan'.

Originally the company had operated a number of hotels in the

TABLE 11.1   **Turnover and profits by division, 1975**

Division	External sales %	Trading profits %
Hotels, entertainment, catering and public houses	33	41
Milk and food	23	13
Brewing and distribution	13	21
Wines and spirits	18	17
Betting and gaming	13	8

Source: Company Report, 1975

Mayfair district of London, and subsequently broadened its activities into the industrial catering industry by acquiring Bateman (1967) and Midland Counties (1968).

Its bid in 1969 for Express Dairies, the second-largest milk distributor and processor in the UK, was a significant move for the company as it meant involvement outside the catering field. The Express Dairies acquisition met with opposition both from within the company itself and from investors, many of whom felt that it was an area capable of only slow (if any) growth, and that Grand Metropolitan lacked the expertise to manage it. The following year saw the take-over of Berni Inns for £15m. in shares, and Mecca, the leisure group which owned betting shops, bingo and dance halls.

In 1971 Trumans the brewers, with nearly 1,000 public houses and off-licence outlets, joined Grand Metropolitan. In 1972 Watney-Mann (owners of International Distillers and Vintners (IDV) and the third largest brewer in the UK) was acquired by Grand Metropolitan. This brought the group a further 6,000 public houses, 1,000 off-licences, and 34 hotels.

It was this take-over of Watney-Mann, at a cost of £400m., which took Grand Metropolitan to the forefront of the European brewery industry, and virtually doubled the company's size overnight. By 1975 Grand Metropolitan achieved turnover of £1,201.4m. and profits of £93.3m. across its various activities, as outlined in table 11.1.

During 1975 the company entered into a management agreement for the operation of three additional properties: the Europa Lodges at Newcastle and Gatwick, and the Westmorland Hotel in London. On the industrial catering side, activity was extended in Europe, the Middle East and the Far East, in order to reduce dependency on a reduced UK market. The Bateman Catering subsidiary established regional offices in Bahrain, Tehran, and Jakarta, while Midland Catering (the equipment design company) had gained valuable export orders from Eastern Europe and the Middle East.

By 1976 the UK brewing and distribution operation, which included Websters, Drybroughs and the Coca-Cola franchise, had undergone a major reorganization. The main reasons for restructuring were to bring the company's activities nearer the market-place, and to stimulate greater involvement and participation, both by company personnel and licensed-house tenants.

In 1977 activities continued with the acquisition of the London International Hotel and the Grand Hotel (Birmingham), the expansion of bingo operations, the opening of four new Berni and Schooner Steak Houses in the south of England, and the acquisition of the Yeovil-based Cricket Matherbie Dairies.

Developments from 1978 to 1981

Hotels and catering   The company's determination to provide higher standards of service and facilities for the 1980s was demonstrated by several development and improvement projects to existing sites. These included the opening of new coffee shops in a number of London hotels, and the establishment of public areas at a number of regional hotels.

The Dubai Metropolitan was opened in January 1979, following on the heels of successful business gained by the Industrial Catering Division in Saudi Arabia, Kuwait and Libya. In April 1979 the Hotel d'Angleterre in Copenhagen was acquired, and in the same year a management contract for the Algosaibi Metropolitan Hotel in Saudi Arabia was agreed.

The Berni and Schooner activities were expanded with the addition of eight new branches, and in August 1979 Berni Inns signed a joint venture agreement with Wendy's International Inc of the USA, to operate 'Wendy Old-Fashioned Hamburger Restaurants' in the UK. This partnership was dissolved at the end of 1980, but the new fast-food concept was further developed with the opening of two London-based 'Huckleberry' fast-food stores – a venture development in association with Burger Queen Enterprises of Louisville, Kentucky. By 1980 there were four Huckleberry Stores in the UK, and three 'Barnaby's' (a new catering venture) in the South East.

In 1980 Grand Metropolitan acquired three major hotels in Paris – the Meurice and the Prince de Galles in the luxury class, and the Grand, a fine, four-star standard hotel. During 1980 industrial catering activity was increased in the Middle East, Europe, the USA and Japan, and extended into Mexico and South America.

Milk and foods   The combined profits of Grand Metropolitan's Express Milk and Foods division made steady progress during 1979, mainly due to the benefits of past investment in modernizing production facilities. However, the surplus of milk production in the EEC gave rise to uncertainties in forecasting future profitability, in spite of the Community's attempt to balance supply with demand.

In 1980 negotiations were completed with the State of Vermont in the USA for the leasing of a large cheese whey processing plant.

During this year the US-based Dry Milks Inc was acquired to market the products subsequently produced from the Vermont plant.

Brewing and retailing Following acquisition of the Cadbury Schweppes holding in Cantrell and Cochrane (Great Britain) Limited, a holding company was formed in 1978, to include the latter and Coca-Cola (Southern Bottlers) Limited. Its immediate priority was to increase sales through the promotion of both product lines in the separate specialist markets. The basic importance of the tied trade through pub ownership was explicit in Grand Metropolitan's acquisition of the public houses and taverns of EMI Limited in 1979, for the Chef and Brewer retailing arm.

Wines and spirits Close trading relationships were set up in the USA with Glenmore Distilleries in 1979. In the same period a joint venture, IDV-Dransfield & Co. Ltd, was established with the Fung Ping Tan Co. of Hong Kong, for marketing of IDV products in the Far East. During 1980 a new bottling and distribution facility was purchased in Macon, France and building of a distillery commenced in Sri Lanka.

Leisure During 1978–9 the major developments in Grand Metropolitan's leisure activities included refurbishment of ballrooms and improvements in social clubs.

External sales and trading profits for 1979 and 1980 for each division are shown in table 11.2.

The Liggett takeover

In December 1979 Grand Metropolitan announced that it had made an official filing in connection with the US anti-trust regulations for the purchase of shares in the US-based Liggett Group.

Grand Metropolitan indicated that it intended to acquire, from time to time, depending upon market conditions and other factors, additional shares of Liggett which together with present holdings would result in ownership of in excess of $US15m. of Liggett's outstanding voting securities. At that time Grand Metropolitan owned approximately 4.4 per cent of the ordinary shares of Liggett, at a cost approaching $US15m. In March 1980 the Liggett group was granted a temporary injunction to block Grand Metropolitan's attempt at increasing its shareholding, although on 24 March Grand Metropolitan had increased its shareholding to 9.5 per cent.

On expiration of the injunction in mid-April Grand Metropolitan made its full intentions clear, when it announced an all-out bid for 90.5 per cent of Liggett shares. The proposed tender of $US50 for every ordinary share represented an outlay of approximately £190m. Managing director of Grand Metropolitan, Stanley Grinstead commented:

TABLE 11.2   **External sales and profits by division, 1979 and 1980**

Division	External sales (£m.)	Trading profit (£m.)	External sales (£m.)	Trading profit (£m.)
	1980[a]		1979	
Hotels	360.1	27.3	308.3	27.8
Milk and Foods	539.7	32.6	471.8	27.2
Brewing and Retailing	671.4	65.7	615.1	64.3
Wines and Spirits	474.6	36.2	447.6	36.1
Leisure	381.9	28.7	328.0	23.8

[a] Excludes Liggett's trading figures (last four months)
Source: Company Report, 1980

TABLE 11.3   **Liggett's performance in 1980, by segment**

Segment	$USm.
Cigarettes	24.0
Tobacco	10.4
Wines and Spirits	24.8
Pet Foods	12.0
Soft Drinks	21.1
Sporting Goods	12.7
	105.0

Source: Company Report, 1980

We estimate that although we will come to borrow money, clearly we will still increase earnings per share at the indicated bid price. The bid will obviously raise borrowings as a proportion of shareholders funds to around 50 per cent but we do not envisage this enduring. We will keep an open mind about what interests of Liggetts we keep and what we will eventually sell.[2]

On 16 May a joint statement from the two companies announced the acceptance of Grand Metropolitan's offer by Liggett.

Including its initial stake in Liggett, Grand Metropolitan spent almost $US600m. in completing the deal, but the acquisition also picked up $US97.5m. in cash.

For the last four months of the 1980 financial year, Liggett's contribution to Grand Metropolitan sales and trading profits were £155m. and £22.4m. respectively.

Liggett's overall performance in 1980 amounted to a trading profit of $US105m., broken down by industry segment as shown in table 11.3.

Acquisition of Inter-Continental Hotels

On 21 August 1981 Grand Metropolitan revealed that agreement had been reached to purchase Inter-Continental Hotels from the US-based Pan Am Group. The latter had announced its intention to sell only three days previously.

By moving so fast, the Grand Metropolitan take-over team led by Mr Stanley Grinstead was able to beat off a host of rival contenders, rumoured to have included the giant Holiday Inns group, the Hilton Corporation, and four major airlines.

As a result of the deal Grand Metropolitan, which by now had grown to be Britain's twelfth biggest company, moved into the top echelon of international hotel operators. Its own 66-strong hotels division, including the London International and Europa, ranked second in Britain behind the 800-strong Trusthouse Forte chain.

Stanley Grinstead explained how his group had made a head start in the race for Inter-Continental. Spurred by thoughts that all international airline operators could be running into financial difficulties, his management team began looking for sale possibilities at the beginning of the year.

In July of 1981 the group had been put in touch with Pan Am by investment bankers in the US. Mr Grinstead had put in an offer for the hotels division on 9 July, but been told by Pan Am that the division was not for sale. From then on, however, Pan Am's financial difficulties began to mount and Stanley Grinstead, finance director Mr Orr, and deputy managing director Clifford Smith, flew out for fact-finding talks with the Pan Am board. The talks were only expected to last over the weekend, but on the Sunday Mr Grinstead made a formal offer.

Mr Grinstead said that Grand Metropolitan had been helped in discussions because of Pan Am's fears that rival contenders in the United States could run foul of American anti-trust regulations.

GROUP ACTIVITIES FROM 1982

In January 1982 Grand Metropolitan announced its intention to sell off almost all of its 26 regionally-based hotels – among them the Elizabethan Falcon at Stratford-upon-Avon – to the Queens Moat Houses chain for £30m.

The deal was substantially in cash, with Grand Metropolitan getting a Queens Moat stake of around 7 per cent in growth stock.

The company had already announced a programme of rationalization involving the sale of ten of its 18 London hotels, which included the Europa and Britannia in Grosvenor Square, package-tour properties such as the Mount Royal and the Piccadilly, the St Ermin's in Victoria and the Mayfair.

Grand Metropolitan had originally contemplated expanding its provincial chain, but the cost of some £30m. spread over three to four years was considered inappropriate to the group's plans. The purchase of Inter-Continental Hotels had led to a combined group that was considered to have too large a representation in London compared with the rest of the world.

The Pinkerton chewing tobacco division of Liggett's was sold to its management for $US325m. in May 1984, on the grounds that it 'did not fit in with Grand Metropolitan's corporate plan'.

In 1985 the company disposed of its leisure division (excluding high street betting shops) for a sum amounting to £95m. The disposal represented another management buyout on the basis that the activities did not fit in with Grand Metropolitan's future business portfolio. During this year the company bought US-based optician Pearle Health, for a sum of £280m., and US home healthcare company Quality Care, for £110m.

In July 1986 Grand Metropolitan purchased Leicestershire-based brewery, Ruddles, for £14.2m. The company stated: 'We have been selling Ruddles beers in 500 pubs in the South-East and East Anglia. The future belongs to strong brand names and Ruddles is the best.'[3]

Between 1986 and 1987 the company disposed of Compass Services (industrial catering operations), GM Health Care, Quality Care, Liggett's cigarette manufacturing business, and the Pepsi bottling operations, for sums totalling approximately £720m. A major acquisition during this period was that of Heublein, the 'Smirnoff Vodka' drinks company, for £800m. Grand Metropolitan had been trading with Heublein for several years through its IDV drinks operation, and the acquisition was considered to give Grand Metropolitan a formidable drinks portfolio, with many leading brand names.

However, the most ambitious venture of the 1980s for Grand Metropolitan was the acquisition of US-based food giant, Pillsbury. In early October 1988 Grand Metropolitan made a £3.1 billion cash (£3.5 billion total) offer for the company, whose products were almost all brand leaders in the United States, and included chilled dough, frozen pizzas, tinned vegetables (Green Giant), ice-cream, frozen vegetables, baking mixes, frozen seafoods, and the Burger King chain of fast-food restaurants. The same year, Grand Metropolitan sold the Inter-Continental hotel chain to the Japanese Saison group for £1.2 billion.

There was an implicit admission in these latest disposals of the failure of the earlier US expansion strategy. For example, Quality Care, a home healthcare company, was sold at a £35m. loss compared with the acquisition price, and Pearle Health had not come up to profit expectations. Referring to these moves and to future strategy, Chairman Allen Sheppard commented:

We decluttered the portfolio...we were in danger of becoming all things to all men. We need stable growth and consistency. There hasn't been a fundamental change in strategy...we are just following common sense, which is the basis of good business practice.... We see food as a significant opportunity in the 1990s. Either we will be a major international player in branded foods or we will be out.[4]

By early 1988, Grand Metropolitan's brands included Smirnoff vodka, J&B whisky, Holsten lager, Ruddles bitter, Le Piat d'Or wine, Berni Inns, Eden Vale cheese and Ski yoghurts.

ORGANIZATION AND MANAGEMENT

In 1980 Grand Metropolitan underwent a major reorganization, and six operating divisions were formed (see appendix 1). The company chairman Sir Maxwell Joseph headed a group comprising the managing director (Stanley Grinstead), finance director (Clifford Smith) and the six chief divisional executives. A small group of staff comprising 40 specialists handled matters concerning financial, tax and property affairs. The six divisions covered the following activities:

1 Hotels and catering
2 Milk and foods
3 Brewing and retailing
4 Wines and spirits
5 Leisure
6 Liggett (acquired in 1980).

Grand Metropolitan's divisional operations were run by the six chief executives, who had wide scope to carry out their own strategies, provided they remained successful. These executives met once a month with the managing director to review profit and cash-flow performance.

There was some restriction as to the direction in which a division might grow, in that expansion had to be in a similar field. For example, the expansion of a brewery into hotels would be discouraged. This control of scope was demonstrated when IDV's desire to expand its product lines through acquisition of US distributors was superseded by the group's take-over of Liggett as a whole, rather than merely bidding for its liquor-distribution subsidiaries.

The highly decentralized structure of Grand Metropolitan seemed well suited to its operations. The group had concentrated its activities in consumer products and services where an early knowledge of, and fast response to evolving tastes were considered vital to success. It was Grand Metropolitan, for example, which turned Watneys away from the disastrous standardized 'red pubs' strategy, after it took over the company.

TABLE 11.4   **Grand Metropolitan regrouping (1983)**

	Trading profits	
	1981 £m.	1982 £m.
UK		
Brewing	55.7	68.5
Consumer services	56.3	67.1
Foods	36.4	35.0
Oil and gas	(3.0)	(1.5)
US		
Consumer products	49.7	64.7
International		
Hotels	9.3	22.9
Wines and spirits	72.2	98.1
Total	276.6	354.8

In October 1981 a decision was taken in principle for Grand Metropolitan to merge the Grandmet International and Metropolitan Hotel companies into Inter-Continental Hotels Corporation, with effect from 1 April 1982. The merger of the two companies under a single management would facilitate the development of an integrated marketing approach and increase the ready availability of a larger geographical coverage of hotels for guests. It was intended to maintain and, wherever possible, to improve the standards of all hotels in the context of their categories and their locations.

In February 1983 a new management structure was devised in order to enhance decentralization. The group was reorganized along three main market sectors, subdivided into the distinctive product groups (see table 11.4).

This restructuring resulted from the considerable changes in the geographical commitment of the group arising from the growth strategy.

The previous structure of divisional responsibility to seven chief executives was to be phased out in favour of a system which would allow a greater degree of decentralization and management independence and responsibility.

Individual profit centres would be 'loosely' responsible to just three individual executive directors, who would assist the chairman and group managing director on the development of broad policy.

Further restructuring was undertaken over the period 1984 to 1986, with the sale of the leisure and the industrial catering businesses, and the acquisition of health care operations. However, a further focusing on food and drinks was evident with the acquisition of Hueblein and

TABLE 11.5 **Sectorial analysis, 1987–8**

	1987			1988		
	Turnover	Trading profit	Capital employed	Turnover	Trading profit	Capital employed
Food	1,046.9	69.2	260.2	1,252.6	84.0	310.2
Drinks	2,177.7	256.9	1,503.5	2,581.2	315.8	1,478.5
Retailing	1,467.4	159.8	1,290.3	1,670.9	178.8	1,898.3
Total	4,692.0	485.9	3,054.0	5,504.7	578.6	3,687.0

Pillsbury and the divestment of the betting shops, hotels and health care business over the period 1987–8.

At the end of 1988 the organization was structured along the three major product groups of food, drinks and retailing (table 11.5).

As part of the new management structure a Group Services division was formed to handle personnel, pensions, community relations and legal and secretarial problems (see appendix 2).

Sir Maxwell Joseph

Maxwell Joseph's career had been shrouded in publicity. After leaving school at the age of 16 he started work at 30 shillings (£1.50) a week for a Hampstead estate agent to learn the property business. After serving in the Royal Engineers during the Second World War he moved into the hotel business, and by 1953 he had joined Grand Hotels, which owned the lavish Mayfair Hotel.

By 1955 he owned six London hotels, but it was the purchase of the Mount Royal for £1m. in 1957 that took him into the realms of big business. Following a spate of property deals, Grand Metropolitan materialized in 1962, acquiring Gordon Hotels in 1964. Some two years later Maxwell Joseph had bought banking interests (Lombards) and gaming clubs, branched out into European hotels, joined the board of Cunard, and had taken over Bertram Mills' circus. The speed with which such decisions were taken was reflected in his own philosophy towards acquisitions: 'All I say is "yes" or "no". Once you start delving into tremendous detail you are lost.... You have to look at business in a simple way and keep to the few vital questions.'[5]

Maxwell Joseph sold off the property side of his business in 1970 to concentrate on Grand Metropolitan's activity within the hotel and catering industry. Personal motives played a part in this: 'One of the reasons I got out of the property business was because it is time-consuming and something you have to do yourself.... Unfortunately anyone can go out, do a deal in a week or two and can earn himself more than you can pay him for a year.'[6]

However, it was Maxwell Joseph's experience with property

dealings that no doubt contributed to his successful management of hotels. Once described as the 'wizard of the property scene', his policy of buying freehold or long-leasehold property, and the avoidance of tying up large sums in working capital, paid off handsomely.

With regard to overall control of the business, Maxwell Joseph's style had been described as management by remote control. His method involved delegation of all operating authority to trusted subordinates: 'If you are going to take over a successful business run by men who believe in their ability to make a success of things, then you cannot expect them willingly to accept their orders from head office.'[7]

This did not mean to say, of course, that acquisitions had merely been added to Grand Metropolitan and left entirely unchanged, or that the benefits from synergy and subsequent management reorganization had been ignored. Indeed there were no less than eight divisional chief executives in 1972, with total sales standing at £434m., compared with six (including the new Liggetts division) in 1980, on sales of over £1,200m. The former organization comprised UK Hotels, Popular Catering, Mecca, Trumans, Berni Inns, Watneys, IDV and Express Dairies.

Nonetheless, such changes reflected corporate 'tuning', rather than direct interference with the strategic business units *per se*. In the words of Stanley Grinstead, managing director of Grand Metropolitan:

His [Maxwell Joseph's] management system is almost total delegation to all but the key strategic decisions, relying on his judgement of people to build up for himself a strong management team and his own business and entrepreneurial instincts to guide his company. Joseph has a philosophy akin to that of Charles Clore – he introduced the idea that a public house could and often should be valued as a property rather than just as a beer shop....Joseph's motives are somewhat different from Clore's. He is now going for the industrial logic of supplying your own beer and food through your own outlets.

...In the past the major force which has shaped Grand Metropolitan Hotels has been the stock market and the decisions of key institutions as to who should own and manage assets of companies like Trumans, Watneys, IDV and Samuel Webster.

He [Maxwell Joseph] is supremely confident in Grand Metropolitan...he regards it as socially responsible, managerially efficient and financially sound....He also argues that opportunities for rationalization within his now diversified group have no tendency to reduce overall market competition.

...Maxwell Joseph said in March 1972 'it is one of my objectives to get into the leisure industry as the standard of living rises and incomes grow'. He is, however, convinced and there is a good deal of evidence to support him, that the pursuit of leisure in its own right can be dangerous, i.e. Grand Metropolitan enter-tainment concerns are usually supported by bricks and mortar.[8]

During the aftermath of the Watney Mann take-over Grand Metro-politan suffered a temporary setback, when the share price collapsed from a 1972 high of 276p to 18.5p three years later. Commenting on the situation Sir Maxwell Joseph remarked: 'I wasn't quite insolvent but if the shares had gone down another penny or penny ha'penny I would have been.'[9]

Yet this period was to prove the resilience of the chairman, whose key strengths were considered to comprise a rarely flexible instinct for the worth of both property and people, and an unrivalled eye for the hotel business on which Grand Metropolitan was founded.

Perhaps the best example of Sir Maxwell Joseph's ability to turn on a sixpence is the Watney Mann bid in 1971. On the morning of 27 August 1971, he sat in his office dismissing suggestions that – in the wake of his successful bid for Trumans – he might buy a national brewery chain. In mid-afternoon came a chance to buy a strategic stake in Watney, and he took it without delay.

That bid set a new British take-over record – not only for price but probably for acrimony, too. Sir Maxwell Joseph had said through the 1960s that he had no appetite for contested bids. But with Watney, and with Trumans before it, he proved that he could win the fiercest of fights.

Sir Stanley Grinstead

In December 1982 chairman Sir Stanley Grinstead (then Mr Grin-stead), announced changes in the management structure of Grand Metropolitan.

Stanley Grinstead had taken over from Sir Maxwell Joseph, upon the latter's illness, in September of that year and the changes came about partly as a result of Sir Maxwell's death that November. Stanley Grinstead had joined Grand Metropolitan in its formative years and had been managing director for several years, joining the company from Grand Metropolitan's auditors of the time.

He was largely responsible for the group reorganization into major geographical areas in 1983, and by 1986 he had been instrumental in building up Grand Metropolitan into an international conglomerate.

Allen Sheppard

Mr Allen Sheppard succeeded Sir Stanley Grinstead as chairman of Grand Metropolitan in 1987. Mr Sheppard had joined the company as a director (Watney Mann) in 1975 from Unipart, British Leyland's spare parts division, and in 1982 he headed the brewing, retailing and leisure divisions. During his years at Grand Metropolitan Allen Sheppard gained a reputation for straight talking and toughness. After receiving a BSc in Industry and Trade at the London School of Economics he obtained further qualifications as a chartered accountant and company secretary, while working for the Ford motor company.

About one year after his appointment as Grand Metropolitan chairman, Mr Sheppard commented on the break-up of the hotels side of the business: 'The hotels had been well run individually but inadequately directed from above.... We concluded we could get much better results out of the business.... But with 100 hotels we are still too small. With the same level of overheads we could run 200 hotels.'[10]

Mr Sheppard had pointed to the high price of hotel property and the associated difficulties of building up this side of the business: 'We were becoming increasingly frustrated by the price structure. It was questionable whether we would realize our ambition of being a world leader. If we didn't buy we would in five years' time, have a chain of 120 hotels with perhaps twice the present level of profits.'[11]

The sale of the hotels was considered necessary because the company would be in too many sectors to be able to be a world leader in them all, by the year 2000. Mr Sheppard's strategy required each individual business to come up with ideas and to know where they aimed to be within the next five years.

Asked what he looked for in a manager, Mr Sheppard stated: 'If his first sentence is about production you know you have a management problem. If he talks about the customer, you know you have a chance.'[12]

Commenting on his negotiations with George Walker of Brent Walker, for the sale of the Mecca and William Hill betting shops, Mr Sheppard commented: 'It's the thing I most like about doing business with George.... He cuts out all the crap and gets straight to the point.'[13]

In his statement to shareholders at the end of 1988 Mr Sheppard commented on the reshaping of the organization and the likely future direction:

> At the same time as pursuing our long-term objectives and getting immediate results we have continued to strengthen our businesses. Our brands have benefited from continuing major investment support and several significant add-on acquisitions have been made. Such acquisitions are designed to upgrade earnings immediately, to consolidate our operating base and to build our positions in the markets we serve.
>
> Brand building and distribution are key success factors in most areas of Grand Metropolitan's business. The evidence of Grand Metropolitan's brand-led strategy is excellently illustrated in our wines and spirits operations, where worldwide leadership is constantly being strengthened by the addition and development of new brands, while distribution and sales for well-established brands continues to be reinforced. Widening distribution of our

brands is of major importance and this is being successfully
addressed, both with partners and independently, particularly in
the increasingly important markets of the Far East and, in preparation for 1992, in all countries of the EEC.

Our vision is for Grand Metropolitan during the 1990s to be in
the top half dozen international companies in each of our chosen
sectors of operations – food, drinks and retailing. We are already
the world leader in case sales of wines and spirits.

To make this vision a reality we have had to narrow our range
of operations and to concentrate on those sectors which offer
scope for development and the ability to continue to grow profits
in line with expectations.

Our strategy is pursued through our chosen product sectors but
it is also our aim to get geographical balance between Western
Europe, North America and Japan/Far East. To co-ordinate this
process we have set up three advisory committees covering these
regions, each chaired by a main board director. These committees oversee the group's sector activities in these regions to
enable us to take advantage of opportunities that arise and to
assess the potential for our products in these markets.[14]

FINANCE

On 30 September 1975 Grand Metropolitan announced the under-
writing of a rights issue of ordinary shares at 50p each which was
subsequently 91 per cent subscribed. The proceeds of the issue were
used to reduce borrowings, which had risen from 1973 to 1974 by
£79m. The £37.6m. raised by the rights issue and the sale of Grand
Metropolitan's interest in the Carlsberg brewery was used to reduce
bank overdrafts and short-term borrowings totalling almost £125m.

One of Grand Metropolitan's financial objectives was related to the
improvement of the relationship between borrowing and assets, by
developing a positive cash flow until conditions were right for further
expansion.

Capital spending amounted to £41m. in 1976, while cash flow was
held positive at £32m. During this year the relationship of total
borrowings to shareholders' funds and deferred taxation was 152 per
cent. By the end of 1977 financial gearing had improved to 127 per
cent and, after allowing for capital investments of over £58m., net cash
surplus was £12.8m.

During 1978 profits attributable to ordinary shareholders increased
by over 56 per cent to approximately £81m. (after adjustments) and
earnings per share to 18.5p. During this year interest charges were
substantially reduced by the conversion of 10 per cent convertible
unsecured loan stock and by reduced borrowings. The ratio of total

borrowings to shareholders' funds (less goodwill) had fallen to about 66 per cent, and a cash surplus of £10m. remained after investments in fixed assets of £80m. In 1979 a further rights issue raised £49.6m. (including premiums) and retained profits amounted to £72.6m. Capital expenditure, however, was increased to nearly £125m. and, consequently, short-term borrowings increased by £16m.

After revaluation of the group's assets in 1980 the surplus over previous book values amounted to approximately £565m. This surplus enabled the company to write off all goodwill from the consolidated balance sheet. Following the valuations and including the full effect of the Liggett acquisition, the net borrowings of Grand Metropolitan were equivalent to approximately 46 per cent of shareholders' funds. During 1981 profits from overseas business represented approximately 35 per cent of total profits, as against 26 per cent in 1980. This shift in the geographical balance of business was largely attributable to the organization of Liggett and Inter-Continental, but at the expense of increasing the ratio of total borrowings to shareholders' funds. In spite of the increase in borrowings, the group generated a cash surplus from its operations after investing more than £160m. in new property, plant and equipment.

In mid-February 1983 the company's share price was averaging 349p on a net asset valuation of 293p per share. The share price low for the 1982/83 period was 171p, and during this period the company made a £125m. rights issue, largely to offset some of the debt arising from the purchase of Inter-Continental (net debt down from £934m. to £801m.). This represented net debt to shareholders' funds of 54 per cent.

In 1986 Grand Metropolitan's acquisition of Heublein increased gearing from the lowest in its history so far of 38 per cent, to about the 108 per cent level. The chairman, Sir Stanley Grinstead, considered at the time that the strong cash flow generated from Heublein, coupled with further disposals, would steadily reduce the high borrowings. It was also considered that the increase in borrowings would act as a sufficient deterrent to dissuade any would-be take-over predator.

In early October 1988 Grand Metropolitan's emphasis was on borrowing rather than equity, in the financing of its £3.3 billion acquisition of Pillsbury. It had planned only to raise some £480m. through a rights issue, the rest being raised through dollar borrowings. By 4 October, the company had lined up $US6 billion in floating rate bank credit, and more than 50 per cent of this had been arranged with the big four UK banks, Barclays, National Westminster, Lloyds and the Midland.

Company management estimated that as a result of the deal, earnings per share would not be diluted and that their growth would continue.

As at September 1989, the balance sheet showed:

	1988 £bn	1989 £bn
Intangible assets	0.6	2.6
Tangible assets	3.5	4.0
Net current assets	0.2	0.2
Net borrowings	0.8	3.6

Appendix 1

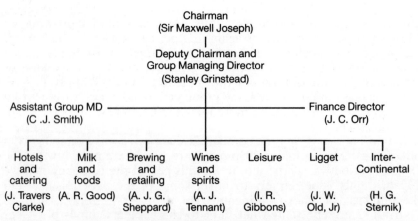

FIGURE 11.1 **Grand Metropolitan board structure in 1981**

Appendix 2

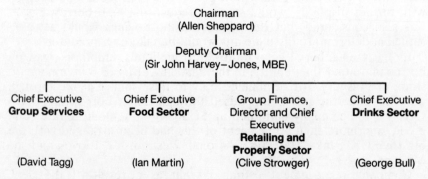

FIGURE 11.2 **Grand Metropolitan board structure in 1988**

Appendix 3

CONSOLIDATED PROFIT AND LOSS ACCOUNTS – 1987 AND 1988

Year to 30 September		1987 £m.		1988 £m.
Turnover		5,705.5		6,028.8
Operating costs		5,141.8		5,386.7
		563.7		642.1
Share of profits of related companies		7.9		11.5
Trading profit		571.6		653.6
Reorganization costs		(9.3)		(24.6)
Profit on sale of property		14.0		39.1
Interest		(120.2)		(93.0)
Profit on ordinary activities before taxation		456.1		575.1
Taxation on profit on ordinary activities		120.1		154.8
Profit on ordinary activities after taxation		336.0		420.3
Minority shareholders' interests	2.3		7.8	
Preference dividends	0.5		0.5	
		2.8		8.3
Profit attributable to ordinary shareholders		333.2		412.0
Extraordinary items		127.8		289.7
Profit for the financial year		461.0		701.7
Ordinary dividends		103.1		129.1
Transferred to reserves		357.9		572.6
Movements in reserves				
Reserves at beginning of year		1,606.5		1,296.2
Capitalization of brands		119.3		608.0
As restated		1,725.8		1,904.2
Retained profit for the year		357.9		572.6
Currency translation adjustments		(42.5)		(19.1)
Premiums on share issues, less expenses		6.0		7.1
Goodwill acquired during the year		(143.0)		(143.7)
Surplus on revaluation of property		–		643.1
Reserves at end of year		1,904.2		2,964.2

CONSOLIDATED BALANCE SHEETS – 1987 AND 1988

Year to 30 September	1987 £m.		1988 £m.	
Fixed assets				
Intangible assets – brands		608.0		588.3
Tangible assets		2,725.2		3,279.4
Investments		177.2		206.1
		3,510.4		4,073.8
Current assets				
Stocks	733.1		761.1	
Debtors	827.5		873.5	
Cash at bank and in hand	113.4		137.8	
	1,674.6		1,772.4	
Creditors – due within one year				
Borrowings	329.7		186.7	
Other creditors	1,166.3		1,301.3	
Net current assets		178.6		284.4
Total assets less current liabilities		3,689.0		4,358.2
Creditors – due after more than one year				
Borrowings	1,141.9		702.4	
Other creditors	103.3		162.6	
		1,245.2		865.0
Provisions for liabilities and charges		70.4		55.1
		2,373.4		3,438.1
Called-up share capital		440.9		442.5
Reserves				
Share premium account	425.8		7.2	
Revaluation reserve	(21.9)		648.4	
Special reserve	–		282.0	
Related companies' reserves	14.2		16.4	
Profit and loss account	1,486.1		2,010.2	
		1,904.2		2,964.2
		2,345.1		3,406.7
Minority shareholders' interests		28.3		31.4
		2,373.4		3,438.1

Notes

1 Statement to Truman shareholders in 1971 inviting them to accept Grand Metropolitan's, rather than Watney's, offer (company sources).
2 *The Times*, 15 April 1980.
3 *The Times*, 26 July 1986.
4 *Sunday Times*, 3 April 1988.
5 *Sunday Times*, 2 April 1972.
6 Ibid.
7 Company Report (1971).
8 A. M. Sewell, Unpublished Paper, University of Bradford, August 1975.
9 Ibid.
10 *Sunday Times*, 14 August 1988.
11 Ibid.
12 *Sunday Times*, 9 October 1988.
13 *Sunday Times*, 10 September 1989.
14 Company Report, 1988.

12   Courtaulds PLC

In 1989 Courtaulds announced that they were proposing to split the company into two distinct autonomous companies. One of these would represent the interests in chemicals and allied products that the company had built up, and the other those in textiles and clothing which had been the foundations of the Courtaulds business. Each of these two companies, Courtaulds and Courtaulds Textiles, would be separately quoted on the International Stock Exchange in London.

In the company annual report for the year ended March 1988 it was stated: 'Courtaulds has sales of £2.4 billion, and employs 68,500 people, 46,000 of them in the UK. It has operations in some 35 countries and is a major UK exporter. In total some 52 per cent of its sales are to markets outside the UK.'

The 1989 report stated: 'Courtaulds is an international group with a world presence in fibres, coatings, films, packaging and textiles and significant positions in fine chemicals and advanced materials. Courtaulds has sales of £2.6 billion and employs 56,000 people in 38 countries.'

These reports also provided other items of information about the company:

'To meet customers' needs faster, better, more distinctively....'

'Our guiding principle is the quality of sustainable earnings....'

'We are continuing to build a dynamic group which is greater than the sum of its parts....'

'...the ultimate test of performance must lie in the earnings per share and the share values to which these give rise.'

'The questions which investors and commentators put to us more than any other are: What are Courtaulds' growth prospects? How resilient is the group now likely to be in a recession? How vulnerable is it to changes in the exchange rates? It is plain from such questions that memories can be long; and that the ghosts of problems and underperformance in the 1970s still walk from time to time in the corridors of investing institutions.'

BACKGROUND

Courtaulds was founded in the early nineteenth century as a silk manufacturer, and a hundred years later was transformed into one of the first manufacturers of man-made fibres, which at that time was rayon. Through a series of acquisitions and diversifications the company, by the mid-twentieth century, was involved in a wide range of related activities such as packaging, film and cellophane, paints, textiles of all kinds and clothing, as well as fibres.

At that time the company was a major supplier of fibres to the Lancashire cotton and allied textiles industry, which was suffering severely as a result of increasing penetration of the market by low-cost countries. The UK government was also concerned about this industry, and passed the 1959 Cotton Industry Act in an attempt to restructure the industry by encouraging the marginal producers to leave. Courtaulds' concerns were also shared by ICI, which was the other major UK producer of man-made fibres. Each developed a strategy to secure the sale of their fibres to the cotton industry. ICI took minority share stakes in certain fibre-users, particularly Viyella and Carrington & Dewhurst, and also made loans to firms to enable them to re-equip with more modern equipment. Courtaulds, on the other hand, preferred to take over companies in the industry. The aim of both was to ensure a healthy cotton industry, capable of using their man-made fibres. These moves created a smaller industry; in that the number of firms fell by 35 per cent between 1959 and 1967, but a more vertically structured and more concentrated industry.

One result of this increasing concentration was the referral of Courtaulds to the Monopolies Commission for its monopoly of the supply of cellulosic fibres, in which it had a UK market share of over 90 per cent. The Commission reported in 1968 and included in its recommendations that Courtaulds should not be allowed to continue to make further acquisitions in any sector of the textiles and clothing industries where such an acquisition would give them more than 25 per cent of the market. In the two sectors of cotton spinning and warp knitting alone, Courtaulds already had market shares of more than 30 per cent.

Nevertheless, the Courtaulds businesses continued to grow, achieving record profits before tax of £118m. in 1975; by the mid-1980s Courtaulds could claim to be one of the world's top six textiles-to-clothing groups, and the world's largest producer of acrylic fibre. By this time the company was a vertically-integrated textile company, with a number of chemical-based interests. It produced the wood pulp which went right through the whole processes to end up as ready-made clothing in the retail shops. Its major market interests were:

- In fibres, Courtaulds were world leaders in three areas: viscose staple which was used in rayon, viscose acetate used in linings and lingerie, and acrylic used mainly in knitwear. Viscose fibres have tended to be in decline and capacity has been cut back drastically, whilst acrylic capacity has been increasing. Acrylic tends to be produced only in the developed world, and is dependent upon advanced neochrome producer-dyeing technology.

- In textiles, the company was involved in spinning both natural and man-made fibres, fabric weaving, especially for clothing and furnishing fabrics, knitting, and clothing manufacture both private label for major retailers and branded.
- In paint, the company was a world leader in the supply of marine paints.
- Other activities covered woodpulp, packaging films, and plastics.

With the exception of the textiles interests most of Courtaulds' businesses operated internationally, with a particular focus on the European Community.

Courtaulds as a commodity producer was always vulnerable to two particular world forces, exchange rates, as commodity products are price-sensitive commodities, and oil prices, as a major man-made fibre producer. The company had always been heavily dependent on the textiles industries, with about 70 per cent of its sales in fibres, textiles and clothing.

In January 1980 Mr Christopher Hogg became chairman of Courtaulds, having previously been in charge at their International Paints subsidiary. He became chairman at a particularly difficult time. The Conservative government had been elected in May 1979 at a time of high inflation, with interest rates beginning to rise steeply, the oil price was rising, the sterling exchange rate was climbing, and UK value added tax went up to 15 per cent in July 1979. The economic environment was extremely difficult, and the profits of most UK companies fell, including those of Courtaulds. In 1981 Courtaulds reported pre-tax profits down to £5m., but they did survive at a time when a quarter of the UK textile industry failed. Appendix 1 provides financial information on the company. Under Hogg, Courtaulds embarked upon a policy of rationalization, with scores of factories closed and tens of thousands of employees made redundant.

The policies of the company were refocused to:

- continue and accelerate the process of decentralization of the management structure, pushing decision making further down, which had been started by Sir Arthur Knight, who was chairman from 1975 to 1979;
- apply a set of rigorous financial disciplines and targets. Criteria were established by which the divisions were to operate and the key decisions were devolved to them. Capital expenditure limits were raised and head office staff was reduced. Each division was given targets for cash generation as a short-term solution to the immediate problems in the company. As a longer-term target,

TABLE 12.1   **Courtaulds operational profile, 1981**

Division	Sales £m.	Trading profit (loss) £m.	Capital employed £m.	Return on capital %	Operating cash flow £m.	Employees
Fibres & yarns	695	1	246	–	28	26,600
Fabrics	419	(7)	140	–	33	16,300
Clothing	362	12	84	15	22	27,200
Paint	268	22	83	28	18	7,600
Packaging	171	3	55	5	15	5,600
Plastics	39	2	9	20	4	2,000
Totals	1,170	33	617	5	132	88,000

For the financial year ending 1981 the results were as follows: Pre-tax profit: £5.1m.; Loss after tax: £16.5m.; Loss after extraordinary items: £114m.

the requirement was a minimum 20 per cent return on capital employed.

An example of the decision-making process arose when Courtaulds decided to exit from the manufacture of nylon. First of all the Fibres Division advised the board that the nylon business could not operate to the cash generation targets which had been set. The board then considered more strategic information designed to determine whether it was a business which would be internationally competitive over the long run. Questions were asked about economies of scale, how value was added, and whether it could be increased and what was the nature of the world-wide competition. They decided that their nylon business did not pass these tests, and should close. It was too small, with only 6 per cent of the European market, compared with ICI'S 20 per cent, consumer demand was collapsing, imports were growing, and it would have required substantial amounts of capital expenditure to bring it up to adequate profitability. Courtaulds closed down two nylon plants, with the loss of nearly 2,000 jobs.

At that time the profile of the company was as shown in table 12.1.

STRATEGIC AIMS

Courtaulds' aims became:

- to reduce the company's dependence on textiles, by cutting capacity in fibres and fabrics, by expanding other businesses and by diversifying into new areas, such as speciality chemicals, which were not so susceptible to cyclical swings;
- to push business abroad, to reduce dependence on the UK market and its sensitivity to the sterling exchange rate;

- to grow overall. The policy was to encourage people with bright ideas by supporting them with cash and allowing them to get on with the job, giving them a limit of two years to show results. Christopher Hogg expected a better success rate than most venture capitalists, who might expect two or three of each ten to succeed. Nevertheless a number did fail, one being the direct mail operation, Scotcade, which failed within one year of Courtaulds taking it on. A further venture was the establishment of 'Courtaulds US Development' to build up a speciality chemical business in the USA. Speciality chemicals were growing at between 3 per cent to 12 per cent per annum, compared with zero growth in bulk chemicals, and were showing a 20 per cent return on capital.

Towards the end of the eighties the biggest issue facing Courtaulds was that of how to grow. The lowly rated shares of the company and its dependence upon slow growth economies and on cyclical markets made this objective very difficult to achieve. In 1986 when the company formed a group executive committee to study the performance and future of the group, a company spokesman had said that:

the formation of the new group reflects the fact that Courtaulds has now reached the point in its development where more top management resources should be focused on performance, future development and expansion of the group . . . the members of the group executive therefore will progressively be detaching themselves from day-to-day operational responsibilities, thus giving greater responsibility to the next level of management.

The formation of the 'group executive' and a task force to deal with strategic development was seen as an important step in marking the change from retrenchment to growth, and freed up the senior management to concentrate on future strategy, in particular on growth. Indeed the chairman said that it was a catalyst to signal to the outside world how much had happened internally, and that they were through the first stage. The task force enabled the chairman to bring in younger people to the higher layers of management. The argument against this was that having a young board would demotivate younger people below, and that the task force or think tank would be left to find all the bright ideas for itself.

Despite the problems associated with growth, by 1987 the company had managed to develop, with the help of a buoyant UK economy and similar developments in export markets, and had recovered to a pre-tax profit of £201m., although employees had fallen further to 46,000.

The company was divided into about 300 profit centres, none of which was under any obligation to buy from any other company in the group, and which reported to about twenty full reporting businesses. Each centre had its own chief executive and was responsible for its own balance sheet and, while it was allowed to budget for a loss, missing targets two years running was not acceptable. The managers of the profit centres were on performance-linked remuneration, and annual targets were set not only on profits but also on earnings per share, dividend cover and gearing. The chief executive of the full reporting business then reported to the main business sector board which in turn was responsible to the group executive, which comprised five main board directors. The decentralized nature of Courtaulds meant that the company had no central marketing or production function, and only an advisory personnel function. However, in product groups where products overlapped, such as some of the textile businesses, approaches to important customers such as Marks & Spencer were co-ordinated.

Even in 1987 the company was still over-dependent on low-quality earning areas such as fibres and parts of the textile industry, and many of its customers, such as the marine and offshore companies which bought from International Paints, were cyclical industries. The textile businesses still accounted for as much as 25 per cent of earnings, even though there were small sectors of growth in a largely static industry. Courtaulds was generally optimistic about its clothing businesses, as it felt that being able to supply retailers in only three weeks was an advantage, compared to twelve weeks from the Far East, and with a number of well-known brand names believed that the quality of earnings would improve. The prospects for fibres growth rested with acrylics, in which there was still world-wide growth, although the European market was static. In 1987 the company made an unsuccessful attempt to buy Du Pont's acrylic plant in USA, in an attempt to secure additional market share around the world. In the chemicals division great hopes were pinned on the prospects for advanced materials, such as carbon fibre, which could be used as substitutes for wood, glass and steel. The Woodpulp Division was profitable, but was a slow growth market, and the decision was subsequently taken to divest it. In the paints division the company had a strong market share in the specialized sector which it occupied, but that market was static or declining, and consideration was being given to entering the decorative sector of the paint business, which accounted for over 50 per cent of the world sales of paint. Flexible packaging was a mixed market with cellophane declining but polypropylene, in which Courtaulds was joint second in Europe, growing. The position of the divisions in 1987 was as shown in table 12.2.

ACQUISITIONS

Although the company had established a business development unit in 1985 to search out acquisitions, Courtaulds had not been involved in a contested bid during Sir Christopher Hogg's chairmanship until

TABLE 12.2   **Courtaulds divisions – sales, 1987**

Division	Sales (£m.)
Fibres	509
Woodpulp	118
Chemicals	168
Coatings	357
Packaging	289
Textiles	935

late 1986 – all previous purchases had been both small and agreed. However, in 1986 Courtaulds made a take-over bid for Fothergill and Harvey, a manufacturer of advanced materials such as carbon fibres. The UK market at that time was worth about £25m. p.a., but Courtaulds expected it to grow to £100m. They initially offered £28.2m. in cash for Fothergill and Harvey, which implied an exit P/E ratio of 16 on the 1985 profits of £2.74m.; subsequently Courtaulds agreed to pay £38.8m. which was accepted by the Fothergill shareholders.

Fothergill's headquarters were at Littleborough near Manchester, and they employed 900 people at a number of sites in the UK and one in USA. Its products were used in a wide range of equipment such as helicopters, jet engines, the nose cone of Concorde, and food factory conveyor belts. The company was divided into twelve companies, each with its own managing director with control over their own expenditures and responsibility for profits. Each of the twelve companies had a particular focus in the market place, but it was not clear how the organization had handled new opportunities which had arisen but had needed the expertise of more than one of the Fothergill companies.

Later in the same year Courtaulds expanded its interests in carbon fibre when it bought an 80 per cent stake in Hysol Grafil, the world's fourth-largest maker of carbon fibre. Further acquisitions followed, and in June 1987 Courtaulds bought a US manufacturer of very high quality performance films for £62m. ($US99m.) in cash, giving an exit P/E ratio of 20. This company had specialized in enhanced polyester film for building and vehicle windows, in order to control glare and heat. It was in a rapidly growing market and was the leader in the USA with sales growing at 18 per cent each year for the previous five years and expected sales of $US50m. for the next financial year. In 1987 this was followed by the purchase of Porter Paints, an American manufacturer of specialist protective coatings and architectural paints, whose sales had been growing at 10 per cent each year for the past four years. Porter's sales were $US105m. and profits were $US9.2m. in the last report; Courtaulds paid £83m. ($US140m.) for the company.

Porter employed 1,000 people in the USA and also owned a chain of 117 stores for professional decorators. Its products were seen as complementary to those of Courtaulds' paint division International Paint, which was the world leader in marine paints with 35 per cent of the world market. Following this purchase International Paints ranked tenth by volume in the world, with North America accounting for one-third of its sales, where it was the fifteenth largest manufacturer of paints, and then had an even world-wide spread throughout the three main markets of North America, Europe, and the rest of the world. International Paints had been maintaining growth in a generally static global paint market as a result of its technology, which had enabled it to increase its market share of marine coatings as other competitors dropped out of the market. This reflected the general trend in the world's paint industry, where there was increasing globalization of high-technology products for specific market sectors. A paint company which controlled the technology for a particular type of industrial coating could thus expect to dominate the market for it world-wide. This factor had led to a great deal of buying and selling of paint companies in the later 1980s, as companies built up their technological and geographical strengths, and disposed of weaknesses.

In 1988 Courtaulds bid for the balance of 43 per cent of the shares which it did not already own in Taubman, an Australian paint manufacturer. Taubman were specialists in protective coatings such as weather resistant paints, and were also the third-largest manufacturer of decorative paints in Australia. In their last financial year Taubman reported operating profits of $A4.9m. on sales of $A165m. and the Courtaulds offer to buy out the minority shareholding put a total value on Taubman of $A92m. The cost to Courtaulds of the minority shares was £18.9m.

In 1988 Courtaulds extended its textiles interests when it acquired Desseilles of France, a lace manufacturer, and Liberty Fabrics, which was one of the largest lace and elastomeric companies in the USA. These purchases cost Courtaulds more than £50m. but made it the biggest single force in the international lace market. The late 1980s had seen a wave of international acquisitions in the world textile industry, and the cause of this had been the increasing levels of automation. The changes in the lace industry exemplified that. For many years lace-making had been an industry dominated by small family firms operating only in their own country, using the same machines for many years, which were generally the Leavers system invented in the 1880s or the Raschel machines from the 1950s. Then the computer-controlled Jacquardtronic machine was introduced, which was faster and more flexible. But it was also much more expensive, so the cost of remaining competitive in lace-making became too high for smaller companies.

A further rationalization of Courtaulds' textile businesses came with the sale in 1989 of the original Samuel Courtaulds weaving business to

Toray of Japan. Toray had been exporting fine polyester fabrics to Europe for many years, but had become concerned that it would not remain competitive without establishing a presence near its customers in the European market.

DIVISIONAL ANALYSIS, 1989

Fibres division

Courtelle   Courtaulds was the world's largest manufacturer of producer-dyed acrylic fibre, with factories in the UK, France and Spain. Its main uses were in knitwear, handknitting, jersey, pile and fleece fabrics, domestic textiles and cotton-type spun yarns for clothing and furnishing fabrics. The acrylic industry in Europe suffered during the year from over-capacity due to a fashion swing and the loss of some large export markets, and increased competition forced prices down.

Viscose staple   A major producer with factories in the UK, Canada and the USA. Main uses were non-woven products for medical, hygiene, disposable and industrial applications, and cotton-type spun yarns for clothing and furnishings. The fashion swing which harmed acrylics helped viscose during 1989, and enabled margins to be improved despite increases in raw material prices. Courtaulds' market share increased in North America.

Acetate yarn   Courtaulds was the leading producer in Europe. All production was in the UK of Dicel and Tricel filament yarns, which was mainly used in dress fabrics, linings and lingerie. Courtaulds also owned 50 per cent of Noveceta, the larger of the two Italian acetate yarn producers.

Chemicals and materials division

Fine chemical intermediates   All production was in the UK, and products included flame-retardant and sulphur-based chemicals, water-soluble polymers and aliphatic esters, including pharmaceutical intermediate chemicals.

Non-woven products   Production was in the UK, and main uses were in the textile, medical and consumer industries. This unit was reorganized during the year, with existing products rationalized and the introduction of products using the new thermal bonding. As a consequence sales were lower than anticipated.

Acetate products   Production was in the UK, with 70 per cent of the output exported. The main products were filter tow, acetic anhydride, acetate flake, and acetate plastics. Main uses were in the chemical, fibre and tobacco industries. Although cigarette consumption in the developed world was declining, the market for filter tow was growing, especially for replacing untipped cigarettes in the newly-industrializing countries.

Advanced materials   Production was in the UK, France and the USA, and included carbon fibre, engineered products, and fibre-reinforced polymer fabrications. Main uses were in aerospace, defence and sports goods, and in general industrial markets. The market for carbon fibre continued to grow rapidly, leading to a shortage of capacity. The market for PTFE-coated fabrics remained static, and the remaining parts of Fothergill and Harvey were consolidated into Courtaulds, with a concentration of the composites business at Coventry.

Coatings division

Courtaulds was a major paint supplier, with operations in 34 countries world-wide. It had leading market positions in heavy-duty coatings for the marine, yacht and onshore steel and concrete markets; in industrial coatings for the metal packaging and coil markets; in powder coatings; and in architectural paints for the professional market. World-wide brands included International, Porter (US) and Taubmans (Australasia). Sales grew over the year by 33 per cent, and margins were improved also. This increase was due in part to the incorporation of Porter's figures for the first time. Powder coatings became the fastest-growing sector of the industrial paint market, being supplied mainly to large industrial customers for direct application to metal packaging.

Films and packaging division

OPP, plastic and speciality films   Courtaulds was a leading producer of co-extruded oriented polypropylene films (OPP) for the rapidly growing Western European market and USA, with factories in the UK and France. They also manufactured polyethylene stretch and shrink packaging. Courtaulds also had a 50 per cent shareholding in an Australian company. The total capacity of the unit was 60,000 tonnes. The market for these products continued to grow.

Cellophane   Courtaulds was the largest world producer of transparent cellulose packaging film, with factories in the UK and Canada, with extensive exports. The market for cellophane was declining, however, and Courtaulds reduced its capacity to 42,000 tonnes.

Performance films   The USA market leader in enhanced polyester film for solar control applications on windows of vehicles and residential and commercial buildings. Also specialized in dyed, coated and metallized films for high-technology industrial applications, with production units in the USA.

Flexible packaging Factories in the UK and eight other countries produced film printing, laminating, bag making and bag-in-box liquid packaging products for their domestic markets.

Rigid packaging and Amtico Collapsible tubes for toothpastes, pharmaceuticals and other products; closures and other mouldings for food, toiletries, pharmaceuticals and carbonated beverages; capsules for wines and spirits. Factories were in both the UK and USA. Amtico made luxury vinyl flooring in the UK for domestic and contract markets, including exports.

Textiles division

The year was a mixed one for the division, with pressure on margins especially in the clothing industry in the UK. The strength of sterling intensified pressures in European markets, as the dollar-related currencies of the Far East made further inroads.

Spinning Spun yarns for clothing fabrics, home furnishing fabrics, knitwear and various industrial end uses, manufactured on the cotton, worsted and woollen spinning systems from a variety of natural and man-made fibres in factories in the UK and France.

Linens Terry towels and towelling products, baby linens and bed linen. Major brands were Christy and Zorbit.

Furnishings Weaving and converting of a wide range of fabrics for curtaining and upholstery. Making up of curtains for the custom-made and ready-made retail markets.

Textile finishing Fabric printing, dyeing and finishing, and the converting of plain and printed fabrics for furnishings, bedding, fashion apparel and workwear.

Fabrics Manufacture of woven fabrics, stretch fabrics, jersey and warp knitted fabrics and lace. Woollen fabrics and specialized fabrics for both shirtings and the automotive industry. Design and converting of linens, silk and prints. Factories were located in the UK, France, Germany, Spain, USA, New Zealand and South Africa.

Contract clothing Clothing which carried retailer's brand names was sold to large chains, mail order and department stores. Major products were underwear, childrenswear, leisurewear and knitwear. Principal production was in the UK.

Clothing brands   Clothing brands included Lyle & Scott knitwear, Jockey and Y-Front underwear, Wolsey knitwear, underwear and socks, Glenalva schoolwear, Gossard and Berlei foundationwear, Aristoc hosiery, and sportswear brands of Dunlop and Slazenger under licence.

Retail   This comprised the Contessa retail chain and the McIlroy department and specialist stores.

Appendix 2 provides further information on the divisional performance and on geographical operations.

THE DEMERGER PROPOSAL

The proposal to demerge the textiles part of Courtaulds into a completely new company, to be called Courtaulds Textiles, which would account for 26 per cent of the operating profits and 20 per cent of the pre-tax profits was to be put for the approval of shareholders at a meeting in March 1990. At the time of the announcement Courtaulds also reported their half-year profits and sales for the six-month period ending 30 September 1989, which showed a fall in pre-tax profits to £85.6m.

Half-year results for the year ending September 1989 and comparative figures for previous half-years are shown in table 12.3.

The demerger proposal to be put forward for approval by the shareholders at the February 1990 meeting was that a new company should be floated on the Stock Exchange, to be called Courtaulds Textiles, and existing shareholders would be given one free share in this new company for each existing four ordinary shares, which they would retain, already held in Courtaulds plc. The existing shareholders would then own the two companies in proportion to their existing shareholding. The new Courtaulds Textiles plc would be listed on the International Stock Exchange in London from 19 March 1990. The performance of the ordinary share price in Courtaulds is shown in appendix 3.

The activities of the two new companies when formed would be as shown in table 12.4.

Sir Christopher Hogg would become chairman and chief executive of the 'new' Courtaulds plc, and also non-executive chairman of Courtaulds Textiles.

Information on UK textile companies, UK expenditure on textile-related products, UK output and income, UK consumer expenditure generally, and retail prices in the UK is included in appendix 4.

TABLE 12.3   **Courtaulds half-year results ending 30 September of each year**

£m.	1984	1985	1986	1987	1988	1989
Sales	1,038	1,051	1,096	1,159	1,270	1,360
Operating profit	59	62	84	99	100	86
Pre-tax profit	54	60	82	102	98	86
Divisional operating profit:						
Fibres	14	19	26	24	13	14
Woodpulp	11	6	10	14	25	–a
Paints/coatings	13	13	13	14	22	24
Chemicals	–	–	6	8	8	13
Packaging	5	4⎫	9	15	16	16
Plastics	2	1⎭				
Spinning	3	6⎫				
Fabrics	7	8⎬	24	28	21	23
Clothing	7	8⎭				
Miscellaneous	(3)	(3)	(4)	(4)	(5)	(4)

a The Woodpulp division was sold in summer 1989.

TABLE 12.4   **Activities of the two new companies and a restatement of the Courtaulds PLC financial figures between the two**

	'New' Courtaulds PLC	*Courtaulds Textiles PLC*
Activities:	Coatings Fibres Films Packaging Speciality materials	Spinning Fabrics Clothing
Sales	£1,743m.	£980m.
Operating profit	£142m.	£50m.
Employees	22,000	31,000

Appendix 1   Courtaulds financial information

PROFIT AND LOSS ACCOUNT, 1988 AND 1989

Year to 31 March	1988 £m.	1989 £m.
Sales	2,421.2	2,609.6
Cost of sales	(1,776.5)	(1,921.8)
Gross profit	644.7	687.8
Selling and distribution expenses	(244.9)	(286.0)
Administrative expenses	(183.4)	(207.8)
Operating profit	216.4	194.0
Share of profits of related companies	16.4	15.0
	232.8	209.0
Interest payable net of investment income	(12.2)	(11.9)
Profit on ordinary activities before tax	220.6	197.1
Tax	(50.9)	(49.3)
Profit after tax	169.7	147.8
Minority interests	(10.5)	(7.9)
	159.2	139.9
Extraordinary items	(15.8)	116.7
Profit attributable to Courtaulds PLC	143.4	256.6
Preference dividends	(0.1)	(0.1)
Profit attributable to ordinary shareholders	143.3	256.5
Ordinary dividends	(47.0)	(50.9)
Transferred to reserves	96.3	205.6
Earnings per ordinary share (pence)	40.9	35.7

BALANCE SHEETS, 1988 AND 1989

Year to 31 March	1988 £m.	1989 £m.
Fixed assets		
Tangible assets	579.7	594.5
Investments	32.0	34.9
	611.7	629.4
Current assets		
Stocks	420.5	434.6
Debtors	404.0	415.5
Cash and deposits	184.8	329.1
	1,009.3	1,179.2
Creditors (amount falling due within one year)		
Loans and overdrafts	(65.7)	(93.7)
Other	(596.2)	(651.1)
	(661.9)	(744.8)
Net current assets	347.4	434.4
Total assets less current liabilities	959.1	1,063.8
Creditors (amounts falling due after more than one year)		
Loans	(274.2)	(251.1)
Other	(22.2)	(25.8)
	(296.4)	(276.9)
Provisions for liabilities and charges	(23.6)	(23.5)
	639.1	763.4
Capital and reserves		
Called-up share capital	101.1	101.3
Share premium account	117.5	118.3
Profit and loss account	395.5	535.3
	614.1	759.9
Minority interests	25.0	8.5
	639.1	763.4

Source: Company Annual Reports 1989

SUMMARY OF FINANCIAL DATA, 1974–87

£m.	1974	1975	1976	1977	1978	1979	1980	1981	1982	1983	1984	1985	1986	1987
Net assets employed														
Fixed assets	354.2	419.0	478.0	514.5	487.5	442.4	428.3	362.5	342.9	337.6	339.6	372.0	422.7	495.5
Investments	16.7	20.5	14.5	15.4	15.5	13.3	19.0	20.0	20.1	25.4	27.6	28.9	30.4	29.2
Working capital	168.0	169.1	235.7	320.8	311.6	313.1	327.2	199.0	176.8	174.2	164.0	212.2	230.0	176.3
Net cash resources	149.8	148.8	75.0	12.5	42.8	42.6	33.6	85.9	127.7	128.0	187.6	190.9	182.4	217.6
Total	688.7	757.4	803.2	863.2	857.4	811.4	808.1	667.4	667.5	665.2	718.8	804.0	865.5	918.6
Financed as follows:														
Ordinary capital	67.6	67.6	68.3	68.3	68.3	68.3	68.3	68.3	68.3	68.3	94.8	94.8	94.8	96.8
Reserves	284.7	352.0	363.9	390.5	374.1	377.6	380.4	254.9	271.9	276.8	367.7	423.9	470.3	559.3
Attributable to ordinary shareholders	352.3	419.6	432.2	458.8	442.4	445.9	448.7	323.2	340.2	345.1	462.5	518.7	565.1	656.1
Preference capital	3.5	3.5	3.5	3.5	3.5	3.5	3.5	3.5	3.5	3.5	3.5	3.5	3.5	3.5
Minority interests	31.5	32.6	37.1	41.7	42.8	43.2	48.5	52.1	59.8	62.2	39.2	30.1	20.5	17.9
Deferred taxation	32.4	37.8	35.0	33.9	31.1	33.0	7.4	6.7	2.1	1.8	3.1	6.8	6.2	3.6
Loan capital	269.0	263.9	295.4	325.3	337.6	285.8	300.0	281.9	261.9	252.6	210.5	244.9	270.2	237.5

continued

continued

£m.	1974	1975	1976	1977	1978	1979	1980	1981	1982	1983	1984	1985	1986	1987
Total capital employed	688.7	757.4	803.2	863.2	857.4	811.4	808.1	667.4	667.5	665.2	718.8	804.0	865.5	918.6
Sales	957	1,134	1,166	1,510	1,576	1,662	1,819	1,710	1,789	1,906	2,038	2,152	2,173	2,262
Operating profit	117.6	119.3	56.3	102.7	75.5	82.9	88.3	29.8	69.6	81.3	129.6	138.9	154.5	213.6
Profit before tax	116.3	118.2	46.3	80.9	53.7	64.0	68.1	5.1	51.1	63.3	117.8	128.2	143.0	201.1
Taxation	26.9	29.3	15.2	19.9	16.9	20.2	20.3	12.1	21.4	21.4	28.4	28.1	26.3	46.6
Minority interests	5.3	6.4	6.9	7.8	6.5	7.2	8.9	9.5	10.8	10.4	11.8	9.3	3.0	9.2
Extraordinary items (credit in 1976)	–	–	(2.1)	5.1	4.9	3.7	2.4	97.6	1.0	28.2	19.7	15.4	9.5	11.4
Attributable Profit (1981 loss)	84.1	82.5	26.3	48.1	25.4	32.9	36.5	(114.1)	17.9	3.3	57.9	75.4	104.2	133.9
Ordinary dividends	13.9	15.1	16.6	18.3	20.7	23.1	23.4	2.7	8.2	8.9	15.8	19.0	24.7	36.6
Retained profit/(loss)	70.0	67.2	9.5	29.6	4.6	9.7	13.0	(116.9)	9.6	(5.7)	42.0	56.3	79.4	97.2
Earnings per share (*pence*)[a]	31.1	30.4	8.8	19.4	11.1	13.4	14.2	(6.1)	6.9	11.5	21.3	23.9	29.9	38.2
Dividends (*pence*) (gross) (net)	7.6	8.5	9.4	10.2	11.3	12.2	12.2	1.4	4.3	4.6	4.2	5.0	6.5	9.5

[a] Before extraordinary items

ANALYSIS OF ORDINARY SHAREHOLDINGS AT 31 MARCH 1988

Size of shareholding	Number of shareholders	Number of ordinary shares Million	Per cent
1–500	36,469	7.9	2
501–1,000	15,684	11.7	3
1,001–5,000	17,452	35.1	9
5,001–100,000	2,172	42.7	11
100,001–1,000,000	332	106.8	27
Over 1,000,000	68	186.4	48
Total	72,177	390.6	100

Appendix 2   Courtaulds PLC, divisional and geographical analysis

ANALYSIS OF OPERATIONS, 1987–9

£m.	Turnover			Operating profit			Capital employed		
	1987	1988	1989	1987	1988	1989	1987	1988	1989
Chemical and industrial products									
Fibres									
Courtelle	278	234	188						
Viscose staple	173	163	197						
Acetate yarn	58	57	61						
Total fibres	509	453	446	59	48	33	113	116	127
Woodpulp	118	103	–[a]	30	33	–[a]	71	79	–[a]
Chemicals and materials									
Fine chemicals	46	47	54						
Non-woven products	18	20	20						
Acetate products	104	146	154						
Advanced materials	–	68	64						
Total chemicals	168	281	292	16	19	20	80	106	110
Coatings	357	385	511	21	28	43	135	134	156
Films and packaging									
OPP	67	84	83						
Cellophane	92	87	78						
Performance films	–	19	35						
Flexible packaging	74	101	115						
Rigid packaging and Amtico	56	58	61						
Total films and packaging	289	333	361	20	30	27	107	133	144
Textiles products									
Spinning	198	205	156						
Linens	80 {	54	52						
Furnishings		29	29						
Finishing	43	23	21						
Fabrics	231	288	356						
Contract clothing	264	281	285						
Clothing brands	121	126	140						
Retail	39	29	34						
Textiles total	935	982	1,001	63	66	50	278	311	330

[a] The Woodpulp Division located in South Africa, was sold in 1988.
The totals do not always agree, due to intragroup sales.

ANALYSIS OF OPERATIONS, 1984-6

£m.	Turnover 1984	1985	1986	Operating profit 1984	1985	1986	Capital employed 1984	1985	1986
Chemical and industrial products									
Fibres	582	665	642	39	37	51	135	164	165
Woodpulp	104	88	77	22	21	14	55	73	73
International Paint	353	382	355	20	21	23	118	119	127
BCL	210	247	220	12	12	8	53	72	81
National Plastics	45	50	60	3	3	2	14	19	20
Textiles group									
Spinning	154	175	189	8	9	13	32	40	43
Fabrics:									
Finishing	–	15	41						
Apparel fabrics	–	135	106						
Home furnishings	–	50	69						
Industrial fabrics	–	41	27						
International fabrics	–	93	103						
Fabrics sub-total[a]	316	334	346	13	18	19	96	104	105
Clothing:									
Contract apparel	–	218	254						
Clothing brands	–	102	110						
Related activities[b]	–	53	54						
Clothing sub-total[a]	356	373	418	16	20	23	78	88	100
Textiles totals	826	882	953	37	47	55	206	232	248

[a] Totals do not always agree due to intragroup sales.
[b] Including retail and wholesale.

ANALYSIS OF OPERATIONS 1981-3

£m.	Turnover 1981	1982	1983	Operating profit 1981	1982	1983	Capital employed 1981	1982	1983
Chemical and industrial products									
Fibres									
Yarns }	695	701	750	1	25	35	246	223	233
Woodpulp									
International paint	268	336	357	22	26		83	104	
BCL	159	171	187	3	5		55	56	
National plastics	39	39	40	2	1		9	10	
Textiles group									
Fabrics	432	332	334	(7)	4	5	140	123	100
Consumer products	350	328	353	12	12	14	84	79	77

GEOGRAPHICAL BREAKDOWN BY MANUFACTURING LOCATION

Turnover (£m.)	1981	1982	1983	1984	1985	1986	1987	1988	1989
United Kingdom									
Home sales	842	816	870	917	929	979	990	1,098	1,077
Exports	414	382	374	433	442	384	430	479	494
UK total	1,256	1,198	1,244	1,350	1,371	1,363	1,420	1,577	1,571
Rest of Europe	192	217	255	262	329	405	440	413	405
North America	174	240	249	266	344	282	264	300	466
Africa	90	104	132	130	113	94	127	73	57
Rest of World	120	159	165	173	133	130	152	192	220
Miscellaneous[a]	(122)	(129)	(139)	(143)	(138)	(101)	(141)	(134)	(109)
	1,710	1,789	1,906	2,038	2,152	2,173	2,262	2,421	2,610

Operating/trading profit (£m.)									
United Kingdom	(7)	23	41	79	78	90	115	131	93
Rest of Europe	6	5	9	11	16	25	46	27	14
North America	8	11	(1)	9	13	9	5	14	35
Africa	15	21	25	22	21	13	30	32	31
Rest of world	12	16	13	13	13	15	15	21	27
Miscellaneous[a]	(4)	(6)	(6)	(6)	(7)	(3)	(7)	(9)	(6)
	30	70	81	128	134	149	204	216	194

Capital employed (£m.)									
United Kingdom	387	330	286	305	336	391	446	489	477
Rest of Europe	60	55	68	52	84	107	103	114	125
North America	44	70	80	88	113	100	84	121	176
Africa	63	57	70	67	84	81	80	82	7
Rest of world	39	51	52	52	40	44	48	47	57
Miscellaneous[a]	(18)	(19)	(18)	(25)	(29)	(20)	(17)	(1)	(19)
	575	544	538	539	628	703	744	852	823

[a] includes elimination of inter-territorial sales, etc.

Appendix 3   Courtaulds PLC

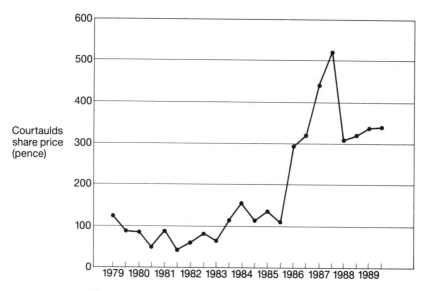

FIGURE 12.1   **Share price 1979 to 1989**

On 1 February 1990 the following information on share prices was available in the *Financial Times*:

	High	Low	Price	P/E
Courtaulds	402	263	386	11.0

On the same day, price:earnings ratios were shown in the *Financial Times* for the following sectors:

	P/E
ALL CONSUMER GROUP	11.06
of which Textiles	10.96
OTHER GROUPS	10.95
of which Chemicals	9.34
Conglomerates	10.53
ALL INDUSTRIALS	11.71

Appendix 4   UK textile companies

PROFILE OF TEN LEADING UK TEXTILE COMPANIES, 1987

	Coats Viyella	Courtaulds	Tootal	Dawson	Crowther	Baird	Readicut	Corah	S. R. Gent	Illingworth Morris
Textiles %										
Fibres	–	34.7	–	7.8	–	–	16.0	–	–	28.9
Yarns										
Thread	19.5	–	41.2	–	–	–	–	–	–	–
H/Knit	17.3	–	–	8.7	–	–	5.3	–	–	–
Other	3.7	11.6	–	19.5	–	–	–	–	–	18.1
Sub-total	40.5	11.6	41.2	28.1	–	–	5.3	–	–	18.1
Fabrics	11.1	19.1	27.6	8.4	6.7	9.8	–	–	–	42.2
Clothing										
Knitted	7.9	6.5	–	29.9	5.3	–	–	21.3	–	2.4
Other	16.2	19.9	25.1	15.9	13.3	90.2	–	67.0	100.0	4.8
Sub-total	24.0	26.4	25.1	45.8	18.7	90.2	–	88.3	100.0	7.2

House/Text										
Carpets	6.3	–	–	–	34.2	–	55.7	–	–	–
Other	10.2	5.5	6.0	9.9	–	–	16.8	5.3	–	–
Sub-total	16.4	5.5	6.0	9.9	34.2	–	72.5	5.3	–	–
Retail	7.9	2.7	–	–	40.4	–	6.1	6.4	–	3.6
TOTAL	100.0	100.0	100.0	100.0	100.0	100.0	100.0	100.0	100.0	100.0
TOTAL VALUE (£m.)	1,643	1,460	398	334	225	164	131	94	84	83
Foreign sales[a] %	41.8	38.4	45.1	40.0	0	6.0	17.7	5.3	7.1	0
Non-textile value (£m.)	107	802	10	0	0	88	16	0	0	5
Share %	6.1	35.5	2.5	–	–	34.9	10.9	–	–	5.7
TOTAL SALES	1,750	2,262	408	334	225	252	147	94	84	88

[a] Sales of foreign subsidiaries, excluding exports from UK.
Source: Barclays de Zoete Wedd Research, September 1987

UK TEXTILE INDUSTRY STATISTICS, 1987

	Output £m.	Year	Index of production Textiles	Clothing
Wool textiles	1,566	1980	100	100
Man-made fibres	969	1981	92	94
Knitting	1,835	1982	89	93
Home textiles	973	1983	92	98
Cotton textiles	1,120	1984	94	102
Finishing	619	1985	98	105
Clothing	4,564	1986	100	108
Carpets	1,071	1987	101	110
Total	13,637			

CONSUMER INCOME AND EXPENDITURES 1977–87 (£m.)

	Personal disposable income	Consumer expenditure				
		All	All	On Clothing	On carpets and floor coverings	On textiles and soft furnishings
	Current prices	Current prices	1985 prices	1985 prices	1985 prices	1985 prices
1977	96,557	86,887	176,016	8,244	1,222	1,346
1978	113,124	100,219	185,950	8,988	1,320	1,372
1979	135,721	118,652	193,794	9,644	1,417	1,323
1980	160,009	137,896	193,806	9,608	1,270	1,256
1981	176,084	153,566	193,832	9,593	1,234	1,256
1982	191,081	168,545	195,561	9,868	1,224	1,266
1983	205,955	184,619	204,318	10,545	1,310	1,326
1984	220,764	197,494	207,927	11,202	1,334	1,321
1985	237,802	217,023	215,267	12,298	1,409	1,513
1986	259,333	239,156	229,105	13,368	1,403	1,562
1987	278,996	261,698	241,382	14,425	1,479	1,781
1988	307,170	293,569	257,918	15,275	1,631	2,050

Source: Annual Abstract 1990, tables 14.2 and 14.9

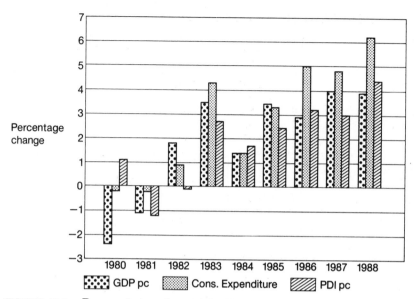

FIGURE 12.2 **Percentage change in income, product and spending per capita (1985 prices)**

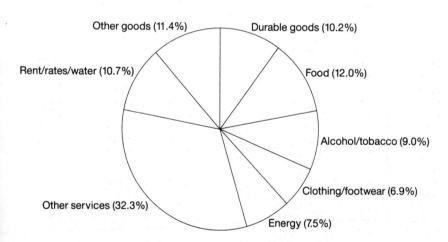

FIGURE 12.3 **Share of consumer expenditure in 1989**

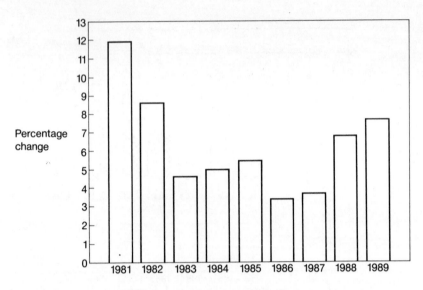

FIGURE 12.4 **RPI percentage change 1981–9**

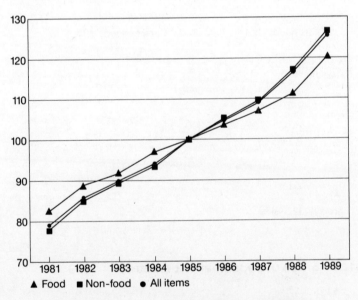

FIGURE 12.5 **General index of prices (1985 = 100)**

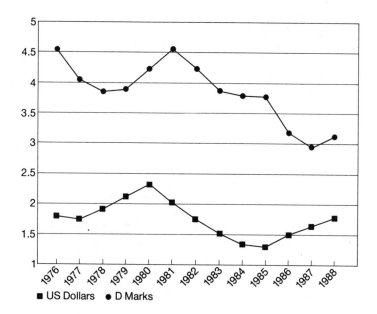

FIGURE 12.6 **Sterling exchange rate 1976–89, £1 = foreign currency equivalent**

13   The DAF–Leyland Merger

BACKGROUND

In 1987 when DAF, the Netherlands-based vehicle manufacturer, took over British Leyland's truck and van operations, the merger appeared to be one of some risk. DAF was a smaller company in an industry where even the main contenders were experiencing their share of problems. The company was a relatively new entrant to the commercial vehicle industry, having come in not long after the Second World War.

During the 1980s the company gradually gained market share, but before the merger with Leyland it remained essentially a second division producer, and was almost totally dependent on the heavy truck sector of 16 tonnes and above.

In 1986 Leyland truck operations were losing more than £1m. a week, and the British government decided they should be disposed of as part of the ending of state involvement in Rover Group. With the loss of old overseas markets, and lacking a continental European sales network, Leyland had become over-dependent on its UK home market. Its debt burden was largely removed to facilitate the DAF take-over. In return for the assets of the Leyland truck and Freight Rover van operations, Rover acquired a 40 per cent equity stake in the Dutch group.

EARLY RESULTS OF THE MERGER

The take-over was completed just as the European commercial vehicle market was moving into high gear, and the Leyland operations became profitable. In May 1989, Aart van der Padt, chairman of the DAF management board, stated that the performance of the British operations had exceeded their most optimistic hopes. The company had beaten its targets in terms of production, sales and productivity.

The merger launched DAF into the European first division, and it had other, just as important, advantages. For example, it had expanded its product range into light trucks – by now Leyland's main area of strength – and vans. Also, it had acquired cheap unused capacity at the Leyland truck plant in Lancashire (its own plants in the Netherlands and Belgium were working close to capacity). Last, but by no means least, DAF had gained a new home market in the UK – Europe's largest single truck market – where Leyland DAF competed with Iveco Ford for overall market leadership and where it led the heavy truck sector.

From its 1986 output of 15,600 vehicles, DAF increased production to 55,767 vehicles in 1988, including 15,678 trucks from the Leyland plant and 20,508 vans from the former Freight Rover operation in Birmingham (renamed Leyland DAF vans). Group turnover climbed from F12.34bn (£653m.) in 1986 to F15.2bn in 1988, while net profit climbed to F1,147.1m. from F133.8m. in 1986.

Integration

The Dutch management team moved with speed to integrate the UK operations into the rest of the group. Mr van der Padt claimed that by the start of 1989, DAF had accomplished one of its first aims, that of implementing a completely integrated organization, from sales and marketing, to R&D, engineering, and manufacturing.

At the same time it pursued the aim of harmonizing the previously separate DAF and Leyland ranges, to eliminate overlaps. The group also aimed to have one integrated product line by 1992. Light and medium trucks up to and including 16 tonnes GVW would be produced at the Leyland assembly plant in the UK, while heavy truck production would be concentrated solely in the Netherlands and Belgium. In the UK, Birmingham was to be the sole source for vans. The Leyland plant in particular was crucial to DAF's expansion, since the heavy truck plants in the Netherlands and Belgium were at full capacity. The rate of output at Leyland had been raised three times in two years, and with an annualized production rate of 16,000 trucks it was producing at twice pre-merger level.

Output and capacity

Through the DAF sales network the merger had opened up the Continent to Leyland's highly competitive Roadrunner light truck range, as well as to the old Freight Rover Sherpa van range. While Leyland truck output rose from 9,144 in 1986 to 15,678 in 1988, exports of the Roadrunner truck range jumped from 114 in 1986 to 1,612 in 1988. A similar pattern was achieved at the Birmingham van plant, with output rising to 20,508 from 18,656, while exports jumped to 2,639 from only 854.

DAF's capacity constraints on the Continent forced it to speed up the transfer of production from Eindhoven in the Netherlands and Westerlo in Belgium to Leyland. It started in late 1988 with the transfer of its 1900 series right-hand drive models from Eindhoven to Leyland, representing an additional output to the UK of 1,000 trucks a year. The second stage began in August 1989 with the gradual transfer over a few months of both right- and left-hand drive 1700 and 1900 models, adding a further output of 2,300 trucks a year.

The transfer of output to Leyland pushed the plant close to single-shift capacity, and a move to double-shift working appeared inevitable, particularly if DAF were successful in its bid for a lucrative military truck contract from the UK Ministry of Defence. It faced stiff competition for the contract, however, from Volvo and from AWD, the privately-owned truckmaker formed from the remains of GM's Beford operation.

Productivity and quality

Revitalized by the merger, Leyland productivity had improved from eight trucks a year per employee to nearly 14. As a result of a two-year quality improvement programme, the average number of defects needing to be rectified as a vehicle came off the assembly line had been reduced from 28 to 10 in two years. The proportion of vehicles coming off the assembly line 'right first time' had risen to 90 per cent of the total from 40 per cent at the beginning of 1987, and the warranty bill had been reduced by around £1m., or 10 per cent, despite the doubling in production. The quality programme had been instituted in 1986 before the merger, and was subsequently considered as a model for the whole of the DAF group.

Product development

One of the biggest challenges facing DAF as a result of the merger was the development of a new van range and the modernization of the Birmingham plant to replace the more than 18-year-old Sherpa van. DAF committed itself to an investment programme of around £150m. over five years in the UK, of which more than two-thirds was accounted for by the van project.

DAF's presence in the European van market was dwarfed by rivals such as Ford with the all-conquering Ford Transit, Volkswagen with its Transporter, and the combined forces of the Fiat/Peugeot Sevel joint venture (Fiat Ducato, Peugeot J5, Citroën C25 and Talbot Express), as well as the Renault Trafic. DAF would have to double production to around 40,000 units a year when the new van was launched in the first half of the 1990s, a daunting task as its much bigger competitors had announced ambitious expansion plans, and Japanese groups were increasingly forcing their way into the sector.

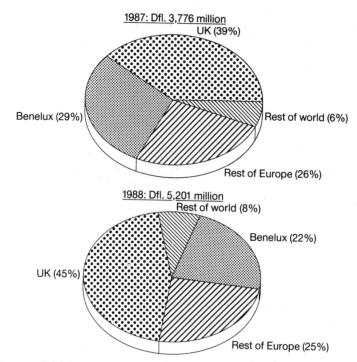

FIGURE 13.1   **DAF's geographical distribution of turnover**

Source: Company report, 1989

Market positioning

From 1987 to 1988 DAF's turnover had risen by nearly 38 per cent, mainly due to the merger. In terms of geographical distribution, the United Kingdom accounted for some 45 per cent, and the rest of Europe (including the Benelux countries) slightly more, at 47 per cent (see figure 13. 1).

Across Europe, DAF had raised its market share for trucks above 9 tonnes (GVW) from some 5 per cent at the beginning of the decade to 10.9 per cent in 1988. It was one of the 'big five' truckmakers in the market above 3.5 tonnes, claiming some 9.4 per cent of the market and edging into fourth place ahead of Volvo. Ahead of DAF were the French state-owned Renault Vehicles Industriels (11.4 per cent), Iveco of Italy (20.6 per cent) and Daimler-Benz of West Germany (23.7 per cent).

Despite the fruits of the merger, DAF was most heavily represented in the heavy-truck segment (16 tonnes and above), with a share of 11.6 per cent. Here, six producers jostled for position, with shares varying between the 13.7 per cent of Volvo and the 8.1 per cent of MAN of West Germany, all trailing Daimler-Benz's 19.1 per cent. However, Daimler-Benz, the world's biggest truckmaker, had begun to look fallible in recent years. Its financial performance had proved disappointing, and its share had fallen from 26.1 per cent in 1986 (trucks above 3.5 tonnes) to 23.7 per cent in 1988.

At the same time Iveco had gained from its merger with the Ford truck operation, increasing its share to 20.5 per cent in 1988 from 18.9 per cent in 1986. RVI had taken its share to 11.4 per cent from 10.6 per cent, and DAF had surged to 9.4 per cent from 5.3 per cent, propelled by the Leyland merger.

THE MARKET

Since the beginning of the 1970s, Europe's commercial vehicles industry had shown sustained if unspectacular growth of close to 1 per cent a year. But in the two decades to 1989 there had been two exaggerated cycles.

From the 1979 peak of sales of 422,000 vehicles (of 3.5 tonnes and above gross vehicle weight – GVW), production plunged under the weight of a European depression and a collapse in demand from Middle East markets. The bottom was reached in 1984, when sales totalled only 333,000. It took until 1987 for demand to rise above the earlier 1979 peak; in 1988 sales were 485,000.

There had been notable casualties along the way. Both General Motors (Bedford) and Ford of the US gave up the struggle in heavy trucks in Europe. GM withdrew completely and Ford ceded management control of its UK-based operations to Iveco, the commercial vehicles subsidiary of Fiat of Italy.

Light trucks and vans

Many of DAF's competitors in the light commercial vehicle market were also strongly positioned in the light truck and panel van markets, where DAF had little presence. This market sector – small vans up to 2 tonnes, medium vans between 2 and 3.5 tonnes – had considerable Japanese market penetration, of between 10 and 12 per cent in 1987. The European leader in this small sector was Ford, with its Transit. However, there also existed another sub-market within this light commercial sector, namely car-derived vans, with companies like Renault being major players.

On the product side, European van and light commercial vehicles production was seen as falling slightly during the last two years of the 1980s, but likely to pick up in the early part of the 1990s. On the demand side, the UK was likely to enjoy the highest growth in demand, with Germany, France and Italy showing little growth.

TABLE 13.1   **European light vehicle (2 to 3.5 tonnes) production, 1986–7**

Model	Manufacturer	No of vehicles produced	
		1986	*1987*
Transit	Ford	105,980	130,266
Type-2	VW	122,325	114,363
Ducato	Sevel	90,254	103,962
Trafic	Renault	52,753	58,741
Bremen	Mercedes	48,520	45,808
Daily	Iveco	32,366	36,138
LT	VW	18,463	20,821
Sherpa	F-Rover	18,364	19,851
Master/B70	Renault	16,090	18,310
Tradevan	Ebro	12,117	15,018
J9	Peugeot	13,082	14,174
MB90–MB180	Mercedes	8,047	11,061
Midi/CF	Bedford	10,920	8,261
C35	Citroën	5,338	6,571
J4	Enasa	3,269	2,467

Source: Automotive Industry Statistics

A prevailing feature of the light commercial sector was the degree of restructuring that was taking place, as manufacturers attempted to rationalize in order to win sales in a highly competitive market. DAF's merger with Leyland gave the company a presence in the light van sector. DAF Leyland made 20,508 vans in 1988, out of production forecast for the European van market of some 610,000 units. While DAF Leyland enjoyed a comfortable market share in the UK, its European-wide market share was relatively small, 3.3 per cent (see table 13.1).

Another feature of this restructuring was the part that Japanese car makers played. Key Japanese car makers signed venture deals with European companies to make Japanese vehicles under licence in the EC. Other strategies employed included the take-over of the van and light commercial vehicle interests from European car makers, who wished to exit from this market sector. Examples of this were Isuzu and Suzuki-derived van designs that replaced the Bedford marque of GM in the UK; the Mitsubishi light vans in Daimler-Benz's Spanish subsidiary; Toyota's joint venture agreement with VW to build a small Japanese-designed van; and Nissan, who had an 80 per cent stake in the Spanish Company Iberica, expanding the European production of its Ebro Tradevan to compete more fully with its Japanese rivals in the

European market. Japanese production in Europe was estimated to grow to over 100,000 units by the end of the decade.

THE FUTURE FOR DAF

While its rivals continued to diversify, DAF determined to invest further in its core business. Its name had repeatedly been linked with the possible acquisitions of Enasa, the Spanish state-owned truck-maker (the two already had a joint venture in truck cabs) and of Steyr, the Austrian truckmaker. Mr van der Padt acknowledged that discussions had taken place, stating simply, 'We are a dedicated truckmaker', implying that DAF would be a European commercial vehicles maker without having to invest at the same time in wash-ing machines (Daimler-Benz), fighter aircraft (Saab-Scania), pickled herring and tomato ketchup (Volvo) or volume cars (Fiat).

In 1989 the objectives of the company were stated as:

- To supply commercial vehicles, bus chassis, components and associated services of high quality at competitive costs to our customers.
- To satisfy the needs of all those with interests in the company: shareholders, employees, dealers, importers and suppliers.

Thus through DAF, stakeholders could take comfort from an uncomplicated investment in the European truck industry, although they might not necessarily draw comfort from the probable imminent maturing of the market. According to Giorgio Garuzzo, chief execu-tive of Iveco, 'It is almost impossible to predict how the market will develop in the short and medium term, even though we are certain that the long-term trend is upwards.'[1]

DAF Leyland fully expected to increase its market share in the wider European market, capitalizing upon its strength in the large truck market, where it had a market share of 9.4 per cent.

Like many other manufacturing sectors, the automobile sector (including trucks and vans), was undergoing dramatic change in the late 1980s. The competitive environment could be summarized as follows:

- increasing globalization;
- over-capacity world-wide;
- a need to be able to make profits from shorter production runs at lower volumes, in order to satisfy more varied tastes;
- massive R&D requirements;
- a search for critical mass and scale.

A recent study by Whipp, Rosenfield and Pettigrew[2] looked at barriers to entry and barriers to success in a case study on the European vehicle industry:

Barriers to entry	Barriers to success
• Competitors on price • Minimum scale of efficient manufacturing plants • Logistics – distribution networks • Universal quality standards • Engineering – R&D tooling etc.	• Application of technology to manufacturing process • Flexibility – of marketing and in changes in technology • Economics of scope and scale • Range of external links and cross-mutuality

Source: adapted from Whipp, Rosenfield and Pettigrew (1989)

They also saw that the key environmental factors that would affect the industry, making for a turbulent environment, were EC harmonization of markets in 1992, increasing deregulation, and the quickening pace of IT take-up in manufacturing industry that would force up scale and increase globalization. These would mean more restructuring, leading to a smaller but more competitive industry.

Appendix 1   DAF

SUMMARY RESULTS

(Dflm.)	1987	1988
Turnover and results		
Turnover	3,776	5,201
Operating profit	106.3	193.1
Profit on ordinary activities before taxation	55.3	154.1
Profit on ordinary activities after taxation	49.6	131.0
Net profit	63.1	147.1
Per share		
Net profit (in guilders)	2.22	5.17
Profit retained (in guilders)	2.22	5.17
Financing		
Net capital employed	1,871.8	2,075.5
Total assets	3,160.8	3,489.1
Group capital and reserves	1,000.3	1,196.9
Cash flow	186.5	299.1
Capital expenditure	209.5	202.9
Workforce		
Number of employees at year-end	16,631	16,491
Wages, salaries and social security	842.3	963.1

CONSOLIDATED PROFIT AND LOSS ACCOUNT

(Dfl 000)	1987[a]	1988
Turnover	3,776,331	5,201,032
Cost of sales	(3,073,257)	(4,233,804)
Gross profit	703,074	967,228
Distribution expenses	(535,452)	(684,857)
General administrative expenses	(77,412)	(94,543)
Other operating income	16,079	5,301
Operating profit	106,289	193,129
Interest payable, net	(50,960)	(39,078)
Profit on ordinary activities before taxation	55,329	154,051
Taxation	(5,766)	(23,041)
Profit on ordinary activities after taxation	49,563	131,010
Profits of non-consolidated companies	15,511	18,154
Group profit after taxation	65,074	149,164
Minority interests	(1,968)	(2,041)
Net profit	63,106	147,123
Earnings per share, per value Dfl 5 (in guilders)	2.22	5.17

[a] The 1987 figures include the full year's results of Van Doorne's Bedrijfswagenfabriek DAF BV and the results of Leyland DAF Ltd for the period since the date of its acquisition.

CONSOLIDATED BALANCE SHEET

(Dfl 000)	1987	1988
Fixed assets		
Tangible assets	1,000,406	1,056,240
Investments	237,364	279,894
	1,237,770	1,336,134
Current assets		
Stocks	1,128,038	1,153,516
Debtors	577,142	670,475
Cash at bank and in hand	217,867	328,971
	1,923,047	2,152,962
Creditors – due within one year	1,289,060	1,413,615
Net current assets	633,987	739,347
Total assets less current liabilities	1,871,757	2,075,481
Creditors – due after one year	676,054	678,266
Provisions for liabilities and charges	195,429	200,273
Group capital and reserves	1,000,274	1,196,942
Minority interests	27,660	27,874
Capital and reserves	972,614	1,169,068

FIVE-YEAR HISTORY

(Dflm.)	1984	1985	1986	1987	1988
Balance sheet					
Fixed assets					
Tangible assets	603	619	655	1,000	1,056
Investments	97	156	155	237	280
	700	775	820	1,237	1,336
Current assets					
Stocks	699	728	734	1,128	1,154
Debtors	373	331	290	577	670
Cash at bank and in hand	56	80	101	218	329
	1,128	1,139	1,125	1,923	2,153
Creditors	696	636	706	1,289	1,414
Net current assets	432	503	419	634	739
Total assets less current liabilities	1,132	1,278	1,239	1,871	2,075
Creditors – due after one year	527	637	596	676	678
Provisions	158	174	165	195	200
Group capital and reserves	447	467	478	1,000	1,197
Minority interests	28	28	27	27	28
Capital and reserves	419	439	451	973	1,169

(Dflm.)	1984	1985	1986	1987	1988
Profit and loss account					
Turnover	1,964	2,202	2,337	3,776	5,201
Cost of sales	(1,522)	(1,694)	(1,810)	(3,073)	(4,234)
Gross profit	442	508	527	703	967
Distribution expenses	(336)	(389)	(398)	(536)	(685)
General administrative expenses	(46)	(47)	(51)	(77)	(94)
Other operating income	6	8	13	16	5
	(376)	(428)	(436)	(597)	(774)
Operating profit	66	80	91	106	193
Interest payable, net	(70)	(66)	(60)	(51)	(39)
Profit before taxation	(4)	14	31	55	154
Taxation	6	(1)	(7)	(6)	(23)
Profit after taxation	2	13	24	49	131
Profit of non-consolidated companies	10	10	12	16	18
Group profit	12	23	36	65	149
Minority interests	(2)	(3)	(2)	(2)	(2)
Net profit	10	20	34	63	147
Profit retained	10	20	34	63	147

Appendix 2   Organization chart

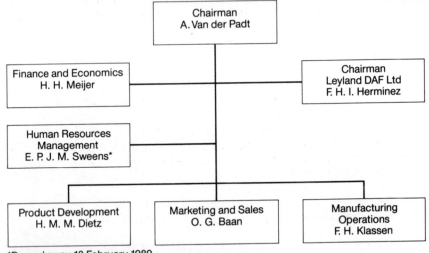

*Passed away 18 February 1989

FIGURE 13.2 **Composition and functions of the board of management since 1 January 1989**

Appendix 3

EXTRACTS FROM THE DAF ANNUAL REPORT, 1988–9

The industrial climate in the main countries of Europe during 1988 was good and helped to further stimulate the road transport industry, DAF's market-place.

This is important, since the years leading up to 1992 will see the competition between European truck makers intensify as the market restructures to meet the challenges of unrestricted trading.

DAF's experience, gained over many years, and broad presence in the European market, provides a sound base from which to meet the challenges of the nineties.

Our commercial vehicle technology and profound knowledge of the transport market further strengthen our position and enable us to ensure continuing successful development.

For DAF, 1988 was a year of progress. It was the first full year when the company could harvest the synergy of the merger which in 1987 brought together DAF Trucks with Leyland Trucks and Freight

Rover. The merger has enhanced many aspects of DAF's operations and has brought significantly higher output and profits.

DAF can expand output still further in the future without major additional investment in manufacturing facilities, thus making the best possible use of facilities and servicing customer requirements even more efficiently.

Production of trucks and vans in Eindhoven, Leyland and Birmingham was at a record level in 1988, totalling 55,767 vehicles. In the market-place, 1988 was a year of real achievement and DAF's share of the market for commercial vehicles of 3.5 tonnes and over in Europe has increased to 9.4 per cent. This was at a time when this market increased by 9.4 per cent.

Considerable efforts will be needed to further improve this position in the future, but it is a sure illustration of the attractiveness of DAF's model programme, the effectiveness of the company's Marketing and Sales organization and the strength of the DAF and Leyland DAF marques in their respective markets.

The 95 series, DAF's top-of-the-range model, voted 1988 Truck of the Year, is an outstanding success with orders in its first year far exceeding expectations.

DAF's Continental dealer network, well proven in trucks, is fully prepared to increase sales of the van and light truck product ranges throughout Europe. This is a gradual process and the results should become steadily more evident. In 1988 the Board of Management announced a substantial investment programme which will be necessary to renew the van changes in the 1990s.

One of the consequences of DAF's success in the market-place has meant that plans to reallocate some production have been brought forward. A first sign of this has been the successful transfer of the DAF 1900 Series right-hand drive models from Eindenhoven to the Leyland DAF Assembly Plant in the United Kingdom.

A direct result of all these achievements, including those of DAF Finance and DAF Special Products which both had a successful year, has been a major step forward in profit performance. The good financial results recorded by DAF provide a healthy basis to pursue a strategy for growth.

This is a strategy which entails the constant improvement and renewal of the model programme, the continual modernization and re-equipment of manufacturing facilities, and the provision of sophisticated and dynamic engineering and marketing techniques.

DAF is committed to the highest standards of quality in all of its products, services and processes. Programmes to further enhance quality throughout the organization are now being actively pursued.

The achievements made by DAF in the period since the merger have been recognized by two important awards.

In the Netherlands DAF received the King William I Award for

Dutch Entrepreneurship. And in the United Kingdom, the Netherlands British Chamber of Commerce granted Leyland DAF the Anglo-Dutch Award for Enterprise.

Mutually rewarding collaborative ventures, whether in manufacturing, development, marketing or sourcing, remain an objective of DAF's forward strategy and much effort will continue to be devoted to pursuing such opportunities.

The decision to seek a listing for DAF on the Stock Exchange of Amsterdam and London was confirmed early in 1989; it is intended that existing shareholders will release approximately 60 per cent of their shares for this purpose. A limited increase in the share capital is also being considered. Subject to market conditions, applications for the listings will be made in May 1989.

The Board of Management lost one of its respected members with the death on 18 February of Frank Sweens. He played an important role in the progress of the company since joining the Board in 1977 with responsibilities for Human Resources.

The Board of Management would particularly like to thank George Simpson, who resigned as a Member of the Board of Management at the end of 1988, for his contribution to making the merger a success. The Board of Management is delighted that his expertise will continue to be available to DAF since he is now a member of the Supervisory Board.

Exploiting the potential of the merged DAF corporation has put considerable strain on employees at all levels. However, there has been a superb response to the challenges which have been presented and I wish to record my sincere admiration of the efforts made.

A Van der Padt
Chairman of the Board of Management

Notes

1 Company Report, 1987
2 Whipp, Rosenfield and Pettigrew (1989): 'Managing Strategic Change via Mature Businesses', *Long Range Planning*, Vol 22, No 6, pp. 92–9

14 TI Group 1979–89

OVERVIEW OF TI GROUP

TI Group, then known as Tube Investments, was founded in 1919 as a holding company for a number of Midlands-based steel-tube companies. After the war it grew rapidly by organic growth and acquisition. Its managerial structure was characterized by minimal bureaucracy and a high degree of decentralization. During the 1960s the increasing complexity of the group led to the adoption of a sizeable divisional management structure.

By 1979 the group was producing a wide variety of capital, consumer and semi-finished goods, with manufacturing and marketing subsidiaries in over 30 countries across the world. The group's operating activities were in five main market sectors: steel tube and steel, aluminium, specialized engineering products, domestic appliances, and cycles and toys.

There then followed a period of rapid decline and restructuring, so that by the summer of 1989, the operations of TI had changed radically: it now operates in only two of its former markets. Its main businesses today are specialized engineering (mainly comprising mechanical seals, thermal technology and aerospace components), specialized tube, and automotive components, of which much has been divested.

1979–82

The year 1979 was one of great disappointment for TI, marring its record of annual yearly increases in profits. All major business areas, with the exception of domestic appliances, experienced a fall in profits. The task of manufacturing was made more difficult than ever by the combination of a reduction in international economic growth,

accelerating inflation, higher interest rates, and the high value of sterling supported by North Sea oil. These difficulties were compounded
by the engineering industry being more affected by industrial labour
disruption than at any time since the General Strike.

Although no part of TI was directly involved in the road haulage
workers' strike, it caused serious disruption to the flow of materials
into its factories and of finished products out of its warehouses. In the
second half of the year the national negotiation between the Engineering Employers Federation and the Confederation of Shipbuilding and
Engineering Unions (CSEU) broke down and led to a prolonged
dispute.

Statement by the chairman, Sir Brian Kellet, Annual Report 1979

As to the general economic background, manufacturing industry – especially that part of TI which seeks to export its goods
or is subject to competition from imports – has been put under
severe pressure by the sequence of events over the past few
years.

Attempts to fulfil expectations for a national standard of living
and quality of social services beyond that which our productivity
has earned have fuelled inflation. That inflation, which is itself
the first enemy of living standards, poses a more serious threat to
the cash flow of businesses. The fight to get inflation under
control has also taken interest rates to progressively higher levels.
North Sea oil has protected national living standards but has
given us a stronger exchange rate than our industrial productivity
would have supported. This adds up to a combination of
circumstances that has put manufacturing industry in the front
line of a battle for survival against interest rates higher than
those of our overseas competitors and an exchange rate which
has reduced our export margins and increased import competitiveness more than has been compensated by savings in import
costs of raw materials.

In 1980, many UK manufacturers were subjected to fierce import
competition, and although wage settlements moved down sharply in
the private manufacturing sector, they continued at much higher levels
in some other sectors, notably in large parts of the public sector where
they were passed on to captive customers through the exercise of
monopoly power. As a major supplier of consumer products and of
intermediate and capital goods to industrial customers, as well as one
of the country's largest employers, TI felt the full force of a squeeze
between rising costs and fiercely competitive prices. Over the two
years to 31 December 1980, it is estimated the combination of relative
inflation and exchange rate movements caused a 30 per cent deterioration in UK competitiveness.

Following the steel strikes there was a sharp decline in consumer spending. The effects on manufacturers were amplified by the distribution and retail trades curbing their purchases severely to avoid overstocking at a time of cash pressures.

The recession was so severe that much of UK industry switched to short-time working, and through the closing months of 1980, TI had 12,000 employees working less than a full week. TI began to introduce overhead and other cost savings in all parts of the group: there were a number of factory closures and about 12,000 redundancies.

Progressive improvements in efficiency and productivity were swamped by the speed and the extent to which market conditions had moved against TI. Among the questions the board had to consider were:

> How much of current volume reduction is due to recession and how much to lack of competitiveness? What is the probable long run level of exchange rates? What is the cost gap between us and our international competitors at those employee rates? How far and how fast can we close that gap by our continual efforts for improved productivity and efficiency?

By 1982, world demand for primary aluminium had fallen in each of the last three years, and was now only about 70 per cent of world capacity. On 29 November, TI's involvement in aluminium smelting came to an end after Alcan's offer to acquire British Aluminium was accepted. The previous year TI had sold its share of Round Oak Steel to British Steel.

Statement by the chairman, Sir Brian Kellet, Annual Report 1982

> What has happened in the world aluminium industry has demonstrated the vulnerability of businesses with products which, apart from price, are undifferentiated between suppliers. The vulnerability of such businesses in times of recession is increased when there is international trade in the product, when prices are affected by exchange rates related to factors other than comparative industrial costs and when there are wide variations in the degree of obligation of different producers to earn profits. Steel and aluminium have been two industries greatly exposed in these ways, from both of which TI has now disengaged.
>
> In contrast, there is in consumer products the greatest scope to compete for customer appeal through product design and performance.
>
> As a product we believe the bicycle has at least equal potential to that of domestic appliances. It is a growth market and design and performance factors are increasingly distinguishing between competitive products in the eye of purchasers. We are in the

throes of a formidable task in reorienting our cycle business to
concentrate on this kind of market and to disengage from former
excessive involvement in supply of commodity-type bicycles to
underdeveloped countries.

1983–JULY 1986

Review of the early 1980s by the chairman, Sir Brian Kellet, Annual Report, 1983

The major problem of mix of its businesses which TI faced some
years ago, namely excessive commitment to primary commodity products, has now largely been dealt with. The latest
arrangements reducing the Group's stake in carbon steel tube
making have increased the emphasis on consumer products and
specialized engineering.

Over the last four years TI has had to bear very large costs for
redundancies and closures. It was only possible to fund this and
maintain a reasonable level of capital expenditure by major
improvements in working capital ratios.

In the 1984 annual statement, the board and its new chairman, Mr
R. Uttiger, promised to take action on the loss-making businesses. The
four loss-makers were Raleigh, Cold Drawn Tubes, Machine Tools
and the Gas Cylinders plant in the USA. They took up rather more
than a half of the group's capital employed, with Raleigh accounting
for a fifth. The board decided that, unless convincing evidence was
produced that profitability could be achieved within a limited period
set by the board, other action would rapidly be taken to eliminate the
losses.

Also, they determined to divest peripheral businesses which
accounted for about 10 per cent of the capital employed in the group
and did not fit the long-term objectives. Disposals of peripheral
businesses realized £16m. in 1985, about half of the programme set in
1984.

During this period, the administratively divisionalized structure was
eliminated and the managing directors of the 25 separate operating
businesses reported directly to a main board director. Uttiger replaced
ten of them and made changes in the board. He recruited three
non-executive directors, Sir John Cuckney, chairman of Investors in
Industry, Derek Edwards, a director of Rio Tinto Zinc, and Michael
Davis, a former director of Imperial Foods. He introduced a bonus
scheme, whereby top management could earn up to 30 per cent of
their salaries if they met specified targets. Control methods were
changed from an annual budget to a four-quarterly rolling forecast,
and at the same time accounting staff was reduced by 30 per cent.

In the summer of 1985, Raschid and Osman Abdullah rapidly built up a stake of just over 20 per cent in TI, through their Evered Company. The board feared that if the bid were successful TI would be broken up into its constituent parts. Fortunately for TI, the Abdullahs delayed making a bid for over a year, which allowed the TI management time to restructure the business.

JULY 1986–MAY 1989

In July 1986, a new chief executive, Mr Christopher Lewinton was appointed. He was formerly chairman of Wilkinson Sword, part of Allegheny International. In August 1986, the Abdullahs sold their TI stake. Once installed, Lewinton took 100 days to 'look inside' TI and develop a new strategy. He went around the City to gain support from the financial institutions for his new plans, and set a target of 10 per cent on sales, as compared with the prevailing 5–6 per cent.

One of Lewinton's first tasks was to formulate a mission statement for the new TI:

TI's strategic thrust is to become an international engineering group concentrating on specialized engineering businesses, operating in selected niches on a global basis. Key businesses must be able to command positions of sustainable technological and market share leadership.

Significant features of the group were stated as:

- High quality of earnings and cash generation.
- A broad international spread of businesses.
- A balanced portfolio of products and markets.
- An emphasis on proprietary skills and technology, with high added value and pricing flexibility.
- Market share position as the number one or number two, or the potential to get there very quickly.
- A small headquarters, strong financial control, fewer and better people, and delegated operational decision making.

The essence of the plan became the TI slogan, 'shrink, concentrate and grow'. The strategy involved the divestment of TI's domestic appliance businesses – shedding its consumer brand names to finance the expansion of its specialist engineeering division into truly international operations.

By early 1987, the implementation of the strategy was under way, with the disposal of Russell Hobbs and Tower to Polly Peck for £12m. This was followed shortly by the announcement to the City that TI was putting its domestic appliances division up for sale. The domestic appliance market in Europe was dominated by Electrolux (25 per cent market share). TI had major interests in gas and electrical appliances.

Its best market segment was free-standing cookers in which it was first (37 per cent share), with Thorn a close second. Ranging across well-known brand names like Creda, New World, Parkray and Glow-worm, the appliance companies accounted for almost 20 per cent of TI's £1bn. turnover in 1986. Within three months they had been sold for almost £210m. TI was left with £9m. of net cash on its hands.

Raleigh was sold to Derby International for £18m. Although it counted for almost half of all UK sales of bicycles, it had suffered losses of £34m. between 1980 and 1986. The disposal meant a £45m. write-off for TI. In 1988, Derby reported profits of £16m. for Raleigh.

Specialized tubing

Fulton, TI's existing small-diameter tubing business, already had a 70 per cent share of the UK market, but no presence in Europe. It supplied 100 per cent of Nissan and Austin Rover's UK needs, and 70 per cent of Ford's; Hotpoint, Electrolux and LEC were also big customers. Armco gave TI a dominant market share of the European automotive brake and fuel line market, together with the refrigerator condenser and shelving market. The trend by automotive assemblers to install rigid fuel and brake-line clusters requires tube manufacturers to liaise closely with assemblers at the design stage. Then in March 1988 TI paid £85m. for Bundy, North America's biggest supplier of specialist small-diameter tubing (with a 60 per cent share of the US market). Along with Fulton and Armco, TI had captured 40 per cent of the world market, and built its tube business up from sales of £10m. to £200m.

Mechanical seals

In September 1987, TI bought John Crane, the world's largest producer of mechanical seals (with an estimated 30 per cent world market share) for a net £196m., as part of a £308m. acquisition of Houdaille Industries. The non-Crane assets were subsequently sold for £112m. to the Houdaille management (down from an agreed £135.2m. prior to the stock market crash in October 1987). There was a certain amount of luck involved in the purchase of Houdaille, which had been the subject of a leveraged buy-out. The subsequent debt burden had constrained capital expenditure, which consequently had handicapped sales and profit growth. Recognition of this had encouraged the existing management to sell off Crane and concentrate on the remaining businesses. Stock turnover at Crane was 96 days compared with 50 days for TI, which is in conflict with UBS-Phillips and Drew's suspicion that the firm had been 'sweated'.

The Houdaille purchase appears expensive at first sight, with a price:earnings ratio of 22 and debts exceeding net current assets.

When the divestment of non-Crane assets is taken into account, the PE ratio is likely to be higher. However, sales margins were high at 15.8 per cent and there was an accumulated tax loss of £27m. available. Stock turnover improvements could potentially release £25m. TI now have control of the only truly global seals business. Close rivals such as Sealol (USA), Durametallic (USA) and NOK (Japan) are large national players with limited overseas involvement, and none have market shares in excess of 8 per cent.

Industrial furnaces

The strategy continued with the £72.5m. purchase of Thermal Scientific. Adding Thermal Scientific's world-leading vacuum furnaces to those of TI's Abar Ipsen subsidiary created the world's largest thermal technology business. The net cost of Thermal Scientific was expected to be in the region of £50m. when property and non-core subsidiaries were divested. It is now the largest manufacturer in a growing world market (1986 estimate of £250m.).

Automotive

Pressures from assemblers, the extended life of components, increased competition from overseas and EC 'emissions' regulations resulted in TI selling its car silencer and Standard Tube Canada subsidiaries for £141m. in January 1989, and in August it sold APA (Spain), manufacturer of shock absorbers and suspension struts, for £36.4m. Together with the proceeds of the disposal of non-core Thermal Scientific companies, these transactions left TI with cash in the bank.

Organization

While the strategy was taking visible form, the TI Board closed its large head office in Birmingham, replacing it with a slim, 50-strong headquarters in Curzon Street in London's West End, and sold its centralized computer facilities in Walsall to local management.

> A lot of people thought we were doing it solely to save money but that wasn't true – it signalled a significant change in culture in the company.
> Only 10 per cent to 15 per cent of our turnover is exported from anywhere. We don't do business *with*, we do business *in* other countries. If you sit at home and export you do not build an international business culture, as some UK companies have been discovering. (Lewinton)

In summer 1987, TI announced the closure of its research establishment at Hinxton, Cambridge in the belief that TI could not afford unfocused research, only applied technology. However, TI realized that new breakthroughs have to be achieved with this strategy of sustainable technology if market share leadership is going to work long term. Research effort will now be concentrated within the various operating companies. Bill Graham, Director of Research at Hinxton: 'Market pull tends only to produce incremental improvements in technology. We need to be aware of the possibility of higher jumps.'

Accounting procedures

Accounting practice insists that companies must depreciate their intangible assets of engineering 'know-how', with a consequent effect of lowering stated profits. TI is concerned that a substantial acquisition would involve goodwill and propel conventional gearing to unacceptable levels, even if interest cover were relatively comfortable. So TI has tried to educate the investment community to its true balance sheet strength by including two calculations for its shareholders' funds, one including and one excluding a deduction for goodwill.

THE FUTURE

To date, TI has taken the relatively low-risk line of acquiring companies in industries where it already had some involvement. With money in the bank and no gearing, TI appears to be looking for a significant new leg to its range of specialized engineering activities.

We'd like to do it [make another acquisition] because no company can stand still but there is absolutely no sense of urgency. Any acquisition would have to complement our existing businesses, be of sufficient size and fit in with our strategy. With our current, balanced spread across products, industries and currency areas, we feel we can't be hurt by unexpected changes within any one category. I would like to see, strategically, the Pacific Rim and Japan become much more important to TI. We have five joint ventures out there and had an office in Singapore for some time but without enough strategic substance. (Lewinton)

Appendix 1   Economic data, 1977–88

	1977	1978	1979	1980	1981	1982	1983	1984	1985	1986	1987	1988
World trade (f.o.b $US bn.)	1,070	1,250	1,576	1,889	1,881	1,743	1,687	1,801	1,997	2,365	2,682	–
Exchange rate ($US:£)	1.75	1.92	2.12	2.33	2.03	1.75	1.52	1.34	1.30	1.47	1.64	1.78
Interest rate (%)	10.0	8.5	13.7	16.3	13.3	11.9	9.8	9.7	12.3	10.9	9.7	10.5
Price index (Jan 1974=100)	182.0	197.1	223.5	263.7	295.0	320.4	335.1	351.8	373.2	385.9	394.5	407.5
Unemployment (m.)	1.25	1.22	1.16	1.49	2.26	2.63	2.86	3.01	3.11	3.18	2.87	2.30
GDP @ factor cost (1985=100)	42.2	48.5	56.2	65.3	71.3	78.0	82.5	91.3	100.0	106.1	116.1	126.6

Appendix 2   TI Group employment and UK manufacturing, 1979–88

	1979	1980	1981	1982	1983
UK employment	53,000	46,500	37,200	26,250	25,100
Total employment	62,000	54,500	45,200	32,500	27,100
UK manufacturing sites:					
>1,000 employees	9	9	9	5	4
500–1,000 employees	26	19	18	8	9
<500 employees	85	72	58	42	37
Total no. of sites	120	100	85	55	50

	1984	1985	1986	1987	1988
UK employment	23,300	22,000	20,000	12,600	7,200
Total employment	29,000	27,100	25,400	21,000	20,700
UK manufacturing sites:					
>1,000 employees	4	3	n.a	n.a	n.a
500–1,000 employees	7	7	n.a	n.a	n.a
<500 employees	39	30	n.a	n.a	n.a
Total no. of sites	50	40	n.a	n.a	n.a

Appendix 3   TI share price

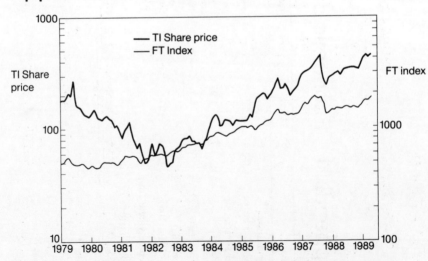

FIGURE 14.1 **TI share price compared with FT ordinary share index, 1979–May 1989**

Appendix 4

TI GROUP FINANCIAL PERFORMANCE – KEY FIGURES, 1979–88

		1979	1980	1981	1982	1983	1984	1985	1986	1987	1988
Turnover	£m.	1,213.8	1,158.2	1,122.0	887.2	914.3	971.2	997.1	1,043.6	855.9	958.9
Profit before interest	£m.	75.3	51.5	6.2	26.0	33.3	39.1	50.7	58.4	65.8	93.1
Profit before tax	£m.	52.2	26.7	-23.1	4.7	16.3	19.0	30.6	43.4	62.3	85.4
Profit after tax	£m.	39.9	16.4	-28.4	1.4	11.8	13.4	18.9	30.5	41.4	57.6
Earnings	£m.	31.6	11.0	-19.4	0.4	11.0	13.2	17.6	27.9	38.4	56.5
Earnings per share	p	26.7	9.3	-16.4	2.9	9.3	11.1	14.8	23.4	29.6	38.1
Sales margins	%	6.1	4.6	0.8	2.9	3.6	4.0	4.7	5.5	7.5	9.3
ROCE	%	13.6	9.8	1.3	7.9	10.6	11.2	15.3	22.0	25.4	25.7
ROI (gross)	%	10.9	4.9	-8.4	0.6	5.6	6.1	8.6	17.7	10.8	11.5
Current ratio		2.0	1.9	1.8	1.8	1.6	1.6	1.6	1.5	1.5	1.7
Acid ratio		0.9	0.9	0.9	0.9	0.8	0.8	0.9	0.9	1.0	1.3
Stock turnover ratio		3.8	3.9	4.0	4.5	4.9	4.7	5.6	7.2	7.2	8.3
Net current assets/sales		87.2	81.4	77.5	67.7	55.2	59.6	54.6	41.8	49.0	71.8
Gearing 1	%	30.0	31.3	46.7	49.6	49.0	42.3	33.0	45.8	0.0	17.4
Gearing 2	%	30.0	31.3	46.7	49.6	49.0	42.3	33.0	45.8	0.0	8.1
Interest cover		3.3	2.1	0.2	1.2	2.0	1.9	2.5	3.9	18.8	12.1

Sales margins $= \dfrac{\text{Profit before interest and tax (EBIT)}}{\text{Turnover}} \times 100$

Return on capital employed (ROCE) $= \dfrac{\text{Profit before interest and tax}}{\text{Capital employed}} \times 100$

Return on shareholders' funds (ROI) $= \dfrac{\text{Earnings for the year}}{\text{Shareholders' funds}} \times 100$

Gearing 1 $= \dfrac{\text{Net borrowings}}{\text{Total shareholders' funds}} \times 100$

Gearing 2 $= \dfrac{\text{Net borrowings}}{\text{Total shareholders' funds} - \text{goodwill}} \times 100$

Appendix 5

TI GROUP DIVESTMENTS, JANUARY 1987–AUGUST 1989

Date	Division	Business	Acquirer	Sale price £m.
Feb. 1987	D D	Russel Hobbs Tower	Polly Peck	11.4
March	C	Raleigh Industries	Derby International	18
April	D	Glow-Worm & Parkray	Hepworth Ceramic	63.5
May	D	New World (cookers)	Birmid Qualcast	18.6
June	D	TI Creda	GEC	125.9
October	ST	Tube Products	MBO	6.8
October	SE	Machine Tools	TMG Engineering	6.5
Dec	ST	Stainless Steel Tube	Sandvik	7.1
March 1988	SE	TI Roberston (eng. dies)	B. Elliot	2
March	SE	TI Serco (fabrications)	MBO	2.5
May	ST	Cold Drawn Tubes (75 per cent) & Seamless Tubes	British Steel	4 (TI share of JV)
August	SE	TI Chesterfield	n/a	7
Dec	SE	TI Flexible Tubes	Senior Engineering	9.75
Jan 1989	A	TI Cheswick & TI Bainbridge	Arvin Industries	110
Jan	A	Standard Tube (Canada)	Ferrum	31
August	A	APA (Spain)	Arvin	36.4

A – automotive; D – domestic appliances; C – cycles; SE – specialized engineering;
ST – specialized tube; MBO – management buy-out

Appendix 6

ANALYSIS OF DIVESTED DIVISIONS

Division	Domestic appliances			
Business	Tower & Russell Hobbs	TI Creda	Parkway & Glow-worm	New World
Year ending	Dec. 1986	Dec. 1986	Dec. 1986	Dec. 1986
Turnover (£m.)	40.4	142.4	71.4	45.1
Profit before interest (£m.)	(2.3)	11.767	7.4	1.6
Capital empolyed (£m.)	11.4	22.587	17.380	9.145
Sales price (£m.)	11.4	125.9	63.5	18.6
Net worth (£m.)	5.4	19.4	15	8.5
EBIT/Sales (%)	–	8.3	10.3	3.5
ROCE (%)	–	52	42.5	33.8
Growth in profit (%)	–	10	10	1.5
Growth in sales (%)	–	12	3.1	10
P/E ratio	–	16.25	13.8	13.9

Division	Cycles	Automotive	
Business	Raleigh	Cheswick & Bainbridge	Standard Tube Canada
Year ending	Dec. 1986	Dec. 1986	Dec. 1987
Turnover (£m.)	143.8	104.6	51.7
Profit before interest (£m.)	(2.4)	9.463	4.420
Capital employed (£m.)	45.6	26.29	21.10
Sale price (£m.)	18	110	31
Net worth (£m.)	–	23.43	11.9
EBIT/Sales (%)	–	9	8.5
ROCE (%)	–	36	36.5
Growth in profit (%)	–	22	28
Growth in sales (%)	0	19	1
P/E ratio	–	18.7	15

Appendix 7

ACQUISITIONS AND RELATED DIVESTMENTS, JUNE 1986–MARCH 1989

Date		Details	Price £m.
June	1986	Exercised its option to purchase Alco Standard's half share in Aber Ibsen (Industrial Furnaces)	12.5
Feb	1987	Purchased small-diameter tubing business of Armco	27
Aug		Bought ITT's 49 per cent stake in Fulton (small-diameter tubing)	4.34
Sept		Bought John Crane (US) and outstanding share of Crane (UK) via the purchase of Houdaille Inc. (mechanical seals)	308
Jan	1988	Sold non-Crane assets of Houdaille	112
March		Acquired Bundy International (small-diameter tubing)	85
Sept		Purchased Thermal Scientific (vacuum furnaces) and disposed of Carbolite and Betolite to the management	72.5
Dec		Acquired Ropac, France (seals)	6
Feb	1989	Other Thermal Scientific disposals	4
March		Disposed of Bundy subsidiaries – Performance Plastics to Flurocarbon Company (US); retained Titeflex	48
March		Purchased Mannesman's (West Germany) 60 per cent share in Mecano-Bundy, subject to regulatory approval	222

Appendix 8

ANALYSIS OF MAJOR ACQUISITIONS AND RELATED DIVESTMENTS, 1986–8

Year ending		Specialized Tube		
		SDT (Armco) Dec. 1986 £m.	Bundy July 1987 £m.	Performance Plastics[a] July 1988 $US m.
Turnover		84.4	26.5	60
Profit before interest		63	22	8.6
Profit before tax		–	15.2	–
Profit after tax		–	8.4	–
Earnings		–	8.4	–
Capital employed		35.7	154.4	42.6
Purchase price		27	154	86
Net worth		29.4	81.8	42.5
Sales margins	(%)	7.5	8.3	14.4
ROCE	(%)	17.6	14.2	–
Profit growth	(%)	–	26	–
Earning growth	(%)	–	14	–
Historic P/E ratio		–	18.3	–

| Year Ending | Houdaille July 1986 $US m. | Specialized Engineering | |
		Crane assets July 1986 $US m.	Thermal Scientific[a] March 1988 £m.
Turnover	358	195.5	51.19
Profit before interest	56.9	30.9	–
Profit before tax	28.3	–	7.383
Profit after tax	23.2	–	4.876
Earnings	36.4 [b]	–	4.876
Capital employed	174	70.2	26.578
Purchase price	500	328	72.5
Net worth	(214.5)	0	17.643
Sales margins (%)	15.8	–	14.4
ROCE (%)	32.7	–	27.8
Profit growth (%)	8.2	8.2	95
Earning growth (%)	2.3	2.3	81
Historic P/E ratio	21.6	–	9.8

[a] Part of Houdaille
[b] Includes pension holiday

Appendix 9

ESTIMATE OF PROFIT INCREASES IN SE ATTRIBUTABLE TO
ORGANIC GROWTH AND RESTRUCTURING

Specialized tube

	1987 £m.	1988 £m.	£m.	1989 £m.	£m.
Reported profit before interest	18.6		34.9		45 [a]
Contribution of Armco (Feb. 1987)	5.8	6.3		6.3	
Contribution of existing businesses (Dec. 1987)	12.8	12.8		12.8	
Contribution of Bundy (April 1988)	–	8.6		13.8	
Divestments – Performance Plastics	–	–		–3.8	
– Others		0.5		0.5	
			28.2		29.6
Increase in profits due to restructuring and organic growth			6.7		15.4

[a] 1989 profits estimated from first-half interim statement

Specialized engineering

	£m.	£m.
Profit before interest estimated for 1989 (Source: UBS Phillips and Drew)		50
Profits from original businesses (1986)	18.6	
Estimate for divestments (using PE ratio of 10)	2.7	
Estimate for 49 per cent share of Aber Ipsen (1986)	0.8	
Contribution of Crane (1986–$US 30.8m at exchange rate of 1.60 $/£)	19.3	
Contribution of Thermal Scientific less estimates for divestments (1987)	5.0	
Estimated contribution from Ropac (using PE ratio of 10)	0.6	41.6
Increase in profits due to organic growth and restructuring		8.4

Appendix 10

ESTIMATE OF TURNOVER BY BUSINESS, JUNE 1989

		Estimated turnover	
		£m.	*%*
Specialized	Seals	180	20
Engineering	Furnaces	90	10
(£422m.)	Aerospace	105	11
	Power transmission		
	Hollow extrusions }	47	5
	Cycle frames		
Specialized	Small-diameter tube	230	25
Tube	Bearing tube	90	10
(£385m.)	Accles and Pollock		
	Apollo, Valti }	65	7
Automotive	Car seats		
(£113m.)	Suspension systems [a] }	113	12
	Silencers (JVs)		

Estimated from June 1989 interim results

[a] Sold August 1989

Appendix 11

TI GROUP BALANCE SHEET 1979–88

(£m.)	1979	1980	1981	1982	1983	1984	1985	1986	1987	1988
Fixed assets										
Tangibles	227.4	247.3	248.5	155.1	154.0	170.0	159.2	132.8	127.9	154.0
Investments	37.0	21.7	7.8	8.8	20.9	21.8	23.6	13.7	16.4	19.5
	264.4	269.0	256.3	163.9	174.9	191.8	182.8	146.5	144.3	173.5
Current assets										
Stocks	319.2	300.1	282.3	195.5	186.0	206.2	176.5	144.7	118.8	115.5
Debtors	245.0	223.4	229.8	163.6	174.1	183.0	178.6	179.9	172.8	175.7
Assets for disposal										71.0
Cash in hand	25.7	13.7	22.9	18.7	13.5	31.3	40.1	54.6	65.2	81.1
	589.9	537.2	535.0	377.8	373.6	420.5	395.2	379.2	356.8	443.3
Current liabilities										
Creditors due within 1 yr	299.9	278.8	296.7	213.3	235.3	261.8	246.0	44.9	17.7	20.2
Other creditors	0.0	0.0	0.0	0.0	0.0	0.0	0.0	214.8	224.1	234.6
	299.0	278.8	296.7	213.3	235.3	261.8	246.0	259.7	241.8	254.8
Net current assets	290.0	258.4	238.3	164.5	138.3	158.7	149.2	119.5	115.0	188.5
Tot. assets less cur. liabilities	554.4	527.4	494.6	328.4	313.2	350.5	332.0	266.0	259.3	362.0

continued

continued

(£m.)	1979	1980	1981	1982	1983	1984	1985	1986	1987	1988
Creditors falling due after more than one year										
Loans & borrowings	100.5	96.5	125.7	93.3	83.5	108.4	86.5	70.7	26.4	101.6
Other creditors	26.6	31.9	30.0	7.6	8.1	9.9	12.1	9.1	11.7	16.5
	127.1	128.4	155.7	100.9	91.6	118.3	98.6	79.8	38.1	118.1
	427.3	399.0	338.9	227.5	221.6	232.2	233.4	186.2	221.2	243.9
Provision for liabilities and charges	0.0	0.0	0.0	0.0	2.0	2.1	1.7	1.2	10.9	8.0
	427.3	399.0	338.9	227.5	219.6	230.1	231.7	185.0	210.3	235.9
Capital & reserves										
Share capital (50p share)	59.3	59.3	59.3	59.3	59.3	59.4	59.5	59.9	73.9	74.3
Share premium	65.5	65.5	65.5	65.5	65.5	65.5	65.6	65.8	84.5	0.4
Other reserves	228.3	213.2	226.3	0.0	0.0	0.0	0.0	0.0	58.5	143.1
Profit and loss account	14.6	0.0	0.0	95.4	86.3	93.3	95.4	46.2	167.7	283.5
Shareholders' funds	367.7	338.0	351.1	220.2	211.1	218.2	220.5	171.9	384.6	501.3
Goodwill written off	0.0	0.0	0.0	0.0	0.0	0.0	0.0	0.0	180.3	268.8
Shareholders' funds – net	367.7	338.0	338.9	220.2	211.1	218.2	220.5	171.9	204.3	232.5
Minority interests	59.6	61.0	53.3	7.3	8.5	11.9	11.2	13.1	6.0	3.4
Total shareholders' funds	427.3	399.0	392.2	227.5	219.6	230.1	231.7	185.0	210.3	235.9

Appendix 12   Breakdown of business by activity and Geography

TURNOVER BY BUSINESS BY VALUE

(£m.)	1979	1980	1981	1982	1983	1984	1985	1986	1987	1988
Aluminium	288.4	291.5	279.3	232.8	254.1	258.1	270.3	297.8	99.0	
Domestic appliances	208.4	216.4	216.0	151.6	162.0	162.0	137.6	143.8		
Cycles	157.1	166.4	153.9	117.3	140.1	167.3	187.6	197.6	232.2	252.8
Automotive			105.0							
Specialized engineering	243.4	256.7	197.6	209.0	206.6	238.8	243.4	259.0	296.0	373.5
Steel/spec. tube	314.4	224.7	168.3	175.3	149.4	143.0	154.2	144.0	229.0	332.0
Other	2.1	2.5	1.9	1.2	2.1	2.0	4.0	1.4	-0.3	0.6
Total	1,213.8	1,158.2	1,122.0	887.2	914.3	971.2	997.1	1,043.6	855.9	958.9

TURNOVER BY BUSINESS BY PERCENTAGE

	1979	1980	1981	1982	1983	1984	1985	1986	1987	1988
Aluminium	23.8	25.2	24.9	26.2	27.8	26.6	27.1	28.5	11.6	
Domestic appliances	17.2	18.7	19.3	17.1	17.7	16.7	13.8	13.8		
Cycles	12.9	14.4	13.7	13.2	15.3	17.2	18.8	18.9	27.1	26.4
Automotive			9.4							
Specialized engineering	20.1	22.2	17.6	23.6	22.6	24.6	24.4	24.8	34.6	39.0
Steel/spec. tube	25.9	19.4	15.0	19.8	16.3	14.7	15.5	13.8	26.8	34.6
Other	0.2	0.2	0.2	0.1	0.2	0.2	0.4	0.1	0.0	0.1
Total	100.0	100.0	100.0	100.0	100.0	100.0	100.0	100.0	100.0	100.0

continued

GEOGRAPHIC DISTRIBUTION OF SALES BY VALUE

(£m.)	1979	1980	1981	1982	1983	1984	1985	1986	1987	1988
UK	780.1	741.7	636.2	506.7	534.0	546.7	571.8	576.5	352.6	220.2
Continental Western Europe	160.2	171.9	179.3	140.0	133.7	152.3	179.2	223.1	255.0	270.6
North America	142.9	126.9	190.3	173.3	161.7	193.0	177.5	173.5	193.1	382.0
Rest of world	130.6	117.7	116.2	67.2	84.9	79.2	68.6	70.5	55.2	86.1
Total	1,213.8	1,158.2	1,122.0	887.2	914.3	971.2	997.1	1,043.6	855.9	958.9
Exports from UK	239.0	235.0	147.0	128.0						
Total exports	433.7	416.5	375.0	381.0						

GEOGRAPHIC DISTRIBUTION OF TURNOVER BY PERCENTAGE

	1979	1980	1981	1982	1983	1984	1985	1986	1987	1988
UK	64.3	64.0	56.7	57.1	58.4	56.3	57.3	55.2	41.2	23.0
Continental Western Europe	13.2	14.8	16.0	15.8	14.6	15.7	18.0	21.4	29.8	28.2
North America	11.8	11.0	17.0	19.5	17.7	19.9	17.8	16.6	22.6	39.8
Rest of world	10.8	10.2	10.4	7.6	9.3	8.2	6.9	6.8	6.4	9.0
Total	100.0	100.0	100.0	100.0	100.0	100.0	100.0	100.0	100.0	100.0
Exports from UK	19.7	20.3	13.1	14.4						
Total exports	35.7	36.0	33.4	42.9						

Appendix 13   Performance of business by margins and return on capital

BUSINESS BY PROFIT BEFORE INTEREST

(£m.)	1979	1980	1981	1982	1983	1984	1985	1986	1987	1988	1989ᵃ
Aluminium	26.8	20.6	-12.8	16.9	22.7	22.1	21.1	20.1	5.3		
Domestic appliances	16.2	10.2	12.9	-7.1	-2.5	-4.5	-6.6	-2.4			
Cycles	3.2	6.4	-10.5								
Automotive			4.8	5.7	8.8	9.3	13.4	14.9	15.1	18.7	6.6
Specialized engineering	13.4	9.0	1.6	8.9	12.2	10.7	12.7	18.4	28.1	41.0	49.0
Steel/spec. tube	15.5	8.5	4.2	3.0	-3.6	4.1	13.4	8.7	18.6	34.9	45.0
Redundancies					-2.9	-1.7	-3.7	-2.4			
Other	1.6	-3.2	6.0	-1.4	-1.4	-0.9	0.4	1.1	-1.3	-1.5	-3.2
Total	75.3	51.5	6.2	26.0	33.3	39.1	50.7	58.4	65.8	93.1	97.4

ᵃ Estimated

DISTRIBUTION OF CAPITAL AMONGST BUSINESSES

(£m.)	1979	1980	1981	1982	1983	1984	1985	1986	1987	1988
Aluminium	168.4	187.2	177.9	61.5	54.2	52.9	61.1	61.6		
Domestic appliances	74.1	66.5	57.0	69.7	68.6	72.0	65.5			
Cycles	74.8	84.5	78.0							
Automotive			42.7	50.1	55.2	58.0	56.7	64.6	69.7	75.4
Specialized engineering	79.8	108.3	96.7	99.2	99.2	105.2	97.0	101.3	119.8	150.5
Steel/spec. tube	168.7	98.5	83.6	73.1	68.3	60.5	60.4	55.6	75.2	131.6
Other	6.8	4.2	-0.3	2.8	1.5	-0.8	-5.9			
Total	572.6	549.2	535.6	356.4	347.0	347.8	334.8	283.1	264.7	357.5

continued

SALES MARGINS BY BUSINESS

%	1979	1980	1981	1982	1983	1984	1985	1986	1987	1988	1989 [a]
Aluminium	9.3	7.1	-4.6	6.3	8.5	8.2	7.9	7.5			
Domestic appliances	6.0	3.8	4.8	-4.7	-1.5	-2.8	-4.8	-1.7			
Cycles	2.0	3.8	-6.8								
Automotive			4.5	4.9	6.3	5.5	7.1	7.5	6.5	7.4	5.8
Specialized engineering	5.5	3.5	0.8	4.3	5.9	4.5	5.2	7.1	9.5	11.0	11.6
Steel/spec. tube	4.9	3.8	2.5	1.7	-2.4	2.9	8.7	6.0	8.1	10.5	11.7

[a] Estimated

ROCE BY BUSINESS

%	1979	1980	1981	1982	1983	1984	1985	1986	1987	1988
Aluminium	15.9	11.0	-7.2	27.5	41.9	41.8				
Domestic appliances	21.9	15.3	22.6	-10.2	-3.6	-6.3	-10.1	30.6		
Cycles	4.3	7.6	-13.5							
Automotive			11.2	11.4	15.9	16.0	23.6	23.1	21.7	24.8
Specialized engineering	16.8	8.3	1.7	9.0	12.3	10.2	13.1	18.2	23.5	27.2
Steel/spec. tube	9.2	8.6	5.0	4.1	-5.3	6.8	22.2	15.6	24.7	26.5

15   Iceland Frozen Foods

In October 1988 Iceland proposed the take-over of its major rival in frozen food retail outlets, Bejam, at a price of £234m. paid for through an issue of ordinary and convertible preference shares. Iceland was the smaller of the two chains, with sales of £154m. from 183 retail outlets in Northern England and Wales, compared with Bejam's sales of £528m. from 267 outlets, largely in the South East of England. The argument put forward in favour of the merger was that Iceland had had the faster growth rate of the two chains over the previous four years. Bejam claimed, however, that its profits and sales per square foot exceeded those of Iceland. Bejam shareholders were convinced by Iceland's arguments, and sold to Iceland in January 1989.

Iceland Frozen Foods had been formed as a private company in November 1980 and floated as a public company in October 1984, when its ordinary shares were offered to the public at 210 pence. Appendices 1 and 2 provide financial information on Iceland and Bejam.

The retail frozen food business had been a rapid growth area within food retailing since frozen peas made their debut in 1955, at a time when few homes had a refrigerator, let alone a deep freeze. Throughout the period since then, the ownership of freezers or fridge/freezers grew rapidly – see figure 15.1.

Frozen foods were sold by supermarkets as well as by freezer chains. The five largest supermarket chains accounted for about 65 per cent of retail frozen food sales, with Sainsbury as the market leader followed by Tesco. It was anticipated that Iceland, with a 4.2 per cent market share, and Bejam with 9.8 per cent, would together take third place.

The major problem posed for the freezer chains was the increasing dominance of the major supermarket retailers, as they opened larger and larger superstores and expanded their product ranges. In the superstores (over 25,000 square feet of selling space) the retailers were able to achieve higher profit margins largely because they could stock

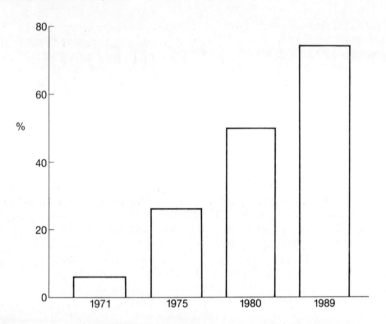

FIGURE 15.1   **Households owning freezer and/or fridge freezer,
1971–89**

a wider range of products. The basic grocery lines such as sugar, canned goods and tea offered low margins, but they had to be stocked, and in stores of less than 12,000 square feet these could take up most of the available space. The larger superstores were able to stock more fresh foods, in-store bakeries and delicatessens, and frozen foods, all of which offered higher profit margins. This, with economies of scale in operations and the application of technology, was encouraging Sainsbury, Tesco, Safeway and Asda towards superstore shopping. Sainsbury, for example, had only increased its number of outlets from 244 in 1950 to 272 in 1988. But they were very different stores (and usually different locations). During that time the average Sainsbury store grew from 10,000 square feet to 18,500, and by 1990 Sainsbury planned to have over 100 stores with over 25,000 square feet, offering nearly 11,000 product lines and achieving annual sales of £822 per square foot. Appendix 3 provides statistics on supermarket sales.

Retailing has traditionally offered opportunities for entrepreneurs to develop a business and achieve rapid growth, and often millionaire status, in a relatively short period of time. The important character-istics of those who have succeeded seems to include the ability to recognize a market opportunity and to take advantage of it by creating a retail image or format which has appealed to the market. Examples are Body Shop, Tie Rack and Sock Shop in the 1980s, Habitat and Mothercare in the 1970s, and Tesco in the 1960s. The key to success in retailing has differed from that in manufacturing industry, for not only are cost control and productivity important, but both image and location play a crucial role. For a retailer, the image is equivalent to the notion of product/market scope for a manufacturer, that is, what products to sell and to which customers. For Habitat it was plain and simple, well-designed furniture to sell to the emerging young middle classes, whilst for Tesco it had been low price/good value groceries aimed at a poorer section of the population.

BEJAM

In 1968 John Apthorp had founded Bejam as a retailer of bulk large-size packs of frozen foods sold alongside freezers, and within ten years recorded sales turnover of nearly £100m. Like other retailers he had previously researched the American market; he felt that unlike America, the smaller size of British supermarkets would not enable bulk sales of frozen foods at that time, but he was convinced that frozen food sales would grow and that a speciality retailer would appeal to the public. He rejected the contemporary method of selling frozen foods by refrigerated vehicles for home delivery. He opened his first outlet in Edgware, London in 1968 with a limited product range of about 100 items, mostly staple products such as peas and fish fingers. The major frozen food manufacturers were reluctant to supply Bejam, in the belief that such freezer centres were a short-term phenomenon and that it would damage the relationships they were then building with the emergent supermarket chains. This meant that Bejam had to make special arrangements with small manufacturers to produce bulk packs. The first freezer centre was successful, and John Apthorp opened four more in the first year and a further ten in the second year. The success continued; by 1974 Bejam was a chain of 100 freezer centres, and by the early 1980s had reached nearly 200.

Bejam's growth was closely related to the changes taking place in society, with more working housewives, more widespread ownership of cars and, especially, increasing ownership of freezers. In 1968 annual sales of freezers in the UK were 50,000. By 1973 over one million homes had a freezer, and with annual sales reaching 500,000 in 1980, over half of all homes by then had a freezer. The growth continued throughout the eighties, such that towards the end of the decade over three-quarters of homes had a freezer.

These early developments were soon followed by competition from others, including the Co-operative Society and Cordon Bleu with chains of specialist freezer centres, but also from supermarket chains which, as their stores grew in size, were able to expand their product ranges to include bulk packs of frozen foods.

The pace of growth which Bejam accomplished was difficult to finance from internal resources, and in order to maintain the rate of expansion, Bejam sold 20 per cent of its equity to a bank in 1971 and in 1973 undertook a public flotation of its shares. In preparation for this flotation Bejam recruited Laurence Don, a former finance director of Tesco, and he assisted in the clarification of the organizational structure, creating a highly centralized multi-tiered heirarchy. Two joint managing directors undertook the day-to-day control of the chain, with each of them responsible for half of the outlets, and one in charge of buying and marketing and the other property, distribution, finance and group services. John Apthorp became executive chairman, and another full-time executive took charge of expansion.

The flotation was a great success, with the shares being over-subscribed many times. Bejam then aimed to maintain tight central control, in order that it could maintain the flexibility of a small company facing the inevitable pressures of growth. Every week the area managers, each responsible on average for about ten freezer centres, were given breakdowns of costs as well as weekly sales figures.

As Bejam grew to become the UK's biggest retailer of frozen foods, they began to be supplied by the major manufacturers. Bejam also decided to sell other, non-frozen, foodstuffs, although frozen foods represented 80 per cent of all foods sold, and they continued to sell freezers (160,000 in 1982). As they grew, their ability to negotiate prices with suppliers improved, with the effect of an improvement in margins whilst being able to sell at prices at least as low as their competitors (especially supermarkets, which Bejam considered their biggest competitors). In 1980 Cordon Bleu, which at the time was the other notable freezer chain, was taken over by the supermarket chain Argyll Foods, which with a further acquisition of 66 Freezer-Fare centres formed a chain of 130 freezer outlets.

Although Bejam considered the growth of supermarket chains, and especially the development of the huge out-of-town superstores, as its main competition, it was not without strengths itself, as its huge cold storage facilities enabled cheaper buying, and its smaller product range enabled the production of a monthly price list for customers, with consequent tight control at store level. Frequently supermarkets could not maintain this competition, as with many thousands of product items in stock, whilst pricing was theoretically established by head office, it was often decided in practice by the supermarket manager. By 1983 Bejam was the equal market leader with Sainsbury in frozen foods, each having 11 per cent share of the market, with the Co-operative Society and Tesco each on 10 per cent and all other freezer centres combined with 12 per cent. Bejam had achieved this position through bulk sales, for its share of the retail-size pack market was only 3 per cent.

INDUSTRY AND MARKET DEVELOPMENTS

The ten-year period between the census of distribution in 1971 and that in 1981 showed dramatic changes in UK food retailing. The number of grocery outlets fell by over 46 per cent, and of these closures the largest share had been in the multiple chain sector, where a deliberate policy of closing small outlets in order to concentrate on opening large superstores had led to a fall of over 50 per cent. After allowing for inflation, real growth in sales by grocery outlets was about 1 per cent per annum, but the multiples had continued their growth at the expense of independents and co-operatives, with a market share rising from 44 per cent to 63 per cent.

The demographic changes of the 1970s which affected retailing were:

1 growth of home ownership;
2 growth in car ownership;
3 increase in working wives;
4 increase in numbers of households with two incomes;
5 reduction in working week and increase in holiday time;
6 increase in numbers of unemployed;
7 increase in proportion of the population retired, and also those at school.

As food retailers moved towards larger out-of-town stores, the additional space enabled them to offer wider ranges of goods with higher margins than those associated with foods. Consumer expenditure on food between 1980 and 1989 increased by only 5.9 per cent in real terms.

The 1979–81 recession caused some retailers to reconsider their product ranges, and a number began to withdraw from certain non-food markets; for instance, Asda withdrew from the 'white-goods' market, i.e. refrigerators, freezers and cookers. The slow growth in food sales led many retailers to turn to categories such as fresh foods and own-label brands as areas of expansion.

Throughout the 1970s and 1980s superstore numbers grew rapidly. In 1970 there were 33 superstores, defined as having a sales area of over 30,000 square feet. In 1980 this figure had reached 278 and by 1986 there were 457 superstores in the UK with an average sales area of 32,700 square feet. These stores were typically built on the edge of town and offered car parking spaces. The principal operators were the major supermarket food retailers such as Sainsbury, Tesco, Asda and Argyll.

MAJOR FOOD RETAILERS

Sainsbury Sainsbury was the leading food retailer, with 16 per cent of the market. Sainsbury was noted for the efficiency it had brought to food retailing, particularly its stock ordering and stock replacement methods. Each product on Sainsbury shelves was coded by a label on the shelf front, and the stock level read every day and sent to regional warehouses, which then despatched the required number of items to bring stock levels up to pre-determined levels. Over 50 per cent of Sainsbury sales were own-label products.

Asda Asda had concentrated from an early stage on superstores, having the advantage of entering the industry later than others, in 1965. It was Leeds-based and started in the North, beginning its expansion in the South considerably later. Each Asda superstore needed a ten-acre site, eight acres of which were for car parking, and a population of 100,000 to provide sufficient customers. Asda was able to convert a higher proportion of each store's total area into sales area, as opposed to warehousing or administration.

Tesco Tesco had for many years been the leading food retailer, and following a struggle for market share with Sainsbury in 1977 the company undertook a major reorganization, moving further into very large stores and closing smaller ones. Unlike its major competitors Tesco was generally represented all over the country, with a market share only slightly lower than that of Sainsbury.

Kwik Save Kwik Save operated 300 stores of an average size of 6,000 square feet, over the North, Wales, and the Midlands. It concentrated on a narrow product range of about 1,000 packaged branded products (compared with about 5,000 in the average supermarket) presented in a rather spartan atmosphere. With no individual pricing of items there was a saving on labour costs, which enabled Kwik Save to offer the lowest prices in the industry on these products.

During the 1980s the Bejam executives had considered the only two constraints to growth to be the availability of appropriate locations for new outlets, and management ability to run a larger operation whilst maintaining flexibility. Over the years the average Bejam store had grown in size, and by 1988 was 4,800 square feet. The stores were still primarily located in the South East and South Midlands, which were the areas where the ownership of freezers was at its highest.

In the mid-1980s the decision was taken to expand in the area of general food retailing, and in 1986 Bejam bought from Tesco, for £10m., the Victor Value chain of 45 supermarkets which Tesco had decided were too small to fit their strategy. In 1987 Bejam began opening the Wizard Wine Warehouses, which had grown to a group of nine by 1989. The wine warehouses operated from low cost sites, had a larger sales area than normal wine retailers, and offered competitive prices and car parking.

*   *   *

Following Bejam's take-over by Iceland, the chain of 53 Victor Value supermarkets was sold to Kwik Save for £15.75m. plus stock at valuation, as well as Wizard Wine Warehouses for £1.2m. Iceland then set about converting the Bejam stores over a two-year period at a cost of £40m. into the Iceland formula. Following the conversion, Iceland would be operating with a sales area of 2.15m. square feet, and the outlets would offer 850 frozen food items including 128 Iceland brand and 67 Bejam brand, with frozen foods comprising 70 per cent of retail turnover. During 1989, whilst the conversions were taking place the sales in Iceland stores were still rising, but Bejam store sales were falling.

Appendix 1   Iceland

FINANCIAL ANALYSIS, 1983–8

£m.	1983	1984	1985	1986	1987	1988
Turnover	46.55	65.24	82.32	116.49	154.54	205.2
Operating profit	2.18	3.24	3.93	5.45	7.30	9.93
Interest	0.36	0.28	0.15	0.34	0.79	0.9
Profit before tax	1.81	2.96	3.83	5.11	7.22	9.03
Profit after tax	1.72	2.85	3.57	3.83	5.42	7.0
Operating profit margin (%)	4.7	5.0	4.9	4.7	4.7	4.8
Pre-tax profit margin (%)	3.9	4.5	4.6	4.4	4.7	4.4
Earnings per share (pence)	6.19	10.0	12.23	13.15	17.21	21.39
Dividend per share (pence)	–	–	3.30	3.75	4.35	5.25
No. of stores at year end	75	81	106	128	164	183
Sales area (net) at year end (000 sq. ft.)	256	312	422	528	672	772
Average store size (sq. ft.)	3,413	3,852	3,981	4,125	4,100	4,218
Share price (pence) High	193	301	295	418	375	404
Low	148	191	240	268	283	273

BALANCE SHEETS

£ thousands	January 1988	December 1988 [a]
Fixed assets:		
Tangible assets	46,973	31,811
Current assets:		
Stocks	9,551	8,041
Debtors	4,443	3,953
Cash at bank in hand	4,309	2,265
	18,303	14,259
Creditors: due within one year	33,036	27,172
Net current assets/(liabilities)	(14,733)	(12,913)
Total assets less current liabilities	32,240	18,898
Creditors: due after one year	(6,210)	(5,415)
Provision for liabilities and charges	(569)	(85)
	(6,779)	(5,500)
	25,461	13,398
Capital and reserves:		
Called-up share capital	3,774	3,550
Share premium account	11,989	1,975
Profit and loss account	9,698	7,873
	25,461	13,398

[a] Year end changed during 1988, from 2 January to 31 December.

Appendix 2   Bejam

PROFIT AND LOSS ACCOUNT

£ thousands	1987	1988
Retail turnover (ex VAT)	496,776	528,660
Cost of sales	(431,561)	(457,545)
Gross profit	65,215	71,115
Other operating income	1,581	1,775
Other operating expenses	(41,670)	(45,672)
Allocation to employee profit-sharing scheme	(854)	(496)
Operating profit	24,272	26,722
Net interest payable	(713)	(1,917)
Profit before exceptional item	23,559	24,805
Exceptional item	–	(495)
Profit on ord. activities before tax	23,559	24,310
Tax on profit on ord. activities	(8,893)	(8,722)
Profit on ord. activities after tax	14,666	15,588
Extraordinary item	250	745
Profit for year	14,916	16,333
Dividends paid and proposed	(5,961)	(6,641)
Profit for year retained	8,955	9,692
Earnings per share	11.72p	12.38p

FINANCIAL ANALYSIS, 1979–88

Year to end June £000 (unless otherwise stated)	1979	1980	1981	1982	1983	1984	1985	1986	1987	1988
Turnover	119,006	157,994	192,847	224,878	252,825	296,245	336,347	399,453	496,776	528,660
Operating profit	5,587	7,896	9,174	11,672	12,338	16,531	19,421	20,518	24,272	26,722
Profit before tax	6,044	8,273	9,021	11,745	12,010	15,671	19,220	19,710	23,559	24,310
Earnings per share	2.41p	3.30p	3.59p	4.62p	4.70p	6.25p	8.74p	9.69p	12.23p	12.54p
Dividends per share	0.98p	1.35p	1.65p	2.20p	2.60p	3.00p	3.75p	4.25p	4.75p	5.25p
Freezer centres: Number of stores at financial year end	151	163	171	184	195	207	215	229	251	267
Sales area: Total at financial year end (000 sq. ft.)	520	575	651	743	821	900	961	1,064	1,177	1,287
Average size of all stores at year end (sq. ft.)	3,400	3,500	3,800	400	4,200	4,300	4,500	4,600	4,700	4,800
Sales statistics: Average food sales per store (inc VAT) (£ per week)	14,400	18,200	20,300	23,100	23,900	26,700	28,500	29,500	30,900	30,000
Freezers, microwaves cookers, refrigerators and dishwashers sold	78,400	75,800	97,400	111,300	149,200	158,700	182,500	201,900	207,700	241,000
Share price (pence) High	–	–	–	–	–	143	196	189	288	206
Low	–	–	–	–	–	102	139	144	148	148

BALANCE SHEETS

£ thousands	1987	1988
Employment of capital		
Fixed assets:		
Tangible assets	108,473	126,854
Investments	639	628
	109,112	127,482
Current assets:		
Stocks	34,367	38,805
Debtors	12,648	16,453
Cash at bank and in hand	1,126	2,407
	48,141	57,665
Creditors falling due within one year	(95,795)	(112,867)
New current assets (liabilities)	(47,654)	(55,202)
Total assets less current liabilities	61,458	72,280
Deferred taxation	(5,265)	(5,276)
Net assets	56,193	67,004
Sources of capital		
Capital and reserves:		
Called-up share capital	12,550	12,651
Share premium account	2,625	3,991
Revaluation reserve	–	741
Profit and loss account	41,018	49,621
Shareholders' funds	56,193	67,004

Appendix 3   Supermarket sales density and profitability

Company	1984	1985	1986	1987	1988	1989
Sainsbury						
Space (000 sq.ft.)	3,944	4,325	4,692	5,034	5,463	5,694
Sales/sq.ft. (£p.a.)	653	710	743	782	809	822
Tesco						
Space (000 sq.ft.)	7,362	7,415	7,502	6,997	8,220	8,542
Sales/sq.ft. (£p.a.)	353	404	447	514	502	552
Kwik Save						
Space (000 sq.ft.)	2,147	2,384	2,656	2,982	3,220	3,800
Sales/sq.ft. (£p.a.)	287	292	287	277	289	311
Asda						
Space (000 sq.ft.)	3,296	3,680	3,843	4,200	4,600	4,975
Sales/sq.ft. (£p.a.)	532	525	654	635	593	544

16   Westbury Homes Group

As Richard Fraser said in his chief executive's statement to the board, 28 February 1985 marked the end of a 12-month period throughout which there had been a great deal of uncertainty about the future ownership of the company. It had in fact been one which began with a feeling of a lot of promise in the air, had pitched into near despair, and yet ended on a high note of optimism with the conclusion of a successful management buy-out and the prospects of strong strategic growth.

At the beginning of the year the directors had announced their decision to apply for a full listing for the Cheltenham-based Westbury Group on the London Stock Exchange. Confidence was high, and a date in July had been set by the issuing house. The rise in interest rates and the sudden decline in the market brought about a temporary halt to the plans. However, by the autumn the economy had picked up and the board was ready to revive the flotation. In October the ultimate shareholder changed his mind and announced his intention of disposing of the whole of his shareholding by offering the company for sale by tender on the open market. Faced with this decision the seven senior directors decided to attempt to construct a bid to secure the business. They formed a new company, gained support from two large institutions, and were successful in acquiring the company.

Despite all this corporate activity the Westbury Homes Group yet again achieved record levels of sales units, turnover and pre-tax profits, and, as to the future, the annual report commented that although the ownership of the company had changed, the management had not, that the market remained good, and that the group had the skills and resources to continue its historic profits growth.

The year was one in which a lot of lessons had been and could be learned, and yet one which may have paved the way for a significant level of strategic initiative.

THE DEVELOPMENT OF A BUSINESS

Westbury Homes evolved out of the initiative and imagination of the two brothers, Bob and John Joiner. In 1966 they sold their existing business to ITT after a period of credit squeeze and a consequent loss of profit. They were not inclined to work for another company as employees, and forbidden by the terms of the sale to re-enter the television business in opposition; they felt that their only real alternative was to set up another business. Their capital gave them the time to think carefully upon the options and to start on a well-planned basis.

They pored over government statistics to find suitable opportunities for their limited resources and decided upon the main criteria to govern their choice. First, the market had to be large enough to accommodate their entry. It had to be able to allow a business to start up and develop without attracting too much competitive attention and aggression. It had to have low entry barriers, given the scale of their capital, and to allow for growth opportunities. Secondly, they wanted to deal with large-value items that might produce rapid cash flow – a unit selling price that was high enough to avoid the need for large selling teams. Thirdly, the product should involve a high labour content which might be sub-divided and sub-contracted out in order to reduce managerial time, attention and risk.

Only house-building and tour-operating fitted the bill and, as the housing business was then in a healthy state of growth, the brothers bought some land at the beginning of 1967. A small estate was contract designed and the construction was subcontracted. Start-up was slow but steady, and the first year saw the completion of just five houses. In 1970 they took on a larger site of 23 units, and profitability was rapidly improved due to the concentration of work in the one site area, thus setting a pattern for future contracts. This was an operation that was largely run by the seat of the pants, with the family making all operational and strategic decisions.

Between 1970 and 1973 Westbury Homes really took off, and company targets were doubled each year. Rapid growth brought with it problems of liquidity and, with a gearing ratio of 9:1 the company was not only under-capitalized, but vulnerable to adverse economic changes.

True to form, in May 1973 interest rates climbed and prices nose-dived. Like Alice in Wonderland who grew too large to get through the door, so too was Westbury Homes faced with a slump of 30 per cent in the market and a mounting backlog of unsold houses. Wisely the brothers swallowed their medicine and took drastic action by slimming down staffing levels and virtually halting new work in order to complete and sell outstanding and uncompleted units.

1974 saw many large housebuilders go to the wall but Westbury just survived and this experience was largely responsible for the introduction and development of an effective financial and management control system which was to serve the company well in the future. Towards the end of 1974 the market improved and the company expanded its geographic coverage. By 1979 the Centre for Inter-firm Comparison had placed Westbury Homes as heading the top ten for return on capital employed of 71 per cent, and second in the league for the fastest growing housebuilder.

THE JOINER BROTHERS

Bob Joiner was the extrovert and visionary of the two brothers, customer-oriented, dynamic and with an ability to motivate his staff; John Joiner could be described as an introvert, planning-oriented, rather uncommunicative, but with attributes which complemented those of his brother. Both brothers typically set themselves objectives which were consistently too high, and consequently operational and financial aspects of the business tended to suffer from a lack of realism.

The two brothers, although professionally unqualified, successfully managed the company from 1964 until the property slump of 1974, when facing imminent financial collapse they handed over management to Geoff Hester as managing director in 1976 and retired into chairmanship positions. It is doubtful that Westbury would have survived the crisis and grown to its present size had they not stepped aside as they found themselves unable to manage a business facing severe problems. This interference in the operational management of the company and the removal of capital sums for private and venture needs, hampered the efficient development of Westbury and left behind little capital for re-investment and re-capitalization.

The brothers certainly could be described as entrepreneurs. Stepping out of operations management, they spread their wings and were responsible for setting up overseas housebuilding operations, one in Canada in 1975 and two in the USA in 1979 and 1983. This 'have a go' attitude of the Joiners enabled them to exploit opportunities as they arrived and was the basis of their business success.

A CHANGE IN MANAGEMENT STYLE

In 1970 Geoff Hester joined Westbury Estates and by 1973 became a director of the company. As managing director in 1976 there can be no doubt that he was largely responsible for taking the company from its relatively small beginnings through to a major housebuilder by the time of his departure in June 1981. Geoff Hester's style of management was a hands-on approach in which typically most operational and strategic decisions were made by him. Known as Mr Westbury, his 'hire and fire' approach to management provided a high staff turnover and earned the company a poor outside image. He was, however, uncomfortable with the large divisionalized company that he had created and, finding himself unable to delegate responsibility adequately, he departed. John Joiner assumed day-to-day control of the company.

For a short period John Joiner's style proved to be a complete contrast; he sought a decentralized form of growth with only a limited amount of control coming from the centre, indeed so much so that it became almost impossible to prepare plans and budgets. This was an exciting period of development – from autocracy to democracy within eight months. The period produced much frustration, especially at top level. John Joiner clashed with the board and its traditional view of growth. In 1981/2 profits dropped for the first time as John Joiner was prepared to lose half a million pounds to get his ideas through. However the tensions were too great and in a boardroom clash John Joiner left and moved off to the United States, leaving his brother Bob as the sole owner of Westbury UK.

Bob Joiner had moved to live in the West Indies in 1977 where the group was now legally registered. His control was thus distant but he still remained financially insistent and demanding.

Richard Fraser was appointed to the position of managing director to bring some sense of control over the erratic pattern of activity. An accountant by profession and with the company since 1973, he had to determine upon a style of management that might rebuild a sense of corporate mission. The new MD encouraged the development of a top-down planning, bottom-up communications style of management. The culture is presently that of a family atmosphere in which employees are encouraged to take pride in their work and in Westburys, in return for higher than average salaries and a management responsive to the needs and development of its staff.

'The company's main resource is its people' says Richard Fraser, 'and I am very much concerned with the welfare and development of my staff, but I have no time for those who cannot shape up to my company expectations. We have to be a slim-line, thinking-based organization in a competitive business and we cannot afford to carry passengers.' The reputation and image of Westburys in the industry and in the public eye is seen as a major concern, and public relations is increasingly occupying both his and the personnel manager's working time. Considerable effort has been necessary to achieve a balanced style after the earlier contrasts, and an incremental and more open method of decision-taking has contributed much to a higher standard of decision-taking. Westburys' image, both internally and externally, was in the process of being changed to fit in with the management's vision of its future role. By March 1984 things had settled down once again and growth was evident in all indices. Bob Joiner and the board wished to go to the market to increase the finance available for fast expansion.

TABLE 16.1   **Recent performance of top ten UK housebuilders**

Parent	Company	Year end	No. of homes sold	Pre-tax profit (% to T/Over)	Return on investment	Approx. land bank (No. of years)
	1. Barratt	June 82	14,000	11.1	18%	3
	2. Wimpey	Dec. 81	7,400	6.4	6%	
	3. Tarmac	Dec. 81	3,980	9.0		
Guardian Royal Exchange	4. Broseley	Dec. 81	3,027	3.3	7%	
P & O	5. Bovis	Dec. 81	2,029	11.0	51%	5
	6. Leech	Aug. 81	1,880	4.2	6%	4½
	7. Bryant	May 81	1,700	13.2	32%	4¾
	8. Westbury	Feb. 82	1,420	6.9	43%	1¾
Carlton Industries	9. Comben	Dec. 81	1,402	6.1	16%	5
Trafalgar House	10. Ideal	Sept. 81	1,300	3.5	20%	
			38,138			

THE PRESENT BUSINESS

Subcontracting is anything and everything in this organization to enable top management to spend its time on doing what it knows best – making money. This principle is still valid today. Subcontractors are part of the family and many of them have been with the firm longer than most of the staff. There are in fact some 300 management and associated staff within Westburys; there are some 2,000 people externally employed.

Figure 16.1 illustrates growth in the group's unit sales over the 10-year period to 1984, compared with total private-sector dwelling completions in Great Britain, making it today the twelfth largest housebuilder.

The group develops housing estates of from 15 to 400 houses for sale to private buyers. Estates typically include a range of detached, semi-detached and terraced houses and in some cases flats. In addition, the group undertakes a limited amount of contract house-building for housing associations and local authorities. In the year ended February 1984 such contract housebuilding amounted to less than 3 per cent of group turnover.

The group's head office is located at Westbury House, Cheltenham. This accommodates the group's centralized design, marketing, land acquisition, planning and finance functions. The operating subsidiaries,

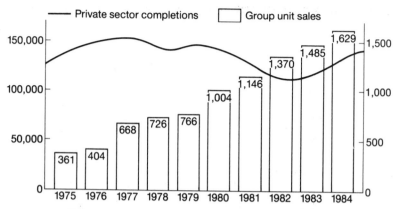

FIGURE 16.1   **Private sector completions compared with group unit sales**

Note: Industry figures (*Source*: Department of Environment) are for the calendar year and are compared with group unit sales for the year to end February in the following year.

which are also based at Cheltenham, are responsible for production and sales in the four operating regions. Figure 16.2 outlines the organization structure.

AREA AND SCOPE OF OPERATIONS

The group's four operating regions are South-West, Severnside, Midlands and Wales (see figure 16.3). Currently the group has 40 estates under development in 12 counties of England and Wales. It is likely that future operations will extend to cover mid and southern England. Within its area of operations, the directors estimate that the group has a market share of approximately 12 per cent locally and about 1 per cent in the national market.

LAND ACQUISITION AND LAND BANK

The success of the group has been founded partly upon an in-depth knowledge of land and planning matters within its expanding area of operations, and to this end a small specialist team exists to deal exclusively with this important aspect of the business.

The group has consistently been able to acquire land with outline planning consent in good locations. Land is not usually acquired without such consent, but the group has developed the use of options on

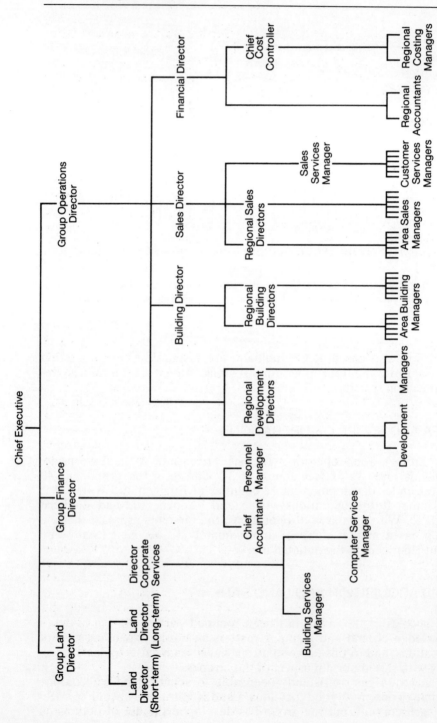

FIGURE 16.2   **Westbury Homes organization chart**

those sites where it is felt that the group's expertise can be used to accelerate the planning consent procedure.

At 31 May 1984 land controlled by the group represented a stock equivalent of two years' usage based on anticipated sales for the year ending February 1983. In addition, at 31 May 1984, the group had options on sites equivalent to a further 2,500 plots. None of these sites presently has planning consent.

ESTATE DESIGN

Reflecting the importance that the group attaches to this key element of the business, a staff of 34 is engaged in the design of housing estates and in carrying out the legal and planning work necessary before site development can commence. These staff have the skills necessary to maximize the estates' appeal to prospective housebuyers and to ensure speedy resolution of planning matters.

HOUSE DESIGN AND PRODUCT RANGE

The group currently has a range of 19 designs for houses, varying in size from one to five bedrooms. In order to maximize customer appeal, each of these designs can be built in a range of external styles. There are currently three distinct styles: Rural, Georgian and Tudor, each of which can be built in a variety of elevations and treatments. Current prices of one-bedroom houses range from £17,750 to £25,000 and of four-bedroom houses from £35,000 t0 £70,000. In the year ended February 1984 some 43 per cent of turnover was made up of sales of one- or two-bedroom homes and the average sale price of all units sold in that year was £27,800.

PRODUCTION AND CONTROL

All construction is carried out by subcontractors, many of whom have developed with the group and therefore understand the group's strict requirements for construction to be completed on time and to high standards of finish. Most subcontractors work almost exclusively for the group. This close relationship with subcontractors has helped the group achieve a production-line approach to building. House construction is divided into eight stages (appropriate to particular subcontract trades) and is closely supervised on each estate by a manager employed by the group and based on that estate. All homes are constructed to National House Building Council Standards and are sold with a ten-year NHBC structural warranty.

Control over house production is achieved by means of a detailed

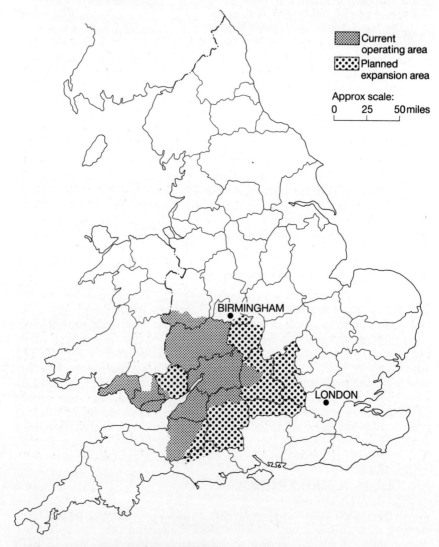

FIGURE 16.3   **Areas of UK operation**

programme, operated by each regional subsidiary, which monitors house production on a weekly basis. This is linked to the group's computerized management information system which provides comprehensive and regular operating and financial reports.

The policy is 'to get it right first time, produce a quality product that the market can afford, and never to miss a completion date for our customers'.

SALES AND MARKETING

The group places great importance on effective on-site presentation and on ensuring that both the house and the estate are presented to customers as attractively as possible. On each estate there is one or more fully furnished show home open seven days a week and staffed by a full-time member of the sales team. Advertising in the local press is controlled by area sales management, who are best placed to assess local conditions and requirements. This is supported, as required, by special promotions and corporate advertising on television and in the national newspapers. On the majority of sites, at least one estate agent is appointed on a 'no sale no fee' basis.

The group considers it important to provide a comprehensive sales service to customers, and to this end employs eight full-time customer service managers who are responsible for accepting houses from production and liaising with customers both before and after sale. The directors believe that this service leads to increased trade-up sales to satisfied customers as well as to new introductions provided by such customers. The group has extensive mortgage allocations with several major building societies and is able to offer the benefit of mortgage assistance to many customers. The group also runs a home exchange plan which operates within strict limits on the number of second-hand houses that can be held by the group at any one time. Each house has a fitted kitchen; however, the group does not normally equip houses with 'white' goods, carpets or curtains as this conflicts with the group's policy of providing maximum value in the building itself.

Effective control, monitoring and target setting are considered vital ingredients of the group's sales success. The sales teams are given targets against which performance is measured. Reservations, contracts and legal completions are all monitored weekly and this information is linked to the group's computerized management reporting system.

OPERATIONAL AND MANAGEMENT CONTROLS

A key feature of the Westbury approach to house building is the emphasis that is placed on effective monitoring and control over all aspects of the business. To this end the group prepares:

- weekly reports of sales, reservations and production by region;
- profit and loss reports after six, eight, ten, 11 and 12 weeks of each quarter for each operating company and for the group as a whole;
- monthly information packs containing a detailed statistical digest plus a cash-flow projection for the next six weeks, and cash-flow comparison with the previous month; and

• quarterly management accounts containing detailed profit and loss accounts and balance sheets compared with budget, backed up by statistical and financial detail; a rolling 12 months' budget which amends the current year's budget; and a detailed management information book which contains a wealth of financial and statistical historical data on the group. This information is produced for each operating company and for the group as a whole.

FINANCIAL STATUS

General

In the year ended February 1984 the group sold 1,629 units, achieving turnover of £45.3m. and pre-tax profits of £3.6m. Apart from a dip in profits in 1982, the group's unit sales, turnover and pre-tax profits had increased in each of the last ten years.

In the year ending 28 February 1985 the latest management accounts, covering the first 26 weeks of the year, showed a net profit before taxation of £1.86m. The directors expected unit sales of 1,711 and a turnover of £53.3m. for the full year. In the absence of unforeseen circumstances, the directors also expected that the group profit before taxation for the year ending 28 February 1985 would be in the region of £4m. The directors estimated that net tangible assets of the group as at 28 February 1985 would be approximately £9.5m.

The group had intended to seek a quotation on the Stock Exchange in July 1984. These plans were postponed in the light of the market conditions at that time.

Trading record and 1984–5 budget

Set out in table 16.2 is a summary of the trading record of the group for the five years ended February 1984, together with the budget for the year ending February 1985. Further financial information is set out in the Accountants' Report.

ENVIRONMENTAL ISSUES

Of major importance to the growth of the company is the government's ability to control interest rates.

The growth of pressures upon planning authorities to restrict house building means that political power is increasingly occupying the group's time. Contacts with planning authorities, land agencies, solicitors, estate agents, etc., are vital relationships which, if managed well, can facilitate the lead time to construction start-up.

Demographic changes and population movement to the south of England tend to work in Westbury's favour. Previously, 70 per cent of

TABLE 16.2   **Westbury's trading record**
BALANCE SHEETS AT 29 FEBRUARY 1984 (£000)

	The Group
Fixed assets	
Property, plant and equipment	1,116
Investment in subsidiary	–
	1,116
Current assets	
Stocks	22,916
Debtors	1,555
Bank balances, deposits and cash	169
	24,640
Creditors falling due within one year	
Loans (secured)	3,165
Bank overdrafts (secured)	6,548
Creditors	6,554
Dividends	338
Taxation	1,230
	17,835
Net current assets	6,805
Total assets less creditors falling due within one year	7,921
Creditors falling due after more than one year	272
Deferred taxation	160
Net tangible assets	7,489
Shareholders' funds	
Share capital	465
Reserves	7,024
	7,489

continued

families lived in rented accommodation, whereas now 60 per cent own their own homes, and present government policy is to increase that percentage.

The first-time-buyer market, however, peaked in 1967 and potentially the largest market segment is in upmarket houses and residential buildings for the elderly. This is presently contrary to Westbury's market focus, which is on the lower end of the housing price scale.

There is now greater emphasis on inner-city sites for urban renewal and public support for the refurbishment of old buildings, often with the co-operation and support of local authorities.

TABLE 16.2   *(continued)*

PROFIT AND LOSS ACCOUNTS YEAR ENDED 28 OR 29 FEBRUARY (£000)

	1980	*1981*	*1982*	*1983*	*1984*
Turnover	18,697	25,572	31,525	38,354	45,284
Cost of sales	(13,755)	(18,429)	(22,894)	(27,689)	(33,389)
Gross profit	4,942	7,143	8,631	10,665	11,895
Selling costs	(741)	(1,869)	(3,189)	(3,977)	(4,379)
Administration costs	(912)	(1,266)	(1,774)	(2,001)	(2,182)
Operating profit	3,289	4,008	3,668	4,687	5,334
Investment income	13	55	35	92	19
Interest payable	(782)	(1,292)	(1,486)	(1,660)	(1,707)
Profit before taxation	2,520	2,771	2,217	3,119	3,646
Taxation	(19)	(229)	(619)	(738)	(1,537)
Profit after taxation	2,501	2,542	1,598	2,381	2,109
Extraordinary items and non-recurring proprietorial expenses	(428)	(469)	(867)	(577)	(1,070)
	2,073	2,073	731	1,804	1,039
Dividends	(361)	(369)	(212)	(1,113)	(917)
Retained profit	1,712	1,704	519	691	122
Earnings per share	13.4p	13.7p	8.6p	12.8p	11.3p

The requirements of housebuyers are changing, with more demand for houses with purchase appeal and superior living environments.

The technology of this industry is low and traditional building materials and construction methods are favoured. Fortunately, the industry is not highly unionized, and Westbury's policy of making the employees feel part of the company has promoted a highly motivated and loyal workforce.

THE BOMBSHELL

In April 1984 confidence in the company's prospects and the market for housebuilding was high. Expansion prospects existed, but capital for land acquisition was scarce. Bob Joiner was disinclined to invest any further; indeed he wished to liquidate some of his investment tied up in the business.

The proposal to float the company, to draw in outside funding, was a positive and logical move. It did, however, demand a greater

TABLE 16.2   (*continued*)
STATEMENTS OF SOURCES AND APPLICATIONS OF FUNDS YEAR ENDED 28 OR 29 FEBRUARY (£000)

	1980	*1981*	*1982*	*1983*	*1984*
Sources of funds					
Funds generated from operations					
Profit before taxation	2,520	2,771	2,217	3,119	3,646
Depreciation	71	80	122	124	119
Losses/(profits) on sales					
of fixed assets	–	6	28	(14)	(14)
	2,591	2,857	2,367	3,229	3,751
Funds from other sources					
Proceeds from sales of fixed					
assets	13	91	70	173	459
Loan received	–	398	–	–	–
Total sources of funds	2,604	3,346	2,437	3,402	4,210
Applications of funds					
Purchases of fixed assets	261	859	236	124	220
Long-term loan repayments	20	–	58	137	106
Tax paid	82	293	421	301	616
Dividends paid	136	694	147	1,150	625
Extraordinary items and non-					
recurring proprietorial expenses	428	469	867	577	1,070
Total applications of funds	927	2,315	1,729	2,289	2,637
Net sources of funds	1,677	1,031	708	1,113	1,573
Increases (decreases) in					
working capital					
Increases in stocks	2,743	4,075	2,886	1,857	5,462
Increases (decreases) in debtors	543	163	166	254	(330)
(Increases) in creditors	(1,874)	(3,344)	(2,223)	(819)	(3,546)
	1,412	894	829	1,232	(1,586)
Movements in net liquid funds	265	137	(121)	(119)	(13)
Increases in working capital	1,677	1,031	708	1,113	1,573

knowledge of the market and a greater self-awareness than hitherto. It precipitated a search for greater understanding about both policy and strategy, which was to be a great plus when the board came round to negotiating the management buy-out. In the March – June period of 1984 the preparatory work was done, but in June interest rates rose by 2 per cent and a lot of other flotations were on the stocks of the City institutions, and the decision was taken to hold the offer. Everything was flattened out; there was a loss of impetus and emphasis; but by the autumn, with BT out of the way, the merchant bankers recommended a flotation for June 1985. Thus a re-writing of the prospectus was put in hand at some quarter of a million pounds' cost. The board meeting was scheduled for Friday 12 October with the prospectus as the single item on the agenda. Bob Joiner attended that meeting, interrupted the agenda, and announced that he was going to sell.

Bob Joiner had been in ill-health for some time, approaching retirement age and with no immediate family to succeed him. The decision was sudden. He had been advised by his doctor that week to stop work. He determined to cut all UK connections, to sell the company, and concentrate his activities in Florida and the Bahamas where he had lived since 1977.

The sudden nature of the statement was serious enough, but equally significant to an astonished board of directors was the immediacy of the decision. It left so little margin of discretion to them. The announcement to sell was made on Friday 12 October; the timetable for the sale was for close of bid offers by 23 November, and completion of the sale by 20 December. The time period was indeed very short, and therefore it seemed only major companies with large resources could be invited to bid.

All promises were broken and seemingly no options existed. The initial reaction of the board was one of despondency. It could be expected that any new owners would replace or phase out much of the senior management and bring in their own people.

THE MANAGEMENT FIGHT-BACK

Barrie Hall was the architect of the buy-out. Over the weekend he read up an article on MBOs and decided to raise the issue on 14 October at a further board meeting.

As group financial director and Richard Fraser's right-hand man, Barrie Hall had played a major role in shaping the outcome of most major decisions, particularly on financial and control aspects. 'When the Westbury sale was announced, I was motivated more by self-preservation than entrepreneurship. I was determined not just to lie there and do nothing so I started phoning around for details on MBOs and soon the idea became a possibility.' The problem was, of course, whether they could produce the sort of money that would make a credible bid. They needed financial advice and they needed it fast. They needed venture capital and they needed a lot of it. They had to build a credible position out of nothing.

The owner and non-executive directors were against the feasibility of a buy-out from personal views and on the advice of Samuel Montagu, the merchant bankers handling the sale.

Unconvinced by any opposition to his idea, Barrie Hall, and on persuasion, Fraser, decided that further action was necessary and during the first week made active enquiries in London for backers and secured the interest from three venture capital companies, Investors in Industry, Candover and Charterhouse.

The other five senior executives were now approached and they rapidly decided to support the buy-out deal, either because of the opportunity to own their own business and reap the financial rewards, or because failure to secure a deal meant redundancy.

One of the problems was that this was an inexperienced board. Arguments in favour of making a bid were that:

- the company was well-known in building industry circles;
- it had a small landbank which was rapidly turned;
- the only real asset was people;
- thus the buying prospects for an outsider were somewhat limited;
- the board knew their people and their potential;
- the prospectus had already been designed and thus the board knew far more about the potential than could any outside bidder;
- all the data were at hand.

Against this there was, of course, the time factor and the fact that in the ultimate the main concern of the vendor was to have a signed and sealed contract for cash with immediate delivery.

The first problem was to find a broker to put together the venture capital. Investors in Industry hit it off with Westburys from the first, both in style and penetration. They had ample experience in MBOs. Their past records showed that their success rate on MBOs was high. The company promoted an active policy of liaison negotiation and post-MBO monitoring. The company could secure finance in the time available. They were to take a stake in the equity and therefore were not only committed but personally interested in the success of the deal. Relationships were good right from the initial stages. They put together a deal with, amongst others, the Prudential, sorted out other partners and formulated a proposal. By 10 November a shell company had been set up to acquire the business should the bid succeed.

The buy-out team together with advice from Investors in Industry were able to put together a feasibility plan and, armed with an accountant's audit of Westbury, secure the initial financial backing. Investors in Industry acted as sole agent for a consortium of financial investors representing their interest in the buy-out deal. As the legal and taxation issues in MBOs are complex, a firm of solicitors was engaged to act on Westbury's behalf, but all parties were still under the direction of Investors in Industry.

MBO TACTICS

Richard Fraser was in a difficult position and facing conflicting interests. He was now in the market as a potential bidder. He was also still running the company for the owner and expected to show the company to any alternative bidder in honest and open fashion. He decided that as far as other competitors were concerned his responsibilities entailed that he should willingly answer any questions concerning the company and the sale, but that he was not obliged to volunteer information.

His role as far as the bidding period was concerned was thus a passive one and, in order to allay suspicions, all bidders were fairly informed of his involvement in a buy-out package.

The advantages that the MBO team had over other businesses were that, firstly, they knew the business inside out and were therefore more likely to appreciate its true worth and potential and, secondly and more importantly, they knew exactly what the owner wanted. Surprisingly none of the other competitors actually took the trouble to fly out to the Bahamas where the owner was residing as a tax exile to discover more about him and his needs. Alternative bidders thus had little apparent notion of the personalities involved in the battle and particularly that what Bob Joiner was really after was to be paid in cash on 20 December.

The buy-out team were able to successfully exploit these conditions in their preparation of the bid:

1   The MBO bid/offer was on one page, simple and unaccompanied by masses of legal jargon (made subject to contract) – and was tailored to the owner's needs.
2   The offer was for cash. Other bidders made offers including delayed payments, share offers, and indeed some required extension to the bid deadline.
3   The MBO team had found it possible to raise money and complete the deal within the time stipulated by the owner. Indeed they knew that time was a key factor in the successful outcome of the buy-out team.
4   The working relationship with Investors in Industry was excellent, and this facilitated the process of raising the finance and shortening the negotiating period.
5   Some bidders were put off once they realized that the entire management team was involved in the buy-out. Should the buy-out fail, the new owner was likely to purchase a company divorced from its senior executives and divorced from their goodwill.

Fraser and Hall pitched the offer price just above the expected market level, but they acknowledged that they had very little margin to play with even if it had not been the best offer. In fact the bid was lower than that suggested by Investors in Industry after much deliberation by the three-man board. Fraser felt the need to notify the next level down in the management team as early as possible. Westburys had always been a very open firm and he felt the need to share the problems and the proposals with 25 of the senior managers to enable them to foresee the options open. The main board of seven, of course, owned the problem.

Rumours had got around, indeed many were based upon fact. One subcontractor heard the full story from his bank! The search was now for a secure business. The search told the board a lot about how to run an exposed business, dependent wholly upon market forces. In particular it taught it how to raise its sights to the future. The prospectus had to rise beyond immediate opportunities or threats within the construction industry, and in particular beyond the options limited in the south-west.

Bob Joiner did not really believe that the board could find the money and asked Richard Fraser to sell at the best possible price. When it became evident that an MBO was not only possible but financially acceptable he came round enthusiastically to the idea. It was obvious that with an MBO team involved the competition was increased and indeed the buy-out team might well offer the best price. If he sold to the management the company that he had built up and had had some considerable pride in would maintain its identity and name and would not be lost in a corporate swallow-up. The top management, with whom the owner had worked, would not lose their jobs and additionally the employees would benefit from their years of service.

The management were under no illusions as to the owner's concern with obtaining the highest price and realized that therefore all other influences were of a very secondary nature. However they made every effort to tailor their bid to his needs and sale requirements, and this was seen to be an influencing factor in the success of the offer.

The week-end following Friday 23 November was spent waiting. Would the tender be accepted? On Monday the bid was successfully received. Richard Fraser notified the press and the staff had the immediate notice of success.

VALUATION OF THE COMPANY

The assets of the company totalled some £9.5 million but it was obvious that book value did not represent the going market value of Westbury.

Investors in Industry and Prudential (the key financial backers) were prepared to go up to £14 million and, having spent so much time and effort on the deal, were particularly anxious to achieve a successful bid.

Based on their knowledge of the company and the housebuilding industry and supplemented by snippets of information gathered from private sources and competitor reactions, the buy-out team soon realized that they could substantially drop the price below the ceiling imposed by their backers.

A price incentive deal was therefore negotiated with Investors in Industry, in which the management's share of the company would be 12 per cent for a purchase price of £14 million, but for each £0.5 million below the top price the buy-out team gained an extra 0.5 per cent.

A complicated organic method of valuation was not employed to arrive at the bid offer, but rather a subjective method was used, based on these questions:

- What is the highest bid our competitors are likely to make, based on formal and informal sources of information available to the buy-out team?
- What is the minimum price the owner will accept for his company?

Against advice from their backers, the MBO team trusted their instincts, and their offer of £12m. was successful (only just).

The management stake in Westbury consequently went up to 14 per cent. The £2.5m. over book price represented valuation of goodwill, intangibles, quality of the company's management control systems, and Westbury's market position and growth potential.

THE MBO DEAL

In order to represent the interests of the financial investors, three non-executive directors joined the board, although maintaining a sensible policy of non-interference in the management of Westbury.

The MBO period is expected to last some three to five years before taking the company into public ownership. The issues at stake here are to continue company growth and profitability, and simultaneously to convince the financial community that Westbury is a well-managed company with a highly attractive appeal to potential investors.

The Westbury Homes buy-out consisted of a straight purchase of assets; however, legal and taxation problems posed some major headaches during the contract period. The sale transaction did not initially achieve tax clearance from the Department of Inland Revenue.

The importance of tax warranties and indemnities cannot be over-stressed in any deal of this kind, and both sides took time to arrive at mutually agreeable positions. Discrepancies in the accounts and back tax were typically met by the seller.

In the Westbury Homes deal, £10 million was paid on the due date and the balance with interest, but minus tax debts, paid one year later.

The capital structure was as set out in table 16.3.

TABLE 16.3   **Capital structure of the Westbury Homes buy-out**

Investors	Share price	Type	Amount	Ownership
			£m.	%
Bank	–	Secured	2.0	–
Investors in Industry and Prudential	£7.67	Prefer-ence	9.8	38
Others	£8.45			48
Buy-out	£1.00	Prefer-ence	0.2	14
		Ordinary	12.0	100

Investors in Industry, Prudential and the buy-out team together held 52 per cent of the new company's stock, giving them a majority stake.

WHAT HAS CHANGED?

The MBO has been successfully negotiated and the board has settled down to a programme of strategic development designed to build a prospectus for a market launch in two to three years' time. Barrie Hall sees the company continuing to expand on a steady basis. 'Sticking to what it's good at' is his view of the company.

There has been no change at the lower levels of the enterprise and none in basic operational practices. The firm has always had to operate on tight site controls and that is ever more necessary now. At the top, the group has lost its two founders who built the company. Now the board is able to use its own projected earnings to plan future developments and growth. The venture capital was fixed for two years; if any major shareholder wants to get out then he is required to sell to one of the others. This is a young and hungry company, says Richard Fraser with great and natural pride.

There has been a change of emphasis since the buy-out. The company has become more professional and this has been accompanied by a quicker flow of decisions, says Roger Hughes, the group operations director. 'But our immediate problem concerns lack of finance for growth due to the buy-out debt burden. We can, however, take an enterprising stance on the future of Westbury and would in due course like to see both internal growth and diversification into related fields.' He argues that the buy-out has enabled the company to get its house in order, particularly on consistent decision-making, more effective planning, the use of profits within the business and the encouragement of professional people managing the company without over-interference.

Now the issues are strategic. Richard Fraser is familiar with the operational needs and difficulties but now he says, due to increasing size and complexity, he confines himself to the strategic issues. He now has to adopt an arbitrating role. Although power is vested in his position, his approach to management is to keep in touch with the other key senior executives, looking at the angles, soliciting advice as necessary, listening to the views of interested parties but taking the ultimate responsibility. Strategy is largely developed on an incremental basis still, and although present policy is largely reactive to market needs and geared to short-term horizons, the company is now forced to view long-term planning with equally increasing importance. The structure of the new prospectus will be such as to demand a formal statement of growth strategy. 'Our immediate plan is to go public at the right time and with the right price in order to repay debt and raise finance for corporate growth, and therefore I intend to make Westbury Homes an attractive buy to outside investors.'

PART IV

GROWTH AND DECLINE

17   Silentnight
The UK Bedding Industry

THE MARKET FOR BEDS AND MATTRESSES

Over the 1970s, the bed and mattress market was one of the most stable, and changes in sales levels rarely upset the equilibrium of manufacturers' profitability. However, by 1980 the situation had changed, sales began to decline, profitability began to fall and several companies went into liquidation.

The market for beds is unique in the furniture market in the sense that domestic manufacturers have retained and built upon their long-established reputation for quality products and, so far, overseas competition has been largely repelled.

The three main submarkets in the beds sector are: bases, mattresses and bed ends. The majority of beds are made from wood and upholstery, but there is still a small market for metal mattress supports and bed ends.

MARKET SIZE AND TRENDS

Sales of beds and bases became static in the late 1970s after a steady growth. At the same time, consumers have been trading down in terms of quality and the value of sales has not been keeping pace with inflation.

Some sectors of the bed market have been relatively buoyant as there has been a trend towards storage bases and bunk beds in the late 1970s. Specialist retailers claim that storage beds accounted for 60 per cent of sales whilst non-specialists claimed they accounted for 40 per cent.

There has been a shift away from double beds to single beds, with lower unit values. In 1979, the market was divided approximately evenly between single and double beds; by 1984, however, the single beds were outselling double beds in a ratio of 53:47.

TABLE 17.1 **UK manufacturers' sales of beds and mattresses**

Year	Value £m.	Volume M. Units
1975	95.7	4.9
1976	109.0	6.3
1977	117.9	6.0
1978	143.1	6.7
1979	154.1	6.6
1980	153.2	6.2
1981	162.0	5.5
1982	176.27	5.3[a]
1983	189.47	5.4[a]
1984	198.21	5.6[a]

[a] estimated
Value and share volume figures are calculated on different bases and it is not possible
to determine the unit price of a bed by dividing value by volume.
Source: Business Monitor

TABLE 17.2 **Overseas trade in beds (£)m.**

	1979	1980	1981	1982	1983	1984
Exports	3.03	2.75	2.30	2.76	2.22	2.04
Imports	0.54	0.56	1.00	1.45	2.35	1.86
Balance	2.49	2.19	1.30	1.31	0.13	0.18

Source: Business Monitor

TABLE 17.3 **Structure of the bed products market – % of MSP value**

	1979	1980	1981	1982	1983	1984
Mattresses	54	54	52	52	52	52
Upholstered bases	37	36	37	37	36	37
Bed ends, headboards, bunk beds	9	10	11	11	12	11

Source: Business Monitor

Through the 1970s unit sales of spring mattresses declined each year, and the unit sales of foam mattresses have increased. The trend to cheaper foam mattresses has been helped by a fashion for wooden beds and bunk beds with a foam mattress which are suitable for children. Foam is not important in the double-bed sector but accounts for a large proportion of single-bed mattress sales. The majority of purchasers of single beds are not buying for themselves, but for chil-

TABLE 17.4   **UK manufacturers' sales of convertibles**

Year	£m. MSP
1981	8.3
1982	7.6
1983	13.1
1984	14.9

Source: *Business Monitor*

dren or guests and so may not be as concerned about quality as they might otherwise be.

People buy beds and mattresses when they set up home, when children need them and for guest rooms. This is largely between the ages of 25–34. There is also a large replacement market. In the replacement market which takes place in the 55–64-year-old group of the population, sales of mattresses are higher than those of bases for economic reasons. If the bed is not distorted, then it is cheaper to replace only the mattress.

Growth areas in the market are luxury beds and storage beds. Although orthopaedic beds remain the most popular, consumers are moving away from them towards those which offer more comfort as well as a firm core for spinal support. These premium-priced luxury beds are also more profitable for manufacturers.

Space utilization has increased in importance as more people buy flats and newer houses with smaller rooms. Storage beds, bunk beds and convertibles have increased in popularity. Drawer divans are the most popular, accounting for 75 per cent to 80 per cent of storage beds and divans, and over 80 per cent of all bed sales.

Convertible sofas can look good for seating and also provide a spare bed for guests. As this has been realized, so the market has grown, although convertible sofas have been available for many years. UK manufacturers' sales of convertibles have been steadily increasing since late 1982.

The buying of a bed is not on the whole considered to be an exciting purchase as it is not generally on view to visitors. Bed purchases compete with electrical and durable goods for discretionary spending.

MANUFACTURERS AND MARKET SHARE

By 1982 the number of manufacturers involved in the bedding industry was 80, compared to a total of 460 after the Second World War. This gives an indication of the nature of concentration in the bedding market.

There are a number of important manufacturers and brands in this

TABLE 17.5   **Market share by volume**

	1979 %	1982 %	1984 %
Silentnight Group	20	30	28–30
Airsprung	3–5	9	12
Sykes (Dorlux)	–	8	9–10
Rest Assured	5–6	4–5	6–7
Reylon	3–5	3–4	5–6
Myers	5	6	4–5
Sleepezee	5	5–6	4–5
Dunlopillo	5–6	4–5	4
Others	38–42	17–21	13–21

Source: Mintel/Trade estimates

market, each with between 4 per cent and 9 per cent market share, the exception being Silentnight who overtook Slumberland as brand leader by the late 1970s. The fortunes of other brands have been variable.

There has been a large increase in own-label manufacturing of beds and mattresses in the 1980s. These products are now thought to account for 20 to 25 per cent of sales. Most of the major manufacturers produce own-label products for retailers, but labels usually state the name of the manufacturers to give an assurance of quality.

Silentnight Holdings plc is the leading UK manufacturer of beds and mattresses. In addition to the Silentnight name, the company is also responsible for Sealy Sleep products, Layezee beds and Perfecta bedding. Silentnight has achieved its strong position by cultivation of the retail trade, and an emphasis on the right product at the right price. Silentnight has spent very little on promoting its products to the public, except for selected advertising in particular areas, and as a result, brand awareness is low even though in the past few years efforts have been made to rectify the situation. However, most effort is still below the line to the retailer. In July 1984 the company launched the 'Super Sleeper' into the luxury bed sector with a £500,000 launch budget. It is being produced under licence from the American firm Serta.

The Airsprung group, selling middle-range beds, is second in the market after significantly bettering distribution in all retail areas since the late 1970s. Their share has increased from 4 per cent to 12 per cent in ten years. It supplies MFI with an estimated 20 per cent of its volume going through this retailer.

Slumberland, one of the loss-making concerns of Dupont, was sold to Melatex, a privately owned company, in February 1983 for £470,000, and Silentnight recently backed out of an opportunity to

TABLE 17.6   **Bed purchases by type of outlet**

Outlet	1981	1982	1984
	%	%	%
Bedding and furniture shops	43–45	42–43	43–44
Department stores	15–17	14–15	15–16
Discount warehouses	11–13	15–17	20–22
Mail order	8–10	7–8	5–6
Co-ops	6–7	5–6	5–6
Other	10–14	11–17	6–12

Source: Price Commission/Trade estimates

purchase it. The upmarket trade marks include Somnus and Posture springing. The operation has been very much slimmed down since the takeover of Melatex, and it is reported to be profitable once again.

Relyon and Rest Assured have maintained their market share despite their products being higher priced. In value terms their market shares are higher than in volume terms. Relyon in particular have reported better turnover and profits in 1983 and 1984 compared with earlier years. Sykes (Dorlux), a manufacturer positioned very much at the lower end of the price range, has done very well and gained a significant market share, as consumers have become increasingly price sensitive. Due to the aggressive stance of MFI and Queensway, consumer preferences have shifted towards a premium price segment and a larger low-priced segment, with the middle-range sector declining significantly. Sykes (Dorlux) were well positioned to take advantage of this shift, and those companies aiming at the middle range (for example, Silentnight) have had to rethink their marketing strategies.

RETAILERS AND DISTRIBUTION

The distribution profile for beds is significantly different from that for furniture as a whole. In all other sectors of the furniture market, one outlet or another has a position of some dominance; for example MFI dominates the kitchen furniture and multiple retailers dominate the upholstery sector. Sales of beds, on the other hand, are very well spread across a wide range of outlets.

Harris Queensway and MFI are the two largest firms in the discount warehouse business in the country, with Harris Queensway alone accounting for 7 per cent of all bed sales. Allied Carpets have now entered the bed retailing market, and the importance of discounters is likely to continue.

TABLE 17.7 **Advertising expenditure**

	1982 £000	1983 £000	1984 £000
Orthopaedic Bed Advisory Service	403	905	1,187
Sealy Beds	155	198	132
Dunlopillo Beds	–	–	113
Silentnight Divans	334	1,131	79
Sleepezee	175	38	53
Slumberland	106	–	–
Other brands	172	296	400
Total	1,345	2,568	1,964

Source: Meal/Mintel

ADVERTISING AND PROMOTION

From table 17.7 it can be seen that the main media efforts have been fairly modest. Many major manufacturers spend very little on above-the-line advertising. In fact most of the promotional expenditure by manufacturers is through the retail trade.

From previous national advertising campaigns Slumberland has the highest brand awareness, and also appeared near the top in the share of recall.

SILENTNIGHT HOLDINGS PLC

Introduction

Founded by Tom Clarke after the war, Silentnight is the largest bed manufacturer in the UK. Additionally, a small proportion of group turnover is accounted for by manufacture and sale of bedroom, lounge and kitchen furniture. The family still has a majority (approximately 52 per cent) of the issued ordinary shares which are held in a private investment company which is wholly owned and controlled by them. At the age of 65, Tom Clarke is chairman. The company went public in 1973 and the profit record was excellent until the late 1970s. In 1978 the chairman reported increased sales (up 50 per cent to £38m.) and profits (up 34 per cent to £3.5m.), and he emphasized that Silentnight was a growth business and the EPS had more than trebled in 5 years. In 1979 sales (£50.9m.) and profits (£4.21m.) reached record levels.

1980–1985

In 1980 Silentnight experienced a fall in profits which was caused by a general recession in the UK economy and specifically by very competitive conditions in the furniture market and substantial de-stocking by retailers. During the year there were various sales and closures estimated to result in an after-tax loss of approximately £1m. In 1981 profits continued to fall, and factory closure and reor-ganization costs totalled £1.32m. However, profits increased in 1982, helped by a switch from £402,000 interest charges to an interest credit of £335,000. For the three years to 1984, pre-tax profits and sales remained fairly static.

In the period 1981–5, Silentnight had the largest investment pro-gramme in the industry, of approximately £5 million per annum. Early investment was on capacity extension, and latterly expenditure has been directed towards new manufacturing technology. Most re-cently a new manufacturing plant has been built to produce the new Super Sleeper bed. This bed is constructed on the basis of a completely new system of springs made under licence from a company in the USA where it is reputed to have gained market share since its introduction a few years ago. Silentnight have sole UK manufacturing rights for the Super Sleeper. The basic benefits are that it has a longer life and is more comfortable. Also, there has been greater investment in distribution in order to provide retailers with a better service and reduce delivery times. To this end, delivery route planning has been computerized (£2.5m.) and £1.4m. spent on vehicles. Also a new exhi-bition centre has been opened near Barnoldswick, which is the location of the head office, displaying a wide range of company products.

Recently, two plants have been closed and a Scottish timber mill sold, and the disposal of a leasing company has raised £2.75m. in cash. In an effort to reduce costs and improve efficiency, the group has used its increasing size to introduce economies of scale based on ver-tical integration. Parkinsons, a separate Yorkshire-based company within the group, supplies woollen felt. Another company exists solely as a buying arm for the manufacturing divisions. The group also handles its own softwood imports at Hartlepool and makes some spring units and timber frames. It is now moving towards direct importation of hardwoods.

Products and marketing

Most of Silentnight's promotion and advertising expenditure is to retailers, which is thought more cost-effective than a television advertising campaign. Silentnight have made efforts to improve their marketing with the launching of the Merchandise Development Service unit (MDS). This provides a design service aimed at increasing the sales productivity of floor space and improving retailers' profitability. The MDS is an attempt to gain competitive edge though superiority of merchandise and differentation from competitors through creating and projecting a new Silentnight image.

Silentnight's marketing effort has in the past been aimed at some 7,000 high street stores and mail order houses. In recent years, they have begun to sell to the discount and specialist retailers including Queensway.

Also, Silentnight made a contribution of £65,000 to support Olympic gymnasts in 1984 as 'there's a strong marketing link between beds, good health and fitness-building activities', and it is considered particularly appropriate as Silentnight pioneered 'firmer beds for your good health'.

Several new products have been produced which indicate an increased awareness of changing consumer preferences and environmental conditions, such as the move to single beds, space-saving furniture and home-assembly furniture.

Appendix 1

INDEX OF RETAIL PRICES – ANNUAL AVERAGE

1974	108.5
1975	134.8
1976	157.1
1977	182.0
1978	197.1
1979	223.5
1980	263.7
1981	295.0
1982	320.4
1983	335.1
1984	351.8

Source: *Annual Abstract of Statistics*, 1985

Appendix 2

HOUSING – PERMANENT DWELLINGS COMPLETED (thousands)

1974	280
1975	322
1976	325
1977	314
1978	289
1979	252
1980	240
1981	204
1982	177
1983	198
1984	212

Source: *Annual Abstract of Statistics*, 1985.

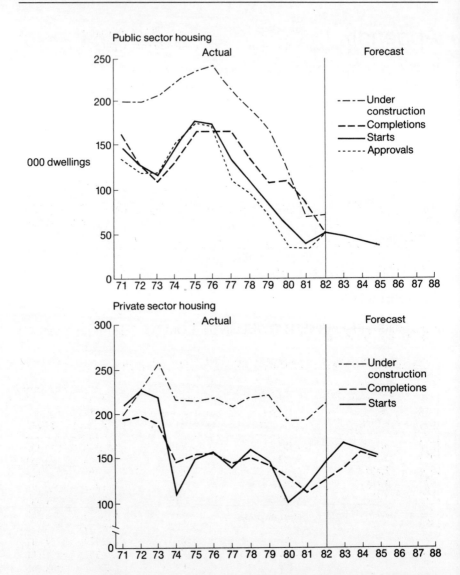

FIGURE 17.1 **Public and private sector housing forecast, 1970–88**

Source: Dept. of Environment housing and construction statistics

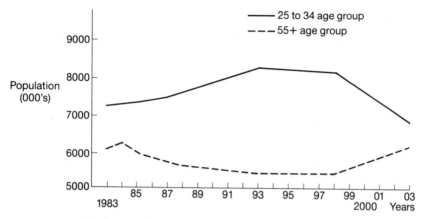

FIGURE 17.2   **Projected population to 2003**

Source: Population census and surveys

Appendix 3

CONSUMERS' EXPENDITURE AT 1980 PRICES (£m.)

	Furniture & floor coverings	Cars, motorcycles & other vehicles	Electrical radio, TV & other durables	Total consumer expenditure	GNP
1974	3,151	4,855	1,497	125,630	216,430
1975	3,278	5,152	1,774	124,748	213,234
1976	3,417	5,325	2,044	125,175	222,144
1977	3,155	4,725	2,305	124,564	222,235
1978	3,322	5,804	2,750	131,373	231,033
1979	3,696	6,668	3,348	137,256	236,357
1980	3,429	6,307	3,584	136,789	230,036
1981	3,354	6,366	3,861	136,429	227,042
1982	3,424	6,570	4,403	137,581	231,111
1983	3,724	7,909	5,018	143,011	238,406
1984	3,754	7,294	5,372	145,241	242,267

Source: *Annual Abstract of Statistics*, 1985

Appendix 4   Silentnight Holdings PLC financial data

FIVE-YEAR SUMMARY YEAR END 31 JANUARY (APPROX) (£000)

	1985	1984	1983	1982	1981
Turnover	79,788	76,667	77,270	72,794	65,926
Profit before taxation	2,233	5,239	5,225	5,110	3,038
Taxation	(598)	30	730	334	829
Profit after taxation	2,831	5,209	4,495	4,776	2,209
Extraordinary items	1,325	–	–	–	1,319
Profit attributable to shareholders	1,506	5,209	4,495	4,776	890
Dividends	1,238	1,238	1,125	1,125	788
Retained earnings	268	3,971	3,370	3,651	102
Earnings per 10p share:					
Before taxation	5.0p	11.6p	11.6p	11.4p	6.7p
After taxation	6.3p	11.6p	10.0p	10.6p	4.9p
Net dividend per share	2.8p	2.8p	2.5p	2.5p	1.8p
Fixed assets	21,770	19,991	18,296	16,260	12,411
Net current assets	7,190	9,264	6,227	4,272	2,983
Long-term liabilities	(6,848)	(7,536)	(2,774)	(2,196)	(762)
Capital and reserves	22,112	21,719	21,749	18,336	14,632
Net tangible asset value per 10p share	49.1p	48.3p	48.3p	40.7p	32.5p
Total borrowings including bank overdrafts to shareholders' funds	24.2%	22.1%	13.9%	13.3%	10.6%

Appendix 5

CONSOLIDATED BALANCE SHEET, 2 FEBRUARY 1985 (£000)

	1985	1984
Fixed assets		
Tangible assets	21,770	19,991
Current assets		
Stocks	6,647	7,688
Debtors	12,671	17,210
Investments	750	1,616
Cash at bank and in hand	2,559	630
	22,627	27,144
Creditors: amounts falling due within one year	15,437	17,880
Net current assets	7,190	9,264
Total assets less current liabilities	28,960	29,255
Creditors: amounts falling due after more than one year	3,947	3,817
Provision for liabilites and charges	2,697	32,557
Minority interests	204	162
	6,848	7,536
	22,112	21,719
Capital and reserves		
Called-up share capital	4,500	4,500
Profit and loss account	17,612	17,219
	22,112	21,719

Appendix 6

CONSOLIDATED PROFIT AND LOSS ACCOUNT, 2 FEBRUARY 1985

	1985	1984
Turnover	79,788	76,667
Cost of sales	56,469	52,172
Gross profit	23,319	24,495
Distribution costs	14,942	13,905
Administrative expenses	5,500	5,030
	20,442	18,935
Trading profit	2,877	5,560
Interest receivable	273	272
Interest payable	(917)	(593)
Profit on ordinary activities before taxation	2,233	5,239
Taxation on profit on ordinary activities	(598)	30
Profit for the financial year	2,831	5,209
Extraordinary items	1,325	–
Profit attributable to shareholders	1,506	5,209
Dividends	1,238	1,238
Profit transferred to reserves	268	3,971
Earnings per ordinary 10p share		
Before taxation	5.0p	11.6p
After taxation	6.3p	11.6p

Statement of retained profits and reserves	1985 £000	1984 £000
Reserves at 28 January 1984	17,219	17,249
Profit retained for the year	268	3,971
Foreign exchange adjustments	125	(1)
Adjustment to deferred taxation account	–	(4,000)
Reserves at 2 February 1985	17,612	17,219

Appendix 7

CHAIRMAN'S REVIEW, 1985 – AN EXTRACT

At our Annual General Meeting last year I was disappointed to have to forecast the results for the year would be half those of the year before. Unfortunately, our financial results for the year confirmed my worst fears with the final profit coming out at £2.2 m. before taxation.

The intense competition in the furniture, upholstery and bedding industry at both retailer and manufacturer level continues unabated.

The retailer is, of course, himself subject to immense competition and consumer pressures, but a continuation of the current trend of buying on price alone can be to no-one's benefit. As major retailers win a larger and larger share of the trade at the expense of the independents, so purchasing power is concentrated in fewer and fewer hands. The squeezing of manufacturers' margins, as a result of being forced to give discounts unrelated to savings, only puts British jobs at risk. It is often overlooked that consumers are also earners, and the price of inadequate investment is ultimately unemployment.

Having seen the damaging effect on other industries of under-investment, we have decided on a policy of continuing to give the consumer quality, choice and value, as we believe this to be the medium-term answer to our present problems. Our fixed assets reflect investment in high-quality equipment and commercial vehicles, continuing our progress towards a more efficient operation. Improved efficiencies, particularly through product innovation linked with quality, will I am sure restore our former profitability.

The amount of money being expended on research and development in the market place, product development and machinery development is now reaching substantial proportions. That which justifies further research and development encourages your directors to re-double their efforts in order to secure a more stable medium-term development of our business.

With regard to our Super Sleeper products, we remain convinced of the superiority of these products over their competitors. Unfortunately, because of the programmed delivery of the machinery, it will be the second half of 1985 before the benefits of this investment begin to show through to the bottom line. We are encouraged by the development of Super Sleeper in the market place, where it has achieved spectacular results for retailers who have supported our marketing effort.

Our investment during 1984 continued at the level of £5 million-plus, principally in the Super Sleeper installation which, when complete in its new building, will be a very fine spring-making investment capable of carrying us into the 21st century.

Five years ago, in the year ended 2 February, 1980, the group employed 3,479 people to produce a turnover of £64m. You will see from these accounts that the number employed is now 2,787, a drop of approximately 20 per cent, for a turnover of £79m. which is a substantial increase in productivity, so that our merchandise is sold in 1985 at very similar prices to 1979, hence my remarks on the need for product innovation and the strengthening of our marketing.

Mr Christopher Burnett will be joining the board of the company as chief executive. He is currently a director of Whitecroft plc and chief executive of the Building Supplies division. Prior to joining Whitecrofts Mr Burnett was managing director of the Fertilizer Division of Fisons plc which he joined from McKinsey & Co. He holds a Master's degree in Business Administration from the Harvard Business School and is aged 44.

18   S. R. Gent

In January 1986 the share price of S. R. Gent plc stood at 64p on the London Stock Exchange, having fallen from the 190p at which they were sold when the company became a public limited company in June 1983. At that time, enthusiastic employees of the company had bought 900,000 shares, when the company offered 25 per cent of its equity to the public, which oversubscribed the offer.

S. R. Gent designed and manufactured ladies' and children's clothing, men's outerwear, and household textiles, primarily for sale to the large retailing chains; Marks and Spencer alone took over 90 per cent of company output. Of nearly 6,000 employees, about 80 were employed in the design department. Company policy was to respond to fashion changes, rather than to set fashion trends, and to do this senior managers and designers regularly travelled abroad to keep up to date with developments. The objective was to produce balanced product ranges for the winter and summer seasons and this required constant development throughout the year. They produced up to 100 new or amended designs for each principal category of product, and these would be presented weekly to the major customers. Following acceptance of the designs, product specifications would be drawn up and quantities and selling prices agreed before volume production started. Over half of the fabrics used were purchased in the United Kingdom, with the balance coming from the rest of Europe, the USA and Japan.

Since the mid-1970s, the management had recognized the need to take advantage of new technology in order to maintain the company's competitive position, especially with regard to production. The emphasis on technical innovation was inspired by their belief that it was necessary to be able to respond quickly to changes in demand. Even though the company spent over £3m. annually on computer-related equipment, which managers agreed was labour-saving and 'de-skilled' staff, the number employed had continued to increase, and stood at 5,887 in 1985. The equipment affected a number of the steps in the process, beginning with designing, which used computer-aided design systems, cutting instructions and computerized sewing machines. In the clothing industry generally, sewing machines were idle about 30 per cent of the time whilst the machinist was preparing material or doing other related jobs, but S. R. Gent's computers enabled this time to be cut significantly such that garments took only half the time to sew that they had previously. The biggest impact, however, was in the cutting rooms, which dealt with about 600,000 square metres of cloth every week, whilst each garment would use about ten pieces. The material was cut in layers up to 300 thick, at very high speeds and at a much higher level of accuracy than was possible with traditional methods. In total, the company was producing about 12 million garments a year in over 1,300 different styles.

The company was located in Barnsley, Yorkshire and had 16 sewing factories within a 30-mile radius of its headquarters. The finished garments were returned to three central warehouses prior to distribution, which was generally by overnight delivery direct to its customers' retail outlets.

The company had established policies to seek a wider customer base and also to widen its product range. It sought more customers both in the UK and overseas, provided it did not harm its relationship with its major customer, Marks and Spencer, which had recorded clothing sales in its year ending in 1985 of £1,423m. Its other customers were five multiples and included Tesco and Richards in the UK, and J. C. Penney in the USA. The chairman, Mr Peter Wolff, was particularly keen to expand the product range as he believed that basic products only had a growth rate the same as the economy, whereas luxury items or impulse purchases could present high-margin opportunities.

The business had originated in 1945 when Edith Wallace began making ladies' blouses for Marks and Spencer, and for many years it had operated from two houses in Barnsley under the ownership of Edith Wallace and her subsequent partner, Ruth Wetzel. In 1966, Ruth Wetzel's son and Peter Wolff took over the management of the company. Peter Wolff had been a merchandising manager with Marks and Spencer for ten years, and he had taken the opportunity of buying a 50 per cent share of S. R. Gent, which at that time had sales of £170,000 and profits of £5,000, for an investment of £12,500.

For its financial year ending in June 1985, the company reported sales turnover up to over £82m. but pre-tax profits were only just over £1m., this being attributed to the problems of the unseasonal weather that the United Kingdom had suffered in both halves of the financial year. (Appendix 1 provides further financial information on S. R. Gent plc.)

THE CLOTHING INDUSTRY

Clothing sales represent a large proportion of UK consumer expenditure, and in 1984 totalled £10.6 billion. In the early 1980s some radical

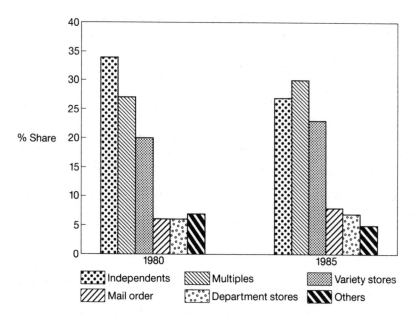

FIGURE 18.1   **UK men's clothing: market share by retailer type**

changes took place in the market-place for clothing which had their foundation a decade previously, when the corner-stone of the large men's retailers (e.g. Burton, and Hepworths, subsequently renamed Next) was undermined by imports of ready-made suits. In response, they searched out new markets, including womenswear, and as a result, the whole face of the high street was transformed. Typically, the shopping areas had been dominated by a mix of department stores, multiple stores, variety chains and independents. The multiples (specialist clothing retailers) took a dramatic lead, with over 25 per cent of all clothing being bought from stores such as Next, Principles, Top Man, Miss Selfridge, etc. Not only did market shares change, but the advent of such stores increased the proportion of own-label brands, at the expense of manufacturers' labels. Figures 18.1 and 18.2 show changes in market share according to the type of outlet in the early 1980s. Figures 18.3 and 18.4 show changes in brands for the early 1980s.

Such changes presented not only challenges for clothing manufacturers, but also opportunities. One result was for retailers to move away from two seasons, i.e. summer and winter clothing, and towards lifestyle clothing and fashion changes on a much shorter cycle.

Clothing sales for 1983 were £9,804m. in a total consumer expenditure of £182,427m. i.e. 5.4 per cent. Table 18.1 gives details of this proportion for the years 1973–82.

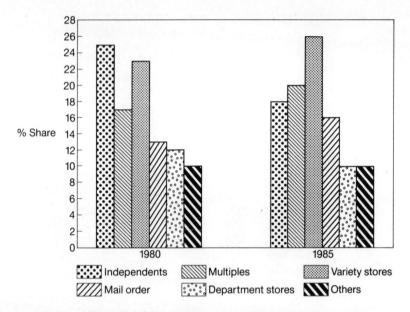

FIGURE 18.2   **UK women's clothing: market share by retailer type**

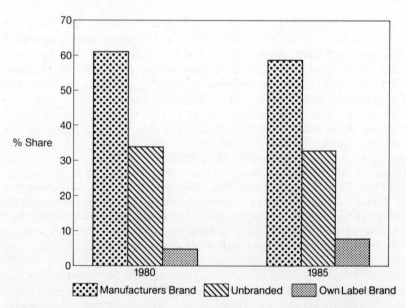

FIGURE 18.3   **UK womenswear: brands in independent stores**

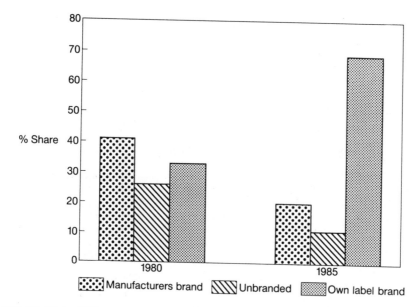

FIGURE 18.4   **UK womenswear: brands in multiple stores**

Despite the apparent decline in percentage terms, sales of clothing had grown over the period, and the period 1980–3 showed a growth of 9 per cent, with a significant increase in men's and boys' clothing.

Of these sales to UK consumers, a significant proportion was imported; the import penetration for various items of clothing varied from 8 per cent for overalls to 86 per cent for woven womens' suits. Table 18.2 shows details of import and export figures.

RETAILERS

There were approximately 10,000 retailers in the UK specializing in the sale of men's and boys' clothing, in addition to the department stores, variety chains and mail order firms. The specialist stores were estimated to account for 42 per cent of men's/boys' wear sales. The more important retailers were as shown in table 18.3.

There were about 22,000 specialist retailers covering the womenswear market, the most important of which are shown in table 18.4.

MANUFACTURERS

There were about 6,000 clothing manufacturers in the UK, employing nearly 220,000 people with exports of approximately £600m.,

TABLE 18.1   **Clothing as a percentage of total consumer expenditure, 1973–82**

1973	1974	1975	1976	1977	1978	1979	1980	1981	1982
7.0	7.1	6.7	6.4	6.4	6.5	6.4	5.9	5.5	5.3

Source: Derived from *Annual Abstract*

TABLE 18.2   **Imports and exports of clothing**

£m.	1980	1981	1982	1983	1984
Sales by UK firms	3,241	2,911	2,922	3,253	3,659
Exports	538	558	540	560	644
Imports	871	997	1,051	1,121	1,417
Home market	3,574	3,350	3,433	3,814	4,432
Import penetration (%)	24.3	29.8	30.6	29.4	31.9

Source: DTI

TABLE 18.3   **Men's/boys' wear retailers' market shares, 1982**

	% by value
Marks and Spencer	14.0
Burton	4.5
C & A	4.0
BHS[a]	2.9
Littlewoods	2.6
Hepworths[b]	2.3
Fosters[c]	2.0

[a] Now part of Storehouse (owned by Habitat/Mothercare)
[b] Now renamed Next
[c] Now part of Sears.

TABLE 18.4   **Womenswear retailers' market shares, 1982**

	% by value
Marks and Spencer	21.0
C & A	6.0
BHS	4.0
Littlewoods	3.0
Burton	2.8

TABLE 18.5 **Size of UK clothing manufacturers, 1978–83**

| Employees | No. of enterprises | | Employment (thousands) | | Gross output (£m.) | |
	1978	1983	1978	1983	1978	1983
1– 99	7,399	5,263	118	81	963	1,137
100–199	301	168	42	28	383	403
200–499	184	132	54	47	503	697
500–999	71	40	49	33	454	550
1,000+	55	14	157	25	1,355	383
Total	8,010	5,761	420	214	3,658	3,170

Source: Census of Production (1983)

representing 26 per cent of industry output. Most of these were very small companies, 74 per cent having a workforce of fewer than 20 employees, 53 per cent fewer than ten; only five firms employed more than 1,500 people.

The UK clothing manufacturers varied both in size and in type of clothing made. Some specialized in menswear, for example, which might be branded (e.g. Peter England shirts) or not (e.g. sold through British Home Stores).

Amongst the larger clothing manufacturers were a group of textile companies which were involved in both non-branded and branded clothing. These included William Baird, Coats-Paton, Courtaulds, Dawson International, and Vantona-Viyella. There was also a small group of large firms involved in knitting clothing items – e.g. Corah, which supplied 70 per cent of its output to Marks and Spencer. And finally, amongst the large firms in the industry were those involved in clothing manufactured from fabric who were not part of the textile industry itself. This group included Aquascutum Group (1,600 employees), which sold its own men's and women's wear through its own retail outlets, as well as to other multiples and department stores; S. R. Gent (5,000 employees), largely involved in womenswear manufacture, with 90 per cent going to Marks and Spencer; Lee Cooper (2,400 employees), manufacturing jeans and casual clothing, and I. J. Dewhirst (3,000 employees), manufacturing men's outerwear, supplying 90 per cent of its output to Marks and Spencer. (Financial information on I. J. Dewhirst is provided in appendix 2, as an example.)

Appendix 1   S. R. GENT PLC

PROFIT AND LOSS ACCOUNTS, 1980–5

Year ended 30 June	1980 £000	1981 £000	1982 £000	1983 £000	1984 £000	1985 £000
Turnover	46,280	53,566	59,742	70,196	79,591	82,823
Trading profit before depreciation	3,727	5,028	6,771	7,372	8,241	4,581
Depreciation	(1,113)	(1,309)	(1,477)	(1,578)	(2,096)	(2,681)
Trading profit	2,614	3,719	5,294	5,794	6,145	1,900
Interest payable	(2,232)	(2,188)	(1,614)	(1,442)	(741)	(1,305)
Share of profits of associated companies	302	383	581	832	711	432
Profit before tax	684	1,914	4,261	5,184	6,115	1,027
Tax	(114)	(155)	(367)	(359)	(821)	(427)
Profit after tax	570	1,759	3,894	4,825	5,294	600
Extraordinary item	–	–	–	–	–	(263)
Dividends	(64)	(61)	(250)	–	(1,080)	(505)
Profit/(loss) retained	506	1,698	3,644	4,825	4,214	(168)

BALANCE SHEETS, 1982–5

Year ended 30 June	1982 £000	1983 £000	1984 £000	1985 £000
Fixed assets				
Tangible assets	12,749	14,590	16,251	17,707
Investments[a]	868	1,424	1,613	1,275
	13,617	16,014	17,864	18,982
Current assets				
Stocks	12,981	16,093	20,590	26,130
Debtors	4,510	9,071	4,734	6,296
Issue proceeds	–	4,992	–	–
Cash	88	31	78	82
	17,579	30,187	25,402	32,508
Creditors (due within one year)				
Finance debt[b]	6,157	10,193	4,022	14,963
Creditors	8,984	10,357	11,932	10,619
	15,141	20,550	15,954	25,582
Net current assets	2,438	9,637	9,448	6,926
Total assets less current liabilities	16,055	25,651	27,312	25,908
Creditors (due after one year)				
Long-term loans	3,430	3,183	811	183
	12,625	22,468	26,501	25,725
Capital and reserves				
Share capital[c]	214	3,600	3,600	3,607
Share premium account	–	4,692	4,591	4,591
Profit & loss account	12,411	14,176	18,310	17,527
	12,625	22,468	26,501	25,725

[a] Investments in subsidiary and related companies including a £44,000 acquisition.
[b] Short-term bank loans.
[c] 36 million ordinary shares plus 71,474 allotted on acquisition of a subsidiary (Sublime Lighting Ltd.) for a value of £124,364.

SEVEN-YEAR RECORD, 1979–85

	1979 £000	1980 £000	1981[a] £000	1982 £000	1983 £000	1984 £000	1985 £000
Turnover	27,601	46,280	53,566	59,742	70,196	79,591	82,823
Operating profit	2,124	2,614	3,719	5,294	5,794	6,145	1,900
Share of profits of related companies	166	302	383	581	832	711	432
Interest payable	(818)	(2,232)	(2,188)	(1,614)	(1,442)	(741)	(1,305)
P B T	1,472	684	1,914	4,261	5,184	6,115	1,027
Tax	(114)	(155)	(367)	(359)	(821)	(427)	(427)
Profit after tax	1,432	570	1,759	3,894	4,825	5,294	600
Extraordinary items	–	–	–	–	–	(263)	–
Dividends	–	(64)	(61)	(250)	(83)	(1,080)	(505)
Retained profits (loss)	1,432	506	1,698	3,644	4,742	4,214	(168)[b]
Fixed assets and investments	6,944	12,081	12,473	13,617	16,014	17,864	18,982
Net current assets	3,153	134	1,249	2,438	9,637	9,448	6,926
Long-term debt	(3,586)	(4,840)	(4,667)	(3,430)	(3,183)	(811)	(183)
Shareholders' funds[c]	6,511	7,375	9,055	12,625	22,468	26,501	25,725
Average number of employees	3,551	4,582	4,238	4,451	5,444	5,740	5,887

[a] 14-month year
[b] After charging an extraordinary item of £263,000.
[c] Including 33 million shares up to 1982, 33.8 million shares up to 1983, 36 million shares up to 1984, and 36.07 million shares up to 1985.

Appendix 2   I. J. Dewhirst PLC

PROFIT AND LOSS ACCOUNT, 1984 AND 1985

Year ended January	1984 £000	1985 £000
Turnover	33,691	43,012
Cost of sales	(29,085)	(37,296)
Gross profit	4,606	5,716
Net operating expenses	(1,634)	(1,977)
Operating profit	2,972	3,739
Net investment income	445	268
Profit on ordinary activities before tax	3,417	4,007
Tax	(915)	(1,363)
Profit after tax	2,502	2,644
Preference dividends	(49)	(49)
Ordinary dividends	(477)	(550)
Retained profit	1,976	2,045
Earnings per share	4.9p	5.18p
Ordinary dividend cover	5.14 times	4.72 times

BALANCE SHEET, 1984 AND 1985

Year ended January	1984 £000	1985 £000
Fixed assets	9,252	11,458
Current assets		
Stock	5,763	7,812
Debtors	994	1,511
Investments	3,600	5,029
Cash	7	8
	10,364	14,360
Creditors (due within one year)	(6,525)	(9,279)
Net current assets	3,839	5,081
Total assets less current liabilities	13,091	16,539
Creditors (due after more than one year)	(56)	(763)
Provisions for liabilities	(249)	(799)
	12,786	14,977
Capital and reserves		
Share capital	4,481	5,513
Share premium account	–	108
Revaluation reserve	876	876
Profit and loss account	7,429	8,480
	12,786	14,977

FIVE-YEAR STATEMENT, 1981–5

	1981 £000	1982 £000	1983 £000	1984 £000	1985 £000
Turnover	20,863	23,186	27,399	33,691	43,012
Operating profit	1,673	2,005	2,441	2,972	3,739
Net investment income	271	512	485	445	268
Profit before tax	1,944	2,517	2,926	3,417	4,007
Tax	403	702	799	915	1,363
Profit after tax	1,541	1,815	2,127	2,502	2,644
Preference dividends	49	49	49	49	49
Ordinary dividends	286	346	404	477	550
Retained profits	1,206	1,420	1,674	1,976	2,045
Ordinary shareholder funds	7,210	8,631	10,306	12,283	14,474
Earnings per ordinary share (pence)	2.98	3.52	4.15	4.90	5.18
Asset value per ordinary share (pence)	14.39	17.23	20.57	24.51	28.89

19 Coloroll

When Mr John Ashcroft arrived as chairman and chief executive in 1978, Coloroll was a small wallpaper manufacturer with 3 per cent of the wallcoverings market. This market share had risen to 30 per cent by 1988; the company had diversified into other areas of home furnishings, and was operating with five divisions: home furnishings, ceramics, glassware, wallcoverings UK, and wallcoverings USA. (It had also entered the carpet manufacturing industry, through the purchase of Wallbridge in 1987 for £8m. The company headquarters were in Manchester, where a small office housed the three-man senior management team of John Ashcroft, Philip Green the managing director, and Eric Kilby, the finance director.

The company had been founded in London in 1923 as an importer of coloured wrapping paper on rolls – hence the name. By the 1960s it had moved to Lancashire, and was manufacturing wallcoverings.

From 1978, following the formation of a management team under the leadership of John Ashcroft, the company had concentrated on achieving a leading position in wallcoverings. It had supported this move with the appointment of two leading designers who created the Coloroll ranges. In addition design was supported by creative marketing, support for the retailers, and tight financial controls; as a consequence, by 1980 Coloroll was the UK's leading wallcoverings manufacturer.

The management team put a strong emphasis on planning, and produced a multi-stage business plan. The first stage of this plan had involved:

- updating the Nelson plant in Lancashire, at a cost of £6m.;
- targeting the out-of-town site retailers;
- cutting delivery time to two days;
- concentrating on high-volume/low-value items, supported by computerized production and financial systems;
- placing considerable emphasis on product design.

These targets were achieved by 1981.

Stage two of the business plan was to create a home furnishings division incorporating co-ordinated ranges of fabrics, bedlinens and the more expensive wallpapers. At that time the latter represented only a fifth of the value of the range, and was the only element manufactured by Coloroll, the other parts being bought in. Subsequently when Fogarty (see below) was bought other parts too were made.

Stage three involved geographical expansion to the USA with the acquisition for £10m. of Wallmates, a wallcoverings manufacturer, which at that time had 4 per cent of the US wallcoverings market. The long-term objective was to build up a UK/US axis with up to 60 per cent of the earnings coming from the USA.

Stage four involved the move into ceramics, first with the purchase of Biltons for £5m., and then Staffordshire Potteries and Crown House. By 1988 Coloroll produced 50 per cent of the mugs manufactured in the UK.

Stage five was the 1988 acquisition of Crowther's carpet interests, and followed the purchase of a small carpet firm (Wallbridge) in 1987. Stage five marked a further move into home furnishing, helping to meet the objective of creating a company with sales of £250m. by 1990, big enough to rank in the list of FT-SE 100 largest companies.

During the period 1978 to 1988 Coloroll had made other acquisitions to fill out the areas it wished to penetrate, and in May 1985 the company was floated on the Stock Exchange with the issue of 13.5 million shares at an offered price of 135p, which gave the company a market capitalization of £40m. Although the offer was oversubscribed many times, the share price fell to 101p when dealing commenced.

A list of the acquisitions since the flotation in 1985, mainly bought through share issues, and which enabled the pace to be stepped up, is shown in table 19.1.

Fogarty Coloroll bought Fogarty for £31m. Within a month 150 of the 1,300 workers were made redundant and a £7m. investment programme had been decided upon. This affected four plants:

- £2.5m. on a central computer-controlled warehouse.
- £2.2m. on a new textile printing plant. Printing had previously been sub-contracted out.
- £1m. on cleaning machinery for the duvet fillings.
- £1m. on computerized hemming machines for duvet covers and pillows.

The new printing plant also enabled Coloroll to produce a wide range of own-label fabric designs for major retail chains. The rotary screen printer could print materials 2.6 metres wide in 14 separate colours. It was forecast that Fogarty would produce sales of £58m. and profits of £5m. in the financial year ending in 1988.

TABLE 19.1   **Coloroll Acquisitions, 1985–9**

1985	Worley – manufacturer of foam vinyl wallcoverings
1985	Alexander Drew – textile commission printers
1986	Bilton – ceramics
1986	Staffordshire Potteries – ceramics
1986	Fogarty – manufacturers of duvets and bedlinen
1987	Wallbridge – a tufted carpet manufacturer
1987	Crown House – ceramics including brand names such as Denby and Edinburgh Crystal
1988	John Crowther plc – cloth, clothing and carpet manufacture with brand names Kosset and Crossley
1988	Barrett – manufacturer of upholstered furniture
1988	Texture Tex – processor of bulk continuous filament nylon yarns for the carpet industry
1989	Burlington – manufacturer of foam vinyl wallcoverings

Staffordshire Potteries   This was the first quoted company to be taken over by Coloroll, and turned out to be the first contested bid.

Wallbridge   Wallbridge was bought for £8m. in 1987, and had reported 1986 sales of £18m., profits of £1m. and net tangible assets of £3.16m. The company had about 2.5 per cent of the UK market in 1986, specialized in nylon tufted carpets, and sold about one-third of its output to the Allied Carpets retail chain.

Crown House   In 1987 Coloroll made an agreed bid for Crown House of £87.3m. The company sold tableware, including Denby stoneware, Edinburgh and Thomas Webb crystal, and George Butler silverware. It also had interests in the engineering industry, which Coloroll sold off for £55m. In the financial year ending 1986 prior to the acquisition, Crown House made profits of £7.2m. on sales of £202m., with £2.8m. from tableware and £4.3m. from engineering. In the last six months before the merger, tableware reported losses of just under a million pounds, attributed to the fall in the numbers of American tourists to the UK.

Crowther   In April 1988 the directors of John Crowther plc, one of the largest carpet producers in the UK, agreed to recommend to their shareholders acceptance of a bid for their company of £215m. from Coloroll plc. At that time Crowther's sales and profits were more than double those of Coloroll. This take-over by Coloroll made the company a major force in the UK home furnishings market.

Crowther had become one of the UK's faster-growing textile companies, with interests in cloth and clothing as well as carpets, and with 10,000 employees worldwide. Its carpet interests had only been purchased in late 1985, and since then the company had struggled to make the carpet division profitable.

Coloroll acquired Crowther with a one-for-one share swap which valued Crowther at £215m. Coloroll kept the carpet manufacturing plants and the stand-alone carpet distribution business, and arranged sale of the cloth and clothing businesses for approximately £90m.

Barrett   Coloroll paid £15m. in cash and shares for Barrett, which was the second largest manufacturer of upholstered furniture in the UK. In 1987 the company had recorded sales of £24m. and pre-tax profits of £1.9m. The cost of entry to the upholstered furniture market was comparatively low, with a highly labour-intensive production process and low levels of automation. Traditionally the £700m. industry had been very fragmented, with many hundreds of small firms, but in 1985 Hillsdown had emerged as a powerful player in the industry when it acquired the well-known firm Christie Tyler.

MANAGEMENT STYLE AT COLOROLL

The company mission statement was expressed in the annual report in these terms: 'understanding what the customer wants and providing it is the basis of Coloroll's success'. This aim was supported by the clearly stated objective to be 'the biggest name in home fashion', based on the following targets:

- 10 per cent return on sales;
- 25 per cent return on capital;
- 20 per cent earnings per share growth;
- 10 per cent dividend growth;
- 30 per cent to 40 per cent range for gearing.

The philosophy, style, culture and operation of the company were written up in a series of books known as the White Book, Yellow Book and Blue Book by chairman John Ashcroft, to guide the company managers.

The White Book was the original five-year business plan designed to take Coloroll into market leadership in its chosen fields. The Blue Book was concerned with management control. In addition there was the Yellow Book, which was generated at operating level as a detailed analysis of the market and competitors in that sector of the industry.

The Blue Book was written in 1986 to show how the central management team would control Coloroll, no matter how big the company grew. It exuded the Coloroll corporate culture to create a hothouse atmosphere for managers. The first event of every Coloroll manager's week was the Monday morning meeting to review the previous week's trading performance. Routine appraisal of sales,

debtors, creditors and stocks ensured that any deviation from financial
targets was identified and quickly corrected. Speed of response
maintained Coloroll's reputation for fast, flexible service to the
retailer. Managers were responsible for their decisions and held
accountable, and they were exposed to the effects of those decisions
through a highly-geared bonus system.

Heads of the five divisions presented their business plans annually
and the plans were supported by updated versions of the Yellow
Book; each operating unit was a profit centre. Each month's financial
data were available five days after the end of the month, in time for
the meeting of the main board of directors on the second Monday of
the following month.

The management style was expressed in the way the new acquisitions were treated. First a team of auditors spent two weeks
examining the company. Then the next step was a management presentation, at which the former managers were interviewed to keep
their old jobs, although typically few of them did. (At Fogarty 13 of
the top 14 managers left within a few days.) Next, the three-man
senior management team of Coloroll considered how they wanted to
restructure the company. After that the 'Coloroll Roadshow' turned
up at the factory and John Ashcroft explained the benefits of working
for Coloroll. Executive facilities such as separate dining areas were
removed, and equal facilities provided for everyone. The management
was then encouraged to adopt the Coloroll style by walking round the
factory twice a week talking to employees and putting up 'How are we
doing' boards with performance details. The procedure of financial
analysis, management presentation and Yellow Book analysis had to
be completed within a month to ensure integration into the group.

The post-acquisition strategy at Staffordshire Potteries was in the
classical Coloroll style. The firm was by no means poorly managed,
and had one of the best production units in the country. Coloroll
believed, however, that it had a 'cultural' problem. This was exemplified by the fact that Staffordshire Potteries did not have a full-
time marketing director, and the claim that a minute of the board had
stated that '...major customers must appreciate that production has to
be phased throughout the year'. The company had many task forces
and committees, but very little information on the market.

Coloroll introduced its management methods, including lines of
responsibility and accountability, the Monday meeting, and full
monthly financial performance data. They closed the directors' bar and
dining room, and saved £500,000 by sacking 50 headquarters staff.

COLOROLL FINANCIAL PERFORMANCE

In 1986 Coloroll entered the retail trade, opening a retail outlet in
London's Regent Street and also buying a site in central Manchester.

TABLE 19.2   **UK 1985 home fashion market**

	£m.
Ceramics/glassware	593
Textiles	810
Window dressings	474
Floorcoverings	1,363
Decorative products	711
Total	3,951

Source: *Textile Sector Review*, C. L. Alexanders Laing and Cruickshank

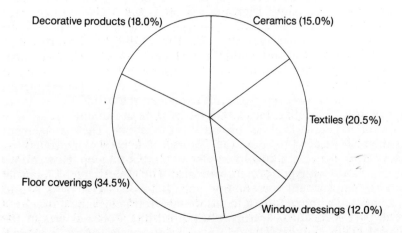

FIGURE 19.1   **UK home fashion market, 1985**

This made it possible to market the full range of products under one roof, and to test proposed new products such as towels. Coloroll's retail customers were considerably upset at the prospect of one of their suppliers becoming a competitor, however, so Coloroll closed the store down. Even so, Marks and Spencer did not relent, cancelling contracts worth over £12m. and continuing to refuse to deal with Coloroll.

By the end of 1988 Coloroll was able to claim that it was the leading company in the UK home fashion market. Table 19.2 and figure 19.1 provide information on this market. With sales for the year ending March 1988 at £260m. Coloroll compared well with its largest rival, Coats Viyella, with estimated sales in home furnishings and carpets of £300m. Following the Crowther acquisition by Coloroll, 1989 carpet sales were likely to add a further £100m. in sales.

TABLE 19.3 Coloroll sales and operating profits, year ending March 1988

	Sales £m.	Operating profit £m.
Home furnishings	84.3	8.9
Glassware	45.9	6.5
Ceramics	43.0	4.9
Wallcoverings UK	52.3	4.4
Wallcoverings USA	38.6	1.1
	264.1	25.8

Table 19.3 shows Coloroll sales and operating profits up to March 1988 prior to the Crowther acquisition.

The figures in table 19.3 vary slightly from those in appendix 1 (financial information on Coloroll), due to foreign currency translations, intergroup trading and income from associated companies and investments.

Divisional reports for year ending March 1988

Home furnishings   This division was the largest producer of quilts and pillows in the UK, with a market share of 30 per cent, and the Fogarty brand was number one in the manufacturer's branded sector of the filled products market, with a 69 per cent share. Coloroll was represented at all price levels in the filled products market, from luxury premium down products to budget man-made items. In the branded linens market, Coloroll was in second place with a 25 per cent market share. In the carpet market the Wallbridge company had increased its market share to 4 per cent. The division claimed high levels of retailer support, with a seven-day turnaround of orders, in an industry where lead times of 21 and 28 days were the norm.

Wallcoverings UK   Projections in this market suggested that sales of wallcoverings would overtake paints in the UK by 1990, making wallcoverings the largest DIY product category. Coloroll maintained its UK market share in wallcoverings at 32 per cent, and was the only UK manufacturer of all seven types of wallcovering, providing a 48-hour delivery service to all UK retailers. Coloroll recorded 35 per cent of wallcoverings exports from the UK. Wallcovering had been the first market entered by Coloroll, and exemplified the company style. Coloroll believed that quality of product and service was unimportant unless it was accompanied by merchandise which appealed to the customer. Therefore Coloroll designers constantly updated designs and created new ones to inspire consumers' home fashion instincts and to complement prevailing colour and style trends. Consequently the wallcoverings catalogue included over a thousand different designs.

Glassware   The newly-acquired companies were successfully integrated and Coloroll claimed 40 per cent of the market of glassware sales to the catering industry, and increased sales to major retailers such as Boots, Debenhams, Asda, House of Fraser and Argos.

Ceramics   In earthenware, Coloroll had a 30 per cent market share and sold over one million coffee mugs per week around the world in over 200 designs. Coloroll's share of the china market was lower, but taking both earthenware and china together it was 20 per cent and the company supplied major retailers such as Asda, Boots, Tesco and the Co-op. An example of the value offered was the 18-piece 'fashion' breakfast set retailed for only £9.99 in 1987. Marks and Spencer had previously been a large customer of Coloroll giftware.

Wallcoverings USA   The 1988 divisional figures were disappointing, being below target sales and profits, and had been further affected by the deterioration of the sterling–dollar exchange rate during the year. The US wallcoverings market was worth $US2 billion at retail prices; domestic sales were about two-thirds of that, and with an 8 per cent market share Coloroll was the fourth largest manufacturer in the USA.

The Crowther acquisition

The Crowther acquisition was first considered in late 1987, but at the time seemed in conflict with Coloroll policy of concentrating on high-volume, low-value items, but the logic of a product area which complemented complete design for the home decided the issue.

John Crowther plc was an old-established textile manufacturer in West Yorkshire which had built up its business on the production of woollen fabrics. After 1981 the company had expanded vigorously by acquisition into a number of related areas, including clothing manufacture, knitwear and yarn spinning. In late 1985 Crowther acquired the UK carpets division of Carpets International. This UK carpets division was the second largest carpet manufacturer in the UK, with well-known brand names such as Crossley and Kosset, but it had been losing money up to 1985 (see table 19.4).

Before the carpets acquisition John Crowther plc was reporting sales and profits as shown in table 19.5.

In order to finance developments, Crowther had borrowed very heavily; as time passed, the Carpet Division had proved sluggish to turn around, and the October 1987 stock market crash had a big effect on the Crowther share price, which fell from 236p to 85p. Early in 1988 the shares had recovered to 108p, when Coloroll started to buy

TABLE 19.4 **Carpets International (UK division) – prior to acquisition by John Crowther plc**

£m.	1980	1981	1982	1983	1984	1985 (6 months)
Sales	68.7	60.4	61.4	59.6	59.6	30.0
Operating profit (loss)	(5.7)	(4.7)	(6.3)	(2.0)	0.3	0.63
Interest	(3.5)	(2.2)	(2.1)	(1.4)	(1.3)	(0.6)
Profit (loss) before tax	(9.2)	(6.9)	(8.4)	(3.4)	–	0.03

TABLE 19.5 **John Crowther plc**

£m.	1980	1981	1982	1983	1984
Sales	3.8	3.6	5.6	7.3	10.8
Operating profit (loss)	0.6	0.07	0.27	0.4	0.8
Profit loss before tax	(0.9)	(0.27)	0.46	0.227	0.514

them. When rumours circulated in the market about a possible take-over bid for the company, Coloroll announced their share-holding and met with the Crowther management to agree a one-for-one share swap.

John Crowther's acquisition and growth policy had continued in 1987 with the acquisition of a further 20 companies at a cost of £100m. paid for mostly in shares, including the leading US manufacturer of dressmaking patterns, McCalls. The largest acquisition in these years was MCD, which was a leading distributor (as opposed to producer) of floorcoverings.

Before the take-over by Coloroll in 1988, Crowther had a decentralized structure with a small senior management group, but it had been plagued by personnel changes. The head of the carpet division left within a year of appointment, and the head of the clothing division stayed only a few weeks. The general structure was as follows:

Cloth division There were nine factories and 780 employees in the division, which produced yarns for apparel, handknitting, carpets, furnishing fabrics and knitwear. It also produced woven woollen fabrics, primarily for better quality ladieswear.

Clothing division   This division produced a wide variety of clothing from 33 factories with 4,075 employees, including some in Ireland. Much of the output was own-label goods for retailers such as Marks and Spencer. In addition there was the hosiery range made for the Pierre Cardin brand name. The expansion into clothing had required a great deal of rationalization, as Crowthers had bought a wide variety of companies, many on the brink of liquidation, in an attempt to bring about a new type of clothing manufacturer. The Crowther strategy was based on the assumption that structural change in the retail sector had created demand for a new type of manufacturer which was big enough to offer sophisticated support in marketing and design, but sufficiently flexible to respond to changes in the market place.

Distribution division   This was formed in April 1986 and included the MCD company which was the largest distributor of floorcoverings in the UK and the WW company which was an importer, wholesaler and distributor of clothing. Together there were 13 distribution ware-houses, and the division employed 800 people.

Carpet division   Crowthers were a major name in carpets, with brand names Kossett and Crossley, and with nine factories employing 3,500 people. The production of carpet yarns and carpets was concentrated at Brighouse in Yorkshire and Kidderminster in the Midlands, with two-thirds of output woven and one-third tufted carpets. The division had a selling operation in the USA and owned 50 per cent of Homfray Carpets in Australia, which had a 20 per cent market share. Since the purchase of Carpets International's UK division in 1985, Crowther had spent over £6m. on rationalizing carpet production, with factory closures and 400 redundancies, but major problems had remained, largely associated with computerization, which delayed deliveries and took a year to resolve. This not only dented retail confidence in the organization but also delayed the general restructuring. In 1987 they spent £1m. on a television advertising campaign for Kossett carpets, which was the first big campaign in carpets for a decade, and were planning to introduce a new range of designs for display at the Harrogate fair in Autumn 1988.

The UK market for carpets had grown in the 1980s, with volume sales growth of 2 per cent in 1987 and value up to about £1 billion at factory prices, but imports had continued to grow at a faster pace – see table 19.6. Figure 19.2 shows the UK domestic carpet market for the years 1983 to 1986, by carpet type.

Figures 19.3 and 19.4 show the breakdown of sales in price ranges. To some extent these were affected by inflation, whilst factors such as technical improvements and increased competition have also affected prices. However, the figures obscure the fact that the share of volume of sales at the very top end of the market (more than £20 per square

TABLE 19.6   **The UK carpet market**

£m.	UK sales at factory prices	UK mfg. sales	Imports	Exports
1983	700	625	150	75
1984	730	630	180	80
1985	810	720	200	110
1986	890	785	225	120
1987	1,000	845	275	120

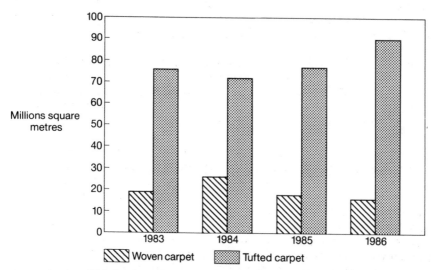

FIGURE 19.2   **UK domestic carpet market by type, 1983–6**

metre) had more than doubled, from 3.2 per cent in 1983 to 7.9 per cent in 1986.

The UK carpet industry was dominated by two groups: Coats Viyella, with nearly 20 per cent of the market, and Crowthers, with about 13 per cent. Other market shares were as shown in table 19.7.

The UK market for domestic carpets was influenced by a number of factors, including changes in consumer expenditure generally, the availability of credit, the extent of house mobility, the number of housing starts, the level of owner occupation, and fluctuations in the value of sterling and associated import penetration.

Although not as high as the record of 1983, housing starts in 1986, 1987 and 1988 were buoyant. Similarly, consumer expenditure rose strongly in that period, although a decreasing proportion had gone on floorcoverings (see table 19.11). A survey on housing moves carried out in 1986 for the Building Societies Association showed that between 1983 and 1986 there was little change in mobility; about 10

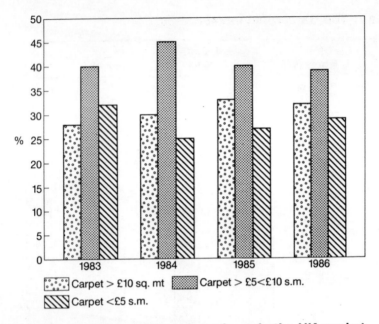

FIGURE 19.3 **Percentage share by volume in the UK market**

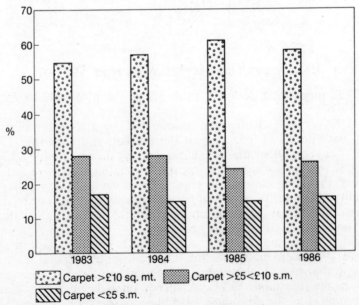

FIGURE 19.4 **Percentage share by value in the UK market**

TABLE 19.7   **Share of the UK market, 1986**

	%
Imports	26
Coats Viyella	18
Crowther	13
Brintons	9
Lamont	5
Stoddard	5
BMK	4
Readicut	3
Tomkinsons	3
Hugh Mackay	3
Abingdon	3
Other UK manufacturers	8

TABLE 19.8   **Length of time in current residence**

	Weighting factor	% of respondents 1983	1986
Unweighted base (100%)		2,501	2,455
Length of residence:			
Less than 12 months	0.5	10	10
1–2 years	1.5	6	7
2–3 years	2.5	7	6
3–4 years	3.5	6	6
4–5 years	4.5	5	5
5–10 years	7.5	18	18
10+ years	10.0	47	47
Mean score		6.9	6.8

Source: Building Societies Association

per cent of adults had moved house in the previous twelve months, whilst 47 per cent had not moved in the previous 10 years. (See table 19.8.)

The structure of the retail market for carpets had changed in the 1980s, as out-of-town multiple retailers increased their share of the market. Best known amongst these were Harris Queensway and Allied Carpets, which had 17 per cent and 7 per cent of the retail market respectively. Table 19.9 shows market shares in 1986.

The carpet industry had been through a difficult period in the 1980s. In 1985 and 1986 almost half the capacity of the industry changed hands as Crowther and Coats took control of a third of the industry. Whilst they were struggling with their acquisitions the smaller firms

TABLE 19.9   **Shares of carpet sales by retail outlet, 1986**

	Volume %	Value %
Independent carpet specialists	35.0	39.8
Multiple flooring specialists	24.7	26.2
Independent furnishing stores	9.3	7.1
Warehouses	5.9	5.1
Mail order	4.9	3.3
Department stores	4.7	5.5
Co-operatives	2.9	3.8
Others	12.7	9.3

Source: TMS

gained ground. Niche players such as Tomkinsons expanded in domestic carpets, and Brinton and Hugh Mackay in contract carpets. In retailing the out-of-town trend began to be challenged by the emergence into the market of retailers such as Next and Marks and Spencer.

In 1988 factors in the UK economy turned against the carpet industry as sterling rose in value, interest rates began to rise and carpet imports rose by 21 per cent in the first six months of the year. The following year opened with falls reported in retail sales and the January inflation figure up to 7.5 per cent.

For the financial year ended in 1987 John Crowther reported the product analysis set out in table 19.10.

Further financial information on John Crowther appears in appendix 2.

Coloroll's share price performance

Coloroll had share price problems following the October 1987 crash, in common with virtually all of British industry, falling from its 1987 peak of 387p to 213p; following the announcement of the Crowther bid it fell further, to 174p.

In October 1988 Coloroll sold off the cloth and clothing divisions for £93m. to the management, and also sold McCalls, a recent acquisition of Crowthers, which was a sewing pattern company in USA, for a further £10m. These parts of Crowther were not felt to fit into Coloroll's overall strategy. At the time of the sale the cloth and clothing divisions were forecasting sales of £185m. and operating profits of £11m. for the 1988–9 financial year. Following these sales it was expected that company gearing would fall to below 40 per cent by the end of the financial year, in March 1989.

Coloroll planned to restructure the carpet companies by concen-

TABLE 19.10 **John Crowther: Product analysis, 1984–7**

£ thousands	1984		1985		1986		1987	
	Sales	Profit	Sales	Profit	Sales	Profit	Sales	Profit
Cloth[a]	10,865	767	19,037	1,119	14,811	1,396	26,297	1,901
Carpets	–	–	18,947	1,514	76,418	5,497	78,898	4,893
Clothing[a]	–	–	–	–	42,412	3,061	98,650	5,927
Distribution	–	–	–	–	90,975	8,505	153,983	13,547
Related company						(56)		3,563
Interest		(253)		(720)		(3,578)		(4,585)
Total	10,865	514	37,984	1,831	224,616	14,825	357,828	25,251

[a] 'Cloth' and 'Clothing' were not recorded seperately until 1986.

TABLE 19.11   **UK consumer expenditure on household goods and services, 1979–87**

Share of total (%)	1979	1980	1981	1982	1983	1984	1985	1986	1987
Furniture	24.6	23.9	23.3	23.0	22.4	21.6	21.0	19.9	19.8
Floorcoverings	11.5	10.7	10.3	10.0	10.1	10.2	9.9	9.4	9.3
Appliances	19.8	20.1	20.1	21.0	22.3	22.8	23.2	24.3	24.2
Textiles/soft furnishings	11.4	11.2	10.8	10.2	9.7	9.3	9.2	8.9	8.9
Hardware	12.5	12.0	12.6	12.3	12.1	12.5	13.1	13.6	14.2
Others	20.2	22.1	22.9	23.5	23.4	23.6	23.6	23.8	23.5
Total value (£ billion)	9.1	10.0	10.6	11.2	12.2	13.0	14.1	15.5	16.8

Source: Central Statistical Office

tration of production at Bradford (Kossett), Kidderminster (Crossley) and Wallbridge (Coloroll). It was hoped that about £3m. economies of scale could be gained through buying of raw materials and improvements in stock control.

Coloroll's success was inevitably related to consumer expenditure, especially in the UK. The London Business School forecast for consumer expenditure, published in June 1988, was as follows:

% change year on year

	1987	1988	1989	1990	1991
Consumer expenditure	+5.2	+4.6	+3.1	+3.4	+3.3

Whilst consumer expenditure on household goods and services generally had grown, the proportion on floorcoverings had fallen – see table 19.11.

The brokers C. L. Alexanders Laing & Cruickshank forecast the UK market for home fashions in 1990 as shown in (table 19.12).

When Coloroll reported their half-year figures in November 1988 the *Financial Times* commented:

> Coloroll, like so many of the companies that flourished in the bull market, has floundered in the current, more cautious climate. Stock market fads aside, it also suffers from doubts about the wisdom of buying as battered a business as Crowther; the impact of higher interest rates on home expenditure; the state of its balance sheet; and a rather raffish reputation. It remains to be seen whether it will really succeed with Crowther. Yet Coloroll has a clear, coherent strategy and – the USA excepted – the established business seems sound. On fundamentals the

TABLE 19.12   **The UK home fashion market, 1990**

	Value (£m.)	Share %	Average market growth 1985–90 % per annum
Ceramics/glassware	859	16.4	7.7
Textiles	1,110	21.2	6.5
Window dressing	628	12.0	5.8
Floorcoverings	1,699	32.5	4.5
Decorative products	934	17.9	5.6
Total	5,230	100.0	5.8

shares should be a snip – with a prospective P/E of 7 at 175p on projected profits of £57m. – but Coloroll faces a tough task in restoring investor confidence. The crunch should come next year when, unless the shares revive, it will be in no position to enliven earnings with another acquisition.

(*Financial Times*, 3 November, 1988.)

Appendix 1   Coloroll Group PLC

PROFIT AND LOSS ACCOUNT

Year ending 31 March	1988 £000	1987 £000	1986 £000	1985 £000	1984 £000
Turnover	257,648	115,233	60,826	37,369	34,963
Cost of sales	(177,529)	(79,178)	(39,607)	(26,174)	(24,737)
Gross profit	80,119	36,055	21,219	11,195	10,226
Distribution costs	(40,848)	(16,455)	(9,434)	(4,995)	(5,031)
Administrative expenses	(14,002)	(8,388)	(5,346)	(2,645)	(2,983)
Income from investments	1,475	119	89	748	–
Other operating income	2,146	357	243	118	95
Trading profit	28,890	11,688	6,771	4,422	2,307
Interest	(2,796)	(1,361)	(541)	(608)	(202)
Profit before taxation	26,094	10,327	6,230	3,814	2,105
Tax	(7,328)	(3,614)	(2,398)	(1,666)	(1,267)
Profit after tax	18,766	6,713	3,832	2,148	838
Minority items	–	–	(193)	–	–
Extraordinary items	(2,604)	–	242	(126)	(1,491)
Attributable profit (loss)	16,162	6,713	3,881	2,022	(653)
Dividends	(6,156)	(3,252)	(1,381)	(962)	(526)
Retained profit	10,006	3,461	2,500	1,060	(1,179)
Earnings per share (pence)	20.8	16.5	13.4	n.a.	n.a.

ANALYSIS OF TURNOVER AND PROFIT BEFORE TAX

£000	1988 Turnover	Profit	1987 Turnover	Profit	1986 Turnover	Profit
Wallcoverings UK	52,257	4,400	46,005	3,707	31,151	2,926
Home furnishings	84,273	8,865	21,709	2,103	9,962	887
Ceramics	43,010	4,942	26,031	2,750	–	–
Wallcoverings USA	38,653	1,051	22,098	1,498	18,236	1,763
Glassware	45,858	6,495	–	–	–	–
Packaging[a]	–	–	3,995	679	3,771	662
Australia	–	–	1,362	2	1,252	(8)
Retail[b]	–	–	439	(412)	–	–
Discontinued activities	2,091	(293)	–	–	–	–
Other	–	634	–	–	–	–
Inter-group	(8,494)	–	(6,366)	–	(3,546)	–
	257,648	26,094	115,233	10,327	60,826	6,230

[a] The Coloroll packaging activities, which comprised the manufacture of plastic shopping bags, were discontinued in 1988.
[b] The retail interests of Coloroll were discontinued in 1988.

GEOGRAPHICAL ANALYSIS

£000	1988 Turnover	Profit	1987 Turnover	Profit	1986 Turnover	Profit
UK	180,427	21,566	75,518	6,014	34,188	3,271
North America	44,803	1,523	25,051	2,962	20,549	2,346
Australia/Far East	3,119	44	1,701	15	1,410	67
EEC	20,724	1,944	10,492	1,107	3,399	403
Other	8,575	1,017	2,471	229	1,280	143
	257,648	26,094	115,233	10,327	60,826	6,230

BALANCE SHEETS

Year ending 31 March	1988 £000	1987 £000	1986 £000	1985 £000
Fixed assets				
Tangible assets	59,732	43,145	13,878	6,894
Investments	9,123	2,711	435	4,442
Current assets				
Stocks	66,332	45,053	21,250	9,389
Debtors	59,714	46,207	17,435	9,574
Cash	12,987	4,059	34	1,379
	139,033	95,319	38,719	20,342
Less:				
Creditors: amounts falling due within one year				
Loans	3,436	12,397	4,713	5,476
Other creditors	86,427	61,343	24,143	12,335
	89,863	73,740	28,856	17,811
Net current assets	49,170	21,579	9,861	2,531
Total assets less current liabilities	118,025	67,435	24,174	13,867
Creditors: amounts falling due after more than one year				
Loans	24,885	6,856	522	324
Other creditors	7,582	1,226	626	735
Provision for liabilities	10,521	9,263	1,703	1,368
	42,988	17,345	2,851	3,427
Net assets	75,037	50,090	21,323	11,440
Capital and reserves				
Share capital	9,256	6,364	2,787	420
Share premium account	24,929	24,821	5,965	–
Other reserves	15,733	4,188	–	13
Profit and loss account	25,119	14,717	11,333	11,007
Shareholders' funds	75,037	50,090	20,085	11,440
Minority interests	–	–	1,238	–
	75,037	50,090	21,323	11,440

Appendix 2   John Crowther Group PLC

FINANCIAL STATEMENTS

Year ending 31 December	1983 £000	1984 £000	1985 £000	1986 £000	1987 £000
Turnover	7,334	10,865	37,984	224,616	357,828
Cost of sales	n.a.	n.a.	n.a.	(157,876)	(258,501)
Gross profit	n.a.	n.a.	n.a.	66,740	99,327
Distribution costs	n.a.	n.a.	n.a.	(17,118)	(29,874)
Administrative expenses	n.a.	n.a.	n.a.	(31,944)	(45,145)
Other operating income	n.a.	n.a.	n.a.	781	1,960
Related companies	1	5	n.a.	(56)	3,568
Interest	(196)	(253)	(720)	(3,578)	(4,585)
Profit before tax	227	514	1,831	14,825	25,251
Tax	(35)	(57)	(159)	(2,666)	(5,009)
Profit after tax	192	457	1,672	12,159	20,242
Minority interest	–	–	–	(87)	(425)
Attributable to members	192	457	1,672	12,072	19,817
Preference dividends	(11)	(11)	(11)	(10)	(10)
Ordinary dividends	(72)	(126)	(310)	(3,350)	(5,208)
Extraordinary items	(141)	(60)	(89)	–	(1,629)
Retained profit/(loss)	(32)	260	1,262	8,712	12,790
Fixed assets					
Tangible	–	2,792	21,097	46,802	67,107
Investments	–	9	19	492	3,903
		2,801	21,116	47,294	71,010
Current assets		5,468	36,663	113,782	181,771
Current liabilities		5,034	23,714	78,242	124,997
Net current assets		434	12,949	35,540	56,774
Total assets less current liabilities		3,235	34,065	82,834	127,784
Creditors due after one year		441	10,803	22,264	37,210
Shareholders' funds		2,794	23,262	60,256	70,054
Minority interests		–	–	314	20,520
		2,794	23,262	60,570	90,574

20 Horizon Travel

During the 1980s the number of Britons who took air-inclusive summer package holidays increased from four million to nearly twelve million. When those travellers making their own arrangements and winter holidays packages were included, probably over a quarter of the British population took at least one holiday abroad a year. (See figure 20.1.)

The holiday companies more than matched this demand with supply and consequently, in real terms, package holiday become cheaper for the customer, but less profitable for the holiday companies. (See table 20.1.)

The larger companies embarked on expansion programmes designed to increase their market shares, and particularly between 1985 and 1988 they engaged in severe price competition.

This concluded in 1989 when the planned supply of summer package holidays totalled twelve million holidays, but only a little over ten million were sold, even with a considerable amount of last-minute discounting.

The results of this were that whilst the larger companies, e.g. Thomson and Intasun, increased their market share, their profits fell heavily. Thus whilst Thomson increased its market share to 39 per cent, it made profits of less than £4m. on package holiday sales of £1 billion. Some of the smaller companies than these became casualties during this period. For example Redwing (a British Airways subsidiary) lost £17m. in the year ending March 1989, and £11m. in the year ending March 1990. British Airways sold the company to Owners Abroad in March 1990. By this time there were two major competitors, Thomson with a 39 per cent market share, and Intasun, with 19 per cent. All the other companies had been taken over, closed down, or were niche competitors.

The growth slowdown of 1989 posed strategic and tactical problems for the holiday companies in their planning for 1990. They could maintain the growth in supply and protect market shares by price cutting

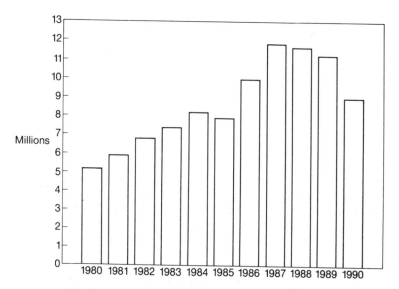

FIGURE 20.1   **Volume of air tour package holidays, 1980–90**

TABLE 20.1   **Price of a typical Thomson summer inclusive tour to Spain[a] 1981–6**

£	1981	1982	1983	1984	1985	1986
7 nights	163	175	147	175	185	159
14 nights	197	215	195	215	228	196

[a] Hotel Taurus Park, Pineda, Costa Dorada: full-board holiday out of London Airport, departing early August.

and late discounting, or they could cut capacity, risking loss of market share through price competition from smaller competitors, while maintaining profitability. Thomson responded by cutting one million holidays from its planned supply of three million for summer 1990. The rest of the industry followed this lead, such that more than two million holidays were cut from the 1990 plans. At the same time the price of a summer holiday rose by about 10 per cent, making 1990 the first real price increase since the early 1980s.

In the event these tactics proved profitable for the holiday companies, as they sold all their planned holidays for 1990 at full prices. However, the contraction in supply created more competition between the high street travel agents, for whom year-on-year growth had been important, as they made their profit through a basic percentage commission.

TABLE 20.2 **Make up of a package price**

	%
Agent's commission	10
Flight	26
Hotel	50
Resort staff/coaches	2
Overheads/marketing	5
Profit	7

The strategies of the holiday companies had varied during the 1980s, as customer needs and tastes changed. A variety of market segments had sprung up, e.g. Italian lakes and long-haul destinations in the Far East.

These typical prices were made up from the percentage costs based on a load factor of 95 per cent (the proportion of seats sold of the seats available) set out in table 20.2.

This case study examines the developments in the industry from the perspective of a company which was one of the major companies at the beginning of the decade, but which by the end had been taken over twice.

HORIZON TRAVEL

In 1965 Bruce Tanner, chairman of Horizon, who was operating a small Birmingham tour operator (as Horizon Midlands), joined with the London-based Horizon Holidays. The result was Horizon London operating from the south and Horizon Midlands operating from Birmingham; this geographical expansion partly explained the early growth of Horizon. At the time when Clarksons, the market leader, went into liquidation in 1974 as a result of offering holidays at too low a price, the Horizon London end of the Horizon operation ran into difficulties, as all the tour operators struggled with the economic problems arising from the quadrupling of oil prices and the devaluation of sterling. Bruce Tanner set about carefully rebuilding the business, conscious that quality control and product consistency were becoming more important in the holiday business; by 1978 Horizon was able to consider setting up its own airline.

By the holiday season of 1979, Horizon had joined the other three big tour operators running their own airline. Thomson Holidays owned Britannia Airlines, Intasun Leisure owned Air Europe, and Cosmos was the owner of Monarch Airways. Horizon's airline was called Orion Airlines; it immediately contributed to company profitability, with £1m. of the company's £7.38m. pre-tax profit for 1980. In 1981 Orion contributed £4m. to pre-tax profits of £13.3m. on sales of £97m. (a 9 per cent market share of the package tour business).

Prior to the establishment of Orion Airlines the company had been paying approximately one-third of its sales revenue to Britannia Airlines (owned by Thomson). Package holiday customers paid, on average, about £35 when booking their holiday (often six months in advance), and the balance eight weeks before departure, whilst the foreign hotel bills were settled when the holidaymakers had returned, so at certain times of the year the tour operators had a very large positive cash flow.

In the early days the original Horizon Midlands had bought ten retail travel agents in main cities which sold competitor's holiday tours as well as Horizon tours.

In 1980 Horizon Travel, as by that time they had been renamed, bought two hotels at Mojacar in Spain, which was not at that time on the tourist map and thus the hotels were virtually worthless unless a big tour operator took an interest in them. Horizon bought them for less than £1m. and subsequently bought and developed a surrounding 20-acre site for self-catering units at a projected completion price of £4.5m., with a forecast contribution of the Pueblo Indalo holiday village, as it would be known, of £1m. per year. It was planned to offer holidays at Pueblo Indalo by 1983 for Spanish holidaymakers as the village reached completion, and subsequently to offer holidays there for UK holidaymakers in 1984.

Following its 1981 financial performance Horizon expected to continue growing, and in 1982 produced record profit figures of £14.3m., even though the 1982 season had not been good for the industry generally. Unlike the other tour operators, however, Horizon had not had to make discount sales of its holidays, although its load factor had fallen to 87 per cent, from 94 per cent in 1981. Each percentage point fall in the load factor meant roughly an overall fall in profits for the industry as a whole of £500,000, as the gross profit margin of 'top-slice' customers was over 40 per cent. (Load factor referred to the planning by the companies regarding the anticipated proportion of holidays sold. The typical load-factor plan in the industry was 90 per cent whereas in the early eighties Horizon had planned on 85 per cent. A load factor of above 90 per cent, the industry termed 'top-slice'.)

By 1983 Horizon Travel was involved in all the stages of the package tour holiday, from retail travel agent (although selling only a minute proportion of their own holidays) to hotel/village ownership and airline transport. In 1983 Horizon Travel offered 525,000 holidays, a 16 per cent increase over 1982.

In March 1985 Horizon plc formed a 50/50 joint venture company with Bass plc, to which Horizon's hotels and holiday centres in Spain, and Bass's holiday clubs in Spain, Greece and Italy were transferred.

In April 1985 Bass bought 26 per cent of Horizon plc's ordinary shares.

In 1986 Horizon sold 590,000 holidays, increasing this to 880,000 holidays in 1987; nevertheless they lost £5.4m. in 1986 and even more in 1987, even though they were the third-largest operator in the industry, with an 8 per cent market share.

In April 1987 the Bass Group bought Horizon for £100m. and subsequently also bought the Wings holiday operator group from the Rank Organization for £10m. That year turned out to be one of the least profitable ever in the tour business; the 30 largest operators totalled losses of over £25m. of which Horizon accounted for £6.8m. In August 1988 both Horizon and Wings were sold to Thomson for £75m. and £17m. respectively, giving Thomson a 39 per cent share of the all-inclusive air package holiday market.

The performance of Thomson Travel Group, comprising Thomson Holidays, Portland Holidays, Britannia Airways and Lunn Poly travel agents is compared with Horizon Travel, comprising Horizon Holidays and Orion Airways in figure 20.2, which illustrates the return on capital employed for the different parts of the businesses for the years 1983 to 1987.

BACKGROUND TO THE INDUSTRY

The package tour holiday companies traditionally began their advertising for the following season before the customers had finished their Christmas dinners; the colder the weather in Britain, the more attractive a two-week stay in the summer sun of Spain and the Mediterranean seemed. Generally, most of the booking was done by the end of February, but in 1983 this had tended to change as customers, in response to the growth in holiday offers, began to book a little later.

The air-inclusive package tour holiday developed after the Second World War. Whereas 600,000 UK residents went abroad by air on a package holiday in 1962, this figure had risen to 1.7 million by 1969, to over 4 million by 1982, and to over 11 million by 1990. The rapid growth of the industry in the 1960s attracted many entrants, and by 1965 there were over 300 companies offering air-inclusive package holidays. However, by the late 1960s the industry had evolved into a smaller group of companies which had survived the development and 'shake-out' periods of the industry growth. In addition, large companies had bought their way into what they saw as a profitable growth market. For example, the Thomson Organization, well-known at that time for its newspapers and television, bought three tour operators in 1965, and by 1982 had become the largest UK operator.

Although the industry continued to grow through the 1970s, there were often problems. The industry was particularly susceptible to

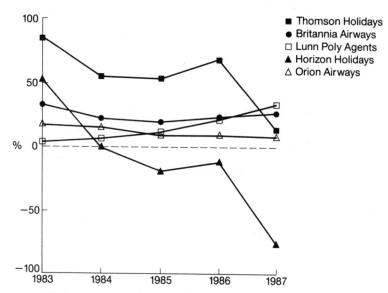

FIGURE 20.2   **Return on capital employed**

TABLE 20.3   **Sterling exchange rates 1976–86**

£1=	US dollars	French francs	Italian lire	German marks	Spanish pesetas
1976	1.805	8.61	1,497	4.552	120.61
1977	1.746	8.57	1,540	4.050	133.11
1978	1.920	8.64	1,628	3.851	146.95
1979	2.122	9.03	1,763	3.888	142.38
1980	2.328	9.82	1,992	4.227	167.10
1981	2.025	10.94	2,287	4.556	185.92
1982	1.749	11.48	2,364	4.243	191.81
1983	1.516	11.55	2,302	3.870	217.48
1984	1.336	11.63	2,339	3.791	214.30
1985	1.298	11.55	2,463	3.784	219.55
1986	1.499	10.79	2,332	3.403	215.78

Source: Economic Trends, Central Statistical Office

fluctuations in sterling, and when sterling was floated by the UK government in 1972, the operators had continually to consider its value from one year to the next.

Table 20.3 shows changes in the value of sterling from 1976 to 1986, and figure 20.3 shows the sterling exchange rate against the Spanish peseta.

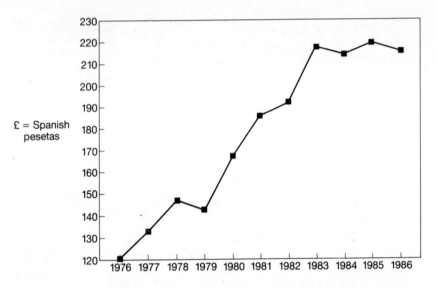

FIGURE 20.3   **Sterling exchange rate against the Spanish peseta, 1976–86**

During the 1970s the economy and industry growth rates had begun to slow down, and profits were not always as easy to make. Clarksons, the industry leader in 1970, reported losses of £2.7m. in 1971, and went into liquidation in 1974.

The *Financial Times* pointed up these problems when it reported on 5 July 1972:

[The companies] are well aware that the last year or so has seen the basis on which package tourism has grown in Britain changed somewhat. Assorted factors have contributed to this, and the problem of the pound is simply the last in a long line. Broadly speaking, the companies have found that:
  (a)   Size gave them greater management problems than they had anticipated
  (b)   Continued growth could not be taken for granted, and
  (c)   Inflation (and now effective devaluation) plays havoc with long-term pricing policies.

The companies which coped best in those difficult times were the Horizons and Wings of the business. It was arguable that this was not necessarily due to the management quality, but rather that they had concentrated on up-market growth by aiming at white collar, middle-class executives who had suffered less in the recessions. In addition, at that time Horizon was more of a regional operator based in the Midlands, and a part of their success may be attributed to the general prosperity of that area at that time. The bigger companies seemed unable to deal with the problems posed. With hindsight it was easy to criticize the tour operators for not buying their currencies or their beds forward, but the environmental turbulence was much more complex than it had ever been before. Some had completed favourable deals, for example Thomson had fixed its beds in Jamaica and Yugoslavia in dollar currency, and when the dollar fell they emerged with a profit. But the currency crisis of 1972 arrived at the very worst part of their year, when the summer rush was about to start, leaving little time to reorganize. The result was that the operators had to involve themselves in the messy business of collecting surcharges at the airports to cover both currency losses and fuel price changes levied by the airlines.

These problems of the early to mid-seventies emphasized the advantages of longer-term planning to the tour operators, and resulted in changes relating to both flights and beds.

Some of the larger companies had recognized that they could cut costs by entering into longer-term contracts (i.e. five to ten years, rather than just a holiday season) with the airlines, and eventually they began to integrate vertically with airline companies. Thomson Holidays bought Britannia Airways, Cosmos bought Monarch Airways, Intasun owned Air Europe, while Laker Holidays and Arrowsmith Holidays were subsidiaries of Laker Airlines, before Laker went into involuntary liquidation in February 1982. In 1990 Airtours, a company specializing in the Caribbean, announced that it would start its own airline for the 1991 season, and that it expected the airline to carry 60 per cent of Airtour customers.

All the holiday tour operators maintained a policy of running their airlines as separate companies from the mainstream holiday business, and even chartered flight seats to other holiday tour operators. For example, Intasun used only 50 per cent of their seats for their own package holidays, the balance being used by as many as 25 different tour operators.

Changes in the methods of acquisition of hotel beds also occurred, particularly in the second half of the 1960s, as there was a shortage of beds in the most popular resorts. Not only were British companies in competition with each other, but they also competed directly with the Scandinavians and the Germans. The tour companies also discovered that British holidaymakers did not take kindly to being accommodated in a hotel dominated by fellow guests of a different nationality – different social habits led to friction and ill-feeling. The original method of obtaining beds was to have an annual contract with the hotelier, and to renew that contract each year. The growing competition for beds led to rapid increases in prices, and consequent uncertainty for the companies. Furthermore, no company could be confident that the beds it had used one year would be available the following year: the hoteliers were in a strong position to negotiate last-minute contracts with competing companies.

As a result, the practice of contracting with a hotelier for a block of beds in his hotel for seven to ten years became increasingly common. The normal contract had three particular features: first, an initial deposit was required, usually amounting to between 10 and 20 per cent of the total value of the contract (sometimes it was as high as 50 per cent), to be repaid over the length of the contract; secondly, the negotiated rate per bed per night increased by an agreed fixed percentage every year, to allow for inflation; thirdly, the company had to give a guarantee that there would be an agreed level of occupancy of the beds, averaged over the whole summer season, below which a financial penalty was incurred.

A third method of obtaining beds also developed. This was the long-term (15–25 years) turnkey lease, in which the company took over a complete hotel, fully equipped and furnished, and was entirely responsible for providing the management. Usually a deposit was required, amounting to perhaps three years' rent in advance. This scheme guaranteed beds for years ahead, and allowed total control over the quality of service provided. There were some problems, however. Local hoteliers resented a hotel leased and managed by a tour company, because the company tended to favour its own hotel, especially in lean years.

Towards the end of the 1980s there were about 550 tour operators in the UK, although the all-inclusive air package holiday was dominated by the largest operators. As the wishes of holidaymakers widened, the tour operators had responded by increasing the range of holidays offered which had created distinct market segments:

- the basic all-in package to the sun, e.g. Spain;
- the holiday for specific target markets, e.g. 18-to-30 age-groups (Club Med) and over-55 age-groups (Saga);
- European city breaks, e.g. weekends, in Paris;
- flight-only packages for those owning property abroad;
- specific geographical areas, e.g. Italian lakes and mountains;
- long-haul travel to the Far East and the Americas.

The different parts of the cost of an all-inclusive holiday varied between operators, but were approximately:

- accommodation 50 per cent of the sales price;
- flight 35 per cent;
- travel agent's commission 9 per cent;
- gross margin of operator 6 per cent.

In 1986 there had been a problem when over 8 million overseas holidays were sold. This had encouraged the big tour operators to increase capacity by about 25 per cent for 1987, whilst trade estimates suggested that demand was only between 10 per cent and 15 per cent higher than the previous year. Spare capacity tended to lead to discounting, and the travel trade believed it was the smaller tour operators which were forced to discount heavily their July and August holidays.

THE PROBLEMS OF PLANNING

Planning for the summer season brochures issued by Thomson, Horizon, Intasun, Cosmos and the other package tour operators began in the November eighteen months perviously. By that time the major operators had already issued their brochures for the next summer and had begun to get some idea of what their sales would be like, as bookings came in from travel agents around the country. By early January the tour operators had to decide what strategic moves they should make. The four major ingredients of the packaged holiday were

1   the hotels;
2   the resorts;
3   the UK airports;
4   the length of stay.

These were determined a year in advance. The brochures, usually led by Horizon or Thomson in the early eighties, went to press in the previous July with prices worked out on the basis of the cost of the four basic ingredients, plus a contribution to overheads and profit. None of the variables was straightforward. The cost of the hotel bed was affected by the exchange rate between sterling and the local currency. Air flight contracts were subject to the price of fuel (always calculated in dollars). Overheads were controllable, but the company had to estimate how many holidays it would sell in order to work out how thinly to spread the fixed costs. Fuel and foreign exchange could be covered by buying forward, but the imponderable remained of how many holidays the public would buy. Horizon had always planned on the basis of a load factor of 85 per cent, that is, they priced on the basis of selling at least 85 per cent of the holidays they offered, whereas other companies planned for a load factor of 90 per cent. The economics of the industry and the slim margins were such that even a slight fall below anticipated demand could cause severe problems for some of the package tour operators. An example of this occurred in autumn 1982 when Horizon launched its 1983 brochures, followed a week later by Thomson with the latter offering one million holidays. By November 1982 the whole trade was reported to be 30 per cent down on bookings compared with the previous year, and Thomson had sold only 200,000 holidays, compared with 240,000 at the same time a year earlier. Horizon, Intasun and Cosmos were each offering about 500,000 holidays, and frequently the latter two had awaited Thomson's announcements before making final commitments on prices, thus expecting in autumn 1982 to be able to offer comparable holidays at slightly lower prices than the market leader.

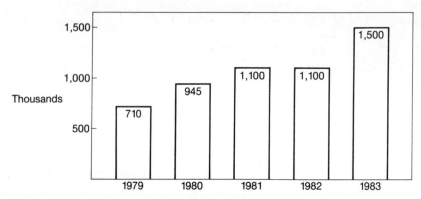

FIGURE 20.4   **Volume of bookings made after April for the summer of each year**

When Intasun and Cosmos produced their 1983 brochures the price differential was more marked than usual, for they priced comparable holidays, often in the same hotels, up to £15 cheaper (on a summer package costing between £175 and £300) with prices guaranteed. Thomson responded by withdrawing its original brochure and issued a new one with price reductions ranging from £5 to £74 on more than half the holidays on offer, with a no-surcharge guarantee at a 'paper' cost to the company of £6m. As forecasts for the 1983 holiday season were of falls of 5 per cent to 20 per cent, Thomson had prepared for the possibility of a price war by splitting its brochure print-run into two parts. The company usually produced 2.75 million copies of its 300-page brochure, but for 1983 it had produced only 1.15 million and had been able to respond to its competitors by producing the second run with the new prices in December 1982. As well as a general fall in demand for holidays in 1983, they had had to contend with an increasing tendency by the buyer to book later and later, such that at one point in summer 1983 it was estimated that the average period between booking and departure had fallen to 20 days. (See figure 20.4.)

The problem which then faced Horizon, Intasun and Cosmos, not to mention the many smaller tour operators, was how to respond to the reissue of Thomson's 1983 brochure. It was a problem of timing as well as cost. Thomson had been able to plan its whole Christmas press and television advertising around the new prices, and it was impossible for the others to produce a new brochure in time to get it out to the 4, 500 travel agents around the country.

Traditionally the first two months of a year produced most of the summer's bookings, so the tour operators had always begun their major advertising efforts at Christmas, aware that by March they would have to start releasing hotel beds and flights, or pay for them with the hope of selling them, but perhaps only at a discount.

TABLE 20.4   **Early growth of the Intasun business**

Year ended 31 March	1977	1978	1979	1980	1981	1982
Holidays sold (000s)	124	238	339	296	417	468
Load factor (%)	88	92	89	90	91	95

As an example of this, by the end of January 1979, 63 per cent of those who eventually took a foreign holiday had booked; by the end of January 1982 this had fallen to 42 per cent. Eventually in 1982, 15 per cent of all holidays were discounted, although Horizon had not discounted any.

As each year progressed those tour operators who got their initial capacity plans wrong had to write to customers explaining changes in departure or arrival-back dates, airports, and even hotels and resorts (with an opportunity for the customer to back out), and this would involve giving the customer an *ex gratia* payment for the inconvenience. Those holidays bought by the tour operator, but not sold, would have to be heavily discounted because by the summer any contribution to overheads and profit would be better than nothing. In the early eighties, however, Horizon had a policy of not discounting its holidays.

OTHER TRAVEL OPERATORS

International Leisure Group

The company began operations in 1971 when Harry Goodman, Stephen Matthews and Michael Prior started Vacation Apartments Ltd. In 1972 they acquired the Intasun name, and by 1977 were operating package holidays from airports all over the UK. In 1978 they decided to acquire their own airline and formed Air Europe, which by 1981 was a wholly-owned subsidiary of Intasun and contributed 28 per cent of the group's profit before tax. Table 20.4 shows the early growth of the Intasun business since it began operating nationally in 1977.

Air Europe planes were regularly chartered to more than 25 other tour operators, although 50 per cent of the capacity was used by Intasun in the peak holiday seasons, but none of the other four operators accounted for more than 8 per cent of the air-fleet's capacity. Like other tour operators, Intasun sold its holidays through ABTA travel agents around the country, who accounted for 95 per cent of the Intasun holidays sold. As a matter of policy the company had made no investments in hotels and negotiated fixed tariffs with hoteliers on a seasonal basis, keeping advance contractual commitments to a minimum. Intasun did sometimes place deposits with hotels, but only when it had already taken sufficient bookings to cover the deposit. It avoided undue dependence on any one hotel group, and believed that its buying power as the second biggest UK tour operator, and its record of taking up its allocations, enabled it to reserve accommodation in advance and to pay only for those rooms occupied.

In common with other overseas air-inclusive tour operators, the company was required to hold a licence issued by the Civil Aviation Authority and hold a bond guaranteeing payment of up to 7 per cent of its estimated gross turnover in the event of failure to meet liabilities to passengers.

In the growth period of the early 1980s, like its competitors, Intasun had planned for growth in the 1983 season, and had increased its number of holidays available by 19 per cent to 634,000, offering a no-surcharge guarantee for all bookings made before the end of February. Both Thomson and Horizon had at that time countered this offer by giving a no-surcharge guarantee regardless of booking date. Such a move was considered by Intasun as contrary to common sense, as they felt that no-surcharge guarantees should be offered in order to encourage early booking.

The history of no-surcharge guarantees was complicated, but in several seasons Horizon had managed to avoid surcharges by getting its buying forward right at times when other operators had been obliged to levy surcharges. The complications arose when an operator found itself in a position of surcharging with the left hand, whilst discounting with the right within the same season. This had befallen Intasun in the past.

International Leisure Group (Intasun) was floated on the Stock Exchange in 1981, and during the decade they increased their share of the market dramatically – see table 20.5. They placed great emphasis on advertising low prices to consumers and developing close relationships with the travel agents. Following the stock market crash of 1987 ILG shares like most others fell sharply in value, and ILG decided to return to private ownership with the management buying back the shares. The reason given was that they wanted to develop a long-term strategy for their airline (*Air Europe*) to build a European network, and they felt that the short-term needs of the stock market would stifle such long-term plans. Also, fluctuations in the package holiday business could affect their ability to raise finance.

At the end of the eighties ILG comprised Intasun, Global, Lancaster, and Club 18–30 holidays.

Thomson Travel

Thomson Travel was a fully-owned subsidiary of the International Thomson Organization plc, and it operated package tours, aircraft charter and travel retailing in the UK through Thomson Holidays, Portland Holidays, Lunn Poly, and Britannia Airways. Thomson

TABLE 20.5   **Market share of the top tour operators**

Percentage share	1983	1984	1985	1986	1987	1988	1989
Thompson Travel Group	17	19	20	27	31	24	39
Intasun Group	11	13	15	18	18	18	16
Horizon Travel[a]	6	6	5	7	8	7	–
British Airways Group[a]	10	7	6	5	5	na	–
Redwing[a]						–	6
Airtours						2	4
Owners Abroad Group						3	4

[a] In 1989, Horizon and Wings were bought by Thomson, and British Airways' loss-making holiday subsidiary, BA Holidays, was merged with the fast-growing Sunmed operation to form Redwing Travel as the third-largest tour operator.
Source: Thomson Travel Group

Holidays was one of the world's largest package tour operators, and by far the largest in the UK, organizing and selling approximately one million holidays a year covering Europe, Asia, Africa and America. It offered every conceivable kind of resort and hotel, from the large and luxurious to the tiny and intimate. Thomson was also the leader in skiing holidays, the number two in villa holidays, and in 1980 had entered the short weekend breaks market.

Portland Holidays was launched in 1980 as a tour operator selling direct to the public. In 1981 over 100,000 holidays had been sold for the first time, and by the mid-1980s Portland Holidays was the leading company in direct sales. Lunn Poly was an expanding retail travel agency, with over 500 outlets.

International Thomson plc was involved in the publishing of newspapers, periodicals and books, and natural mineral exploitation, and had interests in Canada, Australia and USA as well as the UK. It had disposed of its interest in Scottish Television in 1977, and in the *Sunday Times* in 1981. It had taken up its interest in the travel industry when it bought Thomson Travel in 1965.

Although at the beginning of the 1980s the travel company had lost market share, by the end of the decade Thomson was the leading tour operator, with about a 39 per cent market share of package holidays, and over three million customers a year.

Although Thomson Travel's sales more than doubled between 1984 and 1989, it was only in 1988 that its operating income grew significantly. In 1989 no operating profits were made at all, and the first quarter of 1990 produced losses on the travel business. Like most travel operators Thomson generated interest income from the advance payments made on holiday bookings – see table 20.6.

At the end of the eighties Thomson Travel comprised Thomson, Horizon, Portland, and Skytours holidays. Other major operators were Redwing, which comprised Sunmed, Enterprise and Sovereign

TABLE 20.6   **Thomson Travel five-year record**

$Cm.	1985	1986	1987	1988	1989
Sales	888	1,173	1,696	2,047	2,038
Operating profit	49	52	46	60	–

holidays; Owners Abroad, with Falcon, Tjaereborg and Arrowsmith; and Airtours.

TOUR OPERATORS AND THE TRAVEL AGENTS

In 1988 the prospects for package holiday sales had weakened, as up to one million fewer holidays were booked, although demand for winter holidays had been about 40 per cent higher in volume terms than the previous year, and bookings suggested that the following winter would be a record.

For the tour companies, operating on load factors of 85–90 per cent, and for which each additional sale after breakeven represented almost pure profit, the maximization of distribution outlets became increasingly important.

By the end of the 1970s there had already been a distinct move in favour of the largest tour operators, as holidaymakers had seen companies associated with the industry collapse – for example, Clarksons, Courtline, Horizon London, and in 1982 Laker Airlines (including Arrowsmith Holidays and Laker Holidays). Fear of this happening again had encouraged the shift to the industry's more established names.

A gradual move by the tour operators was for some of them to sell their holidays direct to the holidaymakers, thus bypassing the travel agent. For many years they had held off making such a move, fearing retaliation from the travel agents, but the situation was upset when a new tour company entered the market from abroad with experience of direct selling and without any connections with the travel agents. This was the Scandinavian company Tjaereborg. Of the major UK tour operators only Thomson, the largest in 1980 with an over 20 per cent share of the market, launched its own direct-selling operation, Portland, in 1980 which showed a half-million pound profit in 1981, but it did not endear Thomson to the travel agents.

A distinctive feature of the air package holiday industry in the UK was the high proportion of holidays sold through general retail travel agents, and one strategy which had always been open to the tour companies was the acquisition of a chain of independent travel agents. Other than Thomson (with Lunn Poly) such forward vertical integration had not proceeded far, possibly because of the threat of boycott from other travel agents should a tour company make serious inroads into the agency business. Little capital was normally required to set up an agency. Provincial and country town agents were generally very profitable: 75 per cent showed profits in excess of 20 per cent of total revenue (total value of ticket sales less remissions to carriers and tour operators); 40 per cent of suburban agents showed profits in excess of 20 per cent of total revenue, but city shopping centre agents showed only small profits.

It was estimated that travel agents were responsible for booking 83 per cent of inclusive package holidays, as against 77 per cent of airline seats and 68 per cent of sea passages, and the introduction of direct sales did not diminish this significantly. The sale of air package holidays by travel agents represented the most profitable part of their business, since they normally received a commission of 10 per cent on each sale, and occasionally an overriding commission of a variable 2.5 per cent. As a result, any attempt by the companies to bypass the travel agent, by selling direct to the public or using some other outlet, met with strong resistance.

As the holiday business grew there was a brisk demand for retail travel agencies. Consequently, the membership of ABTA (necessary if air-inclusive tours were to be sold) had grown. The Thomas Cook group sold off to its parent company (Midland Bank) the traveller's cheque business, and concentrated on becoming an effective retail chain. There were few economies of scale in retail travel agency, and increased turnover could generally only be achieved by increasing the number of outlets. It may be that too much 'capacity' in retailing holidays was put on the market, and some degree of concentration of ownership might have been expected. The managing director of Pickford's Travel, which operated the country's second-largest chain of 200 retail travel outlets, had proposed one way of cutting the number of travel agents by suggesting that the travel agents, instead of operating on their 10 per cent commission, should be allowed to set their own prices for holiday packages (and hence their own profit margins). This would have enabled a multiple travel agent to negotiate the numbers and prices of holidays bought from the tour operator, and resell them at its own price.

By the late eighties there were approximately 7,000 retail travel agents in the UK; typically at least 60 per cent of a travel agent's turnover was air-related business, either through the sale of airline tickets or through the sale of air-inclusive tours. The role of retailing was supplemented by the sales offices of the major airlines and tour operators, and by agents not appointed by the IATA airlines (such entrepreneurs often being referred to as 'bucket shops'). See table 20.7.

The conventional travel agent was appointed by the IATA airlines to handle the tickets of the IATA airlines operating in the country concerned. Agents' commission on ticket sales was only allowed to

TABLE 20.7   **ABTA travel agents, 1981–8**

	Enterprises	Offices
1981	2,094	4,781
1982	2,211	5,055
1983	2,396	5,299
1984	2,537	5,733
1985	2,647	6,019
1988	>3,000	>7,000

Travel agency chains: number of outlets, 1981–5

	Large (100+)	Medium (20 to 99)	Small (10 to 19)
1981	2	16	11
1982	2	18	10
1983	2	18	12
1984	4	15	10
1985	5	13	7

Major chains' share of holiday market, 1987 and 1988

	1987 (%)	1988 (%)
Thomas Cook	11.5	12.0
Pickfords	7.0	9.0
Hogg Robinson	4.5	4.0
Lunn Poly	10.5	15.0
A. T. May	4.0	4.0

the IATA-appointed travel agents. The IATA appointment was thus highly prized. Deregulation in the airline field extended into this area too: for example, the withdrawal of the large US airlines from the IATA fares-setting traffic conferences meant that they would not see themselves bound by the IATA resolutions on travel agency relations, including the setting of agents' commission.

It was considered at that time that the travel agents were in a powerful position. Since many companies marketed almost identical holidays, and 'brand loyalty' was low, the agents had great influence on whose holidays were sold. They could effectively cut out any company they chose to, without seriously affecting their own volume of business. Furthermore, all the largest travel agents (25 per cent were responsible for 78 per cent of business in 1968; by 1988 the top five controlled over 40 per cent of package tour sales) were closely linked through ABTA and could in theory, if they so wished, act

TABLE 20.8 **The economics of travel agencies (1986)**

	% of income
Salary & related costs	40
Rent & rates	15
Telephone	12
Advertising	3
Heat & light	2
Postage	2
Equipment, depreciation and other costs	18
Pre-tax margin	8
	100

together against any individual company. This was unlikely, but the threat existed.

About 17 million adults visited travel agents in the UK every year, about 13 million undertaking transactions with them, making about 17 million transactions in all. By value:

- 38 per cent booked package holidays;
- 34 per cent booked air tickets;
- 22 per cent booked bus tickets;
- 13 per cent booked ferry tickets;
- 14 per cent booked rail tickets.

Package tours represented about 50 per cent, business travel about 33 per cent, and the balance was personal travel, e.g. air, ferry, rail and bus tickets and insurances as proportions of travel agents business.

Travel agents worked on an overall margin of about 8 to 9 per cent.

As the number of package holiday bookings fell by 10 per cent in 1989, and with a further fall predicted for 1990, based on early bookings for that year, the Automobile Association responded by cutting out sales of inclusive package holidays at 69 of its 88 travel centre outlets.

Table 20.8 shows the average economics of the travel agent business.

During the seventies and eighties the tour operators saw volume as the key to success, as large numbers enabled them to fill up their charter planes, negotiate cheaper prices with hoteliers, and spread the overhead and administrative costs further. To achieve these volumes Intasun decided in the early eighties to undercut the market leader's prices; Thomson decided to fight back. First in 1982, then in 1983, 1984, and again in 1986, the industry leader cut prices drastically and increased its capacity at the same time. The other operators had no choice but to follow suit. Horizon several times tried to fight the trend by holding prices firm, but it ended up flying half-empty planes to the sun as a result. A major restructuring of the industry was bound to follow.

Late in 1990 Thomson announced its new brochures for the 1991 season, and the managing director stated that in future they would act as an umbrella organization to an increasingly diverse range of holidays available from more and more specialist holiday programmes. By the end of 1990 it was expected that all-inclusive package tour holiday sales would have fallen to below nine million holidays, for the first time since the mid-eighties. Thomson anticipated their sales would be more than 12 per cent down on 1990.

This was the case, despite indications that the whole holiday market was still expanding. Government figures showed that the overall holiday market had grown by 5 per cent in 1989.

The new Thomson brochures promised a wider choice of holiday than the basic charters of previous brochures, for example, villa holidays in the Dordogne, Tuscany and Umbria. Holidays in Spain, the traditional resort, were reduced to less than 45 per cent of the holidays on offer.

Appendix 1 Horizon Travel PLC

PROFIT AND LOSS ACCOUNT, 1984–6

Year ending November	1984 £m.	1985 £m.	1986[a] £m.
Sales	151.94	135.69	198.33
Operating costs	129.66	121.03	180.04
Gross profit	22.28	14.66	18.29
Profit before tax	12.52	14.46	4.59

[a] This was an eleven-month year, due to the sale of the company in 1987 to Bass plc.

TRADING ANALYSIS, 1984–6

	1984		1985		1986	
	Sales £m.	Operating profit £m.	Sales £m.	Operating profit £m.	Sales £m.	Operating profit £m.
Tour operations	129.06	5.54	101.36	11.05	156.76	(18.87)
Aircraft flights	71.48	5.85	62.17	2.77	68.70	4.74
Miscellaneous[a]	7.81	0.81	16.39	(0.39)	22.31	0.67
Intra-group sales	(56.40)	–	(44.23)	–	(49.44)	–

[a] This represented activities such as rentals and the travel agents.

BALANCE SHEETS, 1984–6

	1984 £m.	1985 £m.	1986 £m.
Fixed assets			
Tangible	74.20	77.60	74.58
Investments	5.07	16.59	23.41
	79.27	94.19	97.99
Current assets	23.32	38.01	50.40
Creditors (less than one year)	34.56	28.22	40.73
Total assets – current liabilities	68.03	103.98	107.66
Creditors (more than one year)	22.92	41.80	29.01
Capital			
Equity	13.16	23.40	26.45
Reserves	31.95	38.78	52.21
	45.11	62.18	78.66

NINE-YEAR RECORD, 1978–86

£m.	1978	1979	1980	1981	1982	1983	1984	1985	1986
Turnover	31.27	50.17	72.58	96.83	118.49	124.21	151.94	135.69	198.33
PBT	2.95	3.81	7.38	13.40	14.37	12.57	12.52	14.46	4.59
Capital employed	–	6.57	9.79	16.00	35.79	49.93	68.03	103.98	107.66
Share price (p)									
High	–	–	70	148	235	225	188	–	–
Low	–	–	32	62	136	117	105	–	–

21 Next

Between 1981 and 1988 Next went through a period of extremely rapid expansion, starting as the Hepworth chain of menswear retailers and ending up as Next Retailing (Next Originals, Next Collection, Next for Men, Next Interiors), home shopping (Grattan mail order and other catalogues), a newsagents/confectionery chain (Dillons and Preedy) and 877 outlets taken over from Combined English Stores (CES) comprising clothing and jewellery shops and even campsite placements in holiday resorts (Eurocamp). However, for its financial year ending in January 1989 Next reported pre-tax profits down to £62m., from a record £123m. million in 1988. Appendix 1 provides financial information on Next plc.

In the 1989 annual report Next's new chairman wrote:

During the year to January 1989, it became apparent that the rapid growth, particularly as a result of the Combined English Stores acquisition, was putting the Group under significant financial, managerial and operational strain. It was also apparent that the management style that had been successful in a smaller environment was not as suitable to a Group of such diversity. It was, therefore, agreed by the Board that we should dispense with the services of George Davies, Chairman and Chief Executive.

Notwithstanding these changes, in the financial year ending 31 January 1990, Next plc reported a loss before tax of over £46m. This had an inevitable effect upon the market price of Next shares on the Stock Exchange – see figure 21.1.

This was a remarkable turnaround for a company which throughout the 1980s had been recognized as one of the major growth companies, and had played a significant and pivotal role in changing the shape of UK high streets, with a revolution in the retailing of both women's and menswear. During this decade retail sales of all kinds grew strongly

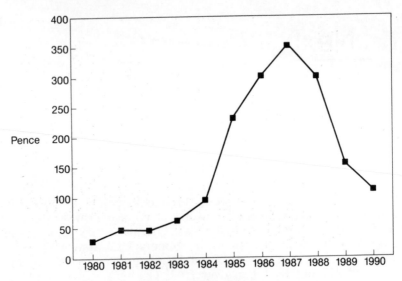

FIGURE 21.1   **Next share price, 1980–90**

throughout the UK – see figure 21.2. Appendix 2 provides general information on consumer income and expenditures.

Next began in May 1981, when J. Hepworth, a chain of menswear retailers, bought 78 Kendalls womenswear retail shops and completely redesigned them under the name Next. Throughout the 1970s Hepworth's, with its reliance on tailored menswear, had suffered – as had Burtons, another menswear retailer – as a result of cheap imports of ready-made men's suits and a growing trend towards more casual clothes. Hepworth's were particularly hit, as not only were they retailers but they also manufactured virtually all of their own retail products. Hepworth finished the decade with pre-tax profits of £5.7m. for year ending in 1980.

The Next image

Kendalls was previously owned by Combined English Stores and was bought by Hepworth for £1.75m. It had not been a profitable chain, and lost over half a million pounds in its first half-year with Hepworth's. It was decided that Next should target the women's 24 to 44 age-group, as most other chains appeared to be targeting the 16-to-24-year-olds at that time. It was thought that the 24 to 44 age-group was poised for an expansion of income and would want both fashion and better quality. A complete change of image was determined for the Kendalls chain, with the change-over to be accomplished quickly, and not on a store-by-store basis. This was achieved, new shopfitting, new facias and new stock, within a period of

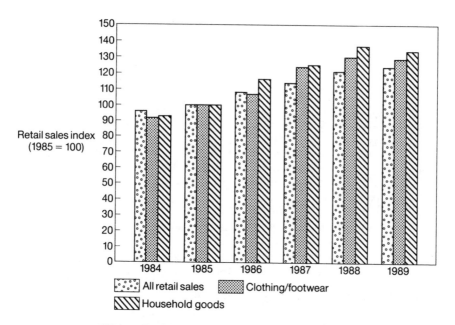

FIGURE 21.2   **All retail sales, clothing and footwear sales, and household goods sales index, 1984–9**

three months. The image for Next was more in line with a continental shop image, rather than the rather hectic style which prevailed on UK high streets at that time. The aim was to be 'cool and sophisticated, and not to dominate the merchandise'. The decor was white and stained grey woodwork, accented with blue and red pinstripes. A trial shop was built in Leicester and customer surveys showed that the shop had an expensive feel. To balance this, more effort was put into window-pricing to show that whilst style and quality were high, prices were not too high. No models were used in the shops, reliance being placed on groups of co-ordinated clothes and accessories.

George Davies joined the Hepworth board in June 1981 to develop and launch the Next concept; eight months later the first Next shops opened as Davies had envisaged them with the help of Conran design. At that time Sir Terence Conran was a non-executive chairman of J. Hepworth plc.

Hired as assistant managing director, George Davies worked on a range of merchandise that would be exclusive to the new stores. Davies believed that his proposed target group bought from the chain Country Casuals, who were more expensive than Davies wanted to be, or from Marks and Spencer, or paid a higher price and went to specialist independents. Davies decided that Next would take on Marks and Spencer who, he felt, it was impossible to ignore. As a result of their prices and quality, Marks and Spencer had at least 15 per cent of the womenswear market, where they competed on volume and by only stocking their own-label brands. Next, it was decided, would open with a range of accessories and outerwear that was entirely its own. Not just style, but yarns and fabrics were to be specially designed and made. The look was to be fashionable, but with the Next interpretation of fashion both quality and price were to be pitched to compare with Marks and Spencer. Another deliberate merchandise decision was to stick, as far as possible, to natural fibres because it was felt that the target market was moving away from synthetics. Davies did not feel that British women were very good at putting clothing together, unlike the French, on whose shops Next drew for inspiration.

Next relied on a speedy turnaround, and delivery of stock and distribution was all-important. By 1983, many thousands of garments were moving in and out of the main warehouse near Leicester, half of which were hanging, the remainder boxed. The company operated a computer-based sales response replenishment system. This meant that every Saturday evening replacement orders were received in Leicester, garments were picked up from the warehouse on Sunday, and deliveries started on Monday. By Tuesday the top branches were replenished and all other branches received their deliveries by Wednesday. On Thursday, the process was repeated for the company's 20 or so top stores. Next used Tibbett and Britten, a specialist clothing transporter, to carry its hanging and boxed garments. They provided the main garmet delivery service from Next's warehouse in Leicester to its stores throughout the country, including the Channel Islands. Both companies had worked together to simplify the distribution procedure, and a loading schedule specifically designed for Next was introduced.

Promotion rather than advertising played the major part in the overall store image of Next. A major section in Vogue was central, not because Next's potential audience was strong on Vogue readers, but because it was expected to give them an instant fashion authority and positioning. The company had a public relations group in London who sent samples from the current ranges to the national newspapers. Colour advertisements also appeared in the columns of the major women's magazines.

In order to further enhance the store image, especially at the beginning of the season when a new range was being launched, cheese and wine parties were held in the stores, and the latest seasonal look was displayed in a fashion show. Small postcards were usually available in most stores, through which customers could obtain the latest Next catalogue.

Particular emphasis was placed on the staffing of the stores, especially the manageresses, who were encouraged to recruit part-time, smart women of the right target age-group, reasoning that they could put the message across better than teenagers.

By 1983, there were 130 branches of Next, one of which was in Germany, and Hepworth's operating profit had increased to £9.27m. for the year ending February 1983, as sales rose to £98.6m.

Following its success with womenswear Next opened its chain of Next for Men, with some stand-alone branches and some sharing with the womenswear shops. The target man was the 25-to-44-year-old partner of the Next woman. Other chains followed their example, and competitors included Hornes with 40 stores with an average 3,000 square feet aimed at the 25-to-45 ABC1 audience, with a price level above Fosters, John Collier and Burtons, but below Austin Reed. John Collier also made changes to half of their 240 stores following a management buyout of the chain, also setting the target audience at 25-to-45-year-old men. At Fosters the target audience was 18-to-35 C1, C2 in 300 of its 500 stores, and the rest of the stores were switched into a discount Your Price chain.

In late 1985 Next applied its retailing principles to the home furnishings market by opening 80 Next Interior stores selling co-ordinated ranges of carpets, curtains, bedlinens, furniture and wall coverings.

Mail order

In 1986 Next turned its attention to mail order and completed a £300m. merger with Grattan mail order. The mail order industry had traditionally operated by selling its goods through agents, who earned 10 per cent commission by selling to their acquaintances and workmates. By giving the customers, who were largely in the C1 and C2 socio-economic groups, the opportunity to pay for the goods weekly over 20 or 40 weeks, the industry had grown to reach 7.3 per cent of the UK non-food retail sales of £23.81 billion by 1976 in current prices. Catalogues were usually about 1,000 pages long, featuring between 10,000 and 20,000 products and cost on average approximately £4 each to produce in 1987. The customer base had fallen over the years from 20.4 million in 1981 to 17.6 million in 1986 and of the 40 per cent of households with a catalogue many invariably had more than one.

Selling their products through the use of agents and a catalogue, five companies dominated the industry. Great Universal Stores Littlewoods, Freemans, Grattan and Empire Stores. See figure 21.3.

Between 1980 and 1986 their fortunes had varied as both GUS and Freemans had increased their market share, whilst both Littlewoods and Empire Stores had declined and Grattan had revived strongly over the last two years. Nevertheless, all five had involved themselves in cost control measures, e.g. weeding out non-productive agents and improving stock control procedures, and in better marketing developments, e.g. using telephone systems for ordering rather than relying on the post. This latter development had been pioneered by Freemans and followed by the rest.

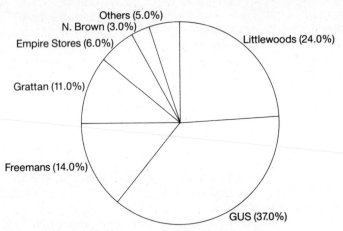

FIGURE 21.3   **UK mail order market shares, 1986**

Other developments included a shift to direct mail, as opposed to agency, to about 15 per cent of the sales. Mail order companies had different cost structures, compared with high street retailers, with lower fixed costs but higher advertising, delivery and staff costs. When a mail order company ran out of stock it was not immediately apparent to the customers who continued ordering, whilst stock which did not sell was difficult to shift with not having a window for sales. One of the major problems in mail order, however, was the high proportion of returned goods which was estimated at 40 per cent on fashion goods and 25 per cent on electrical goods. By 1987, mail order sales had grown to £3.6 billion out of UK non-food retail sales of £57. 97 billion in current prices. The problem facing the industry of attracting new customers had been compounded by the increased competition on the high street between the so-called 'lifestyle retailers' competing for new market segments. As approximately one-third of mail order sales were in womens and childrenswear this increased competition added to the rather drab image the industry had. The main response of the mail order companies was an attempt to attract new customers by introducing new catalogues called 'specialogues' which were designed to appeal to a defined segment of consumers. In addition links were formed with high street retailers to take advantage of well-known brand names. For example, Empire Stores carried inserts for Burton's Top Shops. The expectation behind such links was that the flair for design of the retailer could be combined with the database systems of the mail order company to produce highly targeted catalogues.

The first new catalogue from Next and Grattan was a 360-page catalogue called Next Directory with the promise of a 48-hour delivery based on a telephone ordering service and courier delivery, and to assist with this, Next also bought two chains of newsagents' shops called Dillons and Preedy's. In January 1988 the 'Next Directory' was unveiled and 500,000 copies were ordered. It had taken eighteen months to produce and had cost a total of £24 million including £11 million in stocks and offered an exclusive range of Next products (which were not those then offered in the Next high street shops). It was targeted to break even in six months, make profits within a year and reduce returns to 15 per cent. Traditionally in the industry new catalogues had taken two years to break even.

The Next Directory recorded sales of £20m. in its first ten weeks and suffered only 20 per cent returned goods, a figure well below the industry average. These sales compared well with Next Retail sales, which were then £6m. a week.

In 1987 Next split its womenswear chain into two, Next Collection and Next Too, the latter targeting a slightly younger audience.

By summer 1987 Next was retailing through 565 stores with a total sales area of 900,000 feet, before the Combined English Stores acquisition which added a further 1 million square feet. By 1988, following the take-over, Next was able to claim a 5.3 per cent share of the UK womenswear market and 6.7 per cent of menswear.

The acquisition of Combined English Stores for £335m. in 1987 was followed in 1988 by an active disposal programme of those parts which were not wanted (e.g. Allens Chemists) and then by those which proved not to fit the Next formula (e.g. Zales, Salisbury) and then some more in order to reduce the group's borrowings (e.g. Eurocamp). Paige, Weir and Collingwood were closed as chains, and 300,000 square feet were converted to the Next formula, at a cost of £ 30m. in 1988; the balance was sold. Biba and Mercada were sold in 1989.

Acquisitions

Throughout the 1980s Hepworth/Next bought and sold a variety of retail chains (for example, selling Turner's Shoe Shops (157) in 1983, buying 78 Kendalls outlets in 1981, buying 104 Lord John stores in 1985 (for £11.5m.), buying Preedy's and Dillons in 1987 and selling them in 1988 and 1989, as well as the Combined English Stores group). Consequently it was difficult at any time to estimate sales per square foot in the Next retail outlets. It was believed that the Next stores compared favourably with all their high street competitors, whilst the Hepworth stores did not, and this led to the eventual transformation (or sale) of the latter into Next retail outlets, and also led to the company changing in 1985 both its name, to Next plc, and its headquarters, from Leeds to Leicester.

Table 21.1 gives information on the Combined English Stores acquisition in 1987.

TABLE 21.1   **Combined English Stores acquisition, 1987**

Stores	No. of Shops	Type	Sales £m.	Trading profit £m.
Salisburys	150	Handbags	36.5	6.1
Zales	111	Jewellery ⎫		
Weir	107	Jewellery ⎬	47.1	6.2
Collingwood	137	Jewellery ⎭		
Allens	100	Chemists	28.1	2.1
Biba	56	Fashion	27.1	6.6
Paige	208	Womenswear	43.0	0.7
Eurocamp	–	Camping holidays	15.4	2.1
Mercada		Carpet wholesaler		
Akabrig		Household textiles		

While changing its year end to January in 1988, the company set itself a financial target of an annual growth in earnings per share of 20 per cent.

After the Combined English Stores acquisition and conversions, Next's retail sales space had increased by 17 per cent, but sales per square foot had fallen, so during 1989 radical restructuring was undertaken by the new chief executive, which led to the sale of non-core businesses.

The decision was taken to close down the Next Too chain; this caused some confusion as the merchandise ranges in the womenswear shops were disjointed, having been ordered before the decision was made to close Next Too. In addition, the single buying team for both menswear and Next Directory had been overstretched.

In 1989 clothing and footwear sales represented nearly 7 per cent of total consumer expenditure see figure 21.4.

The decision was taken to rationalize the stores, selling or closing those below 2,000 square feet or above 4,500. The 15 larger stores in particular had been unprofitable, and could be reduced in size. Over 100 Next outlets were closed, leaving the company with 360 and just over one million square feet.

The core was then high street shopping represented by Next Retail, Next Originals, Directory Shops, and Van Dyke; home shopping with Grattan, Next Directory, Kaleidoscope, You & Yours, Streets of London, Scotcade, and Look Again; financial services included Club 24; and the property division. Figure 21.5 shows an analysis of Next sales for the year ending January 1990.

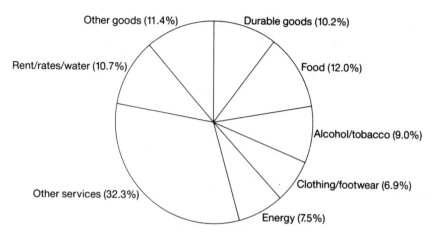

FIGURE 21.4   **Share of total consumer expenditure, 1989**

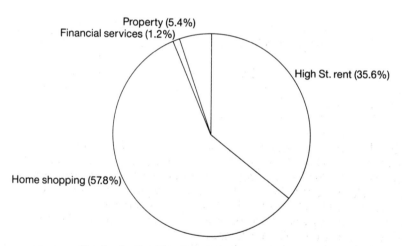

FIGURE 21.5   **Next: analysis of turnover, 1990**

Appendix 1   Next PLC

PROFIT AND LOSS ACCOUNT: FIVE-YEAR RECORD, 1985–90

	Year to 31 Aug 1985 £m.	Year to 31 Aug 1986 £m.	17 months to 31 Jan 1988[a] £m.	Year to 31 Jan 1989 £m.	Year to 31 Jan 1990 £m.
Turnover	146.0	190.0	1,119.7	1,135.9	949.2
Profit before interest	17.7	24.4	131.7	91.8	36.0
Net interest cost	(0.7)	(0.8)	(9.2)	(21.7)	(9.6)
Profit before exceptional items	17.0	23.6	122.5	70.1	26.4
Exceptional items	–	–	–	(7.8)	(73.1)
Profit (loss) before taxation	17.0	23.6	122.5	62.3	(46.7)
Taxation	(7.2)	(8.4)	(41.7)	(22.5)	15.8
Profit (loss) after taxation	9.8	15.2	80.8	39.8	(30.9)
Extraordinary items after taxation	2.1	(0.6)	–	137.7	58.7
Dividends	(5.1)	(11.5)	(29.8)	(27.3)	(17.4)
Retained profit	6.8	3.1	51.0	150.2	10.4
Dividend per share (p)	3.8	5.0	8.7	7.4	4.7
Earnings per share (p)	7.2	10.2	27.4	10.9	(8.4)
Fixed assets (£m.)	100.1	135.0	232.0	267.1	233.8
Stocks (£m.)	29.6	86.4	168.2	194.0	178.4
Debtors (£m.)	19.0	148.4	236.7	293.6	295.8
Shareholder's funds (£m.)	138.0	200.1	224.0	374.0	385.0

[a] Change of year end.

BALANCE SHEETS AT 31 JANUARY

	1988 £m.	1989 £m.	1990 £m.
Fixed assets			
Tangible	232.0	267.1	233.8
Investments	43.6	74.4	73.1
	275.6	341.5	306.9
Current assets			
Stocks	168.2	194.0	178.4
Debtors	236.7	293.6	295.8
Cash	11.6	4.3	51.3
	416.5	491.9	525.5
Current liabilities			
Creditors due within one year	298.3	277.2	277.7
Net current assets	118.2	214.7	247.8
Total assets less current liabilities	393.8	556.2	554.7
Creditors due after one year	166.9	173.5	168.0
Deferred taxation	2.9	7.9	1.7
Net assets	224.0	374.8	385.0
Capital and reserves			
Share capital	37.1	38.0	38.0
Reserves	186.9	336.6	346.9
Shareholders' funds	224.0	374.6	384.9
Minority interests	–	0.2	0.1
	224.0	374.8	385.0

Appendix 2

CONSUMER INCOME AND EXPENDITURE, 1977–87

	Personal disposable income	Consumer expenditure				
		on all items	on all items	on clothing	on carpets and floor-coverings	on textiles and soft furnishings
	Current prices £m.	Current prices £m.	1985 prices £m.	1985 prices £m.	1985 prices £m.	1985 prices £m.
1977	96,557	86,887	176,016	8,244	1,222	1,346
1978	113,124	100,219	185,950	8,988	1,320	1,372
1979	135,721	118,652	193,794	9,644	1,417	1,323
1980	160,009	137,896	193,806	9,608	1,270	1,256
1981	176,084	153,566	193,832	9,593	1,234	1,256
1982	191,081	168,545	195,561	9,868	1,224	1,266
1983	205,955	184,619	204,318	10,545	1,310	1,326
1984	220,764	197,494	207,927	11,202	1,334	1,321
1985	237,802	217,023	215,267	12,298	1,409	1,513
1986	259,333	239,156	229,105	13,368	1,403	1,562
1887	278,996	261,698	241,382	14,425	1,479	1,781
1988	307,170	293,569	257,918	15,275	1,631	2,050

Source: *Annual Abstract* 1990, tables 14.2 and 14.9

PART V

STRATEGY

IMPLEMENTATION

22 Metropolitan Borough of St Helens

COMMUNITY LEISURE

St Helens is a traditional industrial town situated some ten miles to the east of Liverpool and 25 miles to the west of Manchester, in the North West of England. It played a major part in the industrial development of the area following the Industrial Revolution of the eighteenth century, and was the site of Britain's first canal – the Sankey Navigation. Its economic growth during the nineteenth century was founded on the three industries of glass, chemicals and coal, and it remains to this day the largest glass-manufacturing town in Europe.

Before 1974 and the reorganization of local government in England and Wales, St Helens was a smallish borough with a population of about 70,000 people, although part of a much larger urban area containing a number of other small districts. In 1974, St Helens became a metropolitan district within the County of Merseyside and absorbed many of the nearby urban district councils, such as Newton-le-Willows and Rainhill. The population of the enlarged area was 190,000.

Environmentally, as a small borough pre-1974 it was unattractive, with a large acreage of derelict land, coal and chemical tips, low-grade housing intermixed with industrial plants, a poor town centre, and high level of air pollution. By absorbing the surrounding districts, the area to be controlled by the council changed in character overnight. The old town remained, but 48 per cent of the borough's land area was now agricultural (80 per cent grade 1).

In 1990, the total area of the borough was 13,347 hectares. Only two working coal-mines remained, and the design and layout of the town centre showed considerable change from even a decade ago. Pilkingtons Glass remained the largest industrial employer, with 6,000 people; the Health Authority was almost equal, with 5,000, but the local council was the largest total employer, with 8,000. Unemployment, at 8.7 per cent, was still higher than the national average; of the 69,000 households, 60 per cent were owner-occupied. (A range of employment statistics for the Borough is included as appendix 1.)

ST HELENS COUNCIL

Following reorganization of local government in 1974, the new council incorporated many functions and departments, both horizontally and vertically. Whilst its financial control was highly rated, generally the ethos of the council was that of an inward-looking, non-progressive authority, with average or below-average services, and poor co-ordination.

However, in 1984 there was a massive shake-up which, ultimately, resulted in a total restructuring. A key concern was to focus more attention and resources on the Community Service block of the authority, i.e. the departments of Education, Leisure and Personal Services, and to bring about better co-ordination of their service delivery and forward planning. This was not achieved without difficulties, including staff going on strike for two months in protest at the changes. Eight departments were created, namely the Chief Executive's, Administration, Finance, Community Education, Community Leisure, Personal Services (Housing and Social), Technical and Environmental Services, and Operations. The matrix structure still existed with both vertical departments and horizontal functions, but there was every possibility that the streamlining would result in less emphasis on tactical, political activities, and more on the development of longer-term strategies. Indeed, the stated aims of the reorganization were:

1   To provide improved services.
2   To make services more responsive to the needs of the public ('putting the public first').
3   To involve the community in the provision of services by co-ordination with the voluntary sector.
4   To make better use of resources.
5   To pay special attention to disadvantaged groups and areas.
6   To unlock the hidden potential of employees (by involving them more in decision making).

In 1989 the eight departments were reduced to six by combining Administration and Finance with the Chief Executive's department, resulting in one central strategic group serving the needs of the five departments directly concerned with meeting community needs. Technical and Environmental Services later changed its name to Environmental and Design Services.

The elected members, of whom there are 54, comprise the full policy-making unit of the council. They are elected to office for a period of four years, and are advised by professional chief officers of departments, to whom is delegated the responsibility of putting policies into practice and managing service delivery on a day-to-day basis. The council is led by the leader of the party holding the majority of seats. Both the full council and the committees meet on a six-week cycle. The principal committee (also chaired by the leader of the council) is Policy and Resources, with 26 elected members. Six committees covering the five service departments, together with the Development Committee (covering planning, economic development and land and property issues) are formed with varying numbers of elected members on each. Thus, Personal Services (covering housing and social services) is composed of 28 members, whilst Community Leisure has 25 (and these tend to be transitory). The chief officers for each of the five service departments report to their respective committees, and some powers are delegated to the parallel management structure, for which each chief officer is responsible. However, the strategic decision-making is done at committee level.

FINANCIAL PLANNING AND CONTROL

Each of the six service committees/departments and the Policy and Resources Committee operate as profit centres (for the full breakdown of budgeted income and expenditure for 1989–90, see appendix 2). Clearly, some committees (Education and Personal Services) are financially responsible, for larger amounts than others (e.g. Community Leisure), but each is competing for a share of the available resources. Income generation is sometimes restricted by law, particularly where statutory services have to be provided. It may also be restricted by a lack of available resources for the provision of certain potential income-generating services and also by council policy on pricing, particularly to certain groups within the community.

Each of the seven committees may, therefore, be said to be operating as a 'business', with the consequent need to set objectives, to develop strategies to achieve them and to appraise and analyse performance.

COMMUNITY LEISURE

Structure

This department emerged as a result of the 1984 reorganization. Its mission is 'to provide purposeful activities to fill people's spare time' and, to do this, it has developed a range of products and services, divided into four sections.

Libraries and heritage   The Public Libraries and Museums Act of 1964 provides for the statutory provision of a 'comprehensive and efficient library service'. This is the only activity which the department *must* provide.

There are 16 community libraries and one mobile, offering varying combinations of loan services for books, audio and computer software, information services, newspapers and periodicals, all either on site or to day centres, adult training centres, schools, residential homes and to housebound people. The libraries are also venues for community activities such as classes, meetings and exhibitions.

Recreation   This activity, as with all others except library provision, is non-statutory but is provided for by enabling legislation passed over the years.

St Helen has four swimming pools, four leisure centres (providing a range of activities, both sporting and social), numerous soccer and rugger pitches, cricket squares, tennis courts, bowling greens, and a golf course and golf driving range.

A sports development team was formed to foster the growth of participation and to provide coaching and instruction.

Opportunities   This section has a number of services:

1   Community development, through a network of eight community centres.
2   Children's play using over 30 playgrounds, which are particularly active during non-school times such as weekends and holidays.
3   Leisure courses of a non-vocational nature, both day and evening, using 43 centres.
4   Community arts, including youth drama, music, street art and the Citadel Youth Theatre.
5   Rangers operating from four centres in urban and countryside parks and offering talks, walks, leisure courses, conservation projects, exhibitions and displays.

Resources

1   Events and entertainments of an *ad hoc* type, e.g. concerts, and the annual St Helens Show.
2   Landscape management of parks, playing fields, industrial and housing estates.
3   Marketing: market research and promotion of services and facilities.
4   Administration support.

The 1984 restructuring took place against a background of identified weaknesses, including a previous lack of clear management objectives, both strategic and tactical, the absence of an effective method of evaluating performance, a dearth of management expertise, and over-centralization of decision making, leading to inflexibility and fixed attitudes amongst employees, low morale and lack of creativity, with a poor career structure, and, above all, little recognition of the need to shape services to the community or the environment in which they were provided.

The organization structure which evolved (see appendix 3) has a Director of Community Leisure responsible for the four sections, each of which is managed by an Assistant Director. Total full-time staff number 300, of whom 50 are classed as 'managerial'; in addition, there are between 200 and 300 part-time employees. In terms of full-time equivalent, 40 per cent of the staff work in Libraries and Heritage, and 30 per cent in Recreation.

The current structure is designed, *inter alia*, to encourage staff adaptability and mobility, to provide the basis for team working, to create a 'flatter' structure with fewer levels, to encourage delegation of responsibility and accountability to the lowest levels practicable, to provide a career structure and greater participation for employees, to reduce waste and, above all, to ensure that staff are able to involve themselves actively in their local communities, so that services are responsive to local needs and have a high local profile.

Policy and objectives

The policy of the Community Leisure Department is to increase the use of council leisure facilities, primarily by the residents of the Borough.

However, within the council as a whole, a number of target groups have been identified as being worthy of particular attention. These are:

1 the unemployed/low-waged;
2 under-fives;
3 16–18-year-olds;
4 the elderly;
5 the mentally/physically handicapped.

The department tries to balance the desire to increase the use of its facilities and services overall with the desire to increase their take-up by the above target groups.

With respect to the range of activities to be made available to achieve the above, the strategy is to:

1 modernize facilities to maximize their use;
2 diversify existing community facilities to encourage multiple use;
3 combat vandalism and improve security;
4 improve landscaping;
5 encourage community development and co-operation with the voluntary sector.

Finance

The department spends over £9m. annually on its activities (out of a total council spend of £205m. (see appendix 2 for details of actual expenditure for 1987–8, allowed and revised expenditure for 1988–9, and proposed expenditure for 1989–90, by range of activities).

FUTURE CONSIDERATIONS

The above is a summary of the objectives, strategy and structure of the local authority following the 1984 reorganization. However, given the need both to monitor and to pre-empt environmental change, in 1988 the council inaugurated a Unitary Development Plan (UDP) for the borough. A series of Issue Reports was produced by the Department of Technical and Environmental Services, highlighting those key issues which, it was envisaged, would be important in the future planning for the area. The reports cover the environment, the economy, housing, shopping and transportation. They were endorsed by the council in January 1989, as a basis for further consultation and discussion with a wide range of organizations and interest groups.

The UDP is a new type of plan for Metropolitan District Authorities which will replace all existing plans, including structure plans, local plans, and old-style town maps. The UDP will be the council's formal plan for guiding changes in land use, development, protecting the environment and managing traffic, for the ensuing decade. Its purpose is to guide the use of resources to encourage new development and investment opportunities, but in preparing the plan, the council was constrained by the advice contained in the strategic guidance issued by the Secretary of State for the Environment in July 1988; this pays particular attention to the stimulation of economic activity and the promotion of urban regeneration. In this context, the council initiated a number of schemes, including:

- a new link road from the M62 to the town centre;
- the development of a Technology Campus;
- the regeneration of the Ravenhead area, to the south of the town;
- improvements to the Haydock Industrial Estate to the east.

In summary, and covering the major variables of geographic location, image, demographic and social trends and the economy, the principal points to emerge from the UDP are as set out below.

Analysis

In a wider geographical setting, the borough is very much overshadowed by the two major conurbations of Merseyside and Greater Manchester, with their commercial activity, administration, communications and strong cultural development. The designation and development nearby of the two new towns of Warrington/Runcorn and Skelmersdale has brought benefits to the North West as a whole, but has undermined the role and status of St Helens and frustrated efforts to pursue urban regeneration in the borough. The development corporations covering the new towns have now been wound up.

Whilst major events in history furthered the growth and positive image of St Helens, it is today haunted by the ghosts of its past –

derelict waterways, abandoned railways and former colliery sites. Any evidence of recent economic investment is widely scattered and engulfed by large areas of derelict, neglected and under-used land; it is not surprising that the image of St Helens from outside is probably restricted to Pilkingtons and the Rugby League Football Club. Indeed, recent research from the Universities of Warwick and Glasgow placed St Helens amongst those towns in Britain with the lowest quality of life.

Demograph   In contrast to a gradual increase in population throughout the United Kingdom over the next 20 years, St Helens and Merseyside are expected to experience a significant loss. This will continue recent long-term trends which have seen a declining birth rate and significant emigration from the borough as a result of high unemployment and poor prospects of any short-term recovery. However, it is the profile of the emigrants which gives cause for concern; they comprise the young, skilled, virile and energetic elements of the population. Thus, together with those who have sought residence in the outer suburban areas and beyond, the population of the older inner urban area will contain disproportionate numbers of the elderly, less-skilled, and less-prosperous.

The current population is estimated to be 188,000 but, taking into account all aspects of demographic change (see appendix 4 for details), it is forecast that by 2011 the population will be less than 180,000. The short-term increase in pre-school and under-nine-year-old children will be reversed after 2000, the numbers of 10–14-year-olds will decline for the next five years but then show an upward trend to 2005, young adults (aged 15–24) will decline markedly by 2011, adults aged 25–39 will increase until the mid-1990s but then decline sharply, adults aged 40–59 will increase by 2011, and both this group and elderly persons aged 60 or over will represent an ever-increasing proportion of the population, the latter reaching 22 per cent by 2011, a marked increase from its current level of 19 per cent. The Government has also predicted a 39 per cent increase in the number of single-person households over the period 1986–2001.

Increased numbers of elderly persons will generate greater demand for health and social (including leisure) care support services.

A public health report, 'The Winds of Change', produced by the St Helens and Knowsley District Health Authority in 1988 served to highlight certain major health problems of the area, largely attributed to deprivation. The report drew attention to the relatively high death rate from vascular diseases and cancers to which smoking, poor diet, alcohol and lack of exercise have contributed. The report concluded that developments which led to an improved social and physical environment would greatly assist a reduction in mortality.

The economy   Since 1978 the economy of St Helens has been severely affected by structural change, and the closure of a large number of firms resulted in a fall, between 1978 and 1984, in the total number of those employed of 18 per cent (three times the prevailing rate for Great Britain over that period). Despite the decline of traditional industries, however, the workforce continues to exhibit a bias towards manufacturing, and is concentrated in declining sectors. Employment in services achieved a modest growth of 3.5 per cent over the period 1978–84, although this was less than the national average. Public sector services experienced major job losses as a result of enforced cuts in expenditure and reorganization, whilst some increases occurred in catering, banking, finance and insurance services.

Concealed within the overall borough figures are wide variations. Four inner area wards contribute 31 per cent of the unemployed, whilst containing only 21 per cent of the borough's labour force, and the highest rate of unemployment (40 per cent) is to be found amongst young persons (particularly males) aged between 16 and 24.

Finally, 62 per cent of the unemployed aged 30 and over have been out of work for two years or more.

Action

The UDP will not be created within a policy vacuum, as the council has to work within the context of existing plans and constraints which have different origins, time-scales, and levels of discretion. However, economic revitalization is recognized as one of the fundamental components of urban regeneration. Policies in the UDP will need to tackle the problems brought about by a land resource which may be abundant, but a significant amount of which is not regarded as suitable or attractive for industrial use.

The council is committed to the provision of caring and responsive services. Emphasis is given to the provision of special needs, housing, and the clearance and improvement of older housing. With regard to community services, efforts are being made to decentralize the delivery of services to make accessibility easier by the community and to develop stronger neighbourhood focal points. Different degrees of emphasis are needed in different areas of the borough. Attention has been drawn to the opportunities for making greater use of 'urban greenspace' which is more accessible to the concentrations of population living in the inner area. Not all of this space is in the traditionally-accepted form of public open space, recreational facilities and landscaped areas – it may be vacant, derelict or under-used. Some of it is in areas of greatest need and where action by way of physical improvement and the provision of recreational facilities would create the greatest impact and benefits for the community. However, conflict may arise. Evidence indicates growing pressure upon amenity, open space and recreational areas, arising partly from a desire by owners (including the local authority) to realize land assets, and partly on account of development or policy constraints elsewhere. There is also the problem of expensive maintenance. The relative value of amenity, provision and nature conservation must be weighed against the pressure for housing, commercial development, mineral extraction and waste disposal.

In developing the UDP, due regard has been given to the following points:

1   the population of St Helens and its interests are the council's priority;
2   the range and quality of services will be improved;
3   priority is required for those sections of the community who are particularly exposed to poverty, or are otherwise underprivileged or disadvantaged;
4   priority treatment has (and should) become more selective as a result of public expenditure constraints;
5   priority can be expressed not only according to needs but also to opportunities;
6   many of the priorities are based on value judgements. They should be based on more objective criteria and subject to regular review; e.g. the council may wish to maintain certain levels of service regardless of high-cost considerations.

The council is required to consider policy/strategy documents prepared by other large agencies, e.g. the Regional Health Authority, British Coal, Merseyside Waste Disposal Authority, the National Rivers Authority, which have land use planning applications. In some cases, the council has limited influence on these bodies. In addition, various agencies seek to promote economic development and environmental improvement within the area. Finally, private sector initiatives such as retail planning proposals must be considered on their merits and their ability to meet the overall objectives set by the UDP.

LEISURE TRENDS

In 1989, the North West Council for Sport and Recreation (NWCSR) published a report entitled 'Progress through Partnership – a strategy for the development of sport and recreation in the North West (1989–1993)'.

The NWCSR was established in 1976 to provide a forum for sport and recreation interests in the North West, a region comprising the counties of Lancashire and Cheshire and the conurbations of Greater Manchester and Merseyside. Its membership includes representation from all local authorities. Its regional recreation strategy:

● establishes targets for development;
● highlights the policies and priorities of the NWCSR;

- outlines the role which the NWCSR hopes its member bodies might play;
- guides financial investment in sport and recreation.

It places emphasis on target groups, including women, young people, the over-fifties, the rural population, low income groups, people with disabilities, and ethnic minorities.

The strategy stresses the importance of liaison between various local authorities, services and governing bodies of sport to ensure that all coaching staff are suitably qualified and will encourage and assist local authorities, the commercial sector and other bodies to direct funding towards the development of excellence. The NWCSR estimated that capital and revenue expenditure on sport and recreation in the region amounted to £278m. p. a., and expressed a preference for this to increase by stages to £341m. p. a. by 1993 (an additional £10 per person p.a.). The population of 6.36m. was expected to decline by 25,000 by 1993.

Various data on leisure activities from the report and from other sources are given in appendix 5. In summary:

1 Participation in sport and recreation activities between 1977 and 1986 rose from 39.5 per cent of the region's population to almost 46.0 per cent, slightly below the national average.

2 By age-group, compared with national figures, the North West has been more successful in attracting the under-24-year-olds, but less so in stimulating participation in the 'family' (25–44) and 'post-family' (45–59) phases of life, particularly 'amongst females.

3 In terms of actual numbers participating in different activities, between 1983 and 1988, there were large increases for men's and women's indoor activities, a smaller increase for men's outdoor activities and a marginal decline in women's outdoor activities, with considerable variations occurring between age-groups.

4 When participation by gender and age are combined with demographic change over the period, major trends in participation appear, the greatest growth in terms of *actual* numbers participating occurring in both men and women aged 25–44, in both indoor and outdoor activities. Increased numbers of women of all ages are participating in indoor activities, whilst there are decreasing numbers of both young and old men participating in either indoor or outdoor activities, and a considerable reduction of 45–59-year-old women participating in the latter.

5 For the Borough of St Helens, information was obtained by the Community Leisure Department in 1990 on the frequency of use of its services by residents. Libraries, leisure centres, swimming pools and parks and playgrounds were the most intensively used facilities, but there still remained large numbers in the population who never used any of the facilities available.

Appendix 1

ST HELENS EMPLOYMENT, 1987

| | Male | | Female | | |
	Full-time	Part-time	Full-time	Part-time	Total
Agriculture, energy, water supply	2,415	45	258	61	2,779
Manufacture of metals, mineral products, chemicals	5,814	8	1,436	152	7,410
Metal goods, engineering, vehicle industries	3,460	40	791	221	4,512
Other manufacturing	1,661	25	1,860	471	4,017
Construction	2,675	12	195	826	3,708
Distribution, hotels, catering, repairs	4,044	507	2,207	3,395	10,153
Transport, communications	1,926	36	247	128	2,337
Banking, finance, insurance	1,375	60	1,084	600	3,119
Other services	3,625	374	5,289	5,458	14,746
Total	26,995	1,107	13,367	11,312	52,781

ST HELENS EMPLOYMENT CHANGE, 1978–87

	1978	1981	1987	% change 1981–7	% change 1978–87
Agriculture energy, water supply	5,855	5,647	2,780	−50.8	−52.5
Manufacture of metals, mineral products, chemicals	20,039	13,702	7,410	−45.9	−63.0
Metal goods, engineering, vehicle industries	6,701	5,972	4,511	−24.5	−32.7
Other manufacturing	5,013	3,719	4,017	+ 8.0	−19.9
Construction	3,184	3,045	3,709	+21.9	+16.5
Distribution, hotels, catering, repairs	10,989	10,688	10,153	− 5.0	− 7.6
Transport, communications	2,518	2,268	2,337	+ 3.0	− 7.1
Banking, finance, insurance	1,712	2,673	3,120	+16.7	+82.2
Other services	16,284	15,236	14,745	− 3.2	− 9.4
Total	72,295	62,950	52,782	−16.2	−27.0

Appendix 2

ST HELENS METROPOLITAN BOROUGH COUNCIL FORWARD BUDGET ESTIMATE, 1989–90 – SUMMARY OF COMMITTEES

	Education	Community Services			Technical and Environmental Services	Trading Services	Policy and Resources	Sub-total	Adjustment[a] for central administration recharges	Total
		Leisure	Personal services	Total						
	£	£	£	£	£	£	£	£	£	£
Expenditure										
Employees	52,123,930	3,866,689	16,524,214	72,514,833	4,598,934	–	8,835,459	85,949,226	–	85,949,226
Premises	7,967,842	2,182,654	15,669,756	25,820,252	648,671	–	2,955,582	29,424,505	-1,870,462	27,554,043
Transport	1,005,983	126,556	689,951	1,822,490	249,596	–	250,968	2,323,054	–	2,323,054
Supplies and services	7,347,400	1,099,678	2,544,047	10,991,125	520,665	–	3,711,379	15,223,169	-1,949,389	13,273,780
Agency and contracted	8,376,777	346,957	1,107,644	9,831,378	8,192,003	–	2,102,949	20,126,330	–	20,126,330
Transfer payments	4,013,832	5,551	23,251,459	27,270,842	–	–	–	27,270,842	–	27,270,842
Central support	1,276,819	451,536	3,057,675	4,786,030	1,777,793	–	2,679,080	9,242,903	-9,242,903	–
Capital finance	3,596,158	1,054,563	15,007,234	19,657,955	2,306,334	–	3,225,758	25,190,047	–	25,190,047
Bad debts provision	–	–	130,000	130,000	–	–	–	130,000	–	130,000
Sub-total	85,708,741	9,134,184	77,981,980	172,824,905	18,293,996	–	23,761,175	214,880,076	-13,062,754	201,817,322
contingency sum	–	–	–	–	–	–	3,496,600	3,496,600	–	3,496,600
Total expenditure	85,708,741	9,134,184	77,981,980	172,824,905	18,293,996	–	27,257,775	218,376,676	13,062,754	205,313,922
Income										
Customer & client receipts	3,880,888	684,922	24,288,599	28,854,409	2,016,168	50,000	3,390,508	34,311,085	–	34,311,085
Grants, reimbursements and other balances	15,386,117	1,080,386	21,121,248 / 2,552,496	48,587,751 / 2,552,496	4,927,175	–	16,652,207	70,167,133 / 2,552,496	-13,062,754	57,104,379 / 2,552,496
Total income	19,267,005	1,765,308	58,962,343	79,994,656	6,943,343	50,000	20,042,715	107,030,714	13,062,754	93,967,960
Net expenditure	66,441,736	7,368,876	19,019,637	92,830,249	11,350,653	-50,000	7,215,060	111,345,962	–	111,345,962

[a] In order to avoid 'double counting' of central administration recharges. The cost of the central departments are shown initially within the Policy and Resources and Technical and Environmental Services Committees, but are also shown within each service committee's expenditure, with a corresponding figure being included under income within the Policy and Resources and Technical and Environmental Services Committees.

COMMUNITY SERVICES COMMITTEE LEISURE SERVICES REVENUE BUDGET, 1989-90

	Actual 1987-8	Allowed estimate 1988-9	Revised estimate 1988-9	Forward estimate 1989-90
SUMMARY OF NET EXPENDITURE	£	£	£	£
DIRECTORATE	29,471	29,597	30,579	31,683
LIBRARIES				
Assistant Director & Area Management Team	72,936	74,723	77,825	77,581
Community libraries	1,220,474	1,285,995	1,247,482	1,324,634
Information unit	44,362	51,538	49,670	51,516
Bibliographical services	92,253	104,582	106,349	96,235
Community services	112,443	132,158	128,596	133,023
Local heritage	93,818	115,036	116,311	124,749
TOTAL	1,636,286	1,764,032	1,726,233	1,807,738
RECREATION				
Assistant Director & functional management	70,165	74,720	58,933	63,529
Swimming pools	343,067	370,424	364,207	299,734
Leisure centres	626,541	752,133	713,800	631,110
Joint management schemes	109	0	0	0
Outdoor recreation	11,576	36	54,755	48,610
Sport & recreation development team	29,463	51,801	32,895	40,159
TOTAL	1,080,921	1,249,114	1,224,590	1,083,142
OPPORTUNITIES				
Assistant Director & Area Management Team	62,453	73,178	73,881	75,585
Community development	544,900	724,650	689,024	744,884
Children's play	100,622	125,164	139,832	142,811
Ranger service	93,698	94,567	107,891	118,987
Leisure courses	168,118	135,547	132,261	130,910
Parks cafés	3,111	4,376	6,988	5,230
Community arts St Helens	11,289	13,960	14,266	17,898
Public halls	22,604	5,162	13,609	2,955
TOTAL	1,006,795	1,176,604	1,177,752	1,239,260
RESOURCES				
Assistant Director	21,617	23,666	23,719	24,002
Administration	1,032,842	1,120,005	1,102,325	1,133,753
Events	124,427	69,153	95,917	69,644
Land management	1,514,170	1,628,041	1,378,414	1,309,706
Leisure engineering	495,406	352,192	555,729	477,341
Marketing	38,139	43,844	44,143	45,988
TOTAL	3,226,601	3,236,901	3,200,247	3,060,434
DEPARTMENTAL TOTAL	6,980,074	7,456,248	7,359,401	7,222,257

Appendix 3

COMMUNITY LEISURE DEPARTMENT

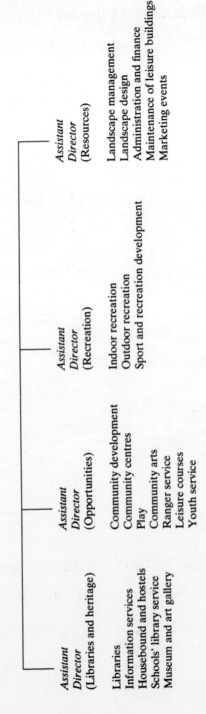

Director

Assistant Director (Libraries and heritage)

Libraries
Information services
Housebound and hostels
Schools' library service
Museum and art gallery

Assistant Director (Opportunities)

Community development
Community centres
Play
Community arts
Ranger service
Leisure courses
Youth service

Assistant Director (Recreation)

Indoor recreation
Outdoor recreation
Sport and recreation development

Assistant Director (Resources)

Landscape management
Landscape design
Administration and finance
Maintenance of leisure buildings
Marketing events

Appendix 4

POPULATION & HOUSEHOLD PROJECTIONS

	Short-term, 1990–6	Medium-term, 1996–2001	Long-term, 2001–11	Overall change
Pre-school (0–4 yrs)	Slight increase	Slight decrease	Continued decrease	Decrease
School-aged population (5–15yrs)	Very slight increase	Continued increase	Decrease	Decrease
Young adults (16–24 yrs)	Sharp decrease	Continued increase	Modest increase	Decrease
Adults (25–39 yrs)	Slight increase	Decrease	Sharp decrease	Significant decrease
Adults aged 40 yrs to pensionable age	Slight increase	Increase	Increase	Increase
Pensioner adults	Static	Static	Modest increase	Increase

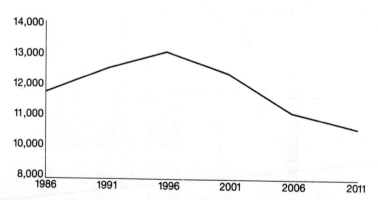

FIGURE 22.1   **St Helens population projection pre-school children (0–4 yrs)**

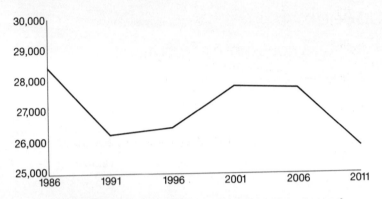

FIGURE 22.2   **St Helens population projection school-aged children (5–15 yrs)**

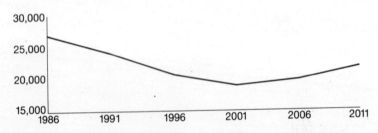

FIGURE 22.3   **St Helens population projection young adults (16–24 yrs)**

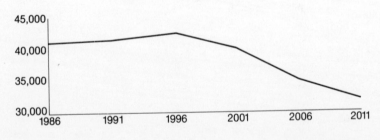

FIGURE 22.4   **St Helens population projection adults aged 25–39**

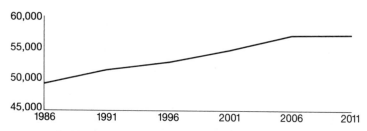

FIGURE 22.5   **St Helens population projection adults aged 40 to pensionable age**

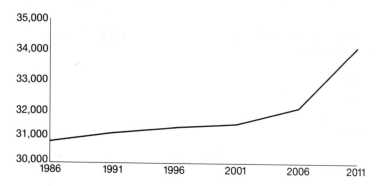

FIGURE 22.6   **St Helens population projection adults of pensionable age**

Appendix 5

CHANGES IN PERCENTAGE LEVELS OF PARTICIPATION IN SPORT 1977–86 (NORTH-WEST REGION)

Age-group	Male (%)	Female (%)
16–24	+ 9	+ 22
25–44	+ 8	+ 13
45–59	+ 9	+ 10
60+	+ 4	+ 8
All	+ 10.5	+ 21.5

Source: General Household Survey

OVERALL PARTICIPATION AND INCREASES IN ACTIVITIES 1983–8 (NORTH-WEST REGION)

	1983 participation	*1988 participation*	*Change*
Men indoor	937.1	1,081.7	+144.6
Men outdoor	994.2	1,070.0	+ 75.8
Women indoor	454.9	721.3	+226.4
Women outdoor	613.5	610.0	− 3.5

Source: The Sports Council 1988

PARTICIPATION TRENDS BY AGE-GROUP AND GENDER 1983–8 (NORTH-WEST REGION)

		Change in participation rate (%)	*Change in numbers (000)*
Men indoor	13–24	+ 3.7	− 11.4
	25–44	+11.7	+130.3
	45–59	+ 7.8	+ 37.6
	60+	− 2.3	− 11.9
Men outdoor	13–24	− 2.3	− 41.3
	25–44	+ 9.3	+108.7
	45–59	+ 4.5	+ 18.9
	60+	− 2.2	− 10.5
Women indoor	13–24	+14.3	+ 63.9
	25–44	+14.3	+140.0
	45–59	+ 7.0	+ 34.4
	60+	+ 3.7	+ 28.1
Women outdoor	13–24	+ 1.0	− 9.4
	25–44	+ 3.2	+ 41.3
	45–59	− 8.0	− 46.6
	60+	+ 1.7	+ 11.2

Source: The Sports Council 1988

USE OF SERVICES IN ST HELENS M. B.

	More than once per week (%)	Once per week (%)	Once per month (%)	Less than once per month (%)	Only occasionally (%)	Never (%)
Libraries	5.0	14.0	16.0	4.0	15.0	46.0
Museum	0.5	0.5	1.0	1.0	20.0	77.0
Leisure centres	8.0	14.0	7.0	1.0	11.0	59.0
Swimming pools	6.0	21.0	9.0	5.0	13.0	45.0
Youth service	0.5	–	0.5	0.5	0.5	98.0
Community centres	2.0	2.0	3.0	2.0	4.0	77.0
Ranger service	0.5	–	0.5	–	2.0	97.0
Arts/drama/music/workshops	1.0	0.5	1.0	–	3.0	94.5
Sports pitches	8.0	9.0	2.0	1.0	7.0	73.0
Parks & playgrounds	12.0	15.0	8.0	3.0	15.0	47.0
Sports courses	2.0	0.5	2.0	2.0	2.0	91.5
Hobby/leisure courses	–	2.0	0.5	–	2.0	95.5
Dances/shows	2.0	2.0	0.5	3.0	12.0	81.5
Others	2.0	5.0	–	–	0.5	–

Source: St. Helens M. B. 1990

23   THF Travelodge

In 1985 the UK-based Trusthouse Forte company, one of the largest hotel and catering groups in the world, launched its budget motel operation, 'Little Chef Lodges', later to become known as 'Travelodges'. The lodges were to be built adjacent to the company's well-established Little Chef roadside restaurants, of which there were over 200, spread throughout the UK.

BACKGROUND

Trusthouse Forte was formed in 1970 by the merger of the Trust Houses Group Limited and Forte Holdings Limited. Trust Houses was formed in 1903 with the main objective of resorting the standards of the old coaching inns, many of which had fallen into decline following the development of the railways. Over the years the company grew into a nationwide group of hotels, with overseas hotel interests as well.

Sir Charles Forte, executive chairman of Trusthouse Forte, founded Forte Holdings Limited in 1935. The major expansion of his company began in the post-war period, and soon Forte activities spanned the whole range of catering: popular and exclusive restaurants, banqueting, airports and in-flight catering, duty-free shops, motorway service areas, and from 1958, hotels in Britain and overseas. By 1970 the company had 41 hotels, a number operating in partnership with BEA and BOAC (now British Airways). The company's sales areas included the United States, Europe and Japan, and achieved a turnover in 1986 of £1,477m. (see appendix 1).

Trusthouse Forte is primarily a hotel company; almost 70 per cent of its profits come from this source. In 1986 THF had more than 800 hotels. These hotels ranged from exclusive hotels, such as the Hotel George V in Paris, to the Post Houses and Inns found in the UK.

The second most important profit centre to the THF organization has been catering, which includes several high-class restaurants and goes down the scale to in-store catering and the Little Chef restaurants. The activities of Gardner Merchant can be included in this section. This company carries out industrial catering contracts, using facilities provided by the client firms.

INVESTMENT POLICY AND GROWTH

The THF board has maintained a policy of keeping the company balance sheets strong, to aid future investment. To this end the various company properties have been revalued at regular intervals, thus preventing understatement. The company looks ahead for investment opportunities that will provide good returns in the future. Profits representing a good return on capital employed have been the hallmarks of Trusthouse Forte. THF's stated initial target return on investment in 1980 was of the order of 15 to 20 per cent, pre-tax and pre-interest.

The company stated at that time that the heaviest investment programme in its history would be maintained, and that the priority areas of expansion for THF were Britain, USA, Europe and the Middle East. It seemed likely that much of this investment would be spent in the hotel industry, but THF's other interests would not suffer any loss of investment as a result. A large proportion of THF's investment in the hotel industry was destined for refurbishing existing and recently acquired hotels.

The company believes in growth by profitable expansion. In the past, this has involved acquisitions and joint ventures. However, such diversification is only undertaken if the board feels the acquisition will complement existing operations.

The THF board believes that providing good customer service in hotels can only be achieved by giving staff extensive well-supervised training. To this end, THF has continuously invested in the provision of full and comprehensive training programmes for its staff at all levels.

MARKETING

In order to maintain good customer service and relations, each individual unit is made responsible for its own profitability. This includes involving hotel management not only in their own regional marketing, but also in the total group marketing policies. THF have found that, overall, this approach reduces the impersonality of such a large organization, whilst still providing all of the advantages of the large organization in terms of general business operation – for example, financial control, management techniques and standards of quality.

Trusthouse Forte is an international company, competing in all the major markets in the world. However, since almost 80 per cent of the company's business comes from its British hotel and catering operations, Britain remains a priority destination to be sold.

THF's marketing activities have been geared towards three objectives:

1   Internationally to increase visitors to Britain from overseas.
2   To increase the number of visitors to THF world-wide.
3   Within Britain to gain a bigger share of the relatively static home business and holiday traffic, particularly during weak or out-of-season trading periods.

THF's marketing problem can be defined in two stages: first, the need to sell Britain as a destination, and second, to sell its own hotel and catering facilities.

To back up the work done by overseas sales staff, THF runs a full programme of promotional, advertising and PR activity, designed to promote the name THF world-wide, thus gaining customer awareness and respect.

In Britain customer awareness of THF is very high, and considered to be better than that any of its competitors, this being the conclusion of an independently commissioned report. Overseas, however, in 1980 the company felt it necessary to launch an international corporate advertising campaign, in order to improve awareness of THF, its hotels and services among European and American audiences.

The major problem to the industry in general is to increase occupancy levels, thus giving a greater base over which to spread the high fixed costs which are inevitable in the hotel industry. THF's occupancy levels are generally 10 per cent to 15 per cent higher than those experienced by the rest of the industry. This has been brought about by three things:

1   THF's well-organized world-wide referral and advanced booking system;
2   effective marketing positioning;
3   innovative sales effort.

Point 2 refers to the fact that in the UK, each THF hotel has its own character and well-defined position in the market. In 1986 THF's British hotels comprised a number of provincial hotels, including seven airport hotels, 36 Post Houses, and over 70 Inns. Although all of them were in the upper quarter of the tariff range, and each possessed at least two AA/RAC stars there was nevertheless a considerable difference between, say, a Post House, which the Price Commission defines as 'a modern hotel outside City Centre on a major road not offering room service or porterage' and an Inn, a small two-star hotel with food and drink facilities aimed both at residents and at the local trade. Each of these different types of outlet filled an identifiable niche in the market and complemented the rest of the company's business.

Relating to point 3, the company has attempted to identify its 'problem' areas, and has then produced packages aimed specifically at addressing these areas. For example, the business trade for hotels tends to be Monday to Thursday, which means rooms are unoccupied at weekends. If the occupancy can be increased during these slack periods, then the high fixed costs can be spread more thinly, and thus the marginal increase in occupancy will lead to a greater increase in profits.

The company's answer to this problem was to introduce, in 1980, the Weekend Bargain Breaks and Hightime Holiday packages, backed by a vigorous marketing campaign. This resulted in an extra 120,000 sleeper nights being sold in a year when the English Tourist Board recorded a total market decline of 4 per cent. Partly as a result of these special promotional schemes, it is now considered that more than 20 per cent of visitors to THF's UK hotels are British residents on holiday.

The company also successfully introduced its Gold Card system, which is THF's own form of credit card. This is of particular benefit to the frequent traveller, notably the businessman, as the cardholder has access to the full range of facilities provided by THF. THF had identified the credit operations as another way of increasing business, and had introduced other measures aimed at both the individual traveller and the businessman.

One further growth area identified by THF is that of conference services. The company has established a system whereby the conference organizer can ring a central function and be dealt with swiftly, being given advice as necessary. THF's 'Meeting Point' service covered over 200 UK venues in 1986, which offered full conference facilities.

PAST GROWTH AND ACQUISITIONS

Since the formation of THF, the result of a merger in 1970 between the Trust Houses group and the Forte group, its growth has been considerable. The policy of growth was reflected in the building of new interests, notably the Post House operation, and also in the acquisition of existing properties as the result of take-overs. An example of the latter is the acquisition of some hotels previously owned by the Lyons group, which took place in early 1977.

The take-over of the Lyons hotels began in November 1976 and involved THF acquiring 35 hotels in Britain and Ireland, in a deal worth £27.6m. This increased the number of THF's hotels to 800. Sir Charles Forte indicated at the time that it was more or less a natural thing to get together for this deal. Lyons wanted to dispose of their hotels, and THF wanted to expand their business.

The Lyons take-over added an extra 5,500 rooms to the THF group, 3,500 of which were in London. At this time the rooms were to cost THF around £4,000 each, with no leases or associated construction costs to be paid. The cost of construction during this period was estimated at £30,000 per room in London; this represented a considerable saving to THF.

The general industry forecast for 1977 predicted an increase in the numbers of tourists, and also increased margins due to the ending of a price war by the hoteliers over the package tourist. This meant that the London acquisition would pay for itself quite quickly.

By February 1978 THF had increased its presence in London to a total of 14 hotels, offering 6,600 rooms. Prior to this, although larger overall, it had lagged behind its rivals such as Grand Metropolitan, in the number of rooms offered in the capital.

During April 1980 THF announced its intention to invest a further £30m. in its Post House operation. This was the first indication of a major new hotel investment by a British hotel group since 1974, although there had been some expansion in the USA during the period. The estimated average cost per room of the Post Houses was £27,000. The first Post House was due to open in 1980, with three being planned for the 1981 financial year, despite a forecast decline in the tourist trade. In November 1980 THF stated that the building programme was to be accelerated and a fourth Post House was to be built in the 1981 financial year.

Also in November 1980, THF closed a deal which involved the purchase of the greater part of Thorn-EMI's leisure interests. This purchase included such properties as the Prince Edward Theatre, the Empire Cinema and Ballroom in London's Leicester Square, the Blackpool Tower complex, and the Chichester Yacht Marina. The take-over also provided for Lord Delfont to become chairman and chief executive of THF's leisure division. The take-over dovetailed neatly with THF's existing entertainment outlets. THF owned the Talk of the Town in London, which it operated in partnership with Lord Delfont, and the acquisition of premises with catering facilities enabled THF to employ its expertise in this field.

Many of THF's subsequent development policies and actions were pre-arranged; the 1980 and 1981 acquisitions were just the start of a much larger future development. During the course of the 1980 financial year more than £95m. was spent world-wide on building new hotels, acquiring others, refurbishing and redecorating properties, buying new equipment, and developing new markets. THF had stated that its priority regions for expansion were Britain, the USA, Europe, and the Middle East.

The Little Chef catering establishment was expanded in 1981, with the company opening a further 30 new restaurants. This expansion continued into the mid to late-1980s (see appendix 2).

A catering innovation in 1979 had been the Julie's Pantry fast service hamburger restaurants. The first 'in town' operation of Julie's Pantry was in London's Knightsbridge, and there were two others at the Scratchwood (M1) and Corley (M6) motorway service stations. Five others were planned to open during 1980.

The Kardomah chain of restaurants, aimed at the shopper, was restyled during 1981, and there were plans to open or acquire further restaurants during that year.

In October 1980 THF took over the management of the Hotel des Bergues in Geneva, a 143-bedroomed hotel which is ranked highly among the world's most exclusive hotels.

In 1984 the company's revenues exceeded £1.1 billion, with profits of around £105m. By this time, Lord Charles Forte had handed over executive control to his son Rocco, but remained active as chairman.

The years 1985 and 1986 saw a significant improvement in the profitability of the consumer catering operation, with a rise in trading profits of 44 per cent, which was achieved principally from the organic growth of THF's existing businesses. A major acquisition from the Hanson Trust gave an even broader base from which to develop profits in the future. This acquisition brought the 85-strong Pier House Inns chain, incorporating Harvester Steak Houses, Falstaff Bar and Grills, and other emergent brands such as Dômes, giving THF a presence in the rapidly-growing licensed leisure eating business, with challenging growth opportunities for the immediate future. The five Welcome Break Service Areas were added to THF's existing motorway service areas, and the 71 Happy Eater restaurants offered substantial opportunities for futher expansion into the rapidly-growing roadside catering markets.

The Roadside Catering Division continued to develop the Little Chef formula, with 42 new restaurants opened during 1987, bringing the total to 270. Over 25 million customer visits were made during the year, and Little Chef was on target for its goal of 400 restaurants by 1991. Consistency and cleanliness were the corner-stones of the product's reputation with travellers. New developments during the year included the introduction of no-smoking areas, and free baby food for the youngest guests.

DEVELOPMENT IN NORTH AMERICA

In March 1978 THF began further expansion in the USA, with the announcement that its wholly-owned subsidiary Knott Hotels had agreed in principle to acquire Colony Foods, including Colony Foods under the names of Colony Kitchen and Hobo Joe's, mainly in the Western United States.

THF regarded the take-over as a good base for expansion in restaurants in America. Its restaurant position in the USA at this time was quite strong with its trade through the Knotts Hotel group, which amongst its outside catering contracts included supplying all the meals for the UN buildings in New York.

In April 1980 THF withdrew from a further bid in America, after an offer of £38.8m. was said to be insufficient to secure the deal. As a result of reduced gearing during the previous year THF had cash resources of £60m. available for an acquisition; with this cash earning a healthy 20 per cent interest they could afford to wait and be choosy.

Shortly after this Rocco Forte (the then group deputy chief executive) announced on behalf of the group that a new expansion programme was planned for the USA. The programme, which was to take immediate effect, was to include operation of the new Plaza Hotel in Dallas, in which THF had an equity stake.

This highlighted THF's change in investment policy in the USA, where it was minimizing its investment costs by operating in the luxury bracket hotels on long-term management contracts, with as little as a 10 per cent equity investment. Rocco Forte also stated that the group's aim was to have around 15 to 20 hotels in the United States, and the same number in other countries.

During 1981 THF added luxury hotels in Tulsa, Little Rock and Miami in the USA, and Toronto in Canada, to complement its existing North American properties in New York, Dallas and Philadelphia.

From 1985 to 1986 THF's Viscount division added six properties, including the purchase of the former Hilton at Long Beach, California. This expansion included franchised properties and management contracts. It was expected that the development of this segment would continue to have a positive impact on the overall results from North America. Aggressive franchising activity allowed the addition of over 4,000 rooms to the Travel Lodge chain in 1986. This was in addition to the continued programme of upgrading good properties whilst disposing of properties that did not meet THF's current standards.

RESTRUCTURING

In early 1983 Donald Durbin, a director of THF, reiterated the company's strengths in hotels and catering and its concentration in doing what it was good at. He was, in fact, referring to the sale of the company's leisure division to Lord Delfont, for around £37m.

The following year saw the disposal of the Colony Foods restaurants and Eastern Foods Inc (industrial catering), two of the company's US operations.

In 1982 turnover and profitability by activity was as shown in table 23.1. At this time THF was structured along the lines illustrated in figure 23.1. In 1986 the activity analysis was as shown in table 23.2.

TABLE 23.1   **THF sales and profits, 1982**

	Sales £m.	Trading profit £m.
Hotels		
UK	255.1	41.7
USA	68.4	8.8
Europe and else-where	81.0	6.1
Catering	394.2	17.8
UK	25.7	(0.3)
USA	46.8	4.2
Leisure	35.6	2.0
Miscellaneous		

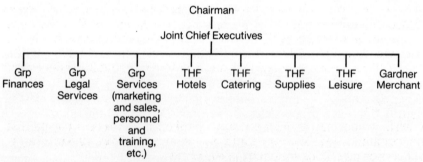

FIGURE 23.1   **The structure of THF (1982)**

TRAVELODGES

In October 1985 THF opened the first of its 'Travelodges' (formerly Little Chef Lodges) at Barton-under-Needwood on the A38 near Burton-upon-Trent, sited adjacent to an existing Little Chef restaurant.

The 'lodge' concept was based on low-cost accommodation, with simplicity as the key theme. For example, there were no conference facilities, no reception area, and hardly any staff. The lodge was managed by the person managing the restaurant, who had undergone extra training.

Specification

Every lodge was designed to look the same from inside, although the design allows for extension in any direction, and up to three storeys high. Being of modular design, each room is factory made and can be delivered complete with fittings to the appropriate site.

Each lodge was planned to have a mixture of between 20 and 30

TABLE 23.2 **THF sales and profits, 1986**

	Sales £m.	Trading profit £m.
Hotels		
UK	380	87
The Americas	127	8
Europe and elsewhere	96	14
Catering		
Contract	552	19
Public	242	22

double and single bedrooms, incorporating very basic fittings. A standard double room offers a king-sized bed and a sofa bed which converts into a full-sized single bed, and includes a pull-out child's occasional bed in its base. Rooms are provided with tea and coffee-making facilities and combined television and radio alarm clock. In 1985 tariffs were £19.50 for single occupancy and £24.50 for a double/family room.

Bookings

Guests – who may or may not have booked in advance – check in at the restaurant reception area and pay on arrival. After 10 p.m. a night supervisor merely hands over the room key.

Building costs

The lodge at Barton-under-Needwood was built in just 16 weeks (after ten weeks of site preparation). Although exact costs were not disclosed, THF's catering managing director, Alan Hearn, intimated that the company was building the lodges at less than half the cost of a Post House. (Post Houses were estimated to cost £41,000 per room in 1985.)

Future developments

In January 1986 a further (30-bedroom) lodge was opened in Bedington, Cheshire, followed closely by a third development in East Horndon, Essex.

Two more firm sites were under review and more than 20 other planning permissions had been obtained around the country.

Although across the UK there were 130 suitable sites, the company had indicated it did not plan to use all of them.

Appendix 1   THF

PROFIT AND LOSS ACCOUNT, 1986

Year ended 31 October	£m.
Sales	1,477
Operating costs	(1,319)
Trading profit before interest	158
Interest	(34)
Trading profit after interest	124
Share of profits of subsidiary company not consolidated	8
Net surplus on property projects and disposals	4
Profit on ordinary activities	136
Taxation	(37)
Profit after taxation	99
Minority interest	(2)
Profit attributable to shareholders	97
Dividends	(47)
Profit retained for the year	50
Earnings per share (pence)	12.5

BALANCE SHEETS, 1986

Year ended 31 October	£m.
Fixed assets	
Tangible assets	1,514
Investments	171
Total fixed assets	1,685
Current assets	
Stock	41
Debtors	253
Short-term deposits and cash	50
Total current assets	344
Creditors due within one year	
Bank and other borrowings	122
Creditors	339
Total current liabilities	461
Net current assets (liabilities)	(117)
Total assets less current liabilities	1,568
Creditors due after one year	
Bank and other borrowings	443
Creditors	12
Total net assets	1,113
Capital and reserves	
Share capital	196
Share premium	70
Revaluation reserve	553
Profit and loss account	281
Shareholders' investment	1,100
Minority interest	13
Total equity investment	1,113

COMPARATIVE RESULTS, 1977–85

£m.	1981	1982	1983	1984	1985
Sales	833	907	963	1131	1245
Trading before interest	72	77	90	115	142
Profit before taxation	52	57	84	109	130
Profit attributable to shareholders	44	48	64	77	87
Total assets less current liabilities	763	805	871	1126	1193
Shareholders' investment	553	583	642	829	916
Net borrowings	168	238	215	270	265
Earnings per share (net) (pence)	6.9	6.1	8.2	9.8	11.1
Dividends per share (pence)	3.0	3.5	4.1	4.7	5.4

Appendix 2

A 'LITTLE CHEF' OPENING EVERY NINE DAYS[1]

The Little Chef name first came to public attention in 1959 when a snackbar with 11 stools opened in Reading, Berkshire.

Last week, the company had 235 Little Chefs in operation but more are opening at the rate of 25–30 a year; 'one every nine days' as Mr Hearn pointed out. The 250th opens just after Christmas. This financial year should see the arrival of 28 – 13 more are under construction.

Originally conceived as a roadside catering operation for the traveller, Little Chef is now developing local business.

The basic formula, though, has not changed – waitress service; limited, graphic, grill-based menu; 60 seats on average; open 364 days a year from 7a.m. to 10p.m.

A three-year redevelopment programme now 18 months away from completion will give all the units a new, softer look; change of emphasis from bright, bold primary colours to pastel shades, from fluorescent to softer lighting. Tables are larger, as are reception areas. Toilet facilities are being improved too. Three-year-old Barton-under-Needwood's ladies' room features fresh flowers, for Mr Hearn believes: 'You can judge a business by the quality of the toilets – you can't walk around the kitchens but you can walk around the loos.'

The change of direction is not intended to encourage longer stays, but is an acknowledgement of the increasing variety of reasons for visiting.

'These are evolutionary moves, not revolutionary moves', Mr Hearn said. 'We're still averaging 60 seats although some units can go to 80. We have to be consistent and work within our existing management skills. Remember, nothing is pre-cooked at a Little Chef and if the number of seats were trebled, we'd have trouble running it.'

Staffing is around 12–15, starting with a manager; a deputy (or two); two or three supervisors to cover the seven-day-a-week, 7a.m.–10p.m. operation; and restaurant catering assistants who cover all duties, with some majoring on griddle work.

The management structure allows upward movement – Little Chef lodges will add a greater career dimension by extending job opportunities. Every manager within Little Chef must have managed a unit at one point in his or her career even if only for a fortnight.

Director-in-charge Peter Smith is not exempt. 'Little Chef', Alan Hearn said, 'is a super breeding ground for young managers. It's probably the quickest route there is within THF'.

Little Chef limits its operation to 'A' roads, equivalent trunk roads or motorways – 11 are operated under franchise by THF's motorway service area division, one at Luton Airport by the airport catering division.

Only one site, in Lewdown, Cornwall, is franchised – to a former Little Chef manager, a relic of a short-lived franchise policy, ditched when it was realized that standards could be better maintained through direct managership.

Little Chef's meteoric development is slowed down by only one thing – the country's road improvement programme, which can knock sites out for a year, or in some cases for ever if, for example, a new bypass is built.

But Mr Hearn reports 100 per cent co-operation from local authorities.

Half the stock is THF-owned, half on lease. 'Our problem is finding, acquiring and building sites. On a 30-mile stretch, for example, there may be only one feasible site.'

The key to Little Chef, offering not a gourmet experience but a consistent, no-risk food formula, is a reluctance to introduce new ideas until management knows they can succeed at 250 units.

'Our managers spend 70 per cent of their time communicating policy and standards to their staff. You'll get the same answers from everyone in the company. Consistency of thinking is the key to consistency for the customers.'

The tables will always be laid in the same way, the food should be of the same standard whether in Glasgow or Gaewan.

The Little Chef consistency has even been noted by *The Tatler* (whose readers one may not expect to see in a Little Chef), which, much to Mr Hearn's delight, recently praised the company for producing food exactly like the picture on the menu.

Notes

1 Extracted from Kate McDermid, 'Lodges Chain Offers Family Rooms at £24', *Caterer and Hotel Keeper*, 3 October 1985.

Appendix   Notes on
              Case Analysis

INTRODUCTION

In the context of business policy education, the case-study approach will generally concentrate on the analysis of the corporate strategy of a company (or companies), usually within an industry setting. This analysis depends heavily upon the application of theory to the evaluation of documented real-life situations and related problem-solving exercises. Such application of theory to reality and reality to theory requires the student to demonstrate innovation and creativity in discussing situations and formulating solutions. It may well be frustrating when companies do not seem to act like textbook models, but it must be recognized that, being 'people-orientated', businesses do not always follow predetermined, mechanistic behaviour. Few of the theories and concepts we have at our disposal are based on 'exact science', but we can take heart fron the fact that the majority of these have evolved from the observation of real-life situations. In working with a probabilistic science the student should avoid dogmatic or over-speculative statements, and should aim for well-supported, constructive arguments based on the selection and application of appropriate concepts and techniques.

THE CASE METHOD

The major goal of using the case-study method as a learning vehicle is for students to consider general problems and concepts of business management, which hopefully will be universally applicable and relevant to approaching strategic problems in tomorrow's world.

The case-study method's particular value to students is in its exposure to the major elements and key success factors of corporate management problem-solving, decision-making, and strategy implementation. Case studies emphasize the management of a firm's resources. Any firm faced by decisions regarding present operations and forward planning in today's real world must consider the key success factors of successful 'money management'.

The concepts, principles, and strategies brought out in case studies should be helpful and professionally constructive to the potential manager considering a career in which the key success factors will be effective and successful decision-making and strategy implementation. The case-study method provides a useful and educational conceptual scheme.

The underlying uniformities of all case-study situations are drawn together in a meaningful whole by the student who works seriously on the assigned cases. The case studies offer a systematic framework for sharpening perception, deepening awareness, improving analytic ability and formulating more creative solutions to problems. Case studies also expose the student to many concepts which will prove useful and helpful in future career paths.

Experience may be the best teacher, but it is often also the most costly. Experience by itself probably produces more failures than successes. The case-study approach to learning allows one to practice and make mistakes, providing the opportunity to develop skills for the future.

A key success factor for the formulation of effective strategic decision-making in business management situations is to isolate possible pitfalls and mistakes before they happen, and to learn how to avoid them. Future managers should make a systematic attempt to improve their practical, personal, and professional competence to handle future business management problems.

Preparation for analysis

From the outset it should be recognized that rarely will a case contain 'complete information' on the company and its environment, nor will its contents be ordered in a manner which readily facilitates the process of logical analysis. Coping with imperfection and uncertainty is part of the learning process and indeed, it is a closer reflection of the reality of the business world. Sorting the wheat from the chaff is part of the creative demand mentioned above – finding the associated skills required takes time and patience.

Thus, at the initial reading of a case it is generally wiser to first sort out the 'picture' rather than attempting to launch straight into problem analysis.

Answers to the following suggested questions should set the scene:

1   What is the nature of the business?
2   What are the major themes?
3   What is the chronology of events?
4   What are the apparent limitations (of data)?
5   What particular analytical concepts and techniques seem (initially) applicable?

If, after the initial reading(s), you feel you know the 'story-line' then it is more likely that confidence will ensue for the more demanding task ahead.

Structure

The following guidelines for case analysis will cover most situations likely to be encountered, although they may vary in the degree of appropriateness from case to case.

Problem recognition and definition   Prioritization of problems is crucial, for if a manager decides to concentrate on the 'wrong' (insignificant, minor, relatively inconsequential) problems, he will more likely ignore the crucial, critical issues. Similarly, it is essential that recognition is given to the time horizon of a problem, insofar as whether it is solvable within a short-term or longer-term period. The analyst can then decide whether a problem requires a short-term or long-term planning horizon, or possibly both.

Analysing the company and its environment   Following problem identification, the next step is to analyse the company with respect to its strengths and weaknesses and the environment within which it exists, with respect to the opportunities and threats facing the company.

In assessing a firm's strengths and weaknesses, the analyst needs to be aware of at least the internal aspects of:

1   general management – objectives strategy structure;
2   finance;
3   marketing;
4   production and manufacturing – research and development;
5   planning, information, and control systems;
6   personnel, training and development, and industrial relations, in so far as one is able to.

In addition, external environmental factors as they relate to the firm will need to be addressed; these include:

1   the competitive situation;
2   the industrial structure within which the firm operates;
3   the state of the economy;
4   business–government relations;
5   technological environment;
6   social environment;
7   factor inputs.

Each of the above corporate functional areas and environmental factors is a necessary strategic problem-solving and decision-making variable in the everyday pressures faced by a firm. All of these areas require attention, because they are all highly interdependent and interactive – that is, a decision in one area will in some way almost always affect other areas of concern.

Selecting options and making a recommendation When (or if) a problem has been identified and the company and its environment has been analysed, the analyst is faced with the task of generating and evaluating feasible, optional solutions. Each possible option to solve a given problem will have pros and cons – reasons for and against implementation. In this position, the analyst is responsible for evaluating both sides of the argument, and one should be able to justify the ultimate choice using a combination of quantitative (numerical) and qualitative (reasoning) supporting criteria.

The hardest part of examining such options is generally the weighting of the relevant pros and cons surrounding each option; the 'best' option should obviously result in the recommendations. However, it is important to recognize that a recommendation needs to be defended, as it is important to know on what grounds a recommendation is given.

The recommendations should be prioritized with respect to the problem as delineated, and they should be practical and pragmatic insofar as the firm might find them feasible and possible to implement, given trade-off analysis and corporate constraints.

Once the firm has delineated its strategy in terms of what is necessary for successful performance, it still faces the tasks of corporate resource allocation and availability. The skill of formulating successful business policy appears to depend on the exploitation of particular strengths within a competitive market situation. To be effective, a plan of action will need to consist of decisions which are co-ordinated successfully. Success in the decision-making process will result from the effective implementation and follow-through of a comprehensive corporate strategy.

Structuring written reports

Where a general written analysis is called for, the stress should be on quality rather than quantity. There is no need to 'rewrite' the case, as the report is not an essay – nor, in the real world of business, do executives have the time to wade through a mass of description. Similarly, it is pointless regurgitating large chunks of the case just to put over a minor analytical point. If the assumption is made that the eventual assessor of the report understands the background to the case, then this tendency will be automatically avoided, for it is futile telling the reader what he already knows.

The analytical framework previously discussed is a reasonably good (and obvious) guide to what should appear in a written report.

However, the 'professional' structure differs slightly from the general order of the analysis, for reasons of visual presentation, information priorities and information accessibility. Nonetheless, it is down to the analyst to decide on the best form of presentation, and the following structure guidelines are put forward merely as a suggestion for improving presentation. In the final analysis it is the validity of the contents, rather than their order, which will determine the quality of the report.

1 *Executive summary*   Should include: the purpose of the report; scope and limitations; main conclusions of the analysis; key recommendations.
2 *Introduction (short)*   Brief background to the company; historical comment.
3 *Main body of the analysis*   Problem definition; internal and external analyses; evaluation of possible alternative solutions.
4 *Appendices*   Graphs; tables; 'SWOT' chart, etc.

Avoid attaching appendices which have played little or no part in the analysis. Likewise, make sure that the appendices are clearly referenced and points are brought into the main body of the analysis where appropriate.